The Reluctant Jew

by

Michael Grossman

Bloomington, IN  Milton Keynes, UK

AuthorHouse™
1663 Liberty Drive, Suite 200
Bloomington, IN 47403
www.authorhouse.com
Phone: 1-800-839-8640

AuthorHouse™ *UK Ltd.*
500 Avebury Boulevard
Central Milton Keynes, MK9 2BE
www.authorhouse.co.uk
Phone: 08001974150

© *2007 Michael Grossman. All rights reserved.*

No part of this book may be reproduced, stored in a retrieval system, or transmitted by any means without the written permission of the author.

First published by AuthorHouse 2/27/2007

ISBN: 978-1-4259-5299-0 (sc)

Library of Congress Control Number: 2006906936

Printed in the United States of America
Bloomington, Indiana

This book is printed on acid-free paper.

Cover photo by Eric McEdward

Dedication

To my wife, Phyllis, and my kids, Aly and Zack, for their constant love, patience, and support, which has allowed me to make time to do something I really enjoy. Thank you, guys.

Table of Contents

Dedication v

Preface ix

Acknowledgments xi

Introduction xiii

Chapter One - The Jewish Centre 1

Chapter Two - The New Rabbi 5

Chapter Three - Adult Ed. 9

Chapter Four - Temple Wife 12

Chapter Five - High Holiday Highs 15

Chapter Six - A Lot of Atoning 21

Chapter Seven - Second Vice-President 25

Chapter Eight - A Spiritual Man 37

Chapter Nine - A Newfangled Regime 44

Chapter Ten - Super Sunday & the "Jewpardy" Competition 51

Chapter Eleven - The Learned Guest Lecturer 75

Chapter Twelve - Prophets and Kings 84

Chapter Thirteen - Everything You've Wanted to Know about Christianity But Were Always Afraid to Ask - Part I: Its Theology and Early History 100

Chapter Fourteen - Everything You've Wanted to Know About Christianity - Part II: The Fall of Rome Through Modern Times 114

Chapter Fifteen - My Brother-In-Law The Muslim 154

Chapter Sixteen - Hindu Homeboys 160

Chapter Seventeen - The Gift Shop 175

Chapter Eighteen - Spreading the Word 182

Chapter Nineteen - The Jerahhi Connection 188

Chapter Twenty - We Already Live in the Promised Land 206

Chapter Twenty One - Jumpin' Jehovahs 214

Chapter Twenty Two - The Singing Rabbi 229

Chapter Twenty Three - At Ease With The Baha'i 242

Chapter Twenty Four - A Concept of God a Modern Can Live With ... 247

Chapter Twenty Five - Why the Resentment? 254

Chapter Twenty Six - The Reluctant Jew 275

Chapter Twenty Seven - The Dinner Dance 281

Chapter Twenty Eight - It's About Time 286

Chapter Twenty Nine - The Last Adventure? 311

Epilogue 319

Bibliography 321

Notes 329

Index 349

Preface

I have tried to describe the events that happened and personalities I encountered while president of Jewish Community Centre of Greenwood Lake as accurately as possible. From time to time, however, for dramatic effect, I have taken poetic license. Sometimes, I have added some details that may not have occurred, at least not exactly as written, or failed to include some details that did. But always, the events and personalities I write about are real. Any changes I've made serve only to better capture, in words, the essence of what actually transpired and the true character of the people I met. Since I've had only positive impressions of everyone I've written about, I don't think I can have offended any of them.

If I've left anyone out or forgotten some important event, forgive me. I've tried to be careful but know, inevitably, I must have overlooked something. Nonetheless, despite any shortcomings, writing this book has brought me incalculable joy and reminds me of one of the most beautiful *midrashes* I've ever read: In the 1800s, there was a renowned Hasidic master who lived with his most devoted student in a small town in the Pale. Every morning, the master said to his student, "Go outside and tell me if the Messiah has come. Go outside and tell me if He has come." This went on day after day, week after week, month after month, and year after long year. "Go outside and tell me if the Messiah has come. Go outside and tell me if He has come." Until one day, the student asked, "But Master, when the Messiah comes, won't you know it," pointing to his heart, "in here?" The Master looked at him, lovingly, and replied, "Ah, my son, no, because in here," placing a hand on his own heart, *"the Messiah has already come!"*

And that's how I feel. No kidding!

Acknowledgments

It would be impossible for me to thank individually all the persons I have relied upon to assemble the information that appears in this book. In particular, I have drawn heavily from the works of Karen Armstrong, James Carroll, Paul Johnson, Walter Keller, Melvin Konner, and Rabbi Joseph Telushkin set forth in my bibliography. In my chapters on Christianity, Jewish history, and Islam, for example, I sometimes use the same quotes from historical personages and sources they used in an effort to forcefully and accurately make my point. I learned the raw information as to dates, events, places, and personalities from them, and the many other authors listed in my bibliography, but the comments and observations I make about that data are mine. I often agree with the viewpoints of the other writers, but many of my insights, I think, are completely original, although there has been so much written about the topics I cover, I can't be 100 percent sure.

There are several people who inspired me to write *The Reluctant Jew*, but above all, there are three. First, Rabbi Mark Blazer, who led our synagogue as spiritual leader from 1995 to 1998. He's the most knowledgeable young man I've ever met. He could recite the names and achievements of all the prophets and sages and all the important Jewish and non-Jewish historical figures: kings, military leaders, physicians, merchants, philosophers, diplomats, scientists and artists, from Genesis through the twentieth century, and then recite them again, backwards. He planted in me a burning desire to learn history. Second, Rabbi Reuben Modek, who was our spiritual leader from August 1998 through August 2002. More than anyone, he brought the joy of Judaism into my life and demonstrated, by his example, its immense beauty. Due largely to his efforts, Jewish Community Centre of Greenwood Lake evolved into Congregation B'nai Torah, a place bursting with spiritual energy. And lastly, Rabbi Brenda Weinberg, who became our religious leader in September 2002. Before that, she'd been our cantor for years. Now she wears both hats. Due to her musical talents, vast knowledge, patience, dedication, and phenomenal teaching ability, I was bar mitzvahed at last, as an adult, in June 2002.

Special thanks also to my brilliant friend and neighbor, Michael Grosso. An experienced author, who's published several works, he taught me how to go about putting this book together. Without his help, guidance, and suggestions, it would never have gotten done. Thanks also to Chuck Noell, a business associate and friend, who pored over my manuscript, edited it, and helped make it flow. Finally, I want to thank my close friend, Bonnie

Kessler, so close that I often think of her as my "temple wife." She is, as this book goes to print, the president of Congregation B'nai Torah. Her encouragement and support during the several years it took to complete this work were beyond anything I had a right to expect.

Introduction

When I joined the Jewish Community Centre of Greenwood Lake in 1994 — now Congregation B'nai Torah — that was the first time I had set foot in a temple, other than for an occasional bar mitzvah, wedding, or funeral, in thirty-five years. Nonetheless, my interest in and excitement about the extraordinary story of the Jews — who've outlived all their ancient conquerors to survive intact into modern times — is intensely passionate. I go to sleep and wake up telling myself the story over and over again. In my dreams, I walk with Samson. Maybe in part, because I'm a lawyer, I've found it exhilarating to learn that story's grand history and then, as though preparing a big case for trial, researching the details I think unconvincing until I prove to myself whether they're right. Incredibly, since my election as president of Congregation B'nai Torah in 1999, I've managed to read 247 books on Judaism, Jewish history, and related subjects, cover-to-cover, including the Hebrew Bible. And I've retained almost everything.

Like many of my contemporaries, I was raised in an almost totally non-observant, non-religious household. Even so, my mother thought I should know at least something about my background, and forced me to enroll in Hebrew school. It was a colossal waste of time and money. I lasted six weeks before being expelled, i.e., physically thrown out of the building for incredible misbehavior. So when I turned thirteen, I was completely unprepared to be bar mitzvahed, and my parents threw a huge birthday party instead. I recall that not a single gift I received had anything to do with "Jewishness," but I did get several books about reptiles and some great camping equipment, things that were much more important to me at the time. I think by then, due to my ignorance, I began to develop an active hostility toward religion. Anyone who approached me telling Old Testament stories or worse, quoting cute little Biblical passages, I looked upon as a narrow-minded idiot and bigot. I had absolutely no respect for the local rabbis or ministers, and felt their true purpose in life was to drag us back into the Middle Ages. Thus began my spiritual development.

But, believe it or not, love and kindness always surrounded me. My parents taught that compassion toward others far surpassed other virtues. And they tried to live what they taught. My father, in particular, opened his heart to everyone. Often, when someone we knew – relative, friend or neighbor – had trouble, my father became physically ill. He felt their pain as deeply as if it were his own. He consoled and comforted them and, when he could, helped them financially. After a while I understood why people called him *"Menshi."* It means *"human being."* I've always felt that quality in him and pray, every day, that some of it has rubbed off on me. My father's love glows in my heart and I know that in my life, no one will ever be so near to me again.

This book is not primarily a history at all, although episodes and teachings from the Jewish past are woven into it throughout. It also touches deeply upon Christian and Islamic history and tries to answer the question, "How should we Jews relate to our modern-day Christian and Muslim neighbors?" There are chapters on Jehovah's Witnesses, the Baha'i, Hinduism, anti-Semitism, the Arab-Israeli conflict, the Jewish holidays and calendar, the Jewish experience in America, and the struggle to understand God. But what it's really about are my numerous and wondrous adventures as president of a small and struggling synagogue in Greenwood Lake, New York. My tenure there lasted four years, from June 1999 through June 2003. Under our constitution, I could not serve longer. That short period, however, was the most educational and meaningful of my life. Because I knew so little when I took office, I began reading everything about Jews I could lay hands on so, when called upon to address the synagogue membership or local community, as often happened, I wouldn't embarrass myself or, more importantly, my congregation. Slowly, I grew confident in my knowledge and found I was capable of contributing intelligently to discussions on Jewish topics. Even more surprising, I was soon leading those discussions.

As I read more and more, I discovered something incredible: the Jews have existed for so long and in so many places that by learning about Jewish history, you learn almost all world history as well. We Jews, as a people, outlasted every one of our ancient oppressors – Egyptian, Assyrian, Babylonian, Persian, Greek, and Roman – to survive whole and undaunted, still what we were then, into this century. We experienced those civilizations firsthand and their histories became part of our own history. The names of the months on the Jewish calendar, for example, *Tishre, Heshvan, Kislev* and the rest, are all Babylonian names. The epic holiday of the Jewish people, Passover, marks the Hebrews' journey to freedom from Egyptian bondage during the reign of Pharaoh Ramses II. Purim celebrates Esther and Mordecai's rescue of the Jews from massacre by Haman, a Persian prime minister. Chanukah celebrates the recapture of the Second Temple by Judah the Maccabee from Antiochus Epiphanes, King of the Syrian-Greeks. And Jesus Christ, undoubtedly the most famous Jew of all time, was executed by the Romans when Pontius Pilate was prelate of Judea. In 70 C.E., when the Romans destroyed the Second Temple, and shortly afterwards, in 136, when the Bar Kochba Rebellion was crushed, Jewish history did not end. We scattered to the corners of the Earth, including

India and China. In exile, over the centuries, we survived rampages of hate by Europeans, Arabs, and Cossacks. We withstood pogroms by Russians and Nazi extermination camps. We lived for nearly two thousand years in the Diaspora without a country, without power, in ghettoes, retaining our customs and beliefs until astonishingly, in the twentieth century, we re-established our ancient homeland.

But we Jews are not just a people; we bring to the fore our religion stretching back more than four millennia. From the early monotheism of Abraham arose Judaism and then, Christianity and Islam. Today, more than half the earth's population — nearly three and a half billion people — follow those religions and owe their very perception of the world to the ancient Hebrews. Although often impossible to believe, they all purport to a universal system of ethics in which love for others is the paramount virtue and each human life is sacred. And I speak from experience. My beautiful wife, Phyllis, is Indian and was born into a Protestant family. She converted to Judaism long before we met. But her mother and father and aunts and uncles are devout Christians, and some of them, Hindus. Her sister, on the other hand, is married to a Muslim and converted to and has been practicing Islam for more than twenty-five years. In addition, I have a first cousin who is married to an Indian woman, and she too is Hindu. Moreover, I have identical twin cousins and both are ordained rabbis. This incredible mixture has not weakened my Jewish identity. Rather, it's ignited in me an unquenchable desire to know about other traditions, and strengthened my belief that each of them seeks justice. At the same time, it's made me more certain than ever of the universality and wisdom of Jewish teachings. Most importantly, it's given me a unique vantage point: I can feel the world through the eyes of the different faiths of my own family members.

My Universalist point of view comes across in the pages of this book. While president, my congregation's visits to mosques, churches, and other places of worship and visits by Bahai, Buddhists, Christians, and Muslims to our synagogue were among the amazing adventures I experienced. Other adventures involved the many weird and also, wonderful personalities I encountered; the often-silly and sometimes-angry political battles I had to navigate between the old and new guards; the numerous new programs I spent hours helping to plan and took great pride in initiating; the lifelong friends I made, and just the never-ending struggle, which took up most of my time, to keep the synagogue solvent and its doors open. But the most exciting adventures, by far, were intellectual and spiritual.

Every book I read on Jewish history, everything I learned in adult Hebrew school classes, ideas and information I absorbed from other members, every fresh insight offered by the congregation's rabbi or cantor, entered deeply into my mind and opened it to whole new worlds. All that I learned about other religions opened it to still more worlds. I tell you, I've come away from my four years as president with the equivalent of a master's, no a doctoral, education in history, culture, and religion. In fact, much of the material in this book draws upon the forty-six articles I wrote for our synagogue newsletter, *From the Lakeside,* during my tenure. Many of those articles were historical and some dealt with Friday night services, the High Holidays, and other observances. Most, however, were about day-to-day business: ideas to make our membership grow, fundraising drives, community dinners, guest speakers, activities, trips, Hebrew school enrollment, award ceremonies, maintaining and improving our building, acquiring more property, annual dinner dances, Board of Trustees meetings, reports about synagogue happenings, community-wide events, and the like. So this book, aside from being an adventure story, is also a journal or how-to manual that I hope will be of interest to presidents-in-training of other congregations, both Jewish and non-Jewish.

As to spirituality, perhaps you'd expect otherwise, but I'm still not what you'd call "religious." In all my life, I've never felt an outside presence guiding or watching over me. But to live a just life, with Torah principles as a guide, does not require acceptance of rigid dogma or an unthinking belief in God. In Genesis, after Abraham's grandson, Jacob, wrestled all night with an angel, God changed Jacob's name to *Israel,* which means *to struggle with the Lord.* So to struggle with the meaning and existence of God, as did Jacob, is well within Jewish tradition. Today, we Israelites struggle to find God, somewhere, and do right as much as the ancients did. Fortunately, there's room in Judaism for a thousand points of view. There'd better be. As the joke goes: Ask two Jews the same question and how many responses will you get? Answer: "Keep counting." And when asked: "Do you really believe in God?" a venerated rabbi replied, "Not yet!"

Writing the pages that follow has been an intense three-year labor of love. But it was not at all an arduous task. Instead, the hundreds of hours I spent forming and setting down my thoughts — as with any undertaking you're really passionate about — was a joyful blessing. If what I've written communicates to you some of my excitement about Judaism and Jewish history and about the small synagogue I presided over, I will consider my efforts to have been a huge success.

Chapter One - The Jewish Centre

I asked my wife, "Phyllis, where is this place already?"

"Don't shout at me," she said. "How am I supposed to know? They said it's on Dutch Hollow Road, but there's no street number."

I looked at her. "Where's Dutch Hollow Road?"

Alyson, my eight-year-old, chimed in, "Why do we have to join a synagogue anyway?"

I almost told her the truth. We had moved to the Town of Warwick from Forest Hills three years ago and, unlike in the City, where 90 percent of the neighbors were Jewish, all of our new neighbors – every God-fearing one of them – were Christian. Living your whole life in New York City, you don't notice things like that. It's almost like living in Israel where, whether you belong to a synagogue or not, you're an authentic Jew just by being there.

"We're joining a synagogue," I thought, "because I'm damned lonely. I'm the only guy up here who doesn't own a gun, I don't go hunting, I don't fix my own porch, and I wouldn't know a Methodist from a Baptist. And if one more Jehovah's Witness knocks on my door," I smiled inside, "I'll convert *him*."

I smelled something. "Is that you, Zack?" I asked my son, the five-year-old.

"It's coming out, Dad. I can't hold it in anymore."

"Zack, we've only driven ten miles from the house. What's wrong with you?"

My wife corrected me. "We've been in the car for almost an hour. You ever hear of a map?"

"Dad," Alyson said, "I'm telling you, it was that brown building back there."

"Brown," I thought. "That building wasn't brown. It was light beige maybe or white, but incredibly grungy and shabby." I turned around.

"God," I thought, "this place hasn't been painted in forty years. It just looks brown."

"See," Alyson said, "there's cars in the parking lot and people."

"Is this the Jewish Centre?" I asked a man.

"Yes," he answered, "there's the front door, but watch the steps. They're loose. And don't use the handrails. They're loose too."

We could see he was limping, badly.

Anyway, we mounted the stairs and carefully, with Phyllis holding Zack's hand, climbed to the top and walked in.

Now, I'm not easily impressed, but Jewish Community Centre, on the inside, was the most gorgeous temple I'd ever seen. It looked right and felt right and exuded charm. Even Zack didn't run to the bathroom immediately. He looked around for a while, smiling. But then he remembered and dashed off. My wife and daughter were smiling too. There were high ceilings crisscrossed with pine beams, soaring arches, inviting corners, casual chairs at tables for sitting and talking, and every wall and all the ceilings had beautiful, knotted, soft wood paneling. It was as though someone had designed it right from a storybook.

We stood awhile, taking the place in. It was completely different from any synagogue I'd been at in Queens or Long Island. It wasn't Jappy, it wasn't glitzy, and it wasn't overbearing. It didn't make me think, "How much are they going to bilk me for to join this place?" Instead, it was amazingly down-to-earth and warm.

The synagogue was starting to fill up. It was Sunday morning and we thought we'd check out the Hebrew school. After a few minutes, a group of kids assembled and began pulling chairs into a circle and seating themselves. There were only eleven of them, but of all ages, and they were chattering excitedly. Another moment passed, when suddenly a deep, sonorous voice boomed out, "Shalom," and Rabbi Harris Goldstein, from a door in the sanctuary, strode in. "Shalom, everyone. Let's pick up where we left off. After Moses came Joshua, and when he died, tribal chiefs ruled the Israelites for 200 years. You remember the tribes, *Asher, Benjamin, Dan, Ephraim Gad...*" He reeled off the names effortlessly, *singing*. And the kids, in unison, sang back the rest: *"Issacar, Judah, Manasseh, Naphthali, Reuben Simeon, and Zeb, the twelve sons of Jacob from Judah to Ben, became the twelve tribes of Israel around two thousand six ten."* Rabbi Goldstein's assistant accompanied on guitar. I realized they were continuing a lesson that must have begun several Sundays ago. The lesson was part history, part music and song, and about fifteen minutes later, part storytelling. I couldn't listen for long, because we had an appointment to meet Susan Lobel, the synagogue president. But from the little I heard, I knew that Harris Goldstein was a phenomenal storyteller. Not only were the kids listening, but most of the adults had gathered around and were listening too.

A woman walked over and greeted us. "Hello, you must be Mr. and Mrs. Grossman. It's good to meet you. Come join us for something to eat. The Hebrew school parents are sponsoring a *kiddush* to celebrate the school's first anniversary." With that, she led us to a room next to the kitchen where some tables had been pushed together and were being set with bagels, whitefish, egg salad, and lox. Already, four or five people were gorging themselves. She said, "Better dig in now. If the other animals get to it first, there'll be nothing left."

I chuckled. "Are you Susan Lobel?" I asked.

"Yes, I remember speaking to you on the phone. Did you have any trouble finding us?"

"Not at all," I started to say. But my wife looked at me, with daggers. And so did Alyson, before running to join Zack, who was listening to the rabbi. I changed the subject.

"This is a beautiful synagogue," I remarked. "I've never been in one this nice before."

"We get a lot of compliments. Believe it or not, it used to be a discotheque, but was completely remodeled in the 1960s. Why don't you come by for services next Friday, when the place will really be decked out?"

Immediately, I started to hem and haw. I wasn't *that* lonely among my new neighbors and I didn't want to get sucked into having to actually be active in this or any synagogue.

"You know, I'm not sure how often we can do that. Mostly, we just want to know about the Hebrew school. We're thinking of signing up our kids."

"I saw them when you came in," Susan said. "They're the most beautiful children I've ever seen." She was buttering me up good. "Can I meet them?"

"Alyson, Zack," I called. "Come over here for a minute. This is Susan Lobel, who is the president of this synagogue. Introduce yourselves."

My daughter was not shy. "I'm Alyson Jenny Grossman. And that's Aly with a *y*."

We waited for my son to speak. We stared at him. "Zachary?" Zack said nothing.

"Oh God!" Aly yelled. "Why does he do that?" Aly continued, "Mrs. Lobel, this is my brother, Zachary, and his middle name is Matthew. Sorry, sometimes he acts a little funny."

Zack finally spoke up. "I was listening to the rabbi's story, you guys. But now you made me miss the end. Thanks a lot, Dad. And tell Aly to shut up." But it was a good sign. Maybe he wouldn't scream too loud when I told him he might be going to Hebrew school Sunday mornings instead of playing hockey all day.

Chapter Two - The New Rabbi

Notwithstanding the fabulous impression the Jewish Community Centre of Greenwood Lake made on us, for some reason, we didn't go back until four months later. When we entered, the same wonderful sensation of friendliness and warmth we felt the first time we visited swept over us. It was now January 1995, and by then, Rabbi Goldstein was no longer there. He had moved to California for warmer weather and a new position at a San Francisco temple. Although Zack hadn't screamed when we first visited JCC, he was starting to scream now. This was his first day of Hebrew school.

As Zack and Alyson and the other students assembled for orientation, I noticed there were still only eleven of them, but this time, the eleven included my two kids. That concerned me. The group was so small it was hard to think of it as a real school, especially without Rabbi Goldstein. However, there were no other choices. Two more Hebrew schools were in the area, but both required attendance not just Sundays, but some weekday nights as well. Given my level of synagogue observance at the time, and my family's – zero – that was out of the question. Also, dues at the synagogues that sponsored those schools were exorbitant, while dues for a family membership at JCC for an entire year — get this — was the ridiculous sum of $150. Even more ridiculous, Hebrew school tuition was an absurd $55. And to boot, unlike any other synagogue I'd ever heard of, there was no one-shot fee, or any fee, for building maintenance. I thought to myself, "No wonder the steps were *lawsuit* dangerous, the building dilapidated and without a paint job for longer than anyone could remember. The place had to be near bankrupt." I was right. I found out later the synagogue was living off a few large bequests and endowments. But those gifts had been given twenty-five to thirty years before by some of the founding members, and were just about gone. JCC was now, by any standard, almost dead broke.

I was very anxious to see who JCC had found to replace Harris Goldstein. Soon, a woman in her mid-twenties, and extremely attractive, walked to where the kids were sitting and began introducing herself.

"No," I thought. "It can't be. No rabbi could look that good."

Susan Lobel, who was standing near me, smirked at the expression on my face. "No, no, Mike. That's not the rabbi. That's Tracy, his wife."

I didn't care. She still looked good.

"Hello, everyone. Welcome to the JCC Hebrew school. I'm Tracy Blazer. You're in for a special time this year. We're going to do everything we can to make sure you learn a lot of new, exciting things and really enjoy yourselves while you're at it. That's a promise. But you have to do something in return. You have to promise me you'll pay attention and participate. Is it a deal?"

The youngest kids immediately said, "Yes, we promise." But the older ones sat stone silent. Tracy smiled at them all.

"First of all, how many of you are nine or younger?" Seven hands shot up. "Good," she said. "You seven are going to be in my class. The rest of you, *you silent types,* are going to be in the new rabbi's class." Her rapport with them was good. They laughed. The kids, I could tell, loved her. Just then, new rabbi Mark Blazer, from an entrance in the back, stepped briskly down from the Bimah, hugged his wife, and stood beside her on the school area floor. He held up a sign:: םולש םכלכ (Hello everyone). A few could read it. He held up another: ם'כורג ,ם'אגה ת'רגע רפס ת'גל ם'אגה ,גוט ,רקוג (Good morning, welcome to Hebrew school.) Only one could read that. Or, maybe, only one wanted to. Rabbi Mark said, "I was just talking to some of your parents and found out that almost half of you have never attended Hebrew school before. Also, I know that a lot of you would much rather be playing with your friends or," turning to Zack, and winking, "hockey."

"My wife," I thought, "or Susan Lobel must have said something."

"Don't worry. You're going to have a better time here than you would just about anyplace else. Your classes won't be boring. We're going to make them fun and different. We're going to have contests, prizes, and trips. We're going to have games and music. We're going to have movies and guests. You're going to learn incredible things here you never knew about before."

He looked up, over the kids, at the parents, who were standing behind the chairs that the kids were sitting on.

"As for you parents, I'm going to be teaching adult Hebrew school classes at least once a month. I've already got four people signed up; there's no extra charge, just a small donation for class materials will do, so if you're interested, let me know. If you're curious about history or want to know more about Judaism, I guarantee you won't be disappointed." He was confident. His manner, like his wife's, was impressive.

Although I was skeptical about the promises they had made, that they were going to make all of us *love* Hebrew school, I took an immediate liking to them anyway. They were intelligent, energetic, enthusiastic, great with kids and — as I learned when I got to know them better — extraordinarily knowledgeable. In particular, talking with Mark, it turned out, was like reading articles from Will Durant's *History of Civilization* or the *Encyclopedia Britannica*. So much fascinating, detailed information came out of him that, whenever he spoke, I always took notes, even when I wasn't in his adult ed. class.

Phyllis and I had some shopping to do, so we left the kids at JCC and headed into town. When we were done, I brought Phyllis home and then drove back to the Hebrew school. When I arrived, the kids' classes were finished, and Mark and Tracy were fielding questions from a number of the parents.

Right away, Zack ran up to me. "Dad, did you remember to bring my hockey equipment?" I had, but it was only 12:15; his game wasn't until 2:00 in Newburgh, about forty minutes away, and I had to drop Alyson off at horseback riding first. I told him we would leave in about thirty minutes and, in the meantime, he should eat the sandwich and soda I'd brought him. Alyson, however, didn't need any distractions. She was fully occupied. She was in deep conversation with her new friend, Robin, President Susan Lobel's daughter.

I walked over to where the rabbi and Tracy were chatting with the adults. I picked up that Mark was a second-year rabbinical student at the Academy for Jewish Religion in Manhattan and not yet, officially, a rabbi. His technical title with JCC was "religious director," but everyone called him Rabbi out of respect. He had, however, at least two more years of schooling to finish before ordination. That made him more affordable for JCC, which was crucial, given the dire state of its finances. It also made him more of an equal with the congregation's lay members and therefore, it seemed, much more approachable. Despite my very limited Jewish knowledge, I even decided to test him. At an appropriate break in the conversation, I brought up a point that was not too asinine.

I said, "Rabbi, my problem with all of this is that there's no evidence. You talk about Moses, Samuel, David, and the rest like they were real people, but there's no archaeological proof at all. If they were so important and had so many followers, how can that be?"

To remember my name, he looked at a list. He said, in front of everybody and without hesitating, "*Um,* Mr. Grossman, you know, you're right. If everything in the Bible really happened, there should be more evidence, lot's more. But did you know that archaeologists have uncovered artifacts in Israel and Palestine in recent years that are mind-boggling and support parts of the biblical text. And even if we can't accept all of the Old Testament narrative as historically factual, that's not what Judaism is about anyhow."

"It wasn't?" I thought, and *"What artifacts?"*

His answer brought me up short. I had been about to pounce because I'd expected the usual responses, "You have to have a little faith, sir" or "Can't you see that the wondrous workings of the world were designed by a *Supreme Being?*" or even, "Would you come with me to services later to pray with others, like yourself, who still find it difficult to believe?" But Mark Blazer was not like that at all. He was open-minded, skeptical, looking for proof himself, and possibly, even though convinced, maybe not completely. I decided that I really liked him and, right there and then, made a donation and signed up for his class.

Chapter Three - Adult Ed.

It was embarrassing to confront the true depth of my ignorance. With my cute little challenge to Mark Blazer concerning Moses, Samuel, and David, I had exhausted my entire store of knowledge and all of my opinions on the subjects of religion and Jewish history. I searched around frantically for some general books about Jews to study, in preparation for my upcoming adult ed. class, so I wouldn't look like an idiot. The most advanced one I could deal with was something called *Introduction to Jewish History - Abraham to the Sages,* by Seymour Rossel. It was a good children's book but too simple for most kids twelve or older. It was the book Aly and Zack were using in their classes. But I found it overwhelming. My upbringing had been so non-observant and so secular that I was conditioned against absorbing anything that smacked of religion, which included, obviously, Biblical and Jewish history. I had to force myself to read the book three times, cover-to-cover, before my resistance began to give way.

After I read it a fourth time and figured out some of the basics – like who the patriarchs were, where the twelve tribes supposedly came from, and when Exodus was supposed to have happened – to my absolute astonishment, I immediately picked up another book, Rossel's *Introduction to Jewish History - Part II,* and devoured it. This took place over a period of just two weeks. And then, I picked up another and devoured it. And then another. I was in shock. This stuff was addictive.

In mid-February, actually in the month of *Adar* on the Hebrew Calendar – *by then, you can see, I was really getting carried away* – I showed up with my kids, ready for Hebrew school. They ran over to Tracy, who today would handle all eleven of the kids with the help of JCC's cantor, Brenda Weinberg. Yes! Despite its desperate financial condition, JCC had a rabbi and a cantor. Although we were very small and very broke, we were the only congregation in the area that had both. I hoped my kids and I wouldn't get too far into our classes, only to see the place soon run out of money and go belly-up.

The adult class was a motley group of characters, eight of us in all, and a good number of them knew less than even I did. The majority wanted to learn about the spiritual, ethical teachings of Judaism first, and the factual, historical basis later. I wanted to do it the other way around. I felt I was already a pretty ethical person and didn't need any sanctimonious religious instruction to tell me how to behave. I mean, did any of us actually have to review the Ten Commandments to know that you don't kill, you don't steal, and you don't spread rumors about people? Not likely! And to conduct myself morally, I certainly didn't need help from a *Supreme Being* who, I was sure at the time, was a fantasy, in our imaginations, and couldn't possibly exist. What I wanted to know were the confirmable facts, i.e., the real events and personalities that gave rise to Judaism. What I wanted to know was whether Abraham, Sarah, Isaac, Rebecca, Jacob, his twelve sons, his sons becoming the twelve tribes, Rachel, Moses, the Exodus, the Commandments, the Ark of the Covenant, Joshua, the Canaanites, Samson, his battles with Philistines, his blinding, Samuel, and kings Saul, David, Solomon, and the rest – were just stories? Just myths? Or could some of it, part of it – any of it – be verified, and actually be true?

Mark, it turned out, favored my approach. He was a serious, *serious* history buff who enjoyed telling anyone who would listen about the Jewish past. He was able to recite a detailed history of every country and kingdom, every city and town, in any era, where the Jews had ever lived or traveled to. He could also, for example, reel off the names, dates, and deeds of all the Egyptian pharaohs, all the Babylonian and Assyrian kings, all the Greek and Roman emperors, all the popes and caliphs and, of course, all the Jewish historical personages, whether ancient or modern, from the very first one to the very last. He was, in short, an amazing teacher. He was better than any of my college or law school professors had been. There was nothing in history I could ask him that he didn't know at least something about.

I was on a roll. It had been three months since I'd read that first book, Rossel's *Introduction to Jewish History,* and I was beginning to get the big picture. By April 1995, our group of eight adults had sat through four of Rabbi Mark Blazer's classes and we were all making phenomenal progress. His emphasis, as promised, was always on history but I suppose it was inevitable that Jewish teachings about spirituality, morality, and God would often weave their way into his lessons. After all, Rabbi Blazer taught that from Abraham forward, the thrust of Jewish history has been our attempt to fulfill the special role we Jews believe God has chosen for us: to complete His work of Creation by bringing justice to the world and being a light unto nations. Some people would say, particularly hardcore doubters like me, "the special role we have chosen for ourselves."

"But Mark," I asked, "if a person truly does justice, does it really matter who did the choosing? Shouldn't the deeds he does in this world count for more than whether he believes there's a next?"

"Believe it or not," Mark said, "I agree with you. In Judaism, what a person does is much more important than what he thinks. And when a person realizes that and acts on it, I think he becomes truly 'Jewish' for the first time. You've probably sensed that all your life. That's why you're here, in this class. You want to know what Judaism really teaches.

"And," he addressed the others, "probably all of you."

It wasn't long before I became friendly with most of the other adult ed. students. There was Gary Birnberg, about my age, quiet and low-key, kind-hearted, and extremely knowledgeable. He was the only one as resolute as I was to master Jewish history. By trade he was a research chemist and would often busy himself fixing wiring, tiling floors, installing shelves, repairing furniture, rehanging doors, or patching the plumbing. Without him, and some of the other handy members, the place would have disintegrated. There was also Joanne, Gary's wife, not as confident as he was about the history, but determined to learn it. Much more important to Joanne was to study Judaism's ethical teachings and incorporate them into her life. She succeeded. So much so that eventually she became JCC's Hebrew school director. Other than president, no job at the synagogue had so many headaches and required so much time and effort. Joanne and Gary communicated their love for the synagogue to their daughter, Sarah, who later became one of the school's star students. I also became close with Pat Weisslander, her husband, Mark, and their three children, Stacy, Jason, and Todd. They were, by far, JCC's most devoted family and almost lived at the synagogue. Pat never missed Friday night services. Never! She held the record for the most consecutive services ever attended by anyone, including rabbis and cantors. Pat's husband, Mark, like Gary Birnberg, was very handy, and helped keep the building from falling apart. As for their kids, for many years, they were the most involved of all the young people at JCC. Especially Todd. He, more than any other kid, or adult for that matter, was willing to do anything that was asked of him for the congregation. I could never turn around without him being underfoot and saying, "Can I help?" And then almost tripping over him.

But the one I really hit it off with from the start, and who became not only my best friend but my wife's as well, was Mrs. Bonnie Kessler. Phyllis and I had so many good times with Bonnie that we gave her a nickname that, no matter how often we used it, made everyone grin. We started calling her "My Temple Wife."

Chapter Four - Temple Wife

Bonnie had just pulled into the parking lot with Jonathan, who was only a year older than Zack. His attitude toward Hebrew school was the same as my son's – lousy. But they were both getting through it okay, in part because they had become friendly and looked forward to seeing each other Sundays. The months were zipping along and it was now September 1995. It was almost Rosh Hashanah.

"Hello Bonnie," I said. We missed you last week. Where were you?"

"Oh, I was around, Temple Husband, but Jonathan was sick and couldn't go to Hebrew school. So we both stayed home. How are you, My Temple Husband?"

I had to laugh. Now, every time she greeted me, she did that. I thought, "Good Lord. What have I started?"

"I'm fine, Temple Wife. Aly and Zack just went inside. You know there's no adult ed. today, so me and Warren are going out for breakfast."

"What do you mean, *you and Warren?* I can tell you right now, you mean you, *me,* and Warren. I'm going too."

It was a riot, teasing her. I said, "Okay. Maybe we'll let you tag along this time."

She said, "You guys? I'm the one who turned you onto the Breezy Point in the first place. It's the best breakfast place in Greenwood Lake. Not only am I tagging along, but you, Temple Husband, are paying for me."

Starting seven weeks before, going to the Breezy Point had become our routine. Whenever there wasn't adult ed. Sunday mornings, the three of us would go there to eat. We piled into Warren's car, and as soon as we did, he turned to me and said, "Did you have to invite Bonnie? Again?" He enjoyed teasing her at least as much as I did.

Warren could be great to hang out with. He always had good jokes. His son, like my kids and Jonathan, was in the Hebrew school, but Warren had no interest whatever in joining the adult ed.class. He wanted his son to be bar mitzvahed, but as for himself, he explained, "It's just not my thing." Unlike with me, Susan Lobel hadn't been able to suck him into being even a little active at the synagogue. Not yet! If Susan had her way, he and the rest of us would've already been on the board of trustees. JCC's active membership was so small that she was always desperate to find people to help her. At the time, however, Bonnie, Warren, and I were unprepared to do anything more than just show up once in a while.

Only five minutes away, we pulled up to the Breezy Point and walked straight to our usual table. We were regulars and the waiters all knew us. I ordered eggs and home fries, Warren ordered pancakes, and Bonnie ordered, *uh,* toast. Just toast, no butter. And juice. She was on one of her diets again. That's something she and Phyllis had in common. Diets. I dug into my eggs and thought, "At least she's a cheap date."

The conversation was animated. We talked about the synagogue, our kids, Israel, our spouses, relatives, local politics, business, and anything else that came to mind. We had lots to say and paused, only occasionally, to take mouthfuls of food. After forty-five minutes, the conversation was still rolling. But for the last several minutes, Bonnie had been talking non-stop about her nieces, Rayna and Andrea, both of whom I had met and were gorgeous. They were still pretty young, but we imagined what they would look like when they grew up.

At that point, Warren turned to Bonnie and, with a mischievous gleam, asked, "How old are you anyway, Bonnie?" I wasn't sure myself. I hadn't thought about it. All I knew was that she was younger than me.

She replied, "Well, Warren, how old do you think I am?"

He looked her over. She felt kind of good that he was examining her. And then, "Oh, I don't know, about forty-six or so?"

Warren and I kept right on talking. Around fifteen minutes later, maybe more, we noticed that Bonnie, my Temple Wife, had not spoken another word. It was as if, physically, she could no longer talk. She had gone red, her eyes bulged, and she was twitching, grimacing, and stammering, almost drooling, trying to whisper something between clenched teeth.

"What's the matter, Temple Wife?" I said. "Speak up. I can't hear you." I thought maybe she was sick. "Are you okay? Are you choking on something?"

"No," she managed, barely audible. And, even less audible, almost gagging: "But, if you don't mind, I'd like to leave, now!"

Even Warren, totally heedless to that point, became concerned. "What's with that twitch? Here," he said. "Drink some water."

"No, thank you," she said. Not 'No, thank you' in a normal voice but 'No, thank you,' in a high, high voice with a tone meaning, 'I wouldn't take your water if it was the last drop on earth and you were the last man.'

He shrugged, excused himself, then burped, and went to wash up.

Then Bonnie turned to me and, with her eyes as well as her mouth, in fact, with her whole body, said, "Did that moron say forty-six? Or so?"

Still not quite getting it, I thought, "What's she so mad about? So what if he was off by a few years."

But at last, she was able to speak, and in a voice so loud I'm certain Warren heard her all the way in the men's room: "I'm not forty-six, you schmucks, I'm thirty-eight, *Ex-Temple Husband*. Got it? *Thirty-eight!* And I'm gorgeous and got a great figure too."

Now I couldn't speak. More accurately, I thought it best to keep my mouth shut until Bonnie blew off more steam. I don't think I had ever seen anyone that insulted before. But it was funny, so funny that Warren and I had to fight back the giggles.

When we got to the car, Bonnie sat by herself in the back, frigid. I was afraid to say anything. But Warren, of course, still pretty oblivious, delivered the finishing touch, "When we go to the Breezy Point next week, Bonnie, maybe we'll let you tag along again – *if you're lucky!*"

Not to be outdone — although I was afraid if I turned around I'd see her burst a blood vessel — I added, "Don't worry, Temple Wife, it'll be my treat."

And with that, we arrived back at the synagogue.

Chapter Five - High Holiday Highs

The moment we stepped through the doors, Susan Lobel hurriedly approached us. I tried to avoid her because I knew what was coming. I had been warned. She was going to insist that we help set up the synagogue for the High Holidays, and take part in the services in a big way. In fact, she was going to ask us to read several lengthy passages from the *Mahzor* prayer book, in front of the entire congregation and all of the guests, during the three days of Rosh Hashanah and the two days of Yom Kippur. At the thought of it, I actually began to shake. I figured I'd better let Bonnie and Warren deal with her. But Bonnie, who had still not recovered from her breakfast date, ran over to Pat Weisslander and started telling her the whole story. Especially the part about how her supposed friend, me, just sat there and let Warren insult her. They were talking loud enough that I heard Pat say, "My God, if I had been there, how old would Warren have said I looked? About sixty-two? Or so?"

To which Bonnie said, "Yeah, and I'm sure Mike would have defended you just like he defended me."

To which Pat responded, "Yeah, right."

As for Warren, when he saw Susan Lobel take her first step in our direction, he hightailed it back to the parking lot to escape into his car with the remark, "I forgot to get gas." Which left only me to face her.

"Hello, Mike. I hear Aly and Zack are doing great in Hebrew school and that you *love* adult ed. Mark says you're one of his best students. That's terrific. Please give Phyllis my regards and thank her for the cookies she made for the kids. And by the way, thanks for paying your dues so quickly, and for the donation you made. I'm certain you know that we really needed the money."

"Damn," I thought, "she was good at this." I wished she'd stop complimenting me so it would be easier for me to outright refuse when she asked me do readings and even, God forbid, prayers, at the High Holidays, instead of my just sitting safely in the audience as I had planned.

"You know, Mike, Rosh Hashanah is only seven days away, and Rabbi Mark and I and the entire congregation really need your help. Keep in mind, Mark's only a second-year rabbinical student and, although he knows his stuff, he's never done the Rosh Hashanah and Yom Kippur services in front of a live audience before. Cantor Weinberg's done them several times, but only in a support role. So Mark badly needs skilled and knowledgeable lay members to back him up. I told him there was absolutely no doubt in my mind we could count on you. Was I right?"

"Damn," I thought again. "She *was* good at this." And, now, she had me by the cajones. "But maybe," I began praying, "I could still get out of it." I would plead ignorance and volunteer to do one, very short English reading, and tell her, "Maybe next year I'll do more."

I said, "Okay, I'll do…"

But before I could finish and limit it to just one reading, Susan said, "Thanks so much. I consider you're volunteering to help, on such short notice, a real *mitzvah*. You'll be doing two or three of the readings from your seat in the audience, but most of them from up on the *Bimah* next to Rabbi Blazer. Isn't that great?" Then she handed me a list of what she wanted me to read. My chest tightened. It was twenty-two pages long. When I looked it over, my chest tightened more. Hard! A quarter of it, although transliterated, was in Hebrew. And another quarter of it, so help me, was songs.

I found Pat. I said, "Listen, you know the services better than anyone except the rabbi and Cantor Weinberg. Look at this, *this book with singing*, Susan expects me to read. I don't know this stuff at all, not even in English! Will you do it for me?"

She said, not entirely jokingly, "After the way you treated me and Bonnie? Are you serious?"

"Pat," I laughed, "you weren't even there. And I didn't mistreat Bonnie. I love Bonnie. We were just teasing her."

"Oh yeah," she replied, "Do you really think that telling a young woman she looks forty-six is funny? I don't. You're lucky she only called you a shmuck. I'd of thought of something worse."

I could tell she was putting me on. But she and Bonnie had decided to try to get me back. And good!

"Pat, you're kidding me, right?"

"Well, you like kidding people, don't you? Now it's my turn."

"And mine," Bonnie called. "I hope you have fun running the High Holiday services, Temple Husband. By yourself! See you next Sunday at Hebrew school."

Boy they were really enjoying this. Zinging me.

"But, I didn't do anything. It was Warren..."

"Well, then maybe you can get *him* to help you. Bye."

Pat said, "And you can't leave yet. You have a meeting with Susan and her High Holiday Committee and with Rabbi Mark and Cantor Brenda, to plan the Rosh Hashanah and Yom Kippur services.

"But I can't," I said, "I have to take my kids home."

"Don't worry," Pat said. "I have to meet my husband in Pine Island and I'll drop your kids off on the way."

"But..." I started.

"I took care of it," Pat added. "I called Phyllis and she knows you'll be late."

Those two had me good. I was trapped. At the meeting of the High Holiday Committee, which consisted of eight people – Susan Lobel, First Vice President David Weinberg, newsletter editor Wendy Dembeck, Tracy Blazer, Gary Birnberg, and me, plus the rabbi and cantor – Susan gave each lay person his or her assignment. No one looked the least bit worried except me. I was terrified. In fact, I was nearly in a faint. I was dying. The only thing that gave me hope I'd somehow get through it was that Mark seemed to understand that, although I was a good history student in his adult ed. class, I knew absolutely *nada* about Rosh Hashanah or Yom Kippur services. Or, for that matter, any of the services. That I showed up at the synagogue once in a while Friday nights, and pretended to mouth the words, he realized meant next to nothing. But my anxiety went beyond even that. That year, 1995, Rosh Hashanah would begin Sunday evening, September 24, and wouldn't end until Tuesday evening, September 26. Even worse, Yom Kippur would begin in the middle of the week on Tuesday, October 3, and end Wednesday evening, October 4. "How many days," I wondered, "could I possibly take off from work?" I had planned to take off a half a day for each holiday. Not the three and a half days, at a minimum, that would be necessary if I had to read everything Susan gave me.

But I saw no way out. I actually started to sweat and get short of breath. Rabbi Mark, however, must have seen my misery, because he cut me a big break. He eliminated from my twenty-two pages all of the Hebrew and all of the singing. And he did it in a way that, if I wanted, I'd only have to be at the synagogue for one full day for each of the holidays. When he did that, I calmed down. I felt my lungs fill with air. I was able to inhale normally again. Now all I had to do was practice aloud several pages of prayer book readings and, as miserable as I knew I would be, deliver them to an audience. That I could handle.

I thought, "Bonnie and Pat better start atoning for their sins now, not wait for Yom Kippur, and hope they didn't run into me in the supermarket this week. I'd kill them." And for once, I wasn't kidding.

Rosh Hashanah arrived on September 24 or, I should say, on the first day of *Tishre*, which is actually the *seventh* month on the Hebrew calendar. That struck me as very strange. Why did Rosh Hashanah, the Jewish New Year, happen then instead of in *Nissan*, which is the first month on the Hebrew calendar? It was the same as if we celebrated the secular New Year in July instead of on January 1. I was embarrassed to ask, but finally mentioned my confusion to member Rich Gedzelman, who explained that in Judaism, there were several New Years, and Rosh Hashanah, though the most important, was only one.

"In fact," he said, "there is a New Year in *Nissan*. It's Passover, the most famous of all Jewish holidays, which commemorates the exodus from Egypt and rebirth of the Jews as a free people. In Jewish history, that event certainly qualifies as a New Year. Rosh Hashanah, on the other hand, celebrates the moment when God said, 'Let there be light,' and created the world. It marks the date five thousand seven hundred fifty five years ago when, according to the Hebrew calendar's reckoning, everything began."

But the one who made the most sense out of it, believe it or not, was Alyson. She said, "Dad, Rosh Hashanah always feels like the New Year to me because every year in September is when I start a new year of school." That felt right to me too.

That first evening's Rosh Hashanah service was relatively short, and my readings, which continued into the next day, came off well. Real well! I didn't garble my words or mumble at all. Even my wife, who knew I was almost in torment attending religious services, let alone participating in them, was kind of impressed. We returned to the synagogue the next morning and, right after Rabbi Mark finished reading the Torah portion, Rich Gedzelman, who was so Jewishly skilled that if needed he could be "acting rabbi," sounded the shofar; hauntingly, beautifully. Later, when I got to know him better, I discovered that was the least of his musical talents. He could play at least three different instruments and his voice was so superb that in a pinch, he could be not only rabbi but cantor too. Eventually, he became the Hebrew school's music teacher and the congregation's choir director as well.

But my kids, I have to say, were bored out of their minds. At about 1:30, just before the end of the afternoon service, that is, the *Mincha* service, with the extra Rosh Hashanah *Musaf* added on, I decided they'd had enough and Phyllis and I promised she'd take them home as soon as the afternoon service was done, and they wouldn't have to come back. I'd completed almost all my readings and had less than two pages left for the evening service, i.e., the *Maariv*. I was actually looking forward to it. There was just one thing left to do before the congregation could break for the afternoon, go home for a bite to eat, and then return for *Maariv*. It was a ritual called *Tashlikh* in which we would symbolically rid ourselves of sin, by throwing bread crumbs into moving water, which at JCC, I discovered could not, for a number of reasons, be performed in a normal way.

From the *Bimah*, after he finished the last *Mincha* prayer, Mark announced, "And now we will do *Tashlikh*. Please join me outside and assemble next to the stream, in the woods to the left of our building."

Zack and I looked at each other. We had been to that stream at the end of August, three weeks earlier, not for any religious purpose, but because Zack wanted to see if there were any frogs to catch. There weren't, and for good reason. The stream was no longer there. It had completely dried up during the unusually hot summer. We tried to warn Mark, but by the time we got to where the stream had been, forty people were already standing around.

"Rabbi Mark," Zack said, "where are we going to throw the bread crumbs?"

Mark, as he opened his *Mahzor* to the correct page for the *Tashlikh* prayers, replied, "Into the running waters of this beautiful brook…" But when he actually looked, all that was there was a dusty, shallow ditch.

We shifted around, a little embarrassed. But then Susan Lobel yelled out, "Let's go to Plan B. We're going to walk over to the lake."

So we all followed her, but when we got there, there was another problem. There was no lake. The water level was so low that it was no longer a lake, but a festering, odiferous swamp.

"Wow!" Zack shouted. "Look at all the frogs. And there's turtles too."

"Look, Zack," said Jonathan, "at those huge water bugs," and then, really excitedly, "and at the size of that water snake."

"Wow," Zack said again. "This is the best part of the whole service."

I thought to myself, "We need a Plan C."

But there was no Plan C. So there, on the shores of the Greenwood Lake Swamp, we performed the *Tashlikh* ceremony on what was, except for Yom Kippur, the holiest day of the year. To his credit, despite the circumstances, Mark did an exceptional job of making the ceremony meaningful and interesting. He even made jokes. The water was so foul and infested with creatures that when it was time to throw in the breadcrumbs, and thereby cast away our sins, Mark said, "I don't know how many more sins this water can take." It was even funnier when we actually started throwing the crumbs in. A freshwater eel, that's how Zack and Jonathan identified it, wiggled to the surface and gobbled them up.

Thus ended *Tashlikh*. Zack had such a good time that he insisted on coming back later for the evening service thinking we might go to the lake again. "Dad," he explained, "night is the best time to catch bullfrogs, because when you shine a flashlight in their eyes, they freeze and it makes them easy to grab."

He was so excited, he even talked his sister into coming too.

Chapter Six - A Lot of Atoning

Now, until that New Year's Day, September 24, 1995, the first of *Tishre* on the Hebrew calendar, 5755, I had never taken part in a *Tashlikh* ceremony. I knew, however, that the one I had just witnessed was unique, to say the least, even in the annals of JCC. I was certain that no other synagogue in the area, maybe in the world, had ever held one quite like it; with a non-existent stream, frogs, turtles, a non-existent lake, water bugs, snakes, eels, and a swamp as part of the ambience. But that was just the beginning. There were more weird and peculiar, but at the same time endearing, things about JCC to come. And sometimes, not so endearing.

By the time Yom Kippur arrived, I was over my panic at having to stand before the entire congregation and do readings. I was relaxed enough that I began to notice things. I observed, for example, that in connection with the High Holidays, other than actually leading the services and singing, which obviously were the responsibilities of the rabbi and cantor, Susan Lobel did almost everything else that needed to be done *by herself*. I thought, "That's not right. How can we expect her do so much alone?" Although some people, especially her husband, Mark, First Vice President David Weinberg, and a precious few others did their share, Susan was the one who seemed to do all the heavy lifting. She set up the *Bimah* and made sure it was spotless, she set out the extra chairs she had rented for the large number of people who would attend, she made sure the microphones and air conditioners were working, she greeted everyone as they entered the synagogue and made them feel welcome, she handed out prayer shawls to all the men, she passed out the prayer books, she adjusted the lighting and overhead fans, she cued everyone who had readings so they would know when it was their turn and, in between, she slaved in the kitchen with her husband, preparing food for the break-fast that would be served after the final Yom Kippur prayer.

If most of the people who attended the Yom Kippur services were even a little bit appreciative of Susan's efforts, I suppose she would have felt a deep sense, or at least some sense, of personal satisfaction in having organized, almost single-handedly, the holiest holiday of the year for the congregation. But that was not the case. By their actions, a significant number of the attendees demonstrated not only that they were not appreciative, but that they felt they were somehow divinely entitled to the benefits of Susan's hard labor. This, despite the fact that, unlike any other synagogue I knew of, JCC charged no one, not even non-members, a High Holiday admission fee at the door. Also, of the more than 150 people who showed up for the services, only a shockingly few felt it incumbent on them to make an appropriate High Holiday contribution to the congregation. Even I, who had virtually no previous experience as to proper synagogue etiquette, knew better. Every other synagogue I'd heard of collected many thousands of dollars in High Holiday contributions from its congregants and guests, in addition to collecting a steep admission fee to get in. At JCC that year, however, the total take for both Rosh Hashanah and Yom Kippur was a pitiful $2,600 and a good amount of that had to be used to pay for the elaborate break-fast spread the members and even their guests felt they had a right to expect.

When I saw people piling food on their plates, I was ashamed of a lot of them. The fact that many of them had made no financial contribution, or at most a minuscule one, didn't stop them from stuffing their faces. Moreover, a small but significant number of those same members were seriously in arrears on their pitifully low annual dues, and had no intention of voluntarily paying up. Several had to be hounded for months before they paid, and a few, when confronted, resigned their membership rather than fork over what they owed. A couple of weeks after Yom Kippur, I learned that my family's High Holiday donation of $175 was the second highest that year. Since I was one of the newest members, I couldn't help thinking to myself, "How selfish and inconsiderate! No wonder this place is broke."

So, to say the least, the pathetic financial support JCC received from its members was among the weird and peculiar, and definitely not endearing things I discovered about my synagogue. On the rare occasions when someone suggested that we immediately raise our absurdly low dues to help cover expenses, someone else — often a congregant who was in arrears — would say, "But then we'll lose half our members." Whenever I heard that, I would think to myself, "If we don't get some money in here soon we won't have a synagogue to lose members from."

All in all, I felt my congregation had a lot to atone for.

Nonetheless, despite its difficult financial situation, somehow JCC continued to exude a warmth and charm that was unique. Whenever we had visitors, including rabbis from other congregations, they always commented how good the place made them feel. It was, I think, something about the ramshackle informality of JCC, as opposed to the pretentiousness of some other synagogues, that attracted everybody. That quality made us overlook many of its severe problems. It was just a run-down old building that had been converted from, well, a dance club and bar, into a synagogue, and several long-overdue major repairs, for which there was never any money, were desperately needed. Otherwise, for example, the leaks in the roof would soon turn into floods, the increasingly noisy antique air conditioners and heaters would soon make it impossible for anyone to hear anything, and all of the doors and windows would literally start falling out of their rotting frames. Sometimes, our unpaved dirt parking lot became so rutted and muddy that it was impassable and we were forced to cancel services. Also, if the front steps weren't repaired soon, we really would have a lawsuit on our hands. There had been a couple of bad injuries already but we just didn't have the wherewithal to fix the broken stairs. Instead, we warned people, verbally, to be careful. I thought to myself, "A lot of good that'll do when we get sued. The last thing we need is for our insurance premiums to go up." Due to its state of severe disrepair, people who might have joined JCC as new members sensed that we were broke. They sensed that its existing membership simply did not have the income to support a full-fledged operation. Unfortunately, they were right, and for that reason, usually went elsewhere. But, despite our inability to make repairs, JCC's charm never failed to make everyone who entered smile. We always seemed to get just enough new members to keep going. That was one of the weird things about the place.

Given our financial limitations, another thing that was weird, but gave us character, was that JCC employed a rabbi *and a cantor*, albeit both part-time. From a budget standpoint, that was impossible to justify. We were seldom open during the week, or even on Saturdays, and most of the services and activities usually took place only on Friday evenings, and Hebrew school classes only on Sundays. Some of the newer members thought it would be better if we took the salary we were paying our cantor, used it to pay our rabbi more, although less than their combined salaries were together, and asked him to start conducting services on Saturdays as well as on Fridays, and conduct Hebrew school classes one evening during the week as well as on Sundays. That way, we would be a much more full-service synagogue and, at the same time, would save money by eliminating one of the salaries. They pointed out that no other synagogue in the county, including the larger and richer ones that could afford to if they wanted, had a paid cantor on staff. Cantor Brenda Weinberg, however, was so popular that the vast majority of the membership refused to even consider the idea. And even if they had, Brenda's husband, David, was the first vice president, and chairman of the board of trustees. Getting anything detrimental to his wife past him, even a small but necessary salary cut, would have been well-nigh impossible.

I also noticed that, like our building, most of JCC's membership was tired and worn out. A good 60 to 65 percent of them were over sixty years old, with about 33 percent well into their seventies. Many of these older members had already devoted several years of their time and energy to the synagogue and had become a bit distressed and frustrated that the congregation had, for the last decade or so, been unable to attract enough younger people to infuse the place with new energy and keep it vibrant. Aside from the parents of the kids in JCC's very small Hebrew school, a few of whom were in their thirties but most in their mid-forties or even fifties, no one thirty-five or younger had joined the congregation in years. That would have to change, or JCC would simply fade out of existence.

But to me, the weirdest thing of all that happened at our synagogue, by far, was when Susan Lobel came over to me about eight months after the High Holidays and said, "Mike, how would you like to be second vice president?" I actually thought, and am not kidding, she had downed one too many glasses of Kiddush wine and was drunk.

Chapter Seven - Second Vice-President

When Susan asked me that, I blew her off right away. I said, "You can't be serious, Susan. You know I have absolutely no religious training or background. You know I don't speak or read Hebrew, that I can barely follow the services, and I was never even bar mitzvahed. And you've heard me try to speak Yiddish and know that I mispronounce every word. My accent, in fact, is a joke around here. Not only that, I don't even think there's a God. How can I possibly be part of the leadership of this, a conservative synagogue, or any synagogue? Why don't you ask Pat or Gary Birnberg? Or even Warren? You'd be better off with him."

She said, "Well, you're here participating, aren't you? You go to adult ed. You come to synagogue activities and show up at services now and then. Give it a shot. If it doesn't work out, you can step down. Will you think about it?"

I said, "Okay, I'll think about it. But, *please,* don't count on me."

Every day at work that week, I couldn't help thinking how far-fetched the idea of my becoming a vice president of the Greenwood Lake Jewish Community Centre was. My motives for joining the synagogue in the first place were clear: to enroll my kids in Hebrew school so they would know something about their Jewish heritage and, maybe, to find some friends for me and Phyllis to socialize with. That's it. Nothing more. And, although I'd become extremely interested in learning Jewish history as a result of Rabbi Blazer's adult ed. classes, that was just a way for me to fill in the huge gaps in my knowledge about history in general. The Jews had been around for so long, in so many places, that by learning Jewish history, I was automatically learning a lot of world history as well. But when it came to identifying myself as part of the Jewish people or as a serious adherent of the Jewish faith, any attraction I felt was overridden by my much stronger identity as a twentieth-century American who valued the ideas of freedom and free thought and, following from that, my self-image as a modern, secular thinker who did not believe in the God of the Scriptures. If I agreed to become second vice president of JCC, I would have to pretend otherwise. I would have to pretend that I accepted ideas I had long ago rejected. That I couldn't do. I was only a sort of amateur Jew at best and knew it.

Strangely, even though many months passed, I couldn't dismiss Susan's offer from my mind. I wondered why. Although I felt very secure with what I considered to be my broad identity as a worldly, open-minded American, at the same time, my underlying Jewish identity — submerged though it might be — tugged at my thoughts. One night, as I lay awake in bed, remembering back to my student years in Ann Arbor at the University of Michigan, the reasons I couldn't ignore Susan's offer started to hit me. Those years, 1968 to 1972, was the only time, other than since I moved my family to Warwick in 1991, that I'd ever lived outside of New York City and outside, therefore, of a predominantly, or at least extremely influential, Jewish culture. In retrospect, I realized that while at the university, I had often tried mightily, albeit mostly subconsciously, to downplay, and sometimes outright conceal, the fact that I was Jewish – even that my last name was *Grossman* – so I could more easily socialize with and be accepted by the people I encountered, 85 percent of whom were Christian. But my efforts didn't matter. Although I didn't identify myself as Jewish, almost all of the non-Jews I became acquainted with did. And that's not to say that any of them, except for an inconsequential handful, ever hinted at harboring any anti-Jewish feelings. To be fair, I have to add that when I met people, after first noticing their sex and then their race, I too thought that the next most important identifying information about them was their religion. There was no avoiding it. The divide between the Jewish world, which I had never consciously thought myself a part of, and the Christian world, which maybe most of them didn't much think about either, was nonetheless real. It was much more noticeable in the Midwest than it had been on the East Coast in New York City, and always seemed an unspoken yet tangible and, at times, uncomfortable presence. However, no one, even when the opportunity arose, wanted to talk about the frightening core reason for that divide. We were all, in truth, subconsciously too afraid to bring it out into the open; too fearful of the ingrained hatreds that might be brought to the surface. How could it be otherwise? For to honestly face what the Christian/Jewish divide was all about, we would have to acknowledge this: "From its very inception 2,000 years ago, Christianity has taught that the Jews murdered God. Tortured him! Not the Romans. Not Pontius Pilate. The Jews. The Church taught that the Jews had rejected Jesus Christ, their own messiah, and were, until they begged forgiveness and accepted him, deservedly cursed. By their own despicable beliefs and actions, they had brought upon themselves Christendom's eternal and justified hatred." Every student on campus, including the most fundamentalist, Bible-thumping, God-fearing Christians among us, dreaded having to admit that. And no one, except the most overt anti-Semites, ever had the guts to openly say it. In truth, only a very few Jews wanted to think about it either.

My remembrance of that core reason for the Christian/Jewish divide was why I couldn't stop thinking about becoming JCC's second vice president. I was reassessing and confronting, for the very first time in my adult life, my basic identity.

The next night, I thought some more about my college years. My two best friends there were Michael McChrystal, a Roman Catholic from Traverse City in northwestern Michigan, and Wiley Livingston, a southern Presbyterian from Birmingham, Alabama. On college forms, in the box next to Religion, they would check off *Christian*, but like me, were almost totally non-observant. They both fell into the category of "extremely liberal Christians" who didn't take religion too seriously and, by the time I met them during my second year at Ann Arbor, couldn't care less that I was Jewish. Living on a big college campus had given them experience they hadn't had before in relating to and socializing not only with Jews, but with students who were Muslim, Hindu, Buddhist, and even Bahai or Sikh. I discovered, however, that although they had gotten used to and were comfortable with Jews, some of their friends and family members at home were not.

During spring break in 1970, which coincided with the Easter holiday, Mike McChrystal invited me to spend a week at his parents' house in Traverse City. "City" is a misnomer, because even today, it's a remote, midsize, country town, and its population remains well under 20,000. Back when I visited, the population was thousands smaller, and the moment I got there, it was almost as though I was a visitor from another planet. His family, however, was great. They were gracious and kind and went way out of their way to make me feel welcome and at ease. But somehow they didn't quite know what to make of me. A couple of times, I heard his parents ask him if I was all right, if they were treating me okay, and even if I needed something special to eat. They just weren't accustomed to Jewish guests. Some of his childhood buddies, however, a few of whom had never traveled further than Detroit, were something else. After touring around with Mike and a couple of them for a day or two, it struck me that in Traverse City, there was not a single synagogue and not a single Jewish neighborhood. In Traverse City, in fact, there was not a single Jew. Except me.

About halfway through my week with Mike, he and his family had to visit some relatives in a town thirty miles away. While they were gone, Mike arranged for me to go water skiing and boating on nearby Lake Michigan with a group of his buddies. He told me, "Don't worry, I told these guys to take good care of you. A few of them are big beer drinkers and real local yokels, but you'll be fine." But I could see he was a little concerned.

At around 9:00 that morning, twelve of Mike's friends, some of whom I had already met, pulled up in a van. A guy named Marty yelled out, "Welcome aboard, Mr. Mike Grossman, hop in. What'll it be, Bud

Light or Miller?" And with that and a pleading look in my eyes, I waved goodbye to the McChrystal family and, for the first time since I'd arrived in Traverse City, felt not only as though I was from another planet, but that these buddies of Mike's were aliens too.

By the time we arrived at the lake, Marty had already downed three Buds. Rodney, his cousin, was working on his fourth. For the first two hours, a few of them worked at readying the water skiing equipment and boat, but mostly, they all just milled around, telling jokes, blasting country music, playing touch football, and guzzling more beers. And they didn't leave me out. They shoved at least six beers at me, four of which I poured into the lake when they weren't looking. I tried to join their conversations, but felt like such an outsider that I couldn't think of a thing to say. Finally, one of them, Tommy, came and sat next to me.

He said, "I hear you're from New York City."

"Yeah?" I said, getting set for a fight, "What about it?"

He heard my defensive tone. "Mike, stay calm. No offense intended. I just wanna know, what's it like living over there?"

I relaxed. "Not bad," I answered. "I love it. There's millions of people everywhere and tons of things to do. But," trying to make a joke, "not much water skiing. Ever been there yourself?"

"Naaw, but I've been to Detroit two times and my girlfriend and me are gonna drive to Chicago next summer. It should be good."

I looked at him. Tommy had to be at least three years older than me, which would make him about twenty-three, but in his entire life, he had never left his home state. His trips to Detroit, *Michigan* were the furthest he had ever been from Traverse City, *Michigan*. And he wasn't the only one. Of the twelve guys in our group that day, a third of them had never traveled outside Michigan, and none had ever been to New York. Mike wasn't kidding when he had told me "A few of them are real local yokels."

Then Tommy said something that bowled me over. He said, "Let me ask you a question and please, don't take it the wrong way. Are you really one of those New York Jews?" And he said it, barely hesitating and without any embarrassment, as though it was the most natural question in the world.

Taken aback, I answered, "Yeah, I'm Jewish. So what?"

He continued, "You know, you're the first Jew I've ever met, and you don't even have horns."

I was stunned. Could this guy be so dumb that he thought what he'd just said was funny and that I was going to start laughing at his insulting, offensive little crack?

I looked at him. He was in stitches and he *was* expecting I'd join in. When I didn't, he got a little nervous. But oddly, his manner was always 100 percent and genuinely friendly. He said, "Don't mind me. I just haven't been around very much. No one in our group, except for Mike McChrystal, has. You really are the first Jew I've ever met."

Still not finished, attempting another joke, Tommy added, "I saw you dump some of those beers in the lake. Would you like some *Manischevitz* instead?"

I got to my feet and said, "No thanks, but you know, I need another beer, bad." And, grabbing a Bud from the cooler, I hurried to the boat, which was at last ready to go.

In truth, I actually had a great time water skiing that day but, as it was happening, I noticed that half the guys, although they tried, couldn't stop staring at me.

The next year, during Christmas week 1971, Wiley Livingston invited me to visit his family in Birmingham, Alabama. With my trip to Traverse City and another year of college behind me, I was much more mature by then and better prepared for what might be some awkward moments. Birmingham, of course, as compared to Mike McChrystal's hometown, was cosmopolitan and had three thriving synagogues. By NYC standards, nevertheless, it was very provincial and, as I was to find out, had enough dangerous-looking rednecks walking around to keep me on my guard. Its total population in 1971 was about 285,000, but only 4,000, less than 1.5 percent, were Jewish. Incredibly to me, however, the Birmingham metropolitan area had more than 1,500 churches.

As we drove the 850 miles from Ann Arbor in Wiley's 1968 Volkswagen Bug, he got me ready for what to expect. His family, he warned, always went wild celebrating Christmas, and every year decorated the front yard with a Nativity scene and thousands of lights, erected an enormous tree, exchanged dozens of gifts, and his father dressed up as Santa Claus. Wiley and I were close enough that we could talk about anything, and I assured him that I really liked Christmas, enjoyed the holiday atmosphere, and looked forward to participating, as best I could, in the festivities. On the outskirts of Birmingham, I even made him stop at a mall so I could buy his parents gifts. I bought a twenty-dollar book about American art for his dad and a twenty-five-dollar silk scarf for his mom. I also bought Wiley a twelve-dollar University of Michigan cap that said "Wolverines Football Team" at a sports outlet At the time, that was a lot of money for me to part with, but I knew that for the next week, I was going to be fed, housed, and entertained like a king. The least I could do was show up with some presents. Not only had Wiley planned all kinds of activities that he told me were already paid for, but his cousin, Mary, who was attending the business school in Ann Arbor and I knew, had set me up on blind dates with two of her girlfriends. One was named – get this – Scarlet Lila Lee, and the other, Susanna Jane York. Nonetheless, I was excited about meeting two attractive girls and, when we pulled into Wiley's driveway, thought, "This has the makings of some great week." But I prayed that Mary hadn't forgotten to tell them what my last name was. For my date with Scarlet, Mary was going to take us, believe it or not, Christmas caroling and, if Scarlet Lila Lee didn't already know and asked me, how would she react when I said *Grossman?* And then, remembering my experience with Tommy, Mike McChrystal's friend, *"Yes, I'm a Jew from New York."*

We arrived at Wiley's house exactly on Christmas Eve. There were five cars in the driveway, fourteen more parked on the street, and the house was packed with almost fifty people. Wiley's relatives were so excited he'd brought a friend home with him for the holidays that they nearly smothered me with their joyful hugs and handshakes. Every one of them told me how honored they were that I'd be spending Christmas with them, and I should consider myself part of the family. One of his uncles said, "Wait till you see the church we're going to for Mass tomorrow. It's 150 years old and a national landmark. It's listed as one of the most beautiful churches in the world, and I know you'll think so too."

Fortunately, Wiley was standing nearby and, before I had to respond or say anything, he said, "Please, Uncle Jim, remember what I told you?" and pulled me into the dining room. My mouth began to water when I saw the mountains of food piled on the table for Christmas dinner. There were so many people that two-thirds of them had to stand, but Wiley found me a chair and was careful to seat me, safely he thought, between him and Mary. For a good half hour, we ate, we talked, and things were going great.

But the liquor had started flowing hours before we'd arrived, and suddenly, Mary's mother, Wiley's aunt Margaret, asked, "It's terrific that you're celebrating Christmas with us but how on earth did you convince your family to let you go? Don't they want you to go to church with them?"

Getting panicky, Wiley tried to speak but could only get out, "Well, he could come because he's…." and then stopped.

Stopped cold. Everyone looked at him. And then at me. Aunt Margaret, a little drunk, tried to guess at what Wiley had left out. "He could come because his parents are overseas or he's…. he's an orphan?"

I clearly was not Hindu or Sikh, but she just couldn't bring her herself to the more obvious conclusion. None of them could.

Wiley, all 190 pounds of him, went completely rigid. Mary froze too and protectively put her hand on my shoulder. I felt like Woody Allen in the scene from *Annie Hall*, where Allen becomes so self conscious while eating at his Christian girlfriend's dinner table that in his mind's eye, he sees himself dressed like a Hasidic Jew with pais down to his knees. But Margaret wouldn't let me off the hook. She kept her eyes on me, insisting I give her an answer. And, boy, did I give her one. I said, "Well, my family let me come because we just don't celebrate Christmas. We never do."

There was a stunned moment of silence. Margaret's mouth, along with half the other relatives', literally dropped open. I continued, "You see, I'm Jewish and we celebrate Chanukah instead."

The effect that had is hard to describe. For nearly two minutes, no one said or did anything. I was squeezing Mary's arm so tight that she started using her other hand to pry open my fingers. I felt like I was wearing a tallis, phylacteries, a yarmulke, and that the pais were now down to my feet. Finally, mercifully, Wiley's dad said, "Michael, I know you're Jewish. Wiley told us two months ago. It's only some of my idiot relatives who forgot. Wiley says you and he are best friends and I can see why. From the way you handle yourself, you seem like a very bright and decent young man. Now, please dig in and eat some more. While you're in my house, we're going to treat you as though you were Wiley's twin brother."

And for the rest of the week, all of them did.

The next day was Christmas morning and Wiley woke me up at 9:30. After we showered and went downstairs, I could see that a lot of his relatives, including Aunt Margaret, Uncle Jim, and Cousin Mary, had stayed over. Fifteen of them were already assembled in the living room around the tree and there were at least sixty Christmas presents stacked beneath it. Sure enough, after a minute or two, Wiley's dad appeared in full

Santa Claus costume. He shouted, "Merry Christmas, everybody," walked straight to the tree, and started handing out the gifts. I got a shirt and tie from Mr. and Mrs. Livingston, an atlas from Mary, and a book about the Civil War from Wiley. The gifts I had bought at the mall were under the tree too, and his mom kissed me when she opened hers. Then his dad said, "Mike, can you hand me that one over there?"

I went to grab it but gasped. It was so heavy, that as I tried to lift it, I yelled *"Jeeesus Christ,"* but stopped, I thought, just in time to change it to *"Geees, Uh, Gee Whiz."*

I did it so smoothly, thank God, that nobody seemed to notice.

The gift I had tried to lift was a set of two fifty pound weights that were one of Wiley's gifts from his parents. He was a second-degree black-belt judo expert and the weights were for his home gym in the garage where he worked out.

After the gift-giving was over, we all sat down for a huge breakfast in the kitchen. This time, somehow, I ended up sitting between Aunt Margaret and Uncle Jim. Margaret turned to me and said, "You know, not all of us down here in the South are that bad. In fact, I want you to know that I think you're very brave, coming to visit total strangers, not really knowing what to expect. And I'm fascinated listening to you. Around here, there's just not that many Jewish people to talk to."

The way she spoke made me relax, and I wasn't nervous, even though Wiley and Mary had gone to the other end of the kitchen to sit at a counter.

I said, "I'm really glad I'm here. Thank you for making me feel so welcome."

But then she added, "By the way, when you yelled out *Jeeesus Christ* back there and tried to cover it up, that was a pretty good try. You almost pulled it off. But I was standing right next to you and heard every word. Next time, try not to say that so loud in a Christian household, under the Christmas tree, on the holiest Christian day of the year. But don't worry about it. You think I don't know that before Jesus became God to Christians, he was Rabbi Jesus to Jews?"

Then she reached over to Jim, who handed her a small box

This is for you," she said. "Last night, I remembered that I've had it for years."

So I tore open the package and unwrapped her gift. Inside was a silver bracelet with six golden charms. She was three times my age, but what she gave me made me love her. The charms were alternating crucifixes, Muslim crescents, and Jewish stars.

Wiley warned me that not everyone in Birmingham was as welcoming as his family. So a few days later, when it came time for my date with Scarlet Lila Lee, Mary and Wiley decided that it would be best to forget about Christmas caroling, and we went to a James Bond movie instead. Mary must have really read the riot act to Scarlet, because she was so friendly and protective that I was taken aback. Five minutes after we were introduced, she took hold of my hand and didn't let go until the date was over. Before the movie started, as we walked along the street, we ran into several people Mary, Wiley, and Scarlet knew. When Scarlet introduced me and told them my last name, she glared at them with daggers if they became the least bit unfriendly. And, unfortunately, a few did become unfriendly. Some of them turned distant and cold, and some even hostile. Especially the guys, when they realized Scarlet was actually on a date with me. She had grabbed onto my hand because she was trying to shield me from the antagonism she knew I'd get from some of her acquaintances. She said, "There are a lot of jerks and rednecks around here, but I swear I'll kill anyone who gives you a hard time."

I looked at her. Aside from being very attractive, there was a lot to like about her.

The rest of the date went well. After the movie, we went out to eat and then to a Christmas party. I got some more unfriendly looks, but nothing too menacing.

When the evening ended, we dropped Scarlet off at her house. As I walked her to the door, Mary and Wiley waited in his Volkswagen Bug with the windows rolled down. Scarlet put her arms around me and offered her lips for a good night kiss. But, although I wanted to, I couldn't do it. She said, "What's the matter? I didn't know you were so shy." And she tried again.

But I still couldn't do it. As attractive as she was, I was scared. Not of her but of some of the locals she had introduced me to who had turned outright hostile when they learned I was Jewish. Also, I remembered that at the party there had been a distinct undercurrent of disapproval from several of the guests that I was even there. I still felt like a total stranger in Birmingham, surrounded by threatening rednecks. She sensed what was bothering me and said, "I used to go out with that tall guy we spoke to, but

I'll be damned if I'll let him tell me who to hang out with. Why don't you give me a call before you leave so we can see each other again?"

And with that, she yanked me close and planted a deep kiss on my mouth. I turned red, quickly said goodbye, and dove into the car.

On the way back to Wiley's house, he couldn't stop laughing.

"You shmuck. What the hell's wrong with you? You're not like that in Ann Arbor. All you had to do was touch her and she would have invited you in."

Even Mary got in on the act.

"What were you thinking? I didn't set you up with a nun. Boy, did you blow that."

Maybe so. In fact, after we got back to Ann Arbor, it took me almost a year to get Scarlet and what I'd missed out on out of my mind. You see, back in my college days, despite the education I was getting about Christian-Jewish relations, the truth is that I spent a good deal of my time trying to date girls, no matter what their religion. But the thing I remembered most about my trip to Birmingham, aside from the palpable resentment of some of the locals, was the kindness of Wiley's family. That's stuck with me all my life.

***

The vast majority of my fellow students at the University of Michigan, more than 42,000 in all believe it or not, Jewish and non-Jewish, were worldly and knowledgeable. Ann Arbor was more like a university megacity than a normal campus, and was a hotbed of political and "Woodstock Generation" activity. There were so many rallies, demonstrations, lectures, rock concerts, foreign films, political organizations, and other extracurricular events going on that I could never decide what to do or who to listen to first. It was the home base of the Black Panthers and the even more radical White Panthers, had major chapters of SDS (Students for Democratic Society) and its militant offshoot the Weathermen, was at the epicenter of the anti-Vietnam War protest movement, and was heavily involved with the ultra-radical group of student leaders called the Chicago Seven (Abbie Hoffman, Jerry Rubin, David Dellinger, Tom Hayden, Rennie Davis, John Froines, Lee Weiner, and Bobbie Seale, which actually makes eight but Seale's case was severed and prosecuted separately) who were indicted and tried for instigating riots at the 1968 Democratic National Convention.

In the midst of all this frenzied activity, there was little time to dwell for long upon the differences between Jews and Christians. There were also nearly twelve hundred Muslims on campus and, until Robert Kennedy was assassinated by Sirhan Bishara Sirhan in June 1968, there was certainly no time to think much about that divide either. Instead, the anti-Vietnam War movement united nearly all 42,000 of us, with the exception of ROTC (Reserve Officer Training Corps) students, behind a vision of the United States using its vast power to "Make Peace, Not War."

With all that was happening, including the murder of Martin Luther King, Jr. in spring, 1968, only two months before Robert Kennedy was shot, it was no wonder relatively few people focused on the momentous changes that had begun to take root in the Catholic Church. In 1962, Pope John XXIII (1958-1963) had convened the Second Vatican Council, attended by 2,600 bishops from around the world, during which, at his insistence, a declaration of new church policy vis-à-vis the Jews called *Nostra Aetate* (In Our Time) was issued. That declaration was like none before, for it specifically repudiated the 2,000 years of previous church teachings blaming the Jews for Jesus's execution and condemning them to eternal damnation. John's successor, Pope Paul VI (1963-1978), passionately embraced this new policy and opened his arms to "especially the Jews, of whom we ought never to disapprove and whom we ought never mistrust, but to whom we must show reverence and love…" Since Catholics made up more than half of the world's 2 billion Christians, these changes were also spreading to Protestant churches and, therefore, throughout all Christendom.

As I lay in my bed in Warwick, now living once again among mostly Christians, I reflected deeply upon the Church's new attitude toward Jews and how Pope John Paul II (1978-2005), appeared more determined than even his immediate predecessors to embed that attitude permanently into all Catholic teachings. Living in the Pine Island section of Warwick, with a large population of non-Jewish Polish farmers and trades people, I suspected I would soon get the opportunity to put those new Church teachings to the test. I reflected even more deeply, however, upon my own attitude toward Jews. All my life, until I'd joined the Jewish Community Centre of Greenwood Lake, it struck me that I had kept myself almost totally ignorant, purposely it seemed, about Judaism and the Jewish people. Unconsciously, probably, I thought that the less I knew about the Jews, the less I would have to come to grips with being one. But now, in my mid-forties, I was too old to delay it anymore. Would I continue, as in my college years, keenly aware but blissfully uninformed about my background? Would I continue, as in my college years, afraid to expose a raw nerve by confronting the core reason for the divide between Jews and their Christian neighbors? Or now, finally, would I face the truth, embrace my neighbors nonetheless, and embrace *myself* as a Jew? – And as a modern, secular American as well?

The time had arrived for me to reassess my identity. And if I became vice president of my synagogue, I would be forced to reassess it as never before. "Besides," I thought, "what did it really mean to be a Jew anyway?" It was time I found out.

I told Susan I was ready to accept her offer in September 1996. I said, "But before you announce it to anyone, tell me again what my responsibilities as second vice president will be. I want to make sure I'm going to have time for this"

She said, "Well, aside from standing in for me and the first vice president from time to time, and helping to run things around here, there'll be some special projects. And the first thing I'll want you to do and pretty soon is start interviewing candidates to take over as rabbi. Mark Blazer, I'm sorry to say, will be leaving this summer."

That came as an unwelcome surprise to me and virtually the entire congregation.

Chapter Eight - A Spiritual Man

I fervently hoped she was wrong. Not only had Mark and Tracy been phenomenal teachers but, as a spiritual leader, I couldn't imagine finding a replacement as inspiring as Mark had been. He was the one who had motivated me to learn some Jewish history and basic Judaism in the first place, and was the major reason I had even considered accepting Susan's offer. "Maybe," I convinced myself, "as second vice president, I could talk him into staying."

At JCC, however, the office of second vice president had been vacant for nearly five years. "No one," I was told, "in their right mind wanted it." It was a job that came with responsibilities but, under the synagogue's constitution, no real authority. The first vice president, on the other hand, was specifically empowered to convene and chair all board of trustees meetings, and it was the board that made 95 percent of the decisions about synagogue policy and business. This was done to serve as a check on the president's authority, which was considerable, and included the power to convene and chair meetings of the General Membership, the decisions of which trumped even those of the board, manage the day-to-day affairs of the congregation, approve the expenditures of money, within limits, in his or her sole discretion for synagogue events and activities, and appoint, without board approval, the chairpersons of all synagogue committees, as well as create new committees as he or she deemed fit. Also, and very importantly, since the rabbi and cantor were part-timers, the president's personality was a dominant factor in setting the congregation's mood and agenda. The second vice president, though, had no independent power to do anything, and was no more than sort of a gofer for the other officers. For this and other reasons, at least three people had turned down the position when asked. So on January 14, 1997, when Susan Lobel told the board of trustees that I'd be willing to do it, they immediately used their authority to fill vacancies and unanimously appointed me. Several months later, in August, I was unanimously elected by the General Membership to serve a full two-year term. Since no one else was running, the election was merely a formality. I was a shoo-in. However, as soon as I was elected, although I didn't feel any more Jewish, something strange began to happen.

I didn't behave any differently than before the election, aside from being much more active in helping Susan organize things like High Holiday services, Purim parties, Seders at the synagogue, Friday night Kiddushes, Hebrew school activities, and building maintenance projects once in a while. And sometimes, when she and the first vice president weren't around, I would make announcements about upcoming events or meetings on their behalf. Yet, simply because I held the title of second vice president, was genuinely concerned about the well-being of the congregation, and was – and everyone knew it – extremely interested in learning about Judaism and Jewish history, some of the congregants began to look upon me, to my utter dismay, as a possible successor, not to the first vice presidency, but to the synagogue presidency itself. Especially several of the longtime officers and board members like Treasurer Sylvia Levy, Financial Secretary Lillian Hilowitz, and Trustees Irving Fishman, Sydel Fishman, Al Levy, Jessie Goldstein, and Nancy Deangelo. But the one who looked to me to succeed to the presidency more than anyone was Susan Lobel herself.

She started dropping hints like, "You know, I've been president now for four and a half years, and elections for new officers are way overdue." Or, "I can't do this forever. Sooner or later, someone else is going have to take my place." And even, "I don't think David Weinberg is going to be able to move up from first vice president because he's too busy with his construction business in the City right now. After him, Mike, you're next in line."

When she said things like that, I looked at her with total, numb disbelief. She and most of her family members had attended conservative synagogues nearly all their lives and were thoroughly familiar with the cycle of Jewish holidays and all aspects of the services. And David Weinberg, the first vice president, was married to JCC's cantor, Brenda Weinberg, and obviously knew vastly more about synagogue practice than I did. As for me, I could just barely say the *Hamotzi* prayer over the challah Friday nights without so misaccenting the words as to embarrass everyone within earshot. In my own mind, I was so unqualified it was ridiculous. Susan would have to find someone else. Without trying too hard, I was able to think of at least half a dozen much more qualified members of our congregation within seconds. At least one of them, I was sure, would step forward.

In the meantime, I took seriously the assignment Susan had given me to find and hire a new rabbi, and I began making inquiries as to how to go about it. After asking around, I decided on a course of action. First, I placed ads in a few of the local Jewish publications and got one or two responses, but nothing very promising. Next, I contacted the Jewish Federation of Greater Orange County, of which JCC was a member, and asked them to let me know if they came across any rabbinical students looking for a part-time position. They told me they would but that they usually received inquiries only from ordained rabbis looking for full-time work and a commensurate salary. Nonetheless, I did get one rabbi-in-training referral from the Federation, but even his salary requirements were too high, so it didn't work out. Then, I contacted several people I knew who were members of other synagogues in nearby Florida Village, Monroe, and Middletown, and asked them to keep their eyes open. They did, but no suitable rabbinical students came their way. Also, of course, I contacted the rabbinical school in Manhattan where Susan had recruited Mark Blazer, The Academy for Jewish Religion, and asked them to help find a replacement. They were very obliging and — after I sent them an e-mail setting forth the job duties and hours of the "religious director," our salary offer, and a detailed description of the synagogue — they got right on it. They drew up a memo, with the details of our job offer, and posted it on bulletin boards throughout their building. However, during the first three months after the bulletin went up, I received only one phone call, and the guy turned out to be so difficult to make an appointment with for a job interview that I gave up. He canceled two appointments due to personal problems and called five minutes before the next appointment was supposed to start to say he would be two hours late. I told him to forget it.

It was now April 1998 and, since Mark and Tracy wouldn't be leaving until August, I still had five months left to find someone new. But I was starting to get a little desperate. So far, not a single suitable candidate had turned up. The problem, Mark and Susan advised, was that I had put out feelers much too soon. Only a very few rabbinical students knew what their schedules would be a year ahead of time but now, with only five months to go, they were certain I would start getting more inquiries. They were right. During May and June, I received calls from four students at The Academy for Jewish Religion and one call from a student at another school who had seen one of my ads, all of whom sounded good on the phone. After a couple of conversations with each of them, I was able to eliminate two from consideration due to what I felt were their unreasonable expectations of secretarial and other support from paid synagogue staff, given JCC's grave financial condition. That left only three candidates for me to interview and then, based on my impressions, to recommend to the Board of Trustees – all three or even just one – who would make the final hiring decision based on their own interviews.

The three candidates who were left were all from the Academy, and I asked Mark whether he knew any of them. He did know two of them quite well, one of whom was his clear favorite. Mark described him as a kind and deeply spiritual man who would be capable of creating an upbeat, joyful mood at the synagogue. However, I wanted to give all the candidates a fair chance, and refused to let Mark's opinion influence me too much without my having met any of them yet. It was now early June and I wanted to finish all my interviews before the end of the month, before we got too deep into the summer and the board members started disappearing on vacations. If we could hire a new religious director no later than June 30, it would give us enough time to have him ready to perform the High Holidays come September. Rosh Hashanah would take place on September 18 and Yom Kippur on September 28.

I conducted two of the interviews on the same Thursday evening, at different times, in The Academy for Jewish Religion's building located at 15 West 86th Street. I was struck immediately by how young they both seemed, compared to Mark Blazer. Mark was actually only about thirty, but these guys were no more than in their mid-twenties, and I got the impression they were both looking, more than anything else, for a small, not-too-demanding congregation in front of whom they would be able to practice performing the religious services they had been learning at the Academy. That was fine, but when I told them I hoped to find a religious leader who would also be able to re-energize our congregation, help us attract new members, teach Hebrew school and adult ed., participate in Greenwood Lake inter-religious community events, and be an effective fundraiser, they both looked befuddled and completely overwhelmed. But I wasn't in a position to be too picky. One of them was not that bad, and I told him I'd schedule the date for JCC's board of trustees to meet him on the third Sunday in June, which was the following week.

I was not, however, happy. I didn't want to have to settle for someone who was just minimally okay, and prayed that the last candidate, Mark's favorite, would really be sensational. His interview was going to take place early on a Friday afternoon at the synagogue and, as I waited for him to arrive, I worried about what I had gotten myself into. How could Susan have left it for me to decide, for all intents and purposes, who was going to be JCC's next rabbi? We were down to our last and only two candidates, and whomever I recommended, barring some completely unexpected objection, was going to be in as our new religious director for the next several years. I waited for our last candidate on pins and needles.

Reuben Modek arrived exactly on time and, when he did, my mood soared dramatically from worry to near elation. The moment he walked in, there was something in his manner, a sort of spiritual radiance, that made me like him immensely. And I know the feeling was mutual. We connected instantly. For starters, for a rabbi, Reuben's appearance was striking. He was very slim, 6'3", had a braided ponytail, and wore on his head a dazzling, multi-colored Bukharan yarmulke. Bukhara is a city in

Southeast Asia in what is now Uzbekistan, where the custom has been to wear large, vividly dyed, knitted *kippot* that cover not just the crown but the entire head. Reuben's was so bright and joyful-looking that I wanted to trade in my small, plain black yarmulke at once so I could put on a Bukharan one right away and join in the fun. Just from his looks and his humble manner, his aura was such that it seemed to me he could be not only rabbi, but also a guru.

After we introduced ourselves and he started telling me about himself I liked what I heard as much as what I saw. He had been born in Israel, had been raised, like me, in a completely non-observant, even atheistic household, had served in the Israeli Army during the 1967 war, had just begun to master Jewish history himself, and, of late, had been earning an income as a tree surgeon and gardener. He was forty years old, more mature therefore than the other candidates, but only in his second year at the Academy because he had only recently decided to become a rabbi. I thought to myself, "Just like I had decided only recently to learn what it meant to be Jewish." Although he already knew a great deal about Judaism, he was dissatisfied with the extent of his knowledge, like I was dissatisfied with mine, and was determined to learn much more.

When I told him I wanted a religious leader who could revitalize the congregation and help rebuild it from the ground up, he immediately said, "You know, this is exactly the kind of synagogue I'm looking for. Your building is incredibly spiritual and welcoming. I feel good just being here. I would love to see this congregation grow in every way possible: financially, organizationally, membership-wise, new programs, an exciting Hebrew school, inspirational services and, most importantly, spiritually. I think I can help do it.

"Also," he added, "this is one of the most beautiful synagogues I've ever seen. I know I'd be happy working and learning here."

I remembered back to the way my family had reacted when we first laid eyes on the place in 1994, four years earlier. We had thought it was the most beautiful synagogue we had ever seen too. Reuben and I felt similarly about that and so many other things that we quickly established a rock-solid rapport.

There was also a quality in him that I noticed which I did not possess but maybe he could teach me. As I looked at him, with his dazzling Bukharin yarmulke, his braided ponytail, his appreciation of the beauty of the synagogue, his humble carriage, I realized he really could be a guru. He exuded caring and concern. He was walking *Tzedakah*. "He would be accepted as holy," I was sure, "in any religion." For it was plain to see, from his demeanor and from what he said, that Reuben Modek was truly a spiritual man.

Some of the board members, however, were not nearly as thrilled as I was about Reuben's appearance. They were used to a much more traditional religious leader and felt he might be unsuitable to take the helm at a conservative synagogue like ours. But JCC was conservative in name only. JCC's membership was so small that we were always desperate for new congregants and never turned away anyone regardless of his or her level of observance, Jewish knowledge, or commitment. Our membership ran the gamut from extremely liberal, non-believing Jews to quite orthodox, deeply observant ones. We had a few congregants who were almost Talmudic scholars and others who, until they had joined JCC, never belonged to a synagogue in their entire lives. Many were attracted to JCC solely because of its insanely low Hebrew school tuition and dues and were just passing through, until their sons and daughters were bar or bat mitzvahed, and would then disappear, never to be seen or heard from again.

When Reuben began his interview with the board, on which I had a seat as did all the congregation's officers, some of the long-timers were so resistant to his unconventional demeanor and style that he must have felt like he was about to be tried before the *Sanhedrin*. A couple of them belligerently cross-examined him; actually, in fact, verbally assaulted him. The board of trustees consisted of all the officers, the president of the Women's Auxiliary, all the elected trustees, and a few honorary trustees. There were supposed to be twenty-six of us altogether but, since several of the trustee positions were vacant, and some trustees were absent, there were only fourteen board members present at the time. That was more than enough, however, to brutally and cruelly work Reuben over.

At the outset, Reuben tried to create an appropriate tone by introducing himself with a few spiritual opening remarks. He said, "To me, every synagogue should be not only a house of worship and not only a house of study and learning, but a place to make deep, lifelong friendships. More than that, it can be a place of intense, joyful spirituality, a place to truly experience the delights of being Jewish." He tried to continue, "I've also learned…" but was rudely cut off.

One of the board members said, "Please don't tell us how to run this synagogue. That's our job. You're only a second-year rabbinical student, and we'll tell you what to do, not the other way around."

Another said, "Listen, we're not really interested in your philosophy or stories. We want to know what your experience has been and what your salary requirements are. So let's cut out all the moralizing and get down to business."

I was so shocked by the hostility of those comments, I was speechless. So also, fortunately, was the vast majority of the board. Those of us who liked Reuben, loved him. Those who didn't just couldn't get past what they considered his eccentric and inappropriate style. They were very concerned, for example, about what kind of services he would conduct Friday nights and on the holidays. They were worried that his services might be so untraditional and avant-garde that they would offend or even drive away some of our more conservative congregants. At my insistence, however, and that of several of the other board members, we let Reuben finish his remarks, questioned him for a while, and then, after much discussion, and after it became clear that most of the board wanted him, those who were still opposed had the good sense and grace to make the final vote in favor of hiring Reuben unanimous. Despite their initial rudeness and hostility, I knew that every anti-Reuben member in the room had JCC's best interests at heart when they had expressed their initial unfavorable opinions. That they weren't comfortable with him was due mostly to a clash of personalities, and not to any specific objection to anything he had said or done. Since I was the person who had recommended Reuben to the board in the first place, however, although I vehemently disagreed with them, I felt it was essential to acknowledge their concerns. I promised I would bring any misgivings they had to Reuben's attention and ask him to address them immediately. In return, when they realized their view would not prevail, they went along with the majority and promised to fully support Rabbi Modek, as best they could, as our new religious director in every way possible. But, throughout his tenure, the "old guard" never really got used to him.

Those who had supported Reuben from the beginning were ecstatic, including my Temple Wife, Bonnie Kessler, who was now recording secretary, Pat Weisslander, who had become corresponding secretary, and our treasurer, Sylvia Levy, and her husband, Al, who was one of our trustees, my two favorite elders at the synagogue. And more than anyone, of course, me. But we all knew that with Reuben as rabbi, things were going to be very different. Reuben was going to be an adventure for all of us.

And there was another piece of the adventure that was about to fall into place.

Chapter Nine - A Newfangled Regime

It happened in August, at least officially, anyway. The truth is that Susan had de facto stepped down three and a half months earlier, near the end of May, and that was even before the board decided to hire Rabbi Modek. She had served as president for an incredible six years, longer than anyone before her and despite the synagogue constitution's prohibition against holding that office more than four years consecutively. She was rightfully entitled to a rest. When she stepped down, she didn't actually say to me, "Mike, you're acting president now." She didn't have to. Although elections were still a ways off, by mid-June, she and almost everybody else at JCC started treating me like president, as though it was already a foregone conclusion. There weren't exactly lines of people jockeying for the job, so it probably was. In fact, there were only two others who seemed somewhat interested, but neither really had the time nor the commitment that would be necessary. I wasn't at all certain I did either. However, both were clearly more qualified than I was, and I figured that sooner or later, one of them would step forward and save me. In fact, in the four or five weeks just before the elections, I tried to lay very low, expecting and hoping, praying actually, that someone in the congregation would come to his senses, realize just how amateur a Jew I really was, and nominate a more suitable prospect. But that didn't happen. Gradually, not fully conscious of it, I began making more and more of the executive decisions for JCC and without even first seeking 100 percent approval from each congregant, lest I commit some faux pas, and be unable to say, "Well, we discussed it beforehand and you agreed. Remember?" And then, on August 29, still praying that some last-minute candidate would come to my rescue, I was unanimously elected by the membership to become JCC's nineteenth president. When I told a twenty-year-long business associate of mine about it, he said, "Boy, if you live long enough, you get to see everything." When I told my closest friend, he yelled, "Mike, have you gone insane?" And when my relatives found out, they were so stunned that they didn't know whether to congratulate me or pity me. Some of my immediate family thought I had become prey to some religious cult and might even start preaching to them. Looking back, I still can't quite believe it myself.

Of all the decisions I made before I was formally elected, the most important, obviously, was my having gotten Reuben hired as rabbi. With him as religious director and me as president, everyone sensed that the whole mood of the synagogue was about to change, for better or worse, dramatically. Unlike many Jews, including a good number of our own congregants, Reuben and I didn't think of Jewish history or Judaism as, more often than not, a series of horrific catastrophes, from *Tish B'av* to the *Shoah*, that had befallen the Jewish people. Instead, with me in total agreement, Reuben always emphasized the boundless joys of Judaism and its intense spirituality. Sometimes, he would spontaneously break into song or even dance. Often, he spoke about *Kabala*. Whenever I watched him – conducting services, singing and dancing, teaching Hebrew school or adult ed., officiating at community or inter-denominational events – I always felt that joyfulness radiating from him, along with a deep inner peace. To a lot of us, the dazzling Bukharin yarmulke he wore was a visible emblem of those wonderful attributes. His optimistic outlook soon spread to most of the congregation and, within a few months, at least a quarter of the men, and even a few of the women, started wearing Bukharin yarmulkes too. It was as though, by putting one on, we were demonstrating our having attained a new spiritual level.

After Mark departed, Reuben tried to hit the ground running and, during the Friday night services leading up to Rosh Hashanah, we got our first opportunity to really see him in action. One huge thing he had going for him was the great chemistry that immediately developed between him and Cantor Weinberg. As a team, they cued off each other so well that they were like *entertainers* who just happened to be great spiritual leaders as well. Together, they were never boring and almost always, with Brenda's singing and Reuben's stories, an inspiration to watch and listen to. The joyful spirituality I had detected in Reuben when I first interviewed him quickly became apparent to everyone. Sometimes, however, I was embarrassed and felt bad that the turnout for their Friday night services was often very small. At least once or twice a month, in fact, we couldn't muster a *Minyan*. Reuben and Brenda's talents were such that they deserved a much larger audience. But Reuben and I were determined to increase attendance and, to an extent, we eventually did. He knew, as did I, that the key to increasing JCC's membership, and thereby enlarging attendance for services, was to have in place a dynamic, enjoyable, and extremely exciting Hebrew school. Every new student we signed up would mean a whole family of new JCC members and some of them, we hoped, would become services regulars. With that in mind, Reuben started laying plans to revitalize our Hebrew school program like his new job and very life depended on it. At the same time, with the High Holidays fast approaching, he spent hours preparing and practicing, so he'd be super-ready to perform the Rosh Hashanah and Yom Kippur prayers. Like Rabbi Mark Blazer three years before, this would be the first time he had ever performed them in front of a live audience, and he wanted to do a spectacular job so the congregation would be proud of him. Equally important, he wanted any non-members who would be in attendance to be so impressed, they'd want to join us. As for me, I was obviously much more of a neophyte when it came to the High Holidays than Reuben was and, since I was going to have to coordinate everything and make several speeches, including the important Yom Kippur *Kol Nidre* appeal for donations, I got to work too.

Although a little rough around the edges, Reuben got through the High Holiday services with mostly good and a few rave reviews. His *Tashlich* service, for sure, wasn't quite as dramatic as Mark Blazer's first performance had been, because by then the lake had filled up, was no longer a swamp, and when we threw the bread crumbs into the water, there were no snakes, turtles, or freshwater eels lurking around. But everyone, with the exception of my son, Zack, and Bonnie's son, Jonathan, considered that a blessing, rather than a setback. Reuben, however, was dramatic in other ways, including his habit of stepping down from the *Bimah* and roaming round the sanctuary to locate members who had volunteered to read portions of the prayers from their seats, and then handing them his microphone. When the reader finished, Reuben, as often as not, would continue the service right from where he was standing. Frequently, he would then take time to explain what was happening and even open the floor to questions or comments. People liked that; it lightened the mood and got everyone involved. As expected, some of the more conservative members were a bit put off by his unconventional appearance and style, but they found themselves in a distinct minority. The overwhelming majority of our members, many of whom had never seen or met Rabbi Modek until the High Holidays that year – because Rosh Hashanah and Yom Kippur were the only times they ever came to services – were impressed. They loved his sincerity and warmth. Also, they knew he was a rabbinical student, so they forgave his inexperience and a mistake or two. And with Cantor Weinberg there, and the great chemistry between her and Reuben, there were many moments of truly intense spirituality and sublime beauty. I usually squirmed and daydreamed through High Holiday services, but that year I was inspired by them.

Kol Nidre arrived. In every synagogue in the world, it is the highlight and most important of all the High Holiday Prayers. Meaning *All Vows*, it is the dramatic prayer sung on Yom Kippur eve during which Jews everywhere ask forgiveness, from God and from those they have wronged, for any sins they may have been committed the previous year. It's called *All Vows* because, in addition to asking forgiveness for their sins, Jews ask that they be released from any vows they made but were unable to fulfill. Traditionally, immediately after the prayer, it's the occasion when most congregations request that all present make generous contributions to their synagogues. At JCC, it had become the custom that David Weinberg, our first vice president, would make that request, usually quite effectively given the small size of our congregation, but it was decided that this year I would back him up by immediately following his request with my own. Our styles were very different, and it was felt I might be able to talk some people into making donations that he had been unable to reach, and vice versa. However, during the Rosh Hashanah services the week before, I had already addressed the assemblage twice, allocating half my time on both occasions to very aggressive appeals for financial contributions, and I was a little fearful of coming on strong yet again. For my efforts, in fact, I had gotten some flack from a few congregants who felt I had insisted a bit too forcefully that everyone – every single member and each of their guests – was *obligated* to make a reasonable donation. This was even before I made my Kol Nidre appeal, which was going to be, by far, my most in-your-face pitch. A typical complaint was as follows:

"You know, Mr. Grossman, people are here for religious services, not to be bothered about contributions. Frankly, I'm offended that you spent so much time asking for money. It's tacky."

I would reply: "Really. Aren't you, your family, and your two non-member guests planning to join us for the break-fast after Yom Kippur services are over? It's a pretty elaborate spread. Whom do you suppose is going to pay for that and everything else that goes on around here? Surely you don't think that your $300 annual dues covers it all. Some people have volunteered to contribute toward the cost of the break-fast, in addition to making separate and generous High Holiday donations, but I noticed that your name is not on the list. I'd appreciate it if you'd help out. How much can I put you down for?"

The reply from people I had to use that spiel on was, almost invariably: "But I don't have much cash on me right now," or "Let me think about it." To which I would say: "That's okay, you can send a check. And there's nothing to think about except how much. Let me put you down for at least $125 and, before you leave, you'll sign a pledge form. As you know, unlike any other synagogue in the area, ours doesn't sell tickets to get in on the High Holidays, so that's the minimum we'd like you to contribute. At least it'll reimburse the synagogue for the food we bought to feed the people in your party. If you contribute more, as others already have, as your separate High Holiday donation, the congregation will consider it a real *mitzvah*. Now, please introduce me to your guests, so I can make sure they picked up donation envelopes on the way in and I can discuss with them appropriate amounts."

After going through this routine a couple of times, word got out that I, *the new president*, meant business and would not back down when it came to congregants fulfilling what were obviously reasonable financial expectations. Rather than risk being confronted by me as above, which I did publicly within earshot of other congregants standing or sitting nearby, most of the recalcitrant members hurriedly handed me envelopes, albeit often reluctantly, containing at least minimal donations before the High Holidays ended and before the break-fast began. If they didn't, I'd approach them before they started shoveling food onto their plates and would say something like: "Sylvia Levy, our treasurer, would like to speak with you before you leave. She tells me you may owe something toward last year's dues and still aren't current on your son's Hebrew school tuition. Also, she has the donation pledge forms I mentioned to you before, and I'd like you to come through on that. Please sign one for at least the amount I suggested. Could you take care of that now, please? The food will still be here when you get back. Sylvia's in the office, waiting for you."

But, despite my efforts, the congregation remained deep in the red. Even though we managed to collect more than $6,000 in High Holiday donations, more than double the year before, it wasn't enough. Not nearly so. Besides, total donations of $6,000 wasn't saying very much. It just looked good because we had been accustomed to collecting only $3,000, often less, in previous years. As compared to most other synagogues, it was still woefully and embarrassingly small. We were still spending thousands more than we were taking in, and JCC's financial condition continued to deteriorate.

Reuben and I knew that the only way to get significantly more donations, not only on the High Holidays but throughout the year, and help start turning things around, was to increase JCC's membership. Without such an increase, even raising JCC's absurdly low $300 annual dues wouldn't be enough. Our current membership consisted of about fifty-five families and five singles who, if everyone was current and not in arrears, which was not the case, collectively paid total dues of $17,250 each year. Raising the dues to $500 for a family membership and $250 for a single would bring the total dues up to $28,750 but our basic expenses, including rabbi and cantor salaries, Hebrew school salaries and expenses, heating and air-conditioning costs, and maintenance and repairs were well in excess of $50,000. Raising the dues alone wasn't going to do it. We needed regular donations and a lot of new members whose numbers, despite the low annual dues we charged and low per-member donations we'd been receiving, would collectively result in a big increase in cash flow. It was an economy of scales issue. We could double or even quadruple our membership, and thereby dramatically increase the money we brought in, but our basic expenses would remain the same. As it stood now, however, JCC was taking in only about $35,000 annually, which consisted of the membership dues, Hebrew school tuitions, the rent we received from a day school that was leasing a portion of our building, interest on our savings, and High Holiday donations which, until Reuben became rabbi and I became president, had been running on average under $3,000 yearly. All in all, we were consistently running an annual deficit of more than $15,000. And it was starting to widen.

Reuben and I had dozens of ideas to attract new members but we never lost sight of the fact that the heart of our efforts had to be the creation of a phenomenal Hebrew school. Happy and eager students, we knew, meant happy parents and happy parents would spread the good word about JCC. They might even get involved in several synagogue activities, such as fundraisers, adult ed., or services and become core, activist members who would help us run and organize things. We desperately needed not just new members, but *those kinds* of new members. Whenever we heard that the parent of a new student would be attending services, even before Reuben reorganized the Hebrew school, we went crazy calling our members and urging them to attend so the new parent would be greeted by at least a half-decent turnout and be impressed. Occasionally, it worked, and that new parent became a regular, more or less, at Friday night services and other activities. When that happened, we would call him or her to make sure he or she would be there whenever we knew another new parent would be coming to services. We'd then repeat the process for the next new parent.

Reuben imported a cutting-edge Hebrew school curriculum from an extraordinarily successful synagogue in Manhattan. That synagogue, within three years of adopting this new curriculum, had increased its Hebrew school enrollment from about thirty to well over one hundred students. The program was exciting and very appealing because it was different and avant-garde and, at the time, only two or three other synagogues in the country were using it. We knew that transitioning to the new program would be a slow process, and it might take a long while to see results. Reuben, therefore, started implementing it immediately. Below is the flyer he drew up that we advertised in most of the local newspapers, ran on the local cable TV station, and posted all around town the summer before the September 2000 semester started:

Michael Grossman

The New Jewish Learning Experience

*a different kind of Hebrew School
opening at the*

Greenwood Lake Jewish Community Centre

*Old Dutch Hollow Road at Lakes Road
Greenwood Lake, New York*

An innovative, exciting program for children ages 4 to 13. The curriculum is designed to match the developmental level and learning style of each child to maximize their enjoyment while they learn Jewish history, culture, holidays, and prayers. A full spectrum of activities including drama, art, debate, singing, movement and dance, story telling, writing, cooking and more helps our students develop their distinctive expressions of Jewish identity. The program draws on the Montessori method.

Classes meet Sundays 10:00AM –12:30PM

Call Mrs. Debra Bloom, Director
***Or* The Jewish Community Centre at (845) 477-3716**

It worked. Within six months, our enrollment increased from sixteen students to twenty; within a year, from twenty to twenty-three; and within a year and a half, from twenty-three to twenty-nine. Since five of our original sixteen students were bar or bat mitzvahed during that period and had graduated, that meant we had signed up seventeen new students, all of whom brought with them their immediate families as new, dues-paying, and sometimes donation-giving, JCC members. A requirement of our new curriculum, although not always enforced, was attendance by our students at services at least one Friday night monthly and on all major Jewish holidays. Invariably, when the students attended services, their parents, and often many of their other relatives, would too. It had started getting easier to put together a *Minyan*.

But then, literally, way before the increased enrollment began to kick in, a miracle happened. Our original little "sixteen-student Hebrew school" accomplished something so incredible and so unexpected that sometimes I think I dreamt it. Whenever I re-read the newspaper headlines about it, however, as astonishing as the accomplishment was, I become a bit more certain it really took place. I should be absolutely certain because I was there, but even so, I still can't quite believe it.

Chapter Ten - Super Sunday & the "Jewpardy" Competition

*"JCC SHOCKS ORANGE COUNTY.
LITTLE DAVID FELLS GOLIATHS. TAKES 2ND PLACE IN JEWPARDY COMPETITION AT SUPER SUNDAY AGAINST SEEMINGLY INVINCIBLE OPPONENTS. JCC DEFEATS FLORIDA AND MONROE TEMPLES IN EARLY ROUNDS. BATTLES TO THE LAST MAN AND WOMAN IN FINALS AGAINST TEMPLE SINAI OF MIDDLETOWN, THE HOST SYNAGOGUE. CONGRATULATIONS TO JCC AND ALL ITS TEAM MEMBERS"*

If an odds maker had been willing to take bets on whether JCC would be able to field anything deserving to be called a team for "Jewpardy," the handicap would have been a staggering thousand to one against us. The chances of our actually participating, let alone placing in the competition would have been much, much longer; off the charts and up there with the odds against winning the New York State Lottery at around fifty-five million to one. And even if some demented bookie had offered those odds, I myself wouldn't have dared bet more than a dollar. So when the above headline ran in just about every Jewish publication and local newspaper in Orange County the week after the Super Sunday that was held on February 6, 1999, some of our congregants, including me, nearly went into a coma. Let me explain.

Super Sunday is sponsored by The Jewish Federation of Greater Orange County (JFOGOC) which is the umbrella organization in which the nineteen synagogues in Orange County, New York and two synagogues in adjoining Sullivan County are members. There are hundreds of similar organizations throughout the country, and they provide invaluable services including ongoing Jewish education and discussion programs, grants for growing Hebrew schools, leadership training for congregation officers, and they organize numerous fundraising drives for Israel and other Jewish causes. In addition, each of these federations sponsors at least one huge annual event, which in Orange County has come to be known as "Super Sunday." Among the attractions and activities at JFOGOC's Super Sundays are guest speakers, name entertainers, table after table of Judaica items available for purchase, musical performances, awards presentations to local Jewish dignitaries and, of course, a huge sumptuous banquet to top everything off. In 1999, rather than look around for an affordable private hall to rent, big enough to handle Super Sunday, as had always been done in the past, JFOGOC persuaded Temple Sinai of Middletown, by far the largest congregation in the county, to host it instead. Temple Sinai's building was enormous and could easily accommodate the crowds of people who would show up, the banquet, all the other activities, and then some. From 1999 forward, every Super Sunday has been held there.

It was shortly after JFOGOC notified its member synagogues about this change of venue that I received a letter from Temple Sinai's religious leader, Rabbi Joel Schwab, inviting JCC to enter what he called the "Jewpardy" competition, which was his brainchild and he was planning as one of the many happenings at Super Sunday on February 6. As it turned out, it was destined to be not just another Super Sunday activity, but the single most anticipated event, with hockey-parent type fans, some of them almost foaming at the mouth, rooting crazily for their own congregations. Modeled after the TV game show *Jeopardy*, each synagogue was asked to put together a team consisting of two adults, two bar/bat mitzvah-age kids, and two younger kids to give the correct "questions" to Jewish-knowledge "answers." For example, Answer: "Abraham's second son"; Correct Question: "Who was Isaac?" Like *Jeopardy*, the answers would range in difficulty from $100 to $1,000 ones with "Final Jewpardy," in which the points would double, at the end of each round. Simple enough, you'd think; except for one disturbing thing: JCC's Hebrew school was so small that it was highly unlikely that we'd be able to come up with enough kids, or enough adults for that matter, with sufficient knowledge to avoid humiliating ourselves. By February 1999, which was six months after I became president, our Hebrew school had grown to sixteen students but was still, by an enormous margin, the tiniest in the county. Temple Beth-El in Florida Village had fifty-five students; the Temple of Liberal Judaism in Monroe well over sixty; and Temple Sinai in Middletown a staggering one hundred plus. Moreover, the Hebrew schools at those synagogues held classes at least two to three days a week, whereas JCC's held classes only on Sundays. At least as discouraging, JCC's adult ed. classes took place only once or twice a month, whereas their adult ed. classes took place once or twice each and every week. And the final, almost overwhelming disadvantage we faced was that those synagogues, and others that were going to participate, had so many qualified students and adults that they were planning to rotate in new team members throughout the competition. Just before each new round, they would take a look at the categories on the Jewpardy board and then send in the students or adults they thought had the best chance of giving correct questions for the answers in the posted categories. There was no rule against it and it was a gargantuan advantage. Some of the kids on JCC's team knew enough about "Jewish History" to hold their own and would be able to give correct questions to the history answers but knew absolutely zip about "Hebrew and Yiddish Expressions" and in that category would fall flat on their faces. But we just didn't have any qualified extras to rotate in. Our four best students and two best adult ed. parents would have to compete in every single round.

On the day of Jewpardy, we arrived early to give ourselves time to get used to the unfamiliar surroundings in Temple Sinai's huge auditorium where the competition would take place. Our six team members and about eight others from JCC, who had come to root us on, took seats in the first two rows. Immediately, we were frightened and almost overwhelmed by how professional the props on the stage looked. The Jewpardy board, the moderator's podium, the lecterns for the competing teams, and the scoreboards were exact replicas from the TV show. And the sound system was modern, crystal clear, and loud. We wouldn't be able to even swallow up there without the entire audience hearing every murmur. As we tried to take everything in and relax a little the auditorium started filling up. Within fifteen minutes of our arrival, it had filled to more than 300 people, and more were still coming in. To try and put ourselves at ease, we looked around for familiar faces but, although several of us had friends from other congregations who were going to compete, for some reason, we didn't recognize anybody. Not a soul. It dawned on us that the reason we didn't recognize anybody was because the other congregations participating were so large that the teams they had sent to compete, along with the supporters cheering them on, represented only a very small fraction of their total memberships. That we didn't know anyone, from among those small fractions, wasn't too surprising. But the unfamiliar faces increased our anxiety tremendously. We were nervous — very, very nervous. And then suddenly, unexpectedly, and much, much too soon, Rabbi Gary Loeb of the Monroe Temple stepped to the moderator's podium and, with his voice amplified by the high-tech sound system and clear as a bell, announced: "Our first round will begin in two minutes. Will the following two teams get ready and start mounting the stage: Temple Beth-El of Florida and Jewish Community Centre of Greenwood Lake."

We all shuddered, some of us uncontrollably. The sound system was so loud and so clear that it was going to be impossible to try to hide, by pretending to have soft voices, what we expected would be our many incorrect "questions". Everyone in the auditorium, now filled with more than 500 people — and I mean everyone, even in the very last rows — would undoubtedly hear each and every stammering word. And each and every one, therefore, of our dumb questions to the answers.

"Please, God," I said to myself, "don't let us embarrass ourselves in front of every Jew in Orange County. Let us give the right questions to one or two answers and we'll sit down, happy. All right?"

Round One

We mounted the stage. I was so nervous, I found it hard walk. I tried to be nonchalant but kept stumbling. The rest of the team didn't look much better. But somehow, we all shuffled over to our lectern and seated ourselves on a bench that had been placed for us alongside it.

Rabbi Loeb said, "Will the two youngest members of each team step forward for the first round."

Temple Beth El's youngest kids jumped to their feet immediately and marched to their lectern. But on our team, no one moved. I looked at Todd Weisslander. It was as though he was frozen. To get him moving, I punched his shoulder, hard. And Jules Osak, our other adult team member, punched his son, Jeremy, too. After making a big deal about rubbing their arms like they were hurt, they finally got up and hesitatingly walked to their lectern.

"JCC has won the coin toss," Rabbi Loeb said. "Would one of JCC's young members choose a Jewpardy category so we can begin?" But again, Todd and Jeremy did nothing.

I whispered, "Pssst, Todd. Choose 'Holidays' or 'History.'" The other categories were "Hebrew & Yiddish Expressions," "Current Events," and "The Torah."

"There's no coaching, Mr. Grossman," Rabbi Loeb yelled. "Next time you do that, your team will be penalized one hundred points." I turned as red as the bright red patterns on my Bukharin Yarmulke and shut up.

Finally, Todd said, "Okay, we'll take 'Holidays.'"

"Good choice," the rabbi said, "which answer in the 'Holidays' category do you want?"

But again, Todd and Jeremy said nothing, as though even that question was too hard. I couldn't help myself: "They'll take the easiest one," I shouted. "The $100 one."

Rabbi Loeb ignored me. "Guys," he said. "Which one?"

Jeremy said, "We'll try the one for $600." My heart sank. And Jeremy's father, under his breath, whispered, "I can't believe that kid."

"Okay, Todd and Jeremy," said Rabbi Loeb. "Here, for $600, is your answer: 'He began the revolt against Antiochus Epiphanies that eventually led to the holiday we call Chanukah.'"

They thought for a second and then Todd yelled, "Who was Judah the Maccabee, Who was Judah the Maccabee?"

"You have a few seconds left," Rabbi Loeb said. "Is that your final question, JCC?"

Jeremy looked at Todd for a moment and then at me. And then, "No, it's not. I got it, I got it! The correct question is 'Who was Mattathias?' I remember from my Hebrew school book. Judah the Maccabee won the revolt but his father, Mattathias, started it."

Jules, Jeremy's father, almost collapsed.

"Excellent," said the Rabbi. "Which answer do you want next?"

But believe me, that was their high point. "We'll try Holidays again, but for $300 this time," Jeremy said.

"Okay, guys. The $300 answer is: 'They are also known as The Days of Awe.'"

When I heard that answer, I figured they'd get the correct question easily. I was wrong. Dead wrong.

Jeremy yelled, "What is Chanukah?"

His father looked at him exasperated and whispered, "What's wrong with you? Not every question is on Chanukah. You just did one on that. This is something different. Think!"

"Come on, Mr. Osak. Like I told Mr. Grossman, no coaching. I won't take 100 points off this time, but this is your last warning. If it happens again, I'll take 200 points off."

Then Todd yelled, "What is Passover?" I had to restrain myself from punching him again, this time in the teeth.

"I'm sorry, JCC. Those questions are incorrect." Rabbi Loeb looked in the direction of the other lectern and said, "Temple Beth-El, for $300 and control of the Jewpardy Board, the answer, again is 'They are also known as The Days of Awe.'"

In unison, the two Beth-El kids shouted, "What are Rosh Hashanah and Yom Kippur?" They then proceeded to give the right questions to almost all of the remaining answers in the "Holidays" category, and the right questions to several of the answers in the "Current Events" and "Torah" categories as well. By the time they got through, the score was a lopsided $4,500 to $1,000. The only reason it was even that close was because Todd had helped to avoid a worse rout by somehow coming up with the correct question for the $400 answer in the "Hebrew & Yiddish Expressions" category. And yes, the Beth-El team captain insisted we be penalized according to the rules and forced Rabbi Loeb to make a deduction for the illegal coaching. So the actual score when Todd and Jeremy sat down was $4,500 to $900.

But it wasn't over. Yet. Now it was time for the bar/bat mitzvah-age kids to give it a try, so Stacey Weisslander, Todd's sister, and Steve Bloom approached the lectern. Todd had just given the correct question for the $400 answer from the "Hebrew & Yiddish Expressions" category, so we had control of the board. It was still JCC's turn.

Rabbi Loeb said, "What category and for how much, JCC?"

Stacey said, "We'll take, uh, 'Torah' for $200."

"Your answer is: This Biblical book ends with the death of Moses."

Without waiting for Stacey, Steve Bloom broke in, "What is the book of Deuteronomy?"

"Correct JCC. What's next?"

"We'll take 'Torah' again, for $500," Steve said.

"God created this on the fourth day."

Steve pondered for a moment and started to say, "The green plants..." but Stacey interrupted him and said, "What are the sun, the moon, and the stars?" She was right. We had a little rally going. The score was now $4,500 to $1,600 and I thought, "Thank you, God, for letting us get a few questions right. Maybe, just maybe, He'd been listening after all."

They continued to hold their own. And before they sat down, they managed to narrow the gap a little more. The last answer for the bar/bat mitzvah-age kids had been selected by the two Temple Beth-El teens from the "Current Events" category for $700: "In 1948, this country unexpectedly voted with the United States and its allies at the United Nations to establish a Jewish homeland in Palestine." One of the Beth-El kids said, "What is Britain?" The other said, "What is France?" Both questions were wrong. Although Britian and France had voted with the United States, neither's vote was unexpected.

Rabbi Loeb said, "JCC, for control of the Jewpardy Board and for 700 points, do you know the country?"

I could tell Stacey was guessing but, with only a second to go before her time ran out, she shouted, "What is the Soviet Union?"

"That is correct, JCC," Rabbi Loeb said. "What a steal. You needed that."

When their round ended the score was 4,800 to 2,300 against us. It was time for the adults.

And in the "Jewish History" category, I noticed, hardly anything had been touched. Of the ten answers in each category posted on the Jewpardy Board, correct questions had been given to only the $100 and $200 "Jewish History" ones. And in Jewish history that day, I was feeling strong.

"Give me 'Jewish History' for $300, Rabbi," I said.

He looked at the board and then at his notes. "This judge anointed Saul as the first king of Israel."

Immediately, I replied, "Who was Samuel?"

"Very good, Mr. Grossman. Let's see if you can keep it going. Which category do you want next and for how much?"

"'Jewish History' again, Rabbi. For $400."

"Okay," he said. "Here it is. 'He was Isaac's grandfather.'"

I had to think but, thank God, it came to me quickly. Isaac's father, I knew, was Abraham and Abraham's father was, uh, Ter… "Who was Terach?" I said.

"You're starting to make a game of it, JCC. But keep your eye on the clock. There's only seven minutes left and you're still a ways back, 4,800 to 3,000. Quickly, give me another category and for how much."

I consulted with Jules for a moment. He was happy to let me run with it for a while longer, but suggested I start picking the harder, bigger-dollar answers to give us a fighting chance to catch up in the remaining time.

I said, "All right, Rabbi Loeb. Give us Jewish History once more, for $900!"

"Mr. Grossman, Mr. Osak, this answer is a little tricky, so think before you say anything. Remember, you can consult with each other and either of you can respond, but no coaching from anyone else. Listen carefully: 'He was the master of a man who had been left for dead but who eventually became prime minister of Egypt.'"

The answer wasn't that hard but I almost fell into the trap. I started to say, "Joseph" but stopped before I blurted it out. Joseph, the most famous of Jacob's twelve sons, had been thrown into a pit and left for dead by his eleven brothers. A passing caravan found him, transported him to Egypt, and sold him into slavery. Years later, Pharaoh, after learning of Joseph's ability to interpret dreams, appointed him his prime minister. But who had been Joseph's master while he was a slave, before he became prime minister?

It was on the tip of my tongue. "Poter ... something?" Jules and I looked at each other wildly.

"Five seconds left, gentlemen. Do you know the question?"

"Who was Poliper?" Jules yelled.

"Three seconds, gentlemen."

"I've got it!" I screamed. "'Who was Potiper?' Right, Rabbi?"

He turned to a woman and two men seated behind him in the front row of the auditorium. "Can we accept that as correct, judges?" First one and then the others, very slowly and overly theatrically it seemed to me, nodded.

Rabbi Loeb said, "The correct spelling is P-o-t-i-p-h-a-r, *Potiphar*. But, congratulations JCC, we'll accept Potiper. That's worth another 900 points. You're getting close and don't forget, Final Jewpardy is coming up."

To our amazement, we were getting so close we were within striking distance. The score was now 4,800 to 3,900.

The Reluctant Jew

"You still have the board, JCC. Do you want to stick with 'Jewish History' or move to another category? Let me know quick, please, there's only three minutes left before Final Jewpardy and the end of the match."

I was exhausted from the excitement and tension and Jules knew it. He stepped to the plate, but decided to play it fairly safe. "Let's try 'Hebrew & Yiddish Expressions' for $300."

The Rabbi said, "These Hebrew words mean the following in English: 'Come, my friend, the Bride to meet, the holy Shabbat let us greet.'"

If ever there was a phrase in Hebrew I should have easily been able to recall, that was it. It was the title and refrain of a song I had sung, in fact, the traditional opening song, at every Friday night service I'd attended for the past several years. And I had attended scores of them. But I drew a complete blank and am, to this day, mortified about it. I was useless.

Fortunately, however, the correct words came to Jules almost instantly. "What are *Leha Dodi likrat kallah, p'ney Shabbat n'kab-la?*"

And we were $300 closer, 4,800 to 4,200.

"Next category and how much are you playing for, JCC? Decide fast, only two minutes left."

Jules said, "We'll take 'Hebrew & Yiddish Expressions' for $1,000."

I and all of JCC's supporters in the audience, all eight of them, gasped and prayed he knew what he was doing.

"In Hebrew, for 1,000 points which will put you ahead, tell me the words that mean: "With everlasting love, You have loved Your people Israel. You have taught us the Torah and its *Mitzvot*. You have instructed us in its laws and judgments."

Again I was useless. But Jules almost got it. Three times, the judges wouldn't accept his response, because he kept leaving out a word or two or transposing them. His time ran out.

"For the steal, Temple Beth-El, do you know the correct Hebrew words?"

Unfortunately for us, they did. One of their adults was Hebrew fluent and shouted, "What are *Ahavat olam beyt yisrael am-havta. Torah u-mitzvot, hukim u-mish-patim otanu limad'ta,*" perfectly.

That made the score 5,800 to 4,200 and we were in trouble.

"There's forty-five seconds left, Temple Beth-El," Rabbi Loeb said. "Time for one more selection before Final Jewpardy. Give me a category and how much, fast."

One of them said, "'Jewish History' for $500."

My eyes brightened. If they blew it, maybe we could steal again and get back into the match. I listened, ready to pounce, if only I'd get the opportunity.

"The $500 answer is: 'All of the Patriarchs and Matriarchs are buried in the Cave of Machpelah in Hebron except this one.'"

I waited, afraid to look at the Temple Beth-El adults. I lifted my head. I could see they weren't sure; they were consulting each other.

"Twenty seconds, Beth-El. Do you know the question?"

They hesitated, they were going to guess.

"Who is Joseph?" one said.

"Sorry, not correct, gentlemen. Try again."

They were worried. "Who is Leah?" the other yelled.

"Wrong again, guys. Five seconds more. Then it goes to JCC for the steal."

They didn't say anything. They were panicking. They just didn't know. Time!

Before the Rabbi could turn to us, I screamed, "Who is Rachel?" which I was certain, beyond doubt, was right. I was beaming. I had just read about the Cave of Machpelah, and who was buried there, in one of the books I was reading.

The score was now 5,800 to 4,700 and, with Final Jewpardy in front of us, it was anybody's game.

No one, including rabbis Loeb and Schwab and all the other rabbis in attendance, could believe we had gotten this far. With only sixteen students in our Hebrew school, common sense and all predictions had led everyone to think, and rightly, JCC would enter the Final Jewpardy round trailing not by only 1,100 points, but by at least 5,000 to 10,000. If that had been the case, even if we won Final Jewpardy, we'd lose the match. But with the score standing at $5,800 to $4,700, we actually had a one in four chance of winning. Remember, we weren't playing for real money, so no team was worried about trying to keep any of the dollars they'd won. The only thing each team was worried about was finishing with more points than the other teams, so as not to be eliminated. With JCC losing $5,800 to $4,700 we weren't going to bet only $700, thinking if we lost Final Jewpardy, we'd still walk away with $4,000 cash (In "Jewpardy" as opposed to "Jeopardy" a wrong "Final Jewpardy question" would result in losing just the amount bet whereas a right "question" would double the amount bet). Or, even if we won the Final Jewpardy round, and doubled the $700 to $1,400, to still lose the match $5,800 to $5,400[1] if Beth-El stood pat and bet nothing. The $5,400 would be worthless. Instead, with the score at $5,800 to $4,700, here were the only real possibilities: (1) Both JCC and Beth-El would bet $4,700; if both gave the correct question for the Final Jewpardy answer, Beth-El would win $10,500 to $9,400[2]; (2) Both teams would bet $4,700; if both gave the wrong question for the answer, Beth-El would win $1,100 to $0;[3] (3) Both teams would bet $4,700; if Beth-El got the question right and JCC got it wrong, Beth-El would win $10,500 to $0;[4] or, and this is what we prayed for, (4) Both teams would bet $4700; if JCC got the question right and Beth-El got it wrong, we'd win $9,400 to $1,100.[5] Other bets were possible, but they wouldn't make sense. Beth-El had to bet $4,700, or close to it,[6] to guard against the bet they knew we were going to make, that is, everything we had, the $4,700.

The excitement in the room was thick. JCC and Beth-El's fans were so tense, they were either on the edge of their seats or out of them, standing. Most were chanting and cheering, shouting encouragement to their respective teams. The rest of the people in the auditorium were going wild too. In my chest, my heart thundered. I perspired. I was flushed.

And then, "Your Final Jewpardy answer is this: 'He became the WCW World Heavyweight Wrestling Champion in July, 1998.'" Rabbi Loeb stopped for a moment while his assistant supplied large oak tag cards on which we would write the amount of our bets and our 'questions' with Magic Markers. He continued, "And he's the only Jewish WCW champion in history. You have thirty seconds starting right" – he hit a timer – "now!"

I figured it was over. Someone from Beth-El had to know it. It would do no good if I knew who it was, and I knew instantly, if Beth-El knew it too. We'd be out of the competition. And in the Final Jewpardy round, the rules permitted all six members on each team to consult with one another;

that is, all six could participate in trying to come up with the correct question. If the adults on the Beth-El team didn't know who the WCW (World Championship Wrestling) champion was, one of the kids on their team undoubtedly would. I mean, the WCW champion was so well-known among youngsters, he was almost like a comic book superhero.

Listlessly, I began writing on the oak tag. I assumed that everyone on my team well knew the name I was writing, and any one of them would have written it him or herself if only he or she had grabbed the Magic Marker first. I assumed that at least someone on the Beth-El team was writing the name down right now too. But, even after I had written out the first three letters – G-o-l – neither Todd, Jeremy, Stacey, Steve, nor Jules seemed to recognize it. At all!

I couldn't believe it. It didn't seem possible.

Jeremy said, "G-o-l? Is that Goliath? Is there a WCW wrestler called Goliath?"

"This is good," I thought. "If my team didn't know, including Jeremy, who was nine years old and exactly the age of kids I thought would most likely know, Beth-El might not either." A voice in my head said, "There's a small glimmer of hope here; maybe more than a glimmer?"

Beth-El held up its card. I looked away, in fact, closed my eyes. My mind told me, 'They had to have gotten it.' I wouldn't look at their card because I'd rather just hear Rabbi Loeb say we lost than have to see it with my own eyes. It would be easier.

I held my breath. I couldn't breathe.

"Who is The Rock?"

"Temple Beth-El," Rabbi Loeb announced, "Very good, The Rock is the WWF champ. However, he's not the WCW champ. They're two different organizations. And he's not and has never been Jewish. You are incorrect."

I was so surprised, I almost fainted.

I was so surprised, I lost hold of my card and it floated into the audience. Some saw what I had written and were smiling.

Rabbi Loeb retrieved the card and, without looking, handed it back to me.

"Mr. Grossman, on behalf of JCC, hold your card high and show it to us." I lifted it, words facing the stage, away from the audience and away from the Rabbi. I stared at what I had written, scribbled actually, making sure it was legible and spelled right. "How could Beth El have missed it? Among most kids, the guy really was a superhero, up there with Spiderman and Flash." Then, slowly, I turned the card, words facing the audience now for all to see:

"Who - Is - Goldberg?"

Even Beth-El's fans applauded.

"That question, JCC, is correct. Next, you'll be playing against the winner of the match between my synagogue, the Monroe Temple of Liberal Judaism, and Congregation Agudas. Congratulations, you've made it into the second round."

"Bring 'em on," we thought. "Yeah," Todd yelled, "let's kick some more butt." This time, his mom, who had been in the audience rooting wildly, punched him. But after winning Round One, nothing that came afterward really mattered. We were euphoric. "This is big," Rabbi Modek kept saying. "Real big." He couldn't wait to announce what had happened in JCC's newsletter. But what had happened was about to get bigger.

The Monroe Temple won its match against Congregation Agudas and also, somewhere along the line, two teams that had signed up for the competition dropped out.

At 3:00, Rabbi Loeb announced, "Jewish Community Centre of Greenwood Lake and Monroe Temple, it's only Round Two but, because of the forfeits, your match is one of the semi-finals. Temple Sinai has already won the other semi-final and the winner of your match will meet Temple Sinai for the championship."

Temple Sinai was Rabbi Schwab's congregation and the host synagogue for Super Sunday.

"This is unbelievable," I said to my teammates. "Are we really heading toward the championships?"

"Not quite," Jules said. "We still have to get by Monroe. And if you thought Florida was tough, wait till you see these guys."

I knew he was right. Surpassed only by Temple Sinai, the Monroe Temple of Liberal Judaism was the second largest in the county and had more than sixty Hebrew school students. With that kind of enrollment, they would have an almost inexhaustible supply of contestants to rotate into their team whenever needed.

In the meantime, between Round One and Round Two, we had lost one of our team members. Todd Weisslander, for some reason, started to feel sick and couldn't continue. Todd was ten years old and had been competing, age appropriately, as one of the younger kids. We didn't have a comparable replacement, but we had to do something so we sent in one of our seven-year-olds. She was Sarah Birnberg, our Hebrew school director Joanne's daughter.

Round Two

At 3:15, Rabbi Loeb said, "JCC and Monroe Temple, please take your places on the stage. We'll begin in exactly two minutes."

This time, we lost the coin toss and Monroe immediately took control of the Board. For eight long minutes, they were like steamrollers. In every category, they got nothing wrong. Finally, with the score 5,600 to 0, they missed something.

Rabbi Loeb said, "Jeremy, Sarah, you need to keep your team in this match. For a big $700 and the steal, the answer again is: *'You sustain the living with loving kindness, and with...'*" It was from a category called "Synagogue Skills." He read three full lines of the Sabbath *Amidah* prayer in English and wanted the Hebrew translation. The Monroe kids had almost gotten it, but the part they recited in Hebrew didn't go with the part Rabbi Loeb had read in English.

Sarah knew the *Amidah* cold. "What is," she said, "... במימחר רבמי מתיח היחמ בדסח מייח מכלכל" and proceeded to rattle off the exact Hebrew translation flawlessly. She kept going, in Hebrew, beyond where the Rabbi had ended and he cut her off.

That'll do, Sarah. That was very good. 700 points for JCC. What catego....?"

"I'll take 'Observances,'" she interrupted, (just to make it interesting in this round, the "Holidays" category was called "Observances") "for $500."

"Okay, Sarah. For 500 points, do you know the question to this answer?: 'On this day, only he may enter once every year.'"

The Reluctant Jew

I had to think. There was something about the phrasing that confused me. The correct question began to form in my mind, but it came to Sarah first. It came to her before anybody, almost at light speed.

She said, "Who is the High Priest on Yom Kippur?"

She was good, apparently, not only in the "Synagogue Skills" category, but at "Observances" too. The score was still daunting but we were on the board, 5,600 to 1,200.

"Nice going, Sarah," Rabbi Loeb said. "There's time for one more answer before I call up the teenagers. What category do you want to try now?"

She said, "Give me 'Observances' again, for $300."

I wished she had picked a harder one, but it was a safe move. She knocked it off easily.

And we were 300 points closer.

Because of Sarah's last correct question, we had control of the board, and Steve picked the category, "The Middle East," for $200. He and Stacy started out all right, and for a minute or two, it seemed they even might gain some ground. But to say the least, and putting it mildly, our teenagers had a very, very rough time.

Rabbi Loeb said, "Here it is, Steve: 'It was the first Arab country to sign a peace treaty with Israel.'"

That was almost too easy. Steve said, "What is Egypt? Give me 'The Middle East' again for $300."

"Here's your answer, Steve: 'He's been the president of Syria for more than twenty-five years.'"

That was easy for Steve too. "Who is Hafez Assad?"

He kept rolling. "I'll take 'The Middle East' for $400."

"This U.S. president negotiated the Camp David Peace Accords with Israeli Prime Minister, Menachem Begin and PLO Chairman, Yasir Arafat."

They were getting a little harder but, even for teenagers, still manageable.

"Who is Jimmy Carter?" Steve asked.

He was doing well. But we were way back. The score was now $5,600 to $2,100, which was still out of Final Jewpardy range. That is, Monroe could bet nothing and even if JCC bet everything and got the Final Jewpardy question right, we'd still lose, $5,600 to $4,200.

"Give me 'The Middle East' again, for $500."

"Israel's desert area in the south is called this."

This was the first question I was worried he might not know. But after hesitating a few seconds to consult with Stacey, he said, "What is the Negev?" which was right.

Then Stacey stood up and, instead of going after the more difficult answers in "The Middle East" category, she went after the easier answers in the "Synagogue Skills" category, almost all of which were still on the board. It was a good strategy and she got the $100, $200, and $300 ones right before she … well, before she and Steve got murdered.

For no reason really, Stacey and Steve blew the $400 "Synagogue Skills" question and the Monroe teens got the steal. That made the score, including the steal, $6,000 to $3,200. Not good, but at least in Final Jewpardy range. That is, if Monroe bet nothing on the Final Jewpardy answer and we bet everything and got it right, we would win $6,400 to $6,000. But in reality, they'd never risk letting just us bet. If we stayed in Final Jewpardy range, Monroe would have to bet. And if they bet and were wrong and JCC was right, we'd come out on top.

But then, the Monroe kids lived up to their reputation. They slaughtered us. By the time the teen round was over, JCC was all but beaten and out of the match. They had wiped us out and widened their lead to a ridiculous $7,900 to $3,200. We were so discouraged that when Steve and Stacey sat down, Jules and I dreaded facing the Monroe adults.

But we got a break. An incredible, lucky break. And that break, we knew, would be our only chance.

When the Monroe adults stood up and positioned themselves at their lectern, Rabbi Loeb said, "You still have control of the Board, Monroe. What category will it be and for how much?"

The only category left that was mostly untouched was "Biblical and Ancient Jewish History." Just the $100, $200, and $400 answers had been used, and the Monroe guys decided to go for the $300 one.

"Your answer," Rabbi Loeb said, "is 'Jacob's eldest son.'"

Without thinking too hard and without consulting with one another both of the Monroe adults shouted, "Who was Judah?"

Jules picked up that that question was wrong immediately, but a split-second later, I realized it too. Surprised by the mistake, Rabbi Loeb looked at them, urging with his eyes that they give it another try. He said, "Monroe, is that your final response?" They looked puzzled. They had been certain "Judah" was right.

Under our breath, Jules and I started murmuring, praying to ourselves.

"Four seconds, three seconds, two seconds, time! Too bad, Monroe, that question is incorrect. JCC, can you ….?"

Jules and I had to move fast, because we knew the match would be over in only a few minutes, and we were still thousands of points behind. So without waiting for Rabbi Loeb to say another word, Jules yelled, "Who was Reuben?" which was right, gave us 300 points, and control of the board.

The Rabbi said, "What category and for how much, JCC?"

And, at that very moment, Jules and I knew our last chance had arrived, and boy did we take it. It was now or never.

I said, "Okay, Rabbi Loeb. Let's get this over with one way or another. Give us 'History' for, uh, for $1,000." If we got it, we'd be within Final Jewpardy range with a chance, not a good chance, but a chance, of winning. If not, we'd be finished and out of the match.

Rabbi Loeb said, "Good luck, JCC. For a big $1,000, your answer is: 'So he could marry Bathsheba, David had him killed.'"

With all the events and details that comprise Jewish history, that's not a name one would likely recall, unless he was a Biblical history buff or had read it very recently. And, incredibly, I had read the story of David and Bathsheba only yesterday. Just to pass time before I had to go somewhere, I had picked up a book from a shelf at home entitled, believe it or not, *David, A Biography*, by Barbara Cohen. Quite by accident, I had flipped to the pages that described how David, upon seeing the beautiful Bathsheba bathing on a nearby rooftop, became obsessed with her and decided she would become his wife. The problem, of course, was that Bathsheba was already married and to an exceptionally brave and loyal officer in David's army. Not to be deterred, David committed the most cowardly and evil act of his life. He ordered his top commander, Joab, to place Bathsheba's husband at the front line, where the fighting with the Ammonites was fiercest, and then have the rest of his men fall back so the officer would be killed. Disgustedly, Joab obeyed. – And I remembered the officer's name.

"Who was Uriah? Who was Uriah the Hittite?" I screamed.

Rabbi Loeb actually smiled. "Well done, Mr. Grossman. That makes the score $7,900 to $4,200. Always remember, in this game, it's never over till it's over." We were in Final Jewpardy range. "What category would you like next and for how much?"

Getting that one right charged me up. It focused my mind, and everything I had ever read about Jewish history seemed to rise from my subconscious to the surface, where I could recall and use it. I said, "Give me 'History' again, Rabbi, for $900."

He said, "Here's your answer: 'When visited by a delegation of prominent Jewish leaders, this pope warmly greeted them with the words, 'Welcome, I am your brother, Joseph.' Do you know the question?"

I was sure I did, but the category was 'Biblical and Ancient Jewish History' and the pope who had said that was from the twentieth century. I hesitated.

"Seven seconds, Mr. Grossman. Can you give me the correct question?

I was confused. I consulted with Jules.

"Three seconds," Rabbi Loeb said. "Watch the clock."

It had to be the pope I was thinking of, but he was a modern one, not ancient.

"One second."

I figured it out. "Who was Pope John XXIII?" I yelled.

The trick was that although John XXIII had been pope in the twentieth century, from 1958-1963, the greeting he used harkened back to the Second

Millennium B.C.E. when the biblical Joseph's eleven brothers, after having left him for dead in the wilderness twenty years before, were forced to travel to Egypt to buy food due to a severe famine back in Canaan. In Egypt, food was plentiful, because by then, Joseph had become the Egyptian prime minister and had strictly enforced his policy of storing surplus provisions during Egypt's seven years of plenty, in preparation for the coming seven years of scarcity. Those years of scarcity were now upon the Middle East. The seven good years to be followed by seven bad years had been foretold in Pharaoh's famous dream: "I dreamed that seven fat cows emerged from the Nile, but later seven lean ones came out." No one but Joseph had been able to accurately interpret it.

When the eleven food seekers from Canaan were brought before Joseph, he recognized them instantly. However, he did not reveal himself, because he remembered, bitterly, what they had done. Finally, Joseph's love for his brothers won out and, weeping tears of joy, he said, "Welcome, for I am your brother, Joseph." Pope John XXIII well knew that remarkable story and, to express his own love for the Jewish people, so long abused by the Church, he used those words too. By the end of his papacy, due to his tolerance for all faiths and respect for all peoples, he'd become the most beloved pope of modern times among both Catholics and non-Catholics. But there's a bit more to the story. John XXIII's real name, you see, the one on his birth certificate and the name he was known by before he became pope, was *Giuseppe* Roncalli. And the name *Giuseppe*, in English, is none other than *Joseph*. – "I," Pope John XXIII said to the Jewish delegation, "am your brother, Joseph."

And we were $900 closer. The score was now $7,900 to $5,200. We were within, well within, Final Jewpardy range, and were determined to stay there. If we did, only sixteen Hebrew school students or not, we could win.

Rabbi Loeb said, "Give me a category and for how much, JCC."

Jules shouted, "He'll stick with 'Jewish History.'"

I added, "For $800."

"The $800 answer," the Rabbi said, "is this: 'Through the centuries, Jewish scholars have been described by different names. From 1480 C.E. to the present day, they've been called *Achoronim*, meaning *latter ones;* from 1038 B.C.E. to 1480 B.C.E., they were called *Rishonim*, meaning *early ones;* from 590 C.E. to 1480 C.E., they were called *Geonim* from *Gaon*, meaning *outstanding scholars;* from 200 C.E. to 590 C.E., they were called

Amoraim, meaning *interpreters of the Mishnah*; and from 310 C.E. to 590 C.E., they were called *this*.'"

When Jules and I heard that one, we stared at each other in numb disbelief. The $800 answer was so esoteric, it should have been worth ten times as much. It made the $1,000 and $900 answers look easy. We had never heard of *Achoronim* or *Rishonim*, and *Geonim* and *Amoraim* were only vaguely familiar. We had made a serious mistake. With the score at $7,900 to $5,200 we were already in Final Jewpardy range, and should have selected a much easier answer, kept control of the board, and not risked giving the Monroe adults an opportunity to steal and make it impossible for us to win.

"Take a guess, JCC," Rabbi Loeb said.

"Who were the *Patriarchs*?" I yelled.

"Wrong," he said. "Three seconds left. Guess again"

Something started to form in Jules's mind. Something with a *T...*?

"Who were the *Torah...Torahnim*?" he shouted.

"Good try, JCC, but that's not it. You're out of time. For the steal and $800, Monroe, do you know the correct question?"

While we had been struggling the Monroe guys had been thinking. They said, "Who were the *Tannaim*?"

"That's it," Rabbi Loeb said. "The *Tannaim*, from *Tanach*, meaning *Hebrew Bible*, is correct. You have 800 more points for a total score of 8,700 to 5,200, and control of the board. What category do you want next and for how much?"

They took "History" for $700 and got it right. And they took "History" again for $600 and got it right. Things were slipping away fast. With their correct questions to those two answers, Monroe's lead was now $10,000 to $5,200. JCC could still win in the Final Jewpardy round, but if Monroe got one more "History" or any other category answer right worth $500 or more, they'd be out of range and we wouldn't be able to catch them. With another $500, their lead would be $10,500 to $5,200 so, in Final Jewpardy, even if they bet nothing and we bet everything, all $5,200, and gave the correct question, JCC would still lose $10,500 to $10,400.

There were ten seconds left.

"What category and for how much, Monroe?"

"We'll take 'History' for $500," one of them said. It was the only answer in the "History" category that hadn't been used.

"For $500," the Rabbi began, "and the *match*, your answer is: 'When Solomon died, this man became King of Judah.'"

Our hearts sank. The chances of their blowing another easy one, as they had the even easier $300 answer earlier, were slim. – Not with the match at stake! But they hesitated and I knew why. After Solomon died, the United Kingdom split into two separate countries. Solomon's son, *Rehoboam*, became king of the Southern country, Judah, and a military leader, *Jeroboam*, became king of the Northern country, Israel. Their names were so similar that I was constantly getting them confused. I wasn't sure, even while I waited with my heart in my throat for Monroe to give their response, which king had ruled which kingdom. Monroe should have reeled off the names quickly, one right after the other, so if the first one was wrong, they'd have time to get in the second. But they waited.

"Less than three seconds," Rabbi Loeb said. "Hurry!"

"Who was *Jeroboam*?" one of the Monroe guys said.

"I'm sorry. That's incorrect. One second."

"Who was.....?"

"Time!!" the Rabbi said. "You're out of time."

The audience was stunned. We were still alive. And, what's more, we were fired up. Once again, Rabbi Loeb's assistant passed out large oak tag cards with Magic Markers. Monroe hadn't wanted to let it get this far and they were angry – *at themselves!* "How much longer," I thought, "could our incredible luck hold out?" As in the previous Final Jewpardy round, we had only a one in four chance of winning, but it had been enough then and maybe it would be now. Our whole team was fired up, which was good. We were focused. We were ready. We listened:

"Your Final Jewpardy answer, said Rabbi Loeb, "is this: 'King Cyrus fulfilled this man's prophecy.' You have thirty seconds."

"That's it? Is he crazy?" I screamed to myself. "What kind of clue is that? Does Rabbi Loeb think we all went to rabbinical school like he did?"

But I noticed that Monroe was stumped too. Nobody on their team was writing anything on their oak tag card either.

Stacey said, "Is it King Nebuchadnezar?" I knew immediately that was wrong. Nebuchadnezar had been king of Babylonia when that country defeated Judah, destroyed Solomon's Temple, and exiled the Jews in 586 B.C.E. But he had made no prophecies I'd ever heard of for a man like Persian King Cyrus to fulfill.

Sarah said to me, "Maybe it's King Ahazeurus?" She was thinking of the Persian king who married Esther and whose prime minister, Haman, had tried to exterminate the Jews. But like Nebuchadnezzar, Ahazeurus and Haman had made no prophecies I knew of that were ever fulfilled by King Cyrus. In fact, King Cyrus was a hero to Jews because he had helped them return to the Promised Land from their exile in Babylon.

Todd said, "What about King Antiochus Epiphanies?" Again, that couldn't be right. Antiochus was king of the Syrian Greeks beginning in 175 B.C.E. It was he who installed statues of Greek Gods in the Jerusalem Temple, thereby triggering the revolt of Mattathias and Judah the Maccabee. But all this happened more than 700 years after King Cyrus died. How then could Antiochus have made a prophecy to be fulfilled by Cyrus, who lived and died seven centuries before him?

Jules said, "We're talking prophecy here, so it's got to be one of the Prophets." A light went on in my head, at last.

I glanced over at Monroe and they were starting to write something. Scared, I forced my fingers to work. There were nine seconds left.

I finished. Four seconds to go. Jules looked at the card. He said, "Are you sure it's him?"

"I think so," I whispered. "He prophesized that the Jews could survive as a people, even in exile, if they obeyed God's laws and eventually they'd return home. He made that prophecy as the Babylonians were burning Solomon's Temple and forcing the Jews into exile. His prophecy was fulfilled when King Cyrus defeated Babylonia and helped the Jews go back to the Promised Land."

"Time!" yelled Rabbi Loeb. "First Monroe. Can we see your question?" Like the round before, I couldn't breathe. With more than 500 people in the room, it was sweltering. I was flustered. I was red. Jules handed me a handkerchief. I mopped myself.

They held up their card:

"Who was Elijah?"

Rabbi Loeb said, "Monroe, I know that was very difficult and yours was a good guess. But I'm sorry, that question is incorrect. JCC, for the *match* and a chance to compete with Temple Sinai in the finals, please show us your card."

I was shaking. I was sweating. I felt faint again. I knew "Elijah" was wrong the moment I saw it, but I still wasn't sure that what I had written was right. I looked at our card, afraid to show it to the audience.

"What are you waiting for?" Rabbi Loeb said. "You can't change it now. Turn it around so we can see."

I did:

"Who – was – Jeremiah?"

I was trembling. I grabbed some tissues from Stacey. If Rabbi Loeb didn't speak up soon, someone would have to give me mouth-to-mouth.

He said, "JCC, congratulations. You're going to the finals."

Now we were stunned. Even if we lost to Temple Sinai, the worst we could do would be second place. It was enough, almost, to make me start believing there really was a God. I absolutely could not believe, along with half the people present, that we had gotten this far.

But in the finals, to put it kindly, we were overmatched. Temple Sinai of Middletown annihilated us. The score they beat us by was something like $14,500 to $1,300. They were so good that we only had control of the board for two or three minutes during the entire match. And in this, the finals round, the answers in the posted categories were much, much more difficult than in the previous rounds. We were so intimidated that we were afraid to go after anything except the easiest answers. While Temple Sinai chose $1,000 and $900 ones, we chose nothing more difficult than $300 ones. We never got into Final Jewpardy range, and even if we had, this time we got the Final Jewpardy answer dead wrong. We weren't even close.

But although they killed us, we weren't humiliated. In fact, we felt incredibly proud and triumphant. From the beginning, with its one hundred-plus Hebrew school students, Temple Sinai had been expected to be the runaway winner by every congregation in the county. That they actually won surprised no one. It was us, "sixteen Hebrew school student JCC," that completely and totally blew everyone's mind. JCC's taking second place was huge! It was an almost miraculous accomplishment. And while president, I never let my congregation, or any other, ever forget it.

It took Reuben about two months before he stopped telling everyone he came across, "This is big, this is very big!" and calmed down. The second-place finish had so energized him that he re-dedicated himself, even more than before, if that was possible, to improving JCC's Hebrew school. "If we could do that well with our little, struggling school," he thought, "what would happen after completely restructuring it and doubling or tripling enrollment?" I had a more realistic view. Energized though I was, I knew that we had been lucky, very lucky. The chances of our besting fifty-plus-student Florida and sixty-plus-student Monroe again, anytime soon, were extremely slim. Slimmer even than our chances of beating them the first time had been. But boy, did that second-place win give us a much-needed boost to our spirits! For many months, it infused a lot of us with newfound levels of enthusiasm and excitement. Reuben was so impressed that a few months after the competition, he invited me to talk to a group of students he was teaching at a temple in Nyack. Since Reuben was working for JCC only part time, he supplemented his income by teaching classes for that synagogue on two or three weekday evenings. I accepted and we set it up for a Thursday, which was the easiest day for me to take off from work early and be in Nyack by 6:00 PM.

Chapter Eleven - The Learned Guest Lecturer

Despite all of my reading and the success of JCC's Jewpardy team at Super Sunday, I was still not confident of my knowledge. The details of Jewish history still seemed as new and confusing to me as ever and had not really sunk in. Since I was unsure of myself, I prepared for my presentation to Reuben's class as if I was about to take oral exams for a doctoral degree in ancient history – and then some. I made voluminous notes, a five-page outline, several maps, and a separate, two-page chronology. Nonetheless, I still thought this was going to be only an informal chat, a discussion at most, with a bunch of eager kids. But when I arrived at the Nyack Temple, Rabbi Modek, to introduce me to his students, brought me not into his classroom but into a small auditorium instead. He had twenty-eight students, seventeen of whom were about thirteen years old and had spent the last six months studying intensely for their upcoming bar or bat mitzvahs. Not only that, most of their parents were there, along with fifteen more advanced students from other classes, and were going to sit in. Altogether, seventy-five people were staring up at the podium. Reuben had billed me as some sort of learned guest lecturer and I thought, "Please, God, help me."

Reuben said, "Ladies and gentlemen, guests and students, I want to introduce you to today's learned speaker, the president of Congregation B'nai Torah in Greenwood Lake and my close friend and colleague, Mr. Michael Grossman. He's going..."

I thought, "Lord, tell me I misheard him. What learned speaker? What if I got dates wrong? What if I forgot names? What if I froze and didn't know Isaac from Isaiah or Jacob from Job? What if I couldn't remember anything? Was he trying to give me a heart attack before I even stood up?"

He continued. "He's going to talk to us today about the history of Israel and the Jewish people, in detail, from Abraham until modern times. You're in for a wonderful, information-packed presentation, and Mr. Grossman will be happy to answer all of your questions when he's finished."

I thought, "Is he trying to kill me? Not only had he gone completely insane but, if he kept it up, I would too."

He said, "And now," motioning me to the podium and microphone, "Mr. Michael Grossman."

I came close to wetting my pants but somehow, I opened my mouth, words came out, and I began.

At least I thought words came out. In truth, for the first two minutes, I was so nervous I couldn't find my voice. Reuben tried to cover for me and buy some time by handing out my outline and maps. Then, one of the kids brought me water and, adjusting my yarmulke and taking a deep breath, at last I spoke:

"In 2000 B.C.E., when Abraham traveled from Ur, his birthplace in southern Mesopotamia, to Haran, in northwestern Mesopotamia, he and his entourage had to cross the Euphrates River. At the time, Akkadian, which evolved into Assyrian and Babylonian, was the area's most widely spoken language, and the locals called the newcomers *Ibirus,* which means *'from the other side'* or *'to cross over.'* *Ibirus* became *Hebrews* and thus arose the first word describing Abraham's followers as a distinct people. *Ivris* is the Hebrew equivalent of *Ibirus* and *Hapirus* the Egyptian."

I looked around. They weren't making faces yet. Instead, they were smiling and I could see, from their looks, wanted more. *What's wrong with these people?* Didn't they know that what I'd just told them was mostly conjecture? No one really knew the origin of the word Hebrews. For centuries scholars had been debating it and, that its source may have been Ibirus, was just an educated guess.

I continued: "Later, when Abraham's grandson, Jacob, wrestled all night with an unknown stranger, who according to Genesis was actually an angel, God changed Jacob's name to *Israel* which means to *'struggle with the Lord.'* Jacob's twelve sons became the twelve tribes of Israel, and from then forward, the Hebrews became known as the *Israelites.* In around 1250 B.C.E., after the 430-year enslavement in Egypt, Moses led the Israelites to freedom and the very frontier of the Promised Land. When Moses died, the mantle of leadership passed to Joshua, who crossed the frontier and conquered the Canaanites."

I looked around again. They hadn't stopped smiling and still no one looked bored. Some of them even seemed interested and wanted still more. I felt my confidence soar and thought, "Maybe this won't be such a fiasco after all." I relaxed, I breathed, my words started flowing.

Then, turning up the microphone so everyone could hear, I stopped being afraid, lifted my head, and this, in brief, is what I said:

"After Joshua, a succession of chieftains ruled the tribes for 200 years. Some of them, the Judges – Gideon, Deborah, Samson, and others – rose to great prominence and wielded authority beyond their own tribal borders. After the Judges, the Israelites united as one kingdom under Saul, who was anointed king by the last Judge, Samuel, in 1020 B.C.E. Saul was killed in battle with the Philistines[1] in 1000 B.C.E. and was succeeded by David, who subdued all of Israel's enemies and ruled forty years. Upon David's death in 961 B.C.E., his son, Solomon, became king, built the First Temple, and ruled the United Kingdom forty years more.

"When Solomon died, the era of the United Kingdom ended and it split into two separate entities. The Northern Kingdom, composed of ten of the tribes, continued to be called Israel, and its first ruler was Jeroboam,[2] who earlier had led an unsuccessful revolt against Solomon and then fled to Egypt. The Southern Kingdom, which included Jerusalem, consisted only of Benjamin, the smallest tribe, and Judah, by far the largest and most powerful. *Judah*, from which is derived *Ju a.k.a. Jew*, was so dominant that the Southern Kingdom was named after it. Judah's first ruler was Solomon's son, Rehoboam, whom the Bible blames for the breakup of the United Kingdom when he told the ten northern tribes, who were petitioning for a reduction of taxes: 'My father beat you with whips, but I will beat you with scorpions.'

"Then, in 722 B.C.E., 200 years after Solomon's death, Assyria conquered the Northern Kingdom and exiled nearly all its inhabitants. They were dispersed and became known as the 'Ten Lost Tribes of Israel.' The Southern Kingdom, however, grew more populous than ever due to the large number of Israelites who, rather than be dispersed, fled there from the North. Many of the Israelites who were dispersed settled in Alexandria, Egypt, where they created one of the largest and most prosperous Jewish communities in the ancient world. The Israelites who remained in what had been the Northern Kingdom, or were somehow able to return, absorbed some of the spiritual practices of new pagan inhabitants installed there by Assyria and became a distinct religious sect known as the *Samarians* a.k.a. *Samaritans* which, according to some linguists, means '*former inhabitants of Israel.*' Judah, which had become more powerful than ever due to its enlarged population, survived 136 years longer, until 586 B.C.E., when the Babylonians overran it and destroyed Solomon's Temple. During the period before Judah was defeated, its most important king was Josiah (648-609 B.C.E.) during whose reign a book of law, the biblical book of Deuteronomy, which had long been forgotten, was rediscovered by workers repairing the Temple. Based on Deuteronomy's instructions, Josiah outlawed all idol worship, reinstituted strict allegiance to the One God,

Yahweh, and began to enforce all laws prescribed by this supposedly lost book. There is a theory, however, that Deuteronomy had never been lost, but was actually written by Josiah himself and then presented to the people as divine law so they would willingly adhere to his concept of Judaism. Josiah's remarkable reign ended in 609 B.C.E. when he was killed in Megiddo, Mesopotamia during battle with an Egyptian army.

"Less than three decades later, when Babylonia destroyed the First Temple, Judah's people, although sent into exile, were never dispersed and did not disappear. In fact, nearly all modern Jews are their descendents. The huge majority resettled in Babylon, where they became one of the greatest centers of Jewish learning outside the Promised Land. In later centuries, scholars of this community wrote the Babylonian Talmud. When Persia defeated Babylonia in 537 B.C.E., the Persian ruler, King Cyrus, encouraged the Jews to return to the Promised Land and, extraordinarily, even helped finance it. There, at the urging of Prophet Haggai, the destroyed temple was rebuilt over twenty-three years and the Second Temple completed in 514 B.C.E.

"The Jews' sojourn under enlightened Persian rule, however, did not last long. The end began in 490 B.C.E. when, at the Battle of Marathon, a Persian army was unexpectedly defeated by a much smaller army of Greeks. Persia's empire, however, did not immediately collapse, and in 458 B.C.E. its rulers allowed Ezra the Scribe, who later authored the biblical book of Ezra, to leave Babylon and travel to the Promised Land. There, he instituted ceremonies and wrote prayers that are still used as part of the core service in synagogues around the world. A few years later, Ezra's contemporary, Nehemiah, persuaded the Persian ruler, King Artaxertes, to appoint him governor of the Jews and was permitted to rebuild Jerusalem's defensive walls. He was so successful that he managed to revitalize the country and bring its economy and Jewish society back to life.

"As Greece slowly took control of Persia's empire, the Greek-Jewish cultural divide became the most intensive battle for ideas in the ancient world. Greeks cherished logic, the arts, and the beauty of man; the Jews cherished spirituality, the law, and the beauty of God.[3] In 331 B.C.E., Alexander the Great put the finishing touch on Persia's long decline when he defeated King Darius's troops and the Persians surrendered to him in the city of Babylon. Shortly before the surrender, Darius was murdered by one of his own officers. When Alexander died in 323, his Greek empire was divided among his four top generals. The area including the Promised Land came under the rule of General Seleucus, whose descendent, the notorious Antiochus Epiphanies, rose to power in 175 B.C.E. He defiled the Second Temple when he insisted on erecting within it statues of Greek gods. Led by Mattathius, of the Hasmonean family, and his son, Judah the Maccabee, the Jews revolted and in 147 B.C.E. re-established a united, independent nation called the Hasmonean Kingdom a.k.a. *Judea*, which was the Greek/Roman name for Judah.

"Independent Judea survived only eighty-four years. Over many decades, Rome subjugated Greece and the entire Mediterranean. In 63 B.C.E., the last independent Hasmonean King, Hyrcanus II, was deposed, and Judea became a Roman province. In 40 B.C.E., Rome installed Herod as the province's king, known later as Herod the Great, who built extensive public works and renovated the Second Temple. He was so murderous, however, having executed his brother-in-law, mother-in-law, wife, uncle, and three of his sons, that shortly before his own death in 4 B.C.E., Emperor Augustus, aware of the Jewish kosher laws, remarked: 'Better to be Herod's pig than his son.' Under subsequent rulers installed by Rome, Jewish anger intensified. A massive revolt began in 66 C.E. but was put down in 70 by Titus, when his soldiers burned the Second Temple. He later succeeded his father, Vespasian, as emperor. The only remnant of the Second Temple left is the famous 'Wailing Wall.' In 72 C.E., the Roman general, Flavius Silva, defeated the last pocket of resistance at Masada, when some 900 Jews, led by Eleazar Ben Yair, committed mass suicide rather than be taken prisoner.

"In 130 C.E., sixty years after Jerusalem's destruction, Emperor Hadrian decided to rebuild the city as a Roman metropolis, with plans to convert the temple site into a shrine to Jupiter. Led by Shimon *Bar Kochba*, which means 'Simon *Son of a Star*,' and Rabbi Akiva, the leading Jewish scholar of the age, another huge uprising began and, for four years, the Jews regained control of most of Judea, including Jerusalem. After staggering losses on both sides, in the hundreds of thousands, Bar Kochba was finally killed and Akiva captured and tortured to death. Rome's losses were so frightening that for the first time in Roman history, when the emperor presented the news to the Senate, he omitted the traditional, "I and the army are well." With the defeat of Bar Kochba, Jews were forbidden to set foot in Jerusalem and they entered the Diaspora and lived as exiles until modern times.

"Then, in 1948, at the close of World War II, nearly 2,000 years after the fall of the Hasmonean Kingdom, and 1,815 years after the defeat of Bar Kochba, the Jews once again established an independent nation, with the critical backing of the United States, its allies and, surprisingly, the Soviet Union. It was decided that the language of this new nation would be modernized *Hebrew* and *Jews* anywhere in the world would be welcomed as citizens. And there was never any doubt that its name would be *Israel*, harkening back to the ancient days of glory in the United Kingdom of David and Solomon."

I stopped, incredibly relieved I had gotten through it. There was some applause. One of the parents said, "You know, on behalf of the entire Nyack Temple, thank you for coming, Mr. Grossman. That was very well done."

I said, "Thank you very much, sir." But inside, I was repeating the compliment to myself, shouting: 'THANK YOU FOR COMING, MR. GROSSMAN, THANK YOU FOR COMING!' It was the best compliment, by far, I'd ever heard.

But then the questions came, a least a dozen or so, and I was thankful that Reuben stood beside me to help answer them. Because of his help, the insane overpreparation I had done for my talk, and my good fortune that the questions they asked were not too difficult, I escaped with my new reputation intact. My reputation as "the learned guest lecturer, from Greenwood Lake, New York."

As I was getting ready to leave, all the students and their parents asked me for copies of the chronology I'd prepared to go with the copies of my maps and outline Reuben had given them. I was flattered and gladly passed them out.

The Great Story's Chronology

DATES PRIOR TO 722 B.C.E. ARE APPROXIMATE. SUBSEQUENT DATES ARE RELIABLE.

DATE(S)	HAPPENING
3100-2000 B.C.E.	SUMERIAN CIVILIZATION IN MESOPOTAMAIA
2350-2100 B.C.E.	AKKADIAN CIVILIZATION IN NORTHERN MESOPOTAMIA
2000 B.C.E.	ABRAHAM - ACCORDING TO BIBLE LIVED 175 YEARS
1750 B.C.E.	JACOB - ACCORDING TO BIBLE LIVED 147 YEARS
1680-1250 B.C.E.	PERIOD OF ENSLAVEMENT IN EGYPT
1250 B.C.E.	MOSES LEADS THE ISRAELITES TO FREEDOM
1210 B.C.E.	JOSHUA ENTERS THE PROMISED LAND
1220-1020 B.C.E.	PERIOD OF THE JUDGES
1150 B.C.E.	PHILISTINES ARRIVE FROM CRETE AND SETTLE ON THE COAST
1020 B.C.E.	SAMUEL ANOINTS SAUL KING
1000 B.C.E.	SAUL KILLED BY PHILISTINES
1000-961 B.C.E.	REIGN OF DAVID
961-922 B.C.E.	REIGN OF SOLOMON
925 B.C.E.	JEROBOAM'S FAILED REVOLT AGAINST SOLOMON
922 B.C.E.	UNITED KINGDOM ENDS – REHOBOAM BECOMES KING OF JUDAH & JEROBOAM BECOMES KING OF ISRAEL
722 B.C.E.	ASSYRIA CONQUERS ISRAEL & EXILES ITS PEOPLE
710 B.C.E.	SAMARITANS ARISE AS DISTINCT RELIGIOUS SECT
680 B.C.E.	LARGE JEWISH COMMUNITY ARISES IN ALEXANDRIA, EGYPT

648-609 B.C.E.	REIGN OF KING JOSIAH IN JUDAH. LOST BOOK OF LAW FOUND IN TEMPLE - PROBABLY BIBLICAL BOOK OF DEUTERONOMY.
586 B.C.E.	BABYLONIA CONQUERS JUDAH – FIRST TEMPLE DESTROYED
537 B.C.E.	PERSIA DEFEATS BABYLONIA – CYRUS PERMITS JEWS TO RETURN TO PROMISED LAND
514 B.C.E.	SECOND TEMPLE IS COMPLETED AT URGING OF HAGGAI
490 B.C.E.	BATTLE OF MARATHON – GREEKS DEFEAT PERSIANS
458 B.C.E.	EZRA THE SCRIBE BECOMES RELIGIOUS LEADER IN JERUSALEM
444 B.C.E.	NEHEMIAH APPOINTED GOVERNOR OF THE JEWS BY ARTAXERXES
356-323 B.C.E.	ALEXANDER THE GREAT
322 B.C.E.	SELEUCUS TAKES CONTROL OF PROMISED LAND
175 B.C.E.	ANTIOCHUS EPIPHANIES IS KING OF SYRIA & RULES JEWS
167 B.C.E.	MATTATHIAS & JUDAH THE MACCABBE LEAD REVOLT
147 B.C.E.	HASMONEAN KINGDOM A/K/A JUDEA ESTABLISHED
63 B.C.E.	HYRCANUS II DEPOSED – JUDEA BECOMES ROMAN PROVINCE
63 B.C.E.-14 C.E.	AUGUSTUS RULES ROME AS ITS FIRST EMPEROR
40-4 B.C.E.	REIGN OF HEROD THE GREAT AS ROMAN INSTALLED KING OF THE JEWS
66 C.E.	JEWISH REVOLT AGAINST ROME
70 C.E.	GENERAL TITUS BURNS SECOND TEMPLE & JERUSALEM
72 C.E.	MASADA – ELEAZAR BEN YAIR VS. FLAVIUS SILVA
79 C.E.	TITUS SUCCEEDS VESPASIAN AS ROMAN EMPEROR
117-138 C.E.	REIGN OF EMPEROR HADRIAN

131-135 C.E.	REVOLT LED BY SHIMON BAR KOCHBA & RABBI AKIVA
135-1948 C.E.	DIASPORA
500-600 C.E.	BABYLONIAN TALMUD COMPLETED
1947 C.E.	SOVIET UNION VOTES YES TO PARTITIONING OF PALESITNE BETWEEN ARABS & JEWS
1948 C.E.	INDEPENDENT ISRAEL RE-ESTABLISHED

Chapter Twelve - Prophets and Kings

I didn't feel like such an amateur Jew anymore. Jewish history and what it meant to be Jewish, as a way to approach every moment of living, was becoming clearer. The Ultra-Orthodox might disagree, but in my readings, I was surprised and delighted to find that in essence, truly being Jewish does not require a mindless adherence to religious ritual or an unthinking belief in a Supreme Being. In fact, to struggle with God, as did Jacob – and to question whether God exists, as did Job – is well within Jewish tradition. Nor is it a system of outdated laws or a cult of ancestor worship, although knowledge of history's lessons is hugely important. And most definitely, it is not, contrary to popular opinion, a belief that the Jewish people are somehow intrinsically superior to others, with us being "the Chosen" and the rest "the Goyim." The concept of chosenness is a factor only insofar as it means that each and every person, Jewish or otherwise, has the power to "choose" to live justly of his or her own free will. The non-Jew who chooses that course is clearly on higher ground ethically than a Jew who does not. Judaism, as I see it, proclaims that the act of choosing to do justice, for one's entire life every day, is the very core, the sine qua non, of what being Jewish means. "Everything else," as Hillel said, "is commentary." If you do not seek justice, you are not living as a Jew, regardless of whether you were born one. Modern-thinking rabbis teach, "God did not choose the Jews; the Jews chose God, i.e., chose to devote their lives to completing his work by building a paradise on earth in the here and now for everyone." But once a person stops seeking justice, he stops, for all intents and purposes, being Jewish, whether he calls himself a Jew or not. The corollary to this is that the tens of thousands of non-religious, non-believing Jews who — like me to an extent — had gone to universities and become active in social causes, while at the same time remaining ignorant of or even denying their backgrounds continued, nonetheless, being Jewish at core.

So, when I thought about a topic for my next newsletter article, the Prophets immediately came to mind. They had spent their lives exhorting the Jewish people and their rulers to be righteous. I was fascinated by the role they played as the consciences and often, enemies of the ancient kings of Israel and Judah. But as I began writing, skeptical as always, my defiant exchange with Rabbi Mark Blazer when I first met him, more than four years before, came rushing back: "Rabbi, my problem with all of this is that there's no evidence. You talk about… Samuel and David… like they were real people, but there's no archaeological proof at all. If they were so important and had so many followers, how can that be?"

He had replied, "Um, Mr. Grossman, you know, you're right. If everything in the Bible really happened, there should be more evidence, a lot more. But did you know that archaeologists have uncovered artifacts... in recent years that are mind-boggling and support parts of the biblical text. And even if we can't accept all of the Old Testament ... as historically factual, that's not what Judaism is about anyhow." When he said that, I had been incredulous, even a bit arrogant and disdainful, and had thought "...*What artifacts?*" But hold on to your hats, because in this chapter, we're going to find out.[1] Before delving in, however, be warned! In places, what follows is very detailed and some parts require serious concentration and slow going. Don't be put off! If the paragraphs reciting the chronology of the prophets and kings become too overwhelming, skip over them. The rest of the chapter will still be meaningful.

Samuel was both the first prophet[2] and last judge. No judge before him had been able to assert authority over all twelve tribes. Even Gideon, Deborah, and Samson, who rose to great prominence, were no more than charismatic tribal leaders around whom, during periods of crisis, many of the tribes temporarily rallied. But the Israelites, feeling increasingly vulnerable to their enemies, particularly the Philistines, grew tired of the decentralized governance of the judges[3] and began longing for the rule of powerful kings with sufficient authority to raise large armies to protect them. Near the end of the Second Millennium B.C.E., Samuel was the most famous and widely respected judge, and the Israelites looked to him to anoint a ruler. He resisted, advising that God was the only true king, and any earthly king would enslave and tax them and, at times, commit unspeakable cruelties. It was with this warning that Samuel transitioned from judge to Israel's first prophet. Nevertheless, he relented, and in 1020 B.C.E. anointed the Benjamanite, Saul, as the first king of Israel. The period beginning with the United Kingdom under Saul and ending shortly after the return of the Jews to the Promised Land in 536 B.C.E., from their exile in Babylon, was the Age of the Prophets.

Most scholars agree that the last prophet was Malachi, 515-445 B.C.E., although some contend it was Jonah, of the whale story, and assign the period 450-400 B.C.E. as the period he was active. Others say Jonah lived much earlier, in the 700s B.C.E., which makes more sense, because those were the years that the Assyrian capital, Nineveh,[4] flourished, and the Biblical description of Jonah's activities mostly took place there. In any event, it is possible that Jonah is not historical at all and the stories about him, only allegories. The same may be said of Daniel, although there is slightly more evidence that he may have lived than did Jonah.

The list of historical prophets between Samuel and Malachi is lengthy, but most of the names are familiar. In approximate chronological order, they were: Nathan (985), Elijah (850), Elisha (825), Joel (790-770), Amos (780-740), Hosea (760-720), Micah (740-700), Isaiah of Jerusalem (742-695), Nahum (663-612), Zephaniah (630-608), Habakkuk (605-600), Obadiah (586-583), Jeremiah (627-580), Ezekiel (593-570), Second Isaiah (540), Daniel (606-534?), Haggai (520-516), and Zechariah (520-515).[5] Each carried forward Samuel's ancient warning and spent his life denouncing the injustices of Israel's and Judah's kings, and exhorting the people to live righteously. Their teachings thunder across the centuries, as powerful today as when they were first spoken more than two and a half millennia ago:

> *"There is no truth, no love, and no knowledge of God in the land;*
> *Swearing and lying, killing and stealing, and committing adultery,*
> *They break all bonds, and blood touches* blood [incest].
> *For Israel has forgotten his Maker,*
> *And built palaces."* - Hosea 4:1-2 & 8:14, and

> Mercy and contentment will come to he ....
> *"Who walks righteously and speaks uprightly;*
> *He who despises the gain of oppression;*
> *Who shakes his hands, lest they hold a bribe;*
> *Who stops his ears from hearing of bloodshed,*
> *And shuts his eyes from looking upon evil"*
> – Isaiah 33:15, and also

> *"Seek the Lord, all you humble of the land,*
> *Who do his commands;*
> *Seek righteousness, seek humility;*
> *And perhaps you may be hidden*
> *On the day of the anger of the Lord."* – Zephaniah 2:3

The words of the prophets comprise a unique literature that even now grips our consciences and shapes our view as to what living justly truly means. That meaning, however, was often totally ignored or conveniently forgotten by the Hebrew kings. The most famous example, perhaps, was when David fell in love with Bathsheba, whom he observed bathing from his palace rooftop. He summoned her, slept with her, but learned she was married to Uriah the Hittite. That Hittite, however, was a captain in David's army, and one of his bravest men. Knowing full well Uriah would loyally follow orders, David sent him into battle against the Philistines on the most dangerous front and then, in secret, ordered the rest of his men to fall back so he would be killed. David promptly married Bathsheba. But he had murdered Uriah. He lived in shame and, in God's eyes, as a criminal for the rest of his life. As punishment, God directed Nathan, the prophet, to tell David this: ..."*God sayeth......Now therefore the sword [bloodshed] shall never depart from thine house; because thou hast despised me and hast taken the wife of Uriah... Behold, I will raise up evil against thee out of thine own house, and I will take thy wives before thine own eyes, and give them unto thy neighbor, and he shall lie with thy wives in the sight of the sun.*"

But David was just one imperfect man, and one king. The long list of them after Samuel anointed Saul is much lengthier than the list of prophets. Including Saul, there were forty-three, the last being Zedikiah, whose reign began in 597 B.C.E. and ended in 586 when Babylonia conquered Judah, destroyed the First Temple, and exiled the Jews.[6] The Babylonian ruler, Nebuchadnezzar, detested Zedikiah for daring to resist, and burned out his eyes. Before blinding him, Nebuchadnezzar forced Zedikiah to witness the torture execution of his two sons. That was the last thing Zedikiah ever saw, and he died with the memory of their mangled bodies seared into his mind. The actions of Nebuchadnezzar, at least as much as those of any of Israel or Judah's rulers, demonstrated beyond doubt the cruelty earthly kings were capable of, that was so feared by Samuel.

That virtually all of the Hebrew kings were real historical personages is now pretty much settled. Several archaeological finds have confirmed passages in the Bible that many, until recently, considered fables or myths. Evidence as to the existence of the two most famous Hebrew kings, however, David and Solomon, has been disappointingly scant. If these men were as widely known and important as the Bible suggests, you'd think they'd be mentioned repeatedly and at length in many contemporaneous, non-Biblical records. But so far, that's not been the case. It seems that to date, only one non-scriptural reference to the "House of David," – contemporaneous with the time when he is believed to have lived – has been found. And it is only *nearly contemporaneous* at that. It is etched in Aramaic on a stone slab that was discovered in Israel at Tel Dan. As to Solomon, the evidence is even sparser. Not a single authentic artifact, tablet, stone, obelisk, or carving bearing his name has ever shown up. As we move forward in time, however, the archaeology is more persuasive. In 1925, for example, a seal with ancient Hebrew lettering was found at ruins on the site of the biblical city of Megiddo, northwest of Jerusalem. It reads: "Shema, servant of Jeroboam." The Bible tells us that after Solomon died and the United Israelite Kingdom ended, Jeroboam became first king of the Northern Kingdom (which continued to be called Israel). The Bible also tells us that Pharaoh Sheshonk attacked Israel during the first year of Jeroboam's reign. Sure enough, at the same archaeological dig in biblical Megiddo, a stone was uncovered bearing the inscription: Pharaoh Sheshonk I. Moreover, the seal with Jeroboam's name and the stone with Sheshonk I's have been dated, and both correspond with the dates given in the Bible for Jeroboam's rule, 922-901 B.C.E.

Jeroboam was followed by four kings who ruled in total less than twenty-four years and about whom, other than what is set forth in the Bible, little is known: Nadab (901-900 B.C.E.), Baasha (900-877 B.C.E.), Elah (877-876 B.C.E.), and Zimri (876 B.C.E.). But about Omri, who became king of Israel in 876 and ruled twelve years, there is reliable information from non-Biblical sources. According to I Kings 16: "[He] bought the hill now known as Samaria from its owner, Shemer, for 4000 shekels and built a city on it, calling it Shemeria in honor of Shemer." The ancient site of that city, which became the capital of Israel, has long been known and it is obvious that Omri, whose kingdom was being threatened with extinction by Assyria, built there for strategic reasons. It sits on a lone hill some 300 feet high and is surrounded by mountains on three sides. Its defenses, apparently, were impressive enough because Ashurnarsipal II, king of Assyria (884-859 B.C.E.), proclaimed in cuneiform writing in his own words: "....I conquered the cities...I caused great slaughter, I destroyed, I demolished, I burned..." but he left Israel and its capital, Samaria, temporarily at least, in peace. Judah escaped for the time being too but, in return, had to pay Ashurnarsipal huge tribute. And as to Omri, the Assyrians left a stunning clue. That they had been extremely impressed by this king of Israel is beyond doubt, because nearly all cuneiform records, even long after his death, refer to the Northern Kingdom not as Israel but as "The House of Omri."

After Omri, his son, Ahab, became king and ruled twenty-two years, 872-850 B.C.E. This is the Ahab that the Bible tells us married Phoenician princess Jezebel and worshipped idols. Like his father, much is known about Ahab's life from non-Biblical sources. During his reign, the Assyrian threat grew darker, but Shalmaneser III, king of Assyria, 859-824 B.C.E., reported, in cuneiform records: "....there were 2,000 chariots and 10,000 horses belonging to Ahabbu (Ahab)." Those forces, fortunately, combined with the forces of Ahab's allies at the time, two Syrian princes, were again impressive enough to hold Assyria at bay.

In I Kings 22, the story of Ahab's "ivory palace" is mentioned. For millennia, that description seemed as mythical as *Shangri La*. Investigation has revealed, however, that although Ahab ruled from Samaria like his father, and occupied the same palace, he extensively expanded and renovated it. During archaeological digs in 1908 and 1931, as mountains of rubble from that palace were being removed and examined, thousands of chunks, pieces, slivers, and shards of ivory were found everywhere, in every room. The obvious explanation is that those fragments are what remain of the tons of ivory King Ahab must have used to decorate his spectacular "ivory palace," which, it turns out, seems really to have existed some 3,000 years ago.

Next to rule Israel were Ahab's sons, Ahaziah (850-849), who lasted only a year before he fell and was fatally injured, and Jehoram (849-842). II Kings 3 describes a revolt during Jehoram's reign by the king of Moab (a vassal state to Israel at the time) and a military alliance between Moab and Judah that was successful in seizing large chunks of territory from Israel. An incredible archaeological find has confirmed this biblical account. In 1868, in Dibon, Palestine, a large basalt stone was uncovered, inscribed with the words of King Mesha, the very Moabite king mentioned in II Kings 3. It is in Moabite dialect and reads: "I am Mesha....king of Moab... My father was king of Moab for thirty years…..I built this sanctuary to Chamosh (Moabite God) …for he saved me from my oppressors and gave me dominion over my enemies. Omri was king of Israel and oppressed Moab many days…And his son succeeded him and he also said I will oppress Moab. In my days he said this but I got the upper-hand of him and his house and Israel has perished forever…" As noticed by Walter Heller in his work, *The Bible as History*, if we take "Israel has perished forever" as meaning simply "The House of Omri has perished forever," the Moabite description fits the biblical one perfectly because King Jehoram, who was Omri's grandson, was the last of Omri's dynasty having been assassinated by a captain in his army, Jehu, shortly after the successful Moabite revolt. Moreover, the basalt stone inscription is a *contemporary account* written by one of the very participants, King Mesha himself, in the war between Moab and Judah on the one hand and Israel on the other. It is certainly, therefore, reliable confirmation of the biblical description of this war, which account, although more widely known, was written much later.

Not only did Jehu kill Jehoram, as mentioned, but, exhorted by the prophet Elisha, he slew Ahab's wife, Jezebel, and King Ahaziah of Judah (842) as well. He was anointed king of Israel the same month by an even more famous prophet, Elijah, and ruled Israel twenty-seven years (842-815 B.C.E.). His power was such that he also ruled Judah, *de facto* if not *de jure,* from his throne in Samaria. But during his reign, Assyria grew steadily stronger and the tribute Jehu was forced to pay all but bankrupted Israel and was a harbinger of worse things to come. In 1845, at a dig on the Tigris River, a novice archaeologist uncovered a black obelisk covered with pictures and cuneiform inscriptions. Beneath a relief showing bearded and capped, Hebrew-looking envoys, the cuneiform reads: *"Tribute of Jaua of Bit-Humri: Silver, gold, a golden bowl, golden goblets, a golden beaker, pitchers of gold, lead, scepters for the king and balsam wood I received from him."* With even my miserable Hebrew language skills, I can undesrstand that one: *Jaua of Bit Humri*, although in cuneiform, is close enough to the Hebrew: *Jehu of Bet-Omri*, and means *King Jehu of the House of Omri* (as Israel was then called). The Bible tells us in II Kings 13 that by the time Jehu died and was succeeded by his son, Jehoahaz, Israel's armed forces had been reduced to "...but fifty horsemen, and ten chariots, and ten thousand men...." This was not due solely, however, to the huge tribute, and resulting drain of Israel's resources, Jehu had agreed to pay the Assyrian king, Shalmaneser III. In fact, that tribute persuaded the Assyrians to eventually back off, but as soon as they did, King Hazael of Damascus savagely attacked because of Jehu's duplicity in making peace with Shalmaneser and leaving Hazael to face him alone. Just two years earlier, Israel and Damascus had agreed to resist Assyria together and, prior to Jehu's betrayal, had been allies. The Bible records that Hazael inflicted staggering losses "....in all the coasts of Israel."

There are scores upon scores of other instances of non-biblical confirmation of events, personalities, and places heretofore known solely from their scriptural descriptions. The above examples, however, at least for me, convincingly demonstrate that the Bible is often amazingly accurate and should more than suffice for even cynics and skeptics. Admittedly, however, there are also scores of examples in which the archaeological or scientific evidence does not support or is flatly at odds with the Bible. The trick, in my opinion, is to try to figure out which portions are real history and which, as Isaac Asimov pointed out in his *Asimov's Guide to the Bible* (1981), are real baloney.

To finish the chronology of Israel's kings: After Jehu, was succeeded by his son, Jehoahaz (815-801), Syria, under the leadership of Hazael's son, Ben-Hadad, further devastaed Israel. As a result, Jehoahaz revived the worship of Asharah, the Canaanite fertility goddess, hoping she might protect the Israelites. From time to time, Omri, and particularly Ahab, had worshipped her too. Jehoahaz was succeeded by his son, Jehoash (801-786) who, strongly supported by the prophet Elisha, defeated Judah's king, Amaziah, and like Jehu, his grandfather, reduced the Southern Kingdom to a vassal state. Jehoahaz was succeded by his son, Jeroboam II (786-746), who ruled an amazing forty years. Not since Solomon had any Hebrew king ruled so long. He recovered most of the lost territory from Moab and Damascus, but was repeatedly denounced by the prophets, Amos and Hosea, for ignoring injustices and permitting idolatry. Next came

Jeroboam II's son, Zechariah (746-745), but he was assassinated within less than a year by Shallum (745) who himself lasted just three weeks before he, in turn, was assassinated by Menahem (745-738). This new king mistakenly believed he could forestall Assyria by paying its new king, the frightening Tiglath-Pileser III (745-727), whatever tribute was demanded. The increased taxes Menahem had to impose to pay that tribute so angered the people that, when Menahem's son, Pekahiah (738-737), succeeded him, he was assassinated almost immediately by an army officer, Pekah, who seized the throne. But by then, the end of Israel was very near. In desperation, Pekah joined Philistines, the king of Damascus, Edomites, Moabites, Phoenicians, and Arabs, in a last-ditch effort to turn back the Assyrians. In these critical circumstances, he tried to force Judah to join the alliance too, but its king, Ahaz, decided to buy his country's safety by paying impossibly high tribute instead. Assyrian cuneiform tablets and the Second Book of Kings are in total agreement as to what happened next: Tiglath-Pileser conquered Damascus, slew its king, and carried off its people to Kir (an Assyrian territory); next, Tiglath captured Hazor, Gilead, Galilee, and all of Naphthali (Israelite territories) and carried away all of Israel's people to Assyria; and finally, Pekah was overthrown and slain by Hoshea (732-722), whom Assyria installed to replace him. They did not leave Hoshea much to rule over. All that they spared was the city of Samaria and a mile or two of surrounding farmland. And, as Assyria dispersed the Israelites to the far corners of its empire and replaced them with a steady stream of non-Israelite immigrants, the area they had lived in since Joshua's time ceased being called Israel, and its people Israelites or Hebrews, but Samaria and Samaritans instead. Soon the city of Samaria itself, the fantastic capital built by King Omri, became so very ethnically mixed that its character as a Hebrew city diluted and disappeared. The ten Northern tribes were lost to history and, except for an odd group once in a while claiming ancestry to one of those tribes, never heard from again.

As to the kings of Judah, who ruled the Southern Kingdom for 136 years more after Hoshea, the last of the Northern kings died and the ten Northern tribes were dispersed, suffice it to say that the same types of archaeological finds that have confirmed much of what the Bible says about Israel's kings have confirmed much of what the Bible says about Judah's kings too. I will not dwell on the archaeology here, as a detailed discussion of most of it is set forth in the references in my bibliography. Very briefly, though, the first king of Judah was Solomon's son, Rehoboam (922-915 B.C.E.), whom the Bible blames for causing the breakup of the United Kingdom when he told the ten Northern tribes: "My father beat you with whips but I will beat you with scorpions." He was followed by his son Abijam (915-913 B.C.E.) and grandson Asah (913-873 B.C.E.), who reigned forty-one years. Asah enforced the laws against idols, defeated a massive attack from Egypt, and repelled an invasion by Israel and King Ben-Hadad of Syria; the same Ben-Hadad whose father, King Hazael, had been betrayed by Israel's King Jehu when he secretly agreed to pay Shalmaneser III ransom and left Hazael to face Assyria alone.

Next, Asah was succeeded by his son, Jehoshaphat (873-849 B.C.E.), who ruled twenty-four years, entered into an alliance with Israel's King Ahab against Syria, and then joined Ahab's son, Ahaziah, in a war against Moab. Alliances shifted constantly, and this was only a couple of years after Judah and Moab had been allies and successfully attacked Israel. Jehoshaphat was succeeded by his son, Jehoram (849-842 B.C.E.), who married Ahab's daughter, Athaliah. During his reign, Edom revolted, regained its independence, and Philistines, together with Arabs, ransacked Jerusalem. Jehoram died after ruling only seven years, and was followed by his son, Achaziah (842), who — as mentioned earlier — was murdered almost immediately by Israel's King Jehu. Upon Achaziah's death, his father's widow, Ahab's daughter Athaliah (842-837 B.C.E.), became Judah's queen. She would have ruled longer, but was thwarted in her efforts to kill Achaziah's son, Jehoash, her own grandson, who took the throne at age six and reigned thirty-seven years (837-800 B.C.E.).

When palace servants assassinated Jehoash, his son, Amaziah (800-783 B.C.E.), replaced him, resoundingly defeated the Edomites, but was assassinated himself after ruling seventeen years. Amaziah's son, Uzziah a.k.a. Azariah (783-742 B.C.E.), took the Judean throne next. The Bible tells us that God struck him with leprosy for refusing to destroy the shrines to idols that were scattered about his realm. He was followed by his son, Jotham (742-733), who had been serving as acting king for years due to his father's illness, and was an experienced ruler. Little, however, is known of him. The next king was Jotham's son, Ahaz (735-715 B.C.E.), who was attacked by Israel's King Pekah and Syria's King Rezin for refusing to join them in a military alliance against Assyria. He had decided to try to buy peace, as had others befor him, by paying tribute instead. To further pacify Assyria, Ahaz permitted worship of their gods throughout his kingdom, for which Isaiah vehemently denounced him.

When Ahaz died, his son, Hezekiah (715-687 B.C.E.), joined an Egyptian-led coalition against Assyria, which was trounced in 701 B.C.E. by Sennacherib, who forced Judah to pay heavy tribute in exchange for not invading. Shortly, however, Hezekiah defied the Assyrians causing Sennacherib (705-681 B.C.E.) to advance on Judah in 690 B.C.E. with 20,000 men. His army, however, was wiped out by plague, described as a miracle in the Bible, and Judah's nearing doom – not by Assyria but a rising new world power – was delayed. The next king, Manasseh (687-642 B.C.E.), Hezekiah's son, was taken prisoner by that power, the Babylonian Empire, which was rapidly eclipsing the Assyrians. During his confinement, the Bible says he repented and was therefore restored to his throne. Manasseh's son, Amon (642-640 B.C.E.), succeeded his father. "He did all the evil things his father had done: he worshiped the same idols, and turned his back on the Lord God of his ancestors." (2 Kings 21). Amon's aides killed him and installed his son, Josiah (640-609 B.C.E.), on the throne. During Josiah's reign, a lost book of law, Deuteronomy, was rediscovered by workers repairing the Jerusalem Temple. Inspired by this book, Josiah reinstituted the worship of Yahweh nationwide, ordered that religious rituals conform to the instructions in the book, and strictly prohibited the worship of idols. Later, he was killed in battle with the Egyptian army of Pharaoh Neco, who was trying to revive the Assyrian Empire and install himself as its king.

Josiah was succeeded by his son, Jehoahaz (609), who reigned only three months before being deposed by Neco who replaced him with Jehoiakim (609-598), Jehoahaz's younger brother. Egypt's influence, however, was in decline and Jehoiakim came under the control of Babylonia after Nebuchadnezzar defeated the Egyptians at the battle of Carchemish in 605 B.C.E. He rebelled against Babylonia around 598, was assassinated, and succeeded by his son, Jehoiachin (598), who ruled only four months before being captured and exiled. Zedikiah (597-586), Jehoiachin's uncle, was installed by Nebuchadnezzar II. Patriots urged him to rebel, while Jeremiah counseled that he continue paying tribute, believing rebellion would mean national suicide. The patriots prevailed, and in 588 B.C.E. Zedikiah led a revolt relying on promises that Egypt would send military help. No help arrived, and in 586 B.C.E. the Babylonians burned Jerusalem to the ground, deposed Zedikiah, forced him to watch the torture execution of his two sons, then blinded him, and the people of Judah were expelled from the Promised Land and carried into captivity.

With the blinding of Zedikiah, the era of Israel and Judah's kings ended.[7] The Age of the Prophets, however, continued on. As Jerusalem fell to Nebuchadnezzar, Jeremiah prophesized, again and again, that the Jews could survive intact as a people, even in exile, if they obeyed God's laws, and they would one day return to the Promised Land. Rather than be captured, he fled from the Babylonians to Egypt, where his voice became silent and he died. Then, in 536 B.C.E., Persia conquered Babylonia, and their monarch, King Cyrus, as if in answer to Jeremiah's prophecies, allowed the Jews to go home. There, due largely to the exhortations of the prophet, Haggai, the Jerusalem temple was rebuilt and the Second Temple completed in 514 B.C.E. It was at this point that the Age of the Prophets began to draw to a close.

Throughout the five centuries of Hebrew sovereignty in the Promised Land, beginning with the anointment of Saul as first ruler of the United Kingdom and ending with the imprisonment and blinding of Zedekiah, the prophets shadowed their rulers like avenging angels. Their influence was such that they could never be ignored. "But why," it is fair to ask, "were they so incensed by idol worship?" Were pagans really so evil, compared to the "pious" Hebrews who believed they were God's Chosen People, and thus much more ethical? The answer is "maybe." For starters, human sacrifice was still being practiced by many of the idol-worshipping societies around them. The Phoenicians, for example, who began flourishing around 2500 B.C.E., more than a millennium before Moses was born, burned men, women, and children at the altar of *Baal a.k.a. Astarte*. The Hebrews' archenemies, the Philistines, who were descendents of the Phoenicians, also worshipped Baal. Some of Canaan's indigenous people worshipped Baal as well and/or a more local god called *El*, to whom human sacrifice was common. *El's* impact on Hebrew thought was appreciable, as is evidenced by God being referred to not always as *Yahweh*, but as *El-Shaddai* ("Almighty God"), *El-Elyon* ("All Highest God"), *El-Olam* ("Everlasting God"), *El-Roy* ("Visionary God") and *Elohim* ("Powerful God") throughout the Old Testament. For the biblical writers to have adopted pagan nomenclature to describe their beloved "One God" so often cannot have been unintentional. The worship of pagan gods by the Hebrews and their kings, after all, was rampant. In the back of their minds, some of the biblical writers may have actually believed in El's presence although in a subordinate role. In fact, such belief would not have contradicted the First Commandment, which reads, word for word: *"I am the Lord your God, who brought you out of the land of Egypt, out of the house of slavery; you shall have no other gods before me."* It does not say there is no other God, only *"…you shall have no other gods before me."* The use of the plural *gods*, by the way, strongly implies the writers' belief that many gods, in addition to Yahweh, the supreme God, existed. The worship of idols of those gods, however, was strictly prohibited by the Second Commandment: *"You shall not make for yourself an idol, whether in the form of anything that is in heaven above, or is on the earth beneath, or that is in the water under the earth, You shall not bow down to them or worship them; for I the LORD your God am a jealous God, punishing children for the inequity of parents, to the third and fourth generations of those who reject me …"* The phraseology, *"I…am a jealous God,"* meaning, presumably, *"jealous of other gods,"* again demonstrates the biblical writers' belief that gods other than Yahweh, although not worthy of worship, existed.

In addition to abhorrent human sacrifice, the pagan societies with whom the ancient Hebrews had contact lacked even nearly as comprehensive and complex a system of laws as had been developed by the Israelites and Judeans. Those laws, as compared to others at the time, were spectacularly egalitarian, and even kings had to obey them. This was in marked contrast to virtually all other Mediterranean, Middle Eastern, or African societies – which to the ancient Hebrews was the entire known world – in which kings were above the law or *were the law;* or even worse, *were gods,* as the Pharaohs considered themselves in Egypt. That's why Samuel had been so reluctant to anoint Saul. He favored the decentralized rule of the Judges, in which no one leader could ever become strong enough to forcefully impose his will on the populace. When the line of Hebrew kings arose, that changed, so the line of prophets arose in tandem to counteract their power. All of the prophets were relentless in reminding their rulers that the only true king was God, and that God's laws applied to all. To them, there was no such thing as a "divine right of kings," which would have been a form of royalty worship akin to idolatry. They railed against idolatry, therefore, in much the same way we rail against Nazism, communism, or despotism today; systems in which the rulers are not answerable to the people, not answerable to the law nor God, but to none but themselves. Although such systems, despite themselves, can occasionally produce beneficent leaders like Cyrus the Great (King of Persia, 550-530 B.C.E.), they more often produce bloodthirsty maniacs with unrestrained power like Nero (emperor of Rome 54-68 C.E.) and Herod the Great (Idumean Jew installed King of Judea by Rome, 37-4 B.C.E.).

Each prophet was associated with a particular king or kings. To get a broad view of the ancient Hebrew timeline and moral landscape, the following charts will be helpful:

Michael Grossman

CHART 1

PROPHET	APPROX. DATES OF ACTIVITY[8]	CONTEMPORANEOUS KINGS	APPROX. DATES REIGNED	KINGDOM OR CITY OF ACTIVITY
Samuel	1025 B.C.E.	Saul	1049-1009	United Kingdom
Nathan	985 B.C.E.	David	1049-969	United Kingdom
Elijah	900 B.C.E.	Solomon, Rehoboam, Ahab, Jehu[9]	969-815	United Kingdom & Israel
Elisha	875 B.C.E.	Rehoboam, Ahab, Jehu	921-815	Israel
Joel	790-770 B.C.E.	Jehoash, Jeroboam II	801-746	Judah
Amos	780-740 B.C.E.	Jehoash, Jeroboam II	801-746	Israel
Hosea	760-720 B.C.E.	Jeroboam II[10]	786-746	Israel
Isaiah	742-695 B.C.E.	Uzziah, Jotham, Ahaz, Hezekiah	783-687	Judah
Micah	740-700 B.C.E.	Jotham, Ahaz, Hezikiah	743-687	Judah
Nahum	663-612 B.C.E.	Hezekiah, Josiah	640-609	Judah
Zephaniah	630-608 B.C.E.	Josiah	640-609	Judah
Habakkuk	605-600 B.C.E.	Johoichin, Zedikiah	598-586	Judah
Obadiah	586-583 B.C.E.	Zedikiah	597-586	Judah?
Jeremiah	627-580 B.C.E.	Zedikiah[11]	597-586	Judah
Ezekiel	593-570 B.C.E.	Babylonian kings	586-536	Babylon
Second Isaiah	540-?? B.C.E.	Babylonian kings	586-536	Babylon
Haggai	520-516 B.C.E.	Persian kings[12]	536-458	Jerusalem
Zecahriah	520-515 B.C.E.	Persian kings	536-458	Jerusalem
Malachi	515-445 B.C.E.	Persian kings	536-458	Jerusalem

CHART 2
ACTIVITIES OF THE PROPHETS

Samuel	Reluctantly anointed Saul king, under whom the twelve tribes united, after having warned that any earthly king would commit unspeakable cruelties.
Nathan	Berated David for killing Uriah and then stealing his wife, Bathsheba. Told David that God's punishment would be "… the sword shall never depart from thine house… "
Elijah	Detested idolaters. Precipitated the fall of Israel's King Ahab and his wife, Jezebel, a Phoenician princess and Baal worshipper. In Jewish folklore, he's reputed never to have died. During Passover Seders, we fill "Elijah's Cup" with wine, hoping he will join us.
Elisha	Disciple and younger contemporary of Elijah who continued the struggle against *Baal* (meaning *idol*).
Joel	A plague of locusts, severe drought, and ongoing famine occurred during his life. Warned of further calamities unless the people repented.
Amos	The economies of Israel & Judah reached almost the prosperity of the old United Kingdom, and the Hebrews became morally lax. Predicted doom unless the people lived ethically. Before he died, a devastating earthquake occurred that killed thousands.
Hosea	Prophesized disaster due to the sins of the people and their kings. Predicted the fall of the Northern Kingdom.
Isaiah	Considered by many the greatest of the prophets. Denounced those who observed religious ritual but ignored injustice. "What need have I of your sacrifices?…sayeth the Lord. I have no delight in lambs and he-goats" (Isaiah 1:11). "Learn to do good and devote yourselves to justice" (Isaiah 1:16).
Micah	Like Isaiah, condemned rituals as meaningless unless bonded to ethics. Reduced the requirements of religion to just three basics: "Doing justice, loving goodness, and walking humbly with God" (Micah 6:8)
Nahum	Prophesized that the Assyrian Empire and its capital, Nineveh, would be destroyed. Probably witnessed the attempted invasion of Judah, during the reign of Hezekiah, by Assyrian King Sennacherib. Judah was saved when Sennacherib's army was wiped out by plague. Afterward, Assyria was eclipsed by a rising new world power, Babylon.

Zephaniah	Prophesized the coming destruction of Judah. Described Yahweh as more than a regional deity but as a God who held sway over all nations.
Habakkuk	Warned that as punishment for its sins, Judah would be destroyed by Babylon, a nation more sinful than even Assyria.
Obadiah	Foretold the destruction of Edom for refusing to help Judah, its brother nation, repel the Babylonians. Considered the two brothers because the Bible says Edom was founded by Esau and Israel by his twin, Jacob, and they thus shared a common bloodline. Predicted the Jews would return from exile and re-inhabit not only their homeland but all of Edom as well.
Jeremiah	Counseled King Zedekiah to offer no military resistance against Babylon realizing that such resistance would mean national suicide. Denounced the immorality of the people but prophesized that the Jews, if they obeyed God's laws, could survive intact even in exile and would eventually return home. The word *Jeremiad*, derived from his name, means *pessimistic complaint*.
Ezekiel	Prophesized Jerusalem's destruction by Babylon but had a famous vision, which foretold that Israel would rise again as (paraphrased), *'living flesh from dry dead bones.'*
Second Isaiah	Was the author of the later chapters of the Book of Isaiah and lived at least two centuries after First Isaiah.
Haggai	Due in large part to his exhortations, Solomon's Temple, which had been totally leveled by the Babylonians, was rebuilt and the Second Temple completed in 514 B.C.E.
Zechariah	Career began about fifteen years after the Babylonian exile ended. Foretold glory for Israel in the "latter days" during the final confrontation between good and evil and the triumph of God's Kingdom.

Malachi, the last historical prophet, was born just as the Second Temple was nearing completion and, upon reaching adulthood, he complained bitterly about its abuses:

> *"Listen, you priests, this command is for you,*
> *Listen to me and take it to heart,*
> *Honor my name, says the Lord Almighty,*
> *Or I will bring a terrible curse against you,*
> *I will curse even the blessings you receive,*

Indeed, I have already cursed them'
Because you have not heeded my warnings;
I will rebuke your descendents,
And splatter your faces with the dung of your sacrifices,
And I will add you to the dung heap." - Malachi 2:2-3

When Malachi died around 445 B.C.E., the Age of the Prophets, as had the era of the kings 141 years earlier, ended.

In modern times, no true prophet – *at least for Jews anyway* – has ever arisen. But the words of the ancients live on, and still shout out to us. My favorite, and among the best known, are those of Amos, whose period of prophetic activity spanned the reigns of five Hebrew Kings. May we never forget them and our purpose as the Jewish people to: "…*[L]et justice rush down like waters and righteousness like a mighty stream."* - Amos 5:25.

* * *

My fellow students and I in JCC's adult ed. classes were finally beginning to master Jewish history and feel comfortable with our new-found knowledge. We definitely weren't neophytes anymore. But when it came to other religions, most of us were almost totally uninformed. As a means of deepening our understanding of Judaism's teachings, we wanted to learn what ethical teachings were important in Christianity and Islam. For my part, I added dozens of books about those faiths to my reading list. In particular, I wanted to know how the minuscule number of Jews in the world "fit in" among their billions of Christian and Muslim neighbors. And, even more important, I wanted to know what they really thought about us. To do that, it was necessary to learn what the world looked like through non-Jewish eyes.

Chapter Thirteen - Everything You've Wanted to Know about Christianity But Were Always Afraid to Ask - Part I: Its Theology and Early History

Although Jesus's religion was Judaism, the religion about him, Christianity, is by far the world's largest. Its adherents today number an incredible 2.2 billion, some 40 percent of the world population, while Judaism's are a mere 15 million, less than 1 percent. It is not widely known, but statistics show that Christianity is now growing more rapidly than even Islam, the other giant, whose adherents by comparison number 1.3 billion. How did Christianity grow so large while Judaism, its parent, grew not at all? And how should we Jews, for centuries condemned and murdered by the followers of one of our own, relate to our modern-day Christian neighbors?

To understand Christianity and answer these questions, we need to know its basic theology and history. Maybe then our understandable fear of it will diminish and we can gain insight into why it has appealed to so many. In our effort to understand Christianity, however, there will be no way to conceal the following horrific truth: From nearly its founding 2,000 years ago, with very few exceptions along the way, the Catholic Church, joined by Protestant churches in the sixteenth century, preached an unrelenting hatred of Judaism that eventually metamorphosized into a racial hatred of people with Jewish blood, and then culminated in catastrophes like the Inquisition and the Holocaust. It is only in modern times, beginning with the issuance of the edict known as *Nostra Aetate* (In Our Time) at the Second Vatican Council in 1962, that the Catholic Church has made a serious, ongoing effort to revise its anti-Jewish theology. That edict repudiated all previous Church teachings that said Jews were "Christ killers and eternally damned." Nonetheless, the Church still maintains that the only legitimate way to salvation is through Jesus, and refuses to extend equivalent legitimacy to any other religion. Even now, most Christians, and a surprising number of Jews, cannot bring themselves to face these disturbing yet undeniable facts.

Nevertheless, if we can lay aside our anger at the way Christianity has treated us, until recently, we may be able to come to at least a grudging appreciation and even respect for the powerful influence it continues to exert over its now 2 billion-plus followers. Needless to say, it has been a tremendous blessing that beginning with Pope John XXIII at the Second Vatican Council, all modern popes appear to have been genuinely committed to reconciling with the Jews and willing to acknowledge, albeit only mildly, the Church's past crimes, accept blame for many of the atrocities committed against Jews, and ask, even if belatedly, our forgiveness.

The Basic Theology

Among the core teachings of traditional Christian theology is this: All of us, men and women alike, are not good, but on the contrary, so sinful and depraved that we're deserving of horrible punishment – even of burning forever in hell. To the Jewish mind, that assessment of human nature seems distorted and severe. But ask yourselves, "Is it wrong?" Although Judaism's view of human behavior is much more optimistic, there is no denying our endless, staggering savagery. In fact, doesn't the historical record of that savagery – war, slavery, torture, mass murder, delight in the suffering of others – clearly show that the Christian view is, well, true? After all, who can confidently argue that we are noble, when not an hour passes without the commission of some unspeakable, mindless cruelty? And also, hasn't Christianity's rampage of hate toward us Jews, until just the last few decades, demonstrated beyond doubt the truth of its own teaching?

If you can accept that man is basically evil, other elements of Christian theology make sense. Christianity says that even though men are evil, we can, nonetheless, do great kindness, *but only with God's help*. It then offers us the opportunity, despite our depravity, to escape eternal punishment by repenting and leading moral lives. In other words, if we accept God's help, past sins will be forgiven and, by avoiding future sins, we'll receive salvation and gain entry into heaven. The key idea is that we cannot and will not do good if left to our own devices. Men are just not capable of it. We must accept God's help or be damned. That core belief is why even the earliest Christian thinkers, including Paul, despite their Jewish roots, so denigrated Judaic theology. To them, the Jewish refusal to accept Jesus's divinity was the same as a refusal to accept the true God and his help. It was a refusal to repent and lead moral lives. That refusal, by the Jews and other non-believers, damned them, deservedly in Christian eyes, to eternal wrongdoing and suffering. What's more, as compared to all other non-believers, Jews were held in special disdain. They had once been the embodiment of the ethics of Abraham, Moses, and the Prophets, but now refused to recognize the very Messiah their own scriptures foretold. A similar charge could not be brought against any other group.

On the question of evil, Judaism's view is markedly different from Christianity's. It acknowledges the depravity men do, but is not premised on the belief that man is basically wicked and incapable of righteous living without divine help. Jewish theology says that when God rested on the seventh day, his work was still unfinished. God left it to us to complete his work by building a paradise on earth here and now, *through acts of loving kindness performed with our own free wills.* That teaching explains why Judaism places much more emphasis on "works" than on "faith." To Jews, God's help and guidance is fine, but the key idea is that men are essentially good and want to be righteous. Moreover, most modern rabbis hold that the quality of being righteous does not depend on any particular set of rigid, dogmatic beliefs concerning a supreme being. In Judaism, what a person does, his "works," is much more important than what he believes.

As to the building of a paradise in the here and now, Christianity says, in contrast to Judaism, that there is no and can never be such thing on earth, which is man's kingdom, but only in heaven in God's Kingdom. For the sick, handicapped, oppressed, unhappy, very poor, disturbed, etc., the here and now is obviously no paradise, and to them and others, this teaching, like the more fundamental one that man is sinful, again seems true. So to Christians, Jesus's spiritual message is one of love for, salvation for, and forgiveness of mankind, despite our evil natures. His purpose in descending from heaven was to make it possible for us to enter the paradise denied us on earth, i.e., to enter God's Kingdom, by unburdening us of our sins. By his crucifixion, Jesus accepted the punishment, for all time, that men deserved and would have suffered but for his sacrifice. To believe in Jesus, then, is to believe he is our savior. The stalwart refusal of Jews to acknowledge Jesus as savior, even in the face of the horrendous pressure brought to bear on us once Christian power solidified and became widespread, served to continuously refuel and deepen Christian hatred. Jewish suffering, in fact, to Christian minds, was irrefutable proof that in God's eyes, Jews really were evil and that, of course, justified Christian hatred. Christian attitudes and behavior became a self-fulfilling prophecy. Why were the Jews suffering? Because they had rejected Christ. That rejection demonstrated our evil. The Jews had brought damnation upon themselves. Only rarely did it occur to some Christians that the real reasons for Jewish suffering were that Jews were prohibited by Christian law from doing most kinds of work, forced to live in isolation in ghettos, required to pay exorbitant taxes as well as protection money to their Christian overlords, and, upon a whim, subject to hanging, burning at the stake, mass slaughter, or even worse, i.e., torture, by Christian mobs or the Inquisition. Jews could end their suffering, but only if they stopped being Jews; that is, if they became Christians.

That's the basic theology – man is evil but can repent; the Jews deserved to suffer because they refused to repent. When the New Testament began to take final form, which was about a century or so after Jesus's crucifixion and decades after the Christians who were originally Jewish had died off, the enmity between the still very large Jewish community and the rapidly growing Christian community dramatically worsened. There were no more Christians alive, except for the few Jews who converted from time to time, who had been born Jewish and once felt as much Jewish as ever they did Christian. The Christians of the second century were virtually all born pagan or of Christian parents of the generation before. As years passed, the Christian memory of their once having been Jewish became ever more distant. By the time of Augustine, in the late fourth and early fifth centuries, that memory was all but lost. Today, the Church reveres Augustine as its greatest thinker, but he is the one who created the philosophical framework that said "the Jews shall be allowed to live but never to prosper; the suffering they must endure bears witness to their sinfulness in refusing to convert." It took hold in the Christian mind that for them to take seriously that they, as believers in the New Testament, were the "New Chosen People," Jews could no longer be permitted to claim that role for themselves. Hence forward, the Chosen People would be those who proclaimed faith in Jesus and the New Testament and no one else.

But here's a tricky part. What exactly do Christians mean when they claim that none but Jesus is the true and only God? How can Jesus be God's son, God, the Father, a man who was crucified, and also the Holy Spirit all at once? And with all these divine entities floating around, how on earth can Christianity hold itself out as a monotheistic religion? From almost its beginning, Christianity has debated and fought over the conflicting answers to these questions. The prevailing view has come to be that the Father, Son, and Holy Spirit are not really a Trinity but a Unity.[1] That is, they are different but equal aspects of the one God described in the Bible. The Holy Spirit is God's ever-present love. The Father is God's strength, mercy, and wisdom. God's son is our savior. And when God's son came to earth, he came as a man so he could perform his sacrificial role. The theological Jesus, therefore, to believing Christians, is God, Father, Son, Man, and Holy Spirit all at the same time. That's why Christian scriptures and sermons use all these terms interchangeably.

The above, obviously, is only a brief, simplistic overview of Christian thought.[2] Most Christians today are as serious as anyone else about making the world as just a place as possible right now. The television evangelists, though sometimes hard to take, really do collect tens of millions for the starving, sick, and poor. And Mother Teresa would be a saint in any religion. It's only the die-hard fundamentalists who still insist that the "flesh" is forever evil and righteousness belongs only to the "spirit" in the otherworld of heaven. And, according to them, most of us won't get there. Their mindset is like that of some ultra-orthodox Jews who endlessly proclaim that they, and only they alone, are the authentic "Chosen People." In recent times, fortunately, there has been a tremendous convergence between mainstream Judaism and mainstream Christianity as to what it truly means to live morally and do justice.

But, setting aside Christianity's view of God, what about its verifiable history? Who was Jesus insofar as can be confirmed by historical facts, who were the major personalities in the religion about him, what were the key events in its development, and what impact has it had on its more than 2 billion followers and on all the rest of us? Needless to say, the whole story can't be told in a few-page chapter. We can, however, albeit with huge gaps, sketch an accurate outline. But be warned! Like the previous chapter about *Prophets and Kings*, this chapter and the next one, also about Christianity, are chock full of detailed historical information. It took me several months to research and write them but, even after several rewrites and hundreds of hours of study, I still can't recall off the top of my head many of the dates, events, and personalities. Nevertheless, please wade in. Do not be deterred! Even if most of the information is completely unfamiliar to you, you'll come away with a basic grounding in the history of Christianity and the Christian world, from Jesus to modern times.

The Early History

To start with, we know beyond serious question that Jesus really lived because, unlike Abraham, Jacob, and even Moses, for example, he is referred to several times in non-biblical nearly contemporaneous sources. The Roman historian, Tacitus, in his *Annals*, completed in 109 C.E., refers to the *"abominable superstition of Christianity,"* to *"Christus, its founder,"* to *"his execution by Procurator Pontius Pilate during the reign of Tiberius,"* and to *"a class hated for their abomination, called Christians, who were exquisitely tortured."* (Notice that Tacitus did not say *"his execution by Jews."* To Tacitus, it was clear that the Romans, not Jews, had crucified Jesus.) Writing even earlier, Josephus, perhaps the greatest historian of the first century and, who although Jewish, became a highly regarded political and military advisor to the Romans, refers in his *Antiquities*, published in 93 C.E., to *"a wise man about this time called Jesus,"* to *"the many people among the Jews and others who became his disciples";* to *"the murder of James by the high priest Ananias in 62AD"* and calls James *"the brother of Jesus, the so called Christ."* He also describes John the Baptist, Jesus's older contemporary, and suggests, indirectly, he was a breakaway Essene (one of the main Jewish sects of the time along with the Pharisees and Sadducees). Other passages attributed to

Josephus to the effect *"Christ was a man of Nazareth, if he was a man?"* were probably forgeries by later Christian writers attempting to strengthen their claim of Jesus's divinity. Pliny the Younger, the Roman letter writer and orator, writing in 112 C.E., says *"they sang many hymns to Christ, as a God"* and *"genuine Christians refused to curse Christ, only non-believers were willing to."* Then Lucian, the Greek satirist, writing in the early second century, says, *"Christ, the man who was crucified in Palestine, introduced a new cult into the world."* Finally, Seutonius, the Roman biographer, writing about 121 C.E., implies that Christians were known during the reign of Claudius (41-54 C.E.), when Jews were being deported from Rome because they were *"making constant disturbances at the instigation of Christus."* However, as Paul Johnson points out in his *A History of the Jews*, Seutonius's chronology is inaccurate because he appears to have thought Jesus was still alive while Claudius was emperor when, in fact, he was crucified in 33 C.E. during Tiberius's rule (14-37 C.E.).

In the still-earlier reign of Emperor Augustus, 23 B.C.E.-14 C.E., when Jesus was conceived, it seems his parents were unmarried. Under Jewish law, he was therefore known as *mamzer*, a term roughly meaning illegitimate but without quite the same stigma. Nonetheless, it marked him as someone with diminished status, not fully equal to those conceived of a sanctified union. That made him something of an outsider and was likely a major reason for his radical revision of Judaism as he grew to adulthood. His mother, Mary of Nazareth, was fifteen when he was born, although by then his biological father, Joseph of Bethlehem, had wed her. Joseph was much older and had sired two sons, James and Joses, in a previous marriage. James, the eldest brother, as recorded by Josephus in *Antiquities*, became leader and first bishop (the official with authority over a particular diocese) of the mother-church in Jerusalem and was one of the most respected and popular Jews, i.e., Jewish-Christians, of his day. His assassination by the Roman-backed high priest of the Second Temple, Ananias, in 62 C.E., for his challenge to established authority, was one of the events that triggered the Jewish revolt in 66. The Romans crushed that uprising in 70 when they destroyed everything in their path, including the Second Temple. Fifteen years before his death, James wrote a lengthy epistle (i.e., letter), to the Jewish community, urging them to live morally. It exhorted *"against wars and killing"*, *"against rich that oppress the poor"*, and that *"not only faith, but good works are necessary."* It was canonized and became a book in the New Testament. Christian tradition holds that James the Apostle is the same James who was Jesus's eldest brother. Historical sources, however, do not confirm this.

The individual who most profoundly influenced Jesus, while he was growing up, was the teacher called Yochanan the Immerser, better known as John the Baptist. Sometime during Jesus's teenage years, Mary decided to bring the family on a pilgrimage to the Jerusalem temple for Sukkoth. Shortly after they arrived, Jesus separated from them and vanished into the crowds. Outside of the city, on the banks of the Jordan River, he met John, whom he decided to stay with and learn from. It is likely he did not see his family again for many years. This is the chronology provided by Paul Johnson and others, and it contradicts the chronology in Luke's Gospel, which has Jesus returning to Nazareth not too long after Mary — distraught by his disappearance — tried to find him. But according to most modern biblical scholars, it is a much more plausible scenario. If Jesus returned to Nazareth within a few weeks, lived traditionally, and became a carpenter, farmer, or journeyman — which is what youths who stayed home most often did — then how and when did his spiritual insights develop and become so powerful that his followers believed he was God? John was a well-known rabbi, with many disciples, whose main teaching was that the washing away of sins, through baptism, opens the way to holiness. That very idea – *repentance brings salvation* – was also Jesus's most fundamental teaching and became the underpinning of all Christian theology. As Jesus's fame grew, his great teacher, according to the Gospel of John (not the same John who was the Baptist) said *"As Jesus rises, so I must diminish."* In about 21 C.E., John publicly berated Herod the Great's son, Antipas, who was the Roman-approved ruler of Judea, for incest and adultery when he married his niece, Herodias, who also, inconveniently, happened to be his sister-in-law. Despite the criticism, Antipas still respected John and would not move against him. Herodias, however, power-hungry and vicious, detested the Baptist and plotted his death. John's life ended when Antipas — vicious himself but no match for his wife — was persuaded by her to order his execution.

Other than Jesus himself, the most influential figure in all Christian history, in fact, one of the most influential in all human history, was the amazingly energetic orthodox Jew, Saul of Tarsus — a city in what is now northern Turkey. In around 36 C.E., while traveling from Jerusalem on the road to Damascus — where he planned to castigate other Jews for the heresy of accepting Jesus's messianic claims — he experienced a life-changing revelation in which he believed he had seen and spoken with the arisen Christ. So powerful was the experience that Saul would say, *"I don't believe Jesus is God, I don't think He's God, I know it."* To mark his break from Judaism, he changed his name to Paul. He went on to preach and win converts throughout the known world and write epistles and sermons that together comprise a huge portion of the New Testament.

Almost single handedly, he brought a Torah-based system of ethics to the pagan world and launched Christianity on its path to becoming the most widely practiced religion on the planet. His role in the development and spread of Christianity was so great that he came to be called Saint Paul, the Thirteenth Apostle. Aside from the twelve apostles who shared Jesus's Last Supper, and Matthias, who was chosen to replace Judas Iscariot after he betrayed Jesus, only Paul has been honored with that title. His life ended in 66 C.E., when Emperor Nero, after a mock trial, had him beheaded. Unlike many Christians at the time, Paul was a citizen of Rome and, under Roman law, could not be crucified.

Of the original twelve Apostles and Matthias, it was their leader, Simon, whose name Jesus changed to Peter, meaning "the rock," who founded the Church of Rome, became its first bishop, and transformed that position into the office of pope – head of the Roman Catholic Church, shepherd of all Christians, and Christ's personal representative on earth.[3] Counting Peter and the current pope, Benedict XVI, but excluding the thirty-nine rivals known as Antipopes, 265 men have held that office. Like Paul, he wrote epistles that became books of the New Testament, and traveled extensively throughout the Greek-Roman world and beyond, preaching the new religion in Samaria, Lydda, Joppa, Caesarea, Jerusalem, Corinth, Antioch, and Babylon. Eventually, he fully established himself as pope in the area that became the Vatican. The Romans, not surprisingly, did not appreciate his efforts and, in 67 C.E., Peter died more cruelly than even Jesus when Nero crucified him upside down.

A Word about the Gospels

Biblical historians are confident that the first of the four *Gospels*, Latin for *Good News*, was authored by Peter's longtime assistant and scribe, John Mark, around 70 C.E., thirty-seven years after Jesus's crucifixion and three years after Peter's. With Jesus long dead and the eyewitnesses to his life old, dying off, or executed, Mark realized the urgent need to record Jesus's teachings before they were forgotten or lost. In this regard the Gospels, which often contradict one another and are extremely confusing in places, should not be viewed as precise historical documents but as an attempt, rather, to preserve the incredible spiritual teacher's lessons for posterity. None of the Gospel writers, including Mark, who was a contemporary of Jesus, ever met him and whatever details they wrote about his life were received by them, at best, second-or third-hand. The details they wrote down, therefore, simply cannot be relied upon as particularly accurate. Nonetheless, the similarities among the first three Gospels are so numerous and striking that it seems likely the basic story they tell, shorn of the miraculous and supernatural that only fundamentalists are able to accept, is for the most part correct. Together, they have come to be referred to as the *Synoptic* Gospels, from the Greek word *synoptikos*, meaning "seen together." Put side-by-side, it becomes immediately clear that Mark, Matthew, and Luke follow the same storyline, agree on most of the important details, and are very alike in structure, wording, and content. Even so, each emphasized different aspects of the Jesus story and wrote for different audiences.

Writing for a gentile audience, i.e. for an audience who had been pagan before they converted, and at a time when early Christians were starting to face severe persecution under Emperor Nero, Mark's purpose was to encourage his readers to remain faithful despite their rapidly mounting hardships. To that end, throughout his narrative, Mark emphasizes Christianity's continuous victories over demonic forces as had been demonstrated – "to all who would but open their eyes to see" – by Jesus's divine powers of healing, ability to cast out demons, performance of other miracles, and ultimate resurrection. Jewish converts, on the other hand, were less in need of such encouragement since their Jewish roots constantly reminded them that, before they became Christians, they had been part of a people who, even at the time of Christ, had a history of brutal persecution that stretched back nearly 2,000 years. Before the Romans, those persecutors included the Egyptians, Babylonians, Assyrians, Persians, and Greeks. Soon, Christians themselves would be added to the list.

The second Gospel was composed by Matthew about 90 C.E. and, unlike Mark's, is addressed primarily to Jewish converts. By trade, Matthew was a tax collector, but he was also a representative of what remained of the Jewish/Christian Jerusalem Church after the murder of its leader, James, the brother of Jesus, by the Roman-installed high priest of the Second Temple, Ananias. To show the relationship between Jesus and God's ancient promises to the Jewish people, Matthew quotes numerous old Hebrew prophecies that he and other Christian thinkers interpreted as having foretold the coming of Jesus as messiah. To further highlight the relationship between Jesus and the ancient Jews, he describes in detail the trip of Jesus's parents, Joseph and Mary, to Egypt as a sort of replay of the Hebrews' 430-year captivity there, and describes Jesus's Sermon on the Mount as echoing the giving of the law to Moses at Mt. Sinai. In fact, the whole structure of Matthew's Gospel is patterned after the Torah, with his five discourses matching the five Books of Moses. Although the earliest Christians had all been Jews, of all the people who heard Jesus's message, the Jews as a group were the most resistant to it. To attract additional Jewish converts, therefore, Matthew felt it was essential to demonstrate to Jews that their own scriptures had foretold and been fulfilled by Jesus's coming.

Lucas, a non-Jew, known now as Saint Luke, wrote the third Gospel sometime in the early 90s. It is the first part of the New Testament book called "Acts of the Apostles" which he completed about three years later. He incorporates accounts from people still alive who knew Jesus, and carefully arranges them in an attempt to tell a logical story. More than Mark or Matthew, he sets the teachings of Jesus against the backdrop of world history and, although clearly addressing himself to a non-Jewish audience, attempts to demonstrate Jesus's love and concern for all humankind. He presents Jesus as both universal savior and the culmination of God's promises to the Hebrew people. Mentioned in one of Paul's epistles as "the beloved physician," Luke was probably a doctor or healer who accompanied Paul on his many travels. Together, the Gospel of Luke and his Acts of the Apostles make up almost a quarter of the New Testament and provide a general history of the early Christian faith.

Of all the Gospels, John's is the one most disputed as to authorship. Written very late in the first century, it is the fourth book of the New Testament and is dramatically different in style, language, and content from the Synoptic Gospels of Mark, Matthew, and Luke. It attempts to be a spiritual synthesis of the previous ones. Unlike them, John's opens with a philosophical prologue in which he identifies the Word of God with Christ and thereby tries to solidify the Son and Father as one spiritual entity. He makes use of the word *Logos*, meaning *reason*, which to the Greeks was the governing principle of the universe. That word, when used in connection with Christian doctrine, came to mean the manifestation of the divine in the creation of the world and the salvation of mankind. After the prologue John's Gospel becomes an historical account but skips over many of the parts included in the earlier Gospels while covering some new material. Only his Gospel, for example, mentions Jesus's miraculous raising of his friend, Lazarus, from the dead and his transformation of water into wine at Cana. But John also records Jesus's restoration of sight to a blind man, which is the one miracle mentioned in all four of the Gospels. Many biblical scholars believe that John's main purpose was to counter *Gnosticism*, meaning *"revealed knowledge,"* which was a rising Christian sect at the time that promised its adherents special intimacy with God. Gnostics believed that divine sparks fell from heaven onto earth and became trapped in human bodies. Those sparks could reawaken the divine in men's souls. Especially relevant and damning for Jews, Gnostics thought the God of the Old Testament was evil and had attempted to prevent humanity from acquiring the Gnostics' *"revealed knowledge"* and remain immersed in eternal ignorance. Some of that thinking, unfortunately, penetrated deeply into the more prevalent orthodox Christianity of the day and contributed to its evolving, virulent hatred of Judaism.

Constantine & Augustine

Two giants in Christian history, Constantine (274-337 C.E.) solidified Christianity's power on earth, while Augustine (354-430 C.E.) solidified its theology, i.e., Christianity's power over the Western mind's perception of God and heaven.

In 336 C.E., Roman Emperor Constantine did for Christianity what Persian King Cyrus had done for Judaism nearly a millennium earlier, only considerably more so. After the Babylonians led by Nebuchadnezzar destroyed Solomon's Temple in 586 B.C.E., the Jews, decimated and dispirited, were removed from their homeland and sent into exile. Scores of thousands were forcibly resettled in their conqueror's capital city, Babylon. But in 537 B.C.E., Persia defeated Babylonia, and the Persian ruler, King Cyrus – almost as though he was messiah – not only permitted the Jews to return to the Promised Land but strongly encouraged and helped finance it. There they remained, sometimes as a fully independent country (the Hasmonean Kingdom, 147 B.C.E.-63 B.C.E.), but more often as a mostly self-governing Persian, Greek, or Roman province, until 70 C.E. when the Romans crushed the Jewish revolt of 66 C.E., burned the Second Temple to the ground and installed a series of governors unquestionably loyal to Rome. Seven decades later, in 136 C.E., Bar Kochba led a second revolt, the Jews were crushed and expelled again, which expulsion, this time, was the beginning of the Diaspora. But for Cyrus, the Jewish territorial connection to the Promised Land might have been severed centuries before it was almost permanently severed by this re-exile which lasted nearly 2,000 years. In many ways, King Cyrus's decision to permit the Jews to return to their biblical homeland was the ancient equivalent of the United Nations' modern-day decision to permit the Jews to return there, after the long Diaspora, and then to recognize the re-established nation of Israel on its age-old site.

As miraculous as King Cyrus's decision must have seemed to ancient Jews, it was nothing as compared to how miraculous Emperor Constantine's conversion to Christianity must have seemed to fourth-century Christians. Born a pagan, and fully devoted to the Roman pantheon of deities, Constantine somehow came to believe that his success in defeating his rivals for the Roman throne was due solely to the direct intervention of Jesus. In 313, a year after he'd defeated Maxentius (an opponent who reigned from

306-312) and became emperor of the Western Roman Empire, he outlawed the persecution of Christians upon penalty of fine, forfeiture of property, or long imprisonment. Prior to that, Christians were still being thrown to Colosseum lions to entertain the masses. That was because the Romans, having crucified the disruptive Jesus in 33, disliked Christians as much as they did Jews, who had repeatedly revolted and inflicted staggering losses on the Roman Army. Both groups were forever rebellious and a constant threat to Roman control. But in 325, shortly after Constantine became emperor of the Eastern (Byzantine) Empire, in addition to the Western, he installed Christianity as the official religion of his entire realm. But for Constantine, Christianity might have remained, in the eyes of the pagan Greek/Roman world, no more than a weak, offshoot Jewish sect. Instead, Christians gained control of the mightiest, most far-flung governing entity on earth and used the Roman Army, Roman treasury, and Roman governing institutions to win millions of converts. In fact, as Christianity became ascendant, it was pagans who disappeared or became, for the most part, weak and unimportant cults. So total was Christianity's ascendancy that when Constantine died in 326, it would not be much longer before the Christian worldview took such hold throughout all Europe and beyond, that the entire Western World became known as "Christendom," with the pope at its head as the single most influential person on earth. After Constantine, with one exception, Julian the Apostate (361-363 C.E.), all European sovereigns ruled as Christians, proclaiming allegiance to Jesus as the only true God, and to the pope as His divinely appointed earthly representative. At long last, with Constantine having firmly established Christianity's worldly power, the stage was set for the full development of Christianity's spiritual power and its deep penetration into the minds and thoughts, emotions and hearts of all who came under its thrall. One such person was the son of Patricius, an undistinguished Roman noble, who, but for his son, would long be forgotten. That son was Augustine.

Although fifteen centuries have passed since Augustine's death in 430 C.E., and many of his ideas are dated and out of vogue, no Christian thinker has since arisen to rival his ongoing influence and appeal. He towers above other Christian theologians (with the exception of Paul), even higher than Maimonides towers above most Jewish thinkers. It would be impossible to overstate his impact and importance. He was born in Algeria and, although to a Christian mother, was pagan like Constantine. He spent his entire youth in North Africa and at age fifteen ended up in Carthage, where he received the bulk of his education, lived with a non-Christian woman till he was thirty, and sired a son by her he named "Gift of God." At age eighteen, he embraced a religion newer than even just four-century-old Christianity, Manichaeism, which at the time was Christianity's most serious competitor. Founded by a Persian aristocrat, Mani (216-276), who claimed to have received God's ultimate revelation, incomplete pieces of which had been revealed to earlier prophets including Zoroaster, Buddha, and Jesus, its main teaching was that the world is composed of two opposing realms, Good (a.k.a. Spirit, a.k.a. Light) ruled by God, and Evil (a.k.a. Matter, a.k.a. Darkness) ruled by Satan, that had become mixed together and were constantly at war with each other. To enter the divine realm, men had to free themselves from their bodies, which were *matter*, and thereby from their carnal desires, including greed, jealousy, hatred, aggression, cruelty, and licentiousness. For whatever reason, however, Manichaeism did not satisfy Augustine and, after many years of vainly trying to weave its teachings into a coherent system, he abandoned it and moved to Italy in 383. There, in Rome, he met and was befriended by Saint Ambrose (339-397), the most celebrated Church Father before the emergence of Augustine's himself, and in 387 Augustine and his only son, "Gift of God," were baptized by Ambrose, the Bishop of Milan.

Shortly after Augustine's baptism and formal conversion to Christianity the decay of the Roman Empire became palpable and it began collapsing around him. The barbarians, as they say, were at the gates and it would not be much longer before Alaric, King of the Visgoths, sacked Rome (410). But Augustine's spiritual achievements soared. In 391, he returned to North Africa, was ordained as a priest, and after a short time, in 395, became Bishop of Hippo (a city in what is now Algeria). His growing body of writings became prolific. Between 386 and 429, he wrote 270 *epistles* (i.e., detailed letters on theological subjects), between 388 and 428 numerous treatises: *On Free Will* between 388 and 395, *On Christian Doctrine* in 397, *On Baptism: Against the Donatists* (a heretical Christian movement) and *Confessions* in 400, *On the Trinity* between 400 and 416, and *On Nature and Grace* in 415. His greatest work, however, *City of God*, was written between 413 and 426, toward the end of his life. In it, Augustine sets forth a Christian philosophy of history. The first half of the book argues against pantheism and paganism, and the second half seeks to establish the Church as the rightful and logical successor to all previous religions. It is so breathtaking in scope, powerful and movingly written, that it makes compelling reading even for non-Christians. He wrote his last major work, *Retractions*, in 428. In line with Augustine's character as an honest seeker of truth, he used that work to correct any conclusions in his early works he now — from the vantage point of long life and wisdom — considered to have been in error. *City of God* to Dark Age Christians was what Maimonides's works, the *Mishneh Torah* and *Guide for the Perplexed*, combined, would become for Jews centuries later. In short, *City of God* tried to explain why one should be Christian, just as Maimonides tried to explain why it made sense to be Jewish.

After the two giants, Constantine and Augustine, the iron grip of the Church on Western minds continued to deepen, and remained virtually unchallenged for more than a millennium. Those who too strongly criticized Vatican theology were frequently punished by excommunication or banishment, and sometimes by death. Not until Galileo (1564-1642), who correctly posited in direct contradiction of central Christian teachings that the earth travels around the sun, not the other way around, was the Church's credibility and good judgment so shaken that its authority began to dramatically diminish. No person had ever before delivered such a staggering blow to the Church as an institution. In 1632, Galileo published a book, *A Dialogue of Two Worlds,* which presented his theories as a dialogue between fictional characters. He used that format in an effort to ward off what he knew would be strong condemnation by the Vatican. He hoped that presenting his theories as a fictional account, as opposed to a scientific treatise, would protect him from imprisonment or worse. His book, however, had enormous appeal to Renaissance minds and instantly became a "bestseller." Galileo was summoned to Rome, brought before the Inquisition, and threatened with torture and ultimate execution unless he recanted. He did recant, muttering under his breath, *"The earth does move."* As a result, Galileo survived but the Church, almost, did not. It was severely, permanently, and nearly mortally wounded. It has never regained its once unassailable position.

Chapter Fourteen - Everything You've Wanted to Know About Christianity - Part II: The Fall of Rome Through Modern Times

Byzantium, The Holy Roman Empire & Christendom

Before Galileo the Church's authority was absolute. No actions could be performed, policies put into effect, or even new ideas written about or discussed without a fearful look over the shoulder to gauge how the Church hierarchy would react. In this respect, the seemingly omniscient and overpowering presence of the Christian authorities back then was as intimidating and invasive as the still all-too-threatening presence of the mullahs and imams in the Muslim world today. Christianity became, like Islam would become in the Middle East beginning in the eighth century, the legitimizing philosophy for all Western rulers. This was due to the dramatic rise of the Christian-controlled successor entities to the ancient Roman Empire – Constantine's Byzantine Empire and, several centuries later, Charlemagne's Holy Roman Empire – and shortly thereafter, the transformation of the entire Western world into an even larger, all-encompassing theological enterprise called "Christendom."

During Augustine's lifetime, the ancient and seemingly invincible Roman Empire, particularly the Western realm, was coming to an end. Although its successor empire in the Eastern realm prospered and would survive for more than a millennium more, into the fifteenth century, it retained only the outward trappings of the ancient Empire and evolved into something with little resemblance to its predecessor. Augustine's contemporary, Theodosius I (346-395), became emperor of the Eastern (Byzantine) realm in 379, and Emperor of the Western in 394. During the six-decade interim between Constantine's death in 337 and Theodosius I's ascendancy to the united throne, the two realms had been ruled by a series of rival, often warring sovereigns. Theodosius I was the last ruler of a united Roman Empire, and his reign over both realms was extremely short-lived, lasting only a year. Upon his death in 395, his older son, Arcadius, inherited the Western throne and his younger one, Honorius, the Eastern. No ruler would ever again be able to assert authority over both domains. In 410 C.E., when Augustine was fifty-six years old, Alaric, King of the *Visigoths* (Western Goths as opposed to Eastern or *Ostrogoths*), captured and sacked Rome. Although he withdrew, the Western realm's total collapse was not far off. In 476, Germanic troops, mostly Visigoths again and supposedly loyal to the Western Roman emperor, Augustulus (475-476), mutinied and chose one of their own tribesmen, Odoacer, as king. Odoacer deposed Augustulus and became the first non-Roman emperor of the Western Empire. With the advent of Odoacer the old Roman political institutions crumbled and quickly disappeared.

The Byzantine Empire, however, much different culturally and politically from the defunct Western Empire, burgeoned. Constantinople became the capital of the Eastern Roman Empire after Constantine renamed the city of Byzantium (now Istanbul, Turkey) after himself in 330. The area encompassed by the Byzantine Empire at its height included Western and Central Turkey, southern Spain, northern Libya and Algeria, western Jordan, northern and parts of eastern Egypt, parts of Romania, and all of present-day Croatia, Slovenia, Macedonia, Serbia, Montenegro, Bosnia and Herzegovina, Bulgaria, Albania, Israel, Cyprus, Lebanon, Italy, and Greece. In fact, the primary language spoken by the Byzantines, known then simply as "Romans," was Greek, while the predominant language of the Western Empire was Latin, which slowly evolved into the Romance languages, including Italian, Spanish, and French. Gradually, the Greek language and culture in Byzantium gave rise there to the Greek Orthodox Church, in contrast to the Roman Catholic Church, which had taken root in the West back during the time of Peter, the apostle and first pope.

Beginning in the seventh century, the Byzantine Empire was confronted by an enemy as threatening and frightening as ever the Goths had been to the Western Empire: the Arabs; enthused, on-the-march, feeling invincible, and convinced they were right by Mohammad (570-632), their prophet and founder of Islam, their new religion. Due to superior military tactics, however, the Byzantines withstood the almost-annual Arab raids, and in the ninth and tenth centuries, reached the zenith of their power. Up until then, the Arabs had been united behind powerful caliphs who exerted authority throughout the Muslim world in much the same way the popes exerted authority in the Christian world, only more so. Unlike many popes, the caliphs controlled and led vast armies. With the decline of the Caliphate, the Byzantine Empire regained some of the territory it had lost to the Arabs, as well as to Western Europeans, its economy vastly improved, and there was a revival of the arts and sciences, albeit a restrained revival due to the often stultifying overbearance of the Greek Orthodox Church. Unfortunately for the Byzantines, they were confronted by enemies besides the Arabs, including some of the constituent peoples of their own empire, particularly the Bulgarians who, after a long rebellion, were finally subdued in 1014. The resources Byzantium had to expend putting down that rebellion and fending off the Muslims were enormous, and considerably weakened it. So much so that by the late eleventh century, the Muslim world, as well as Western Europe, had forged ahead of Byzantium in technology, military organization, and wealth. So far ahead that when the Seljuk Turks arrived on the scene, the Byzantine Army was no match and was crushed at the Battle of Manzikert in 1071. Despite this onslaught of hated Muslims, Christian West Europeans were reluctant to assist their Byzantine co-religionists because of a deep schism that occurred in 1054 between the Latin papacy of the Catholic Church in Rome and the patriarchs of the Greek Orthodox Church in Constantinople.

After a short time, however, the Latins overcame their reluctance, and in 1096, Pope Urban II launched the First Crusade. As a result, when the Seljuk Turks retreated, the Byzantine Empire made a strong but brief recovery. That newfound strength, however, did not last because the Crusaders and their West European backers, particularly the Italians, had exacted a stiff price from the Byzantines for Western support by insisting that Byzantium turn over to them lucrative trade routes and commodities. This, in effect, was demand for a bribe. Within less than 110 years, ongoing payment of that bribe so drained the Byzantines' declining resources, and further weakened their army, that the Crusaders themselves decided to take advantage of the situation, and in 1204, captured and plundered Constantinople. It was not until 1261 that Emperor Michael Paleologus VIII overcame the Latins and recaptured the city. But the end was near. The Ottoman Turks (Seljuk Turk's successors) captured most of Asia Minor, the Balkans, and other areas from the Byzantines in the fourteenth century. As the Goths had been at the gates of Rome in 410, the Ottomans arrived at the gates of Constantinople in 1453 and, after an unrelenting four-month siege, captured the city. After their victory, however, the Ottomans, unlike the Goths, refused to leave and with Constantinople's conquest, the Byzantine Empire and last remnants of the old Roman Empire disappeared.

Meanwhile, in Western Europe, the Renaissance was gathering steam and would soon transform the European continent into the most powerful, wealthy, and creative place in history. Not since Ancient Greece and China had any society come close to accomplishing culturally what Western Europe would accomplish in the next few centuries. But what had been happening there, i.e., in Christendom's Western realm, before the Renaissance, during the several centuries after Alaric and his Visigoths caused Rome's fall?

After Rome's and the Western Empire's collapse, a thousand years before the Renaissance began, Germanic tribes including Visigoths, Lombards, Vandals, Saxons, and Franks established independent kingdoms throughout Europe, as did many non-Germanic tribes such as the Magyars (Hungary) and Bulgars (Bulgaria). Without the old, mighty Roman Army holding them back, these tribes grabbed for themselves as much territory as possible. In the fifth and early sixth centuries, the Visigoths conquered most of Western Gaul (France) and all of Spain, where they came into conflict with the Vandals, who also sought territory there. The Vandals were overpowered, pushed out, and settled in North Africa, where they conquered Carthage in 439. In the late sixth century, the Saxons invaded Britain along with two other Germanic tribes, the Angles and Jutes, where they eventually merged as one mixed race: the Anglo-Saxons (a.k.a the *Angles,* from which is derived, the *English*). At about the same time, the Lombards invaded northern and central Italy and founded the kingdom of Lombardy, which was ascendant until 774, when it was defeated by one of the most renowned rulers in history, Charlemagne, king of the Franks. Prior to then, in the third century, the Franks in large numbers had begun settling and gathering strength along the shores of the Rhine River which, for part of its course, flows through what is now the city of Strasbourg in France before swinging west and north into Germany. Still pagans then, the Franks prospered when they formed an alliance with the Roman Emperor, Julian the Apostate, in 358. He, you'll recall, was the only non-Christian Roman Emperor after Constantine. By the fifth century, they had expanded their reach to north of the Loire River, which is the longest river on today's French territory. Under King Clovis I (481-511), who drove out the last Roman governor of Gaul in 486, the Franks grew stronger. They managed to subjugate all rival tribes including the Visigoths in western Gaul, the Burgundians (who had founded the Bourgogne Kingdom in northern Gaul) and Alamanni (who had conquered what is now the Alsace region in eastern Gaul and a large part of Switzerland). In 496, near the height of his power, Clovis I converted to Christianity, which action, although not quite as dramatic as Constantine's conversion, was destined to give rise to the "Holy Roman Empire." After Clovis I, all his descendents and all Frankish kings thereafter ruled as devout Christians. By the time of his death in 511, the Frankish kingdom included all the territory from the Pyrenees Mountains on the Spanish border in the South to what is today the northernmost province of the Netherlands, and from the Atlantic coast in the East to the Main River in the West, deep in what is now modern Germany. In other words, Clovis I's Frankish Kingdom was considerably larger than the modern day nation of France. Upon Clovis's death, however, the kingdom was divided among his several sons and was significantly weakened. One section was known as Austrasia where a powerful family, the Carolingians, arose and became de facto rulers. In 687, a member of that family, Pepin of Hestral, subjugated two other sections of Clovis I's old realm, Neustria and Burgundy, and reunited the Frankish Kingdom. His son, Charles Martel, whose name is known to all high school students as one of the saviors of Western civilization, defeated the Moors in 732, driving them out of Southern Gaul into their last European strongholds in Iberia. Eventually they would be driven off the continent and back into North Africa. By doing so, he expanded the already-large Frankish Kingdom hundreds of miles further south and westward.

So in 771, when Charles Martel's grandson became sole king of the Franks, the new ruler's realm covered a truly vast area encompassing almost all of Central and Western Europe, including parts of modern-day Spain, 90 percent of France and Belgium, all of Switzerland, huge chunks of Germany and Austria, and parts of Holland, Poland, Hungary, Slovakia, the Czech Republic, Bulgaria, and Romania. During his reign, Martel's grandson would make it even larger. That grandson was Charles the Great, better known in the French as *Charlemagne*, who was destined to become a leader of such celebrated stature that in the Christian imagination, he is rivaled by just one man, and a fictional one at that: the legend King Arthur. In 773, after sitting two years on a real throne, Charlemagne answered Pope Hadrian II's urgent call to defend the Papal States from invading Lombards who already controlled all of northern and large parts of central and southern Italy. Charlemagne attacked, was quickly victorious, assumed sovereignty of the Lombardy kingdom, became the Catholic Church's undisputed temporal protector and guardian, and became, in fact if not yet in title, the first emperor of the Holy Roman Empire.

When Charlemagne became the Church's protector, the institutions that had held the old Western Roman Empire together were gone: the invincible army, the senate, the pantheon of deities, the unified tax system, the single currency, the safe and passable roads, and the all-powerful godlike emperors. In 476, when Visigoth troops mutinied and overthrew Augustulus, the last Western Roman emperor, that empire was at a formal end. As central authority disintegrated and Germanic and other tribes rushed into the void, the areas they controlled began to coalesce into coherent political and cultural entities that were the first glimmers of the modern nation-states that now exist on the European continent. However, in the first few centuries after Rome's collapse, and before full-fledged nation-states evolved, the earliest decentralized fiefdoms began forming, each with a lord and manor, and serfs, although that nomenclature and true feudalism would not come into being until the early tenth century.

Despite the chaos, the Catholic Church tenaciously clung to a vision of a vast, unified Christian empire with the pope at its helm as its most indispensable leader. When Charlemagne rescued the Vatican from the Lombards, Pope Hadrain II tried to transform that vision into a reality. Retaining for himself supremacy in all ecclesiastical matters, he anointed Charlemagne "Patrician of the Romans." In doing so, of course, he had little choice, being totally defenseless without Charlemagne's army. Under this arrangement the pope was to be the spiritual head of the envisioned Christian empire and the Patrician its temporal head. In 799, Pope Leo III, Hadrian II's successor, was confronted by a vicious rebellion in Rome and attacked by an armed gang that attempted to gouge out his eyes and tear out his tongue. Like Hadrian II, he sought help from Charlemagne who intervened, squelched the rebellion, and on Christmas Day 800, Leo III crowned him "Emperor of the Romans," and knelt before him in homage.

Thus began the Holy Roman Empire. It would last, incredibly, at least in name, until 1806, when Napoleon forced the last Holy Roman Emperor, Frederick II, to resign. For centuries before, however, it had long deserved the dismissive description of French philosopher Voltaire (1694-1778) as "neither holy, nor Roman, nor an empire." Nonetheless, during its thousand-year existence, it served, together with Byzantium, as one of the vast spiritual realms of the theological entity called "Christendom" that still persists today, despite Galileo, the Renaissance, Darwin, and modern science, and all true followers of Jesus consider themselves part of, continue to view the world through, and allow to shape their values. "Christendom," which is the holy community of Christians regardless of race, ethnicity, or nationality, is comparable to what Islam calls the "Umma," and for Muslims is their holy community worldwide.

Where were the Jews during all of this? Scattered and in the Diaspora. In 136, after the Romans expelled almost all of them from Judea when the Bar Kochba rebellion was crushed, they traveled to the four corners of the earth. Some trekked deep into central Asia and as far southwest as India and China. Most, however, settled in Central Europe, Spain, Asia Minor, and North Africa. There were no walled ghettos yet but, increasingly after Constantine (274-337), Jews became more and more unwelcome among their Christian neighbors, so they lived in separate, segregated communities. Dispersed and without any territory of their own, there was no Jewish Empire even laughingly comparable to Christendom, which was not just a theological enterprise, but controlled vast areas over which it exercised political authority too.

They lived, rather, very precariously within the borders of the Christian kingdoms around them, ever fearful of sudden eruptions of anger from their far-more-populous neighbors. When Islam arose in the eighth century and swept through Asia Minor, North Africa, and Spain over the next two, Jews living in the Umma found their situation much better than that of their co-religionists living in Christendom. They were physically more secure, in general more prosperous, their religion respected, and they had far more opportunity to rise to positions of importance and influence. Moreover, like Jews, Muslims were kosher and did not eat shellfish or pork. Therefore, they could dine together. Jews were not, however, equals. They were second-class citizens at best and, as in Christendom, subject to sudden outbursts of religious fanaticism that almost always took lives — Jewish ones.

It is interesting to note that although the Jews had no empire comparable to Christendom or the Umma, entities which though chiefly theological in nature exerted territorial authority as well, they did have something — more of a concept than a physical reality — that bound them together through the centuries and propelled them, intact and united, into modern times as the most incredible survivors in history: the idea of *the indestructible Jewish People,* known also by a myriad of other names including *"the holy nation of priests," "the People of the Book,"* and *"the Chosen People."* All Jews, regardless of their level of observance of Judaic rites or the depth of their faith, even agnostics and atheists, and regardless of their nationality or birthplace, were still Jews and considered themselves part of that "Chosen by God" race. But here's the really astonishing thing: The Jews are not a race; in truth, they're a group of disparate people, speaking many different languages and of many, entirely different ethnicities, yet who insist and believe they are a race. Jews take it as inarguable that they are the first to whom the true, monotheistic God revealed himself: *Hear O Israel, God is One* (the Shema and mantra of the Jewish People). In other words, "there is one God for everyone" and the Jews insist they were first to have discovered that "truth." But the time when all Jews spoke Hebrew and could trace their ancestry directly back to the twelve tribes whom the Bible says stood at Mount Sinai and heard God's voice, had been over, even by the time of the twelfth-century Middle Ages, for more than a millennium. The idea of *the indestructible Jewish People,* however, in the minds of Jews and most non-Jews as well, lives on like an eternal, immutable law of nature. Mark Twain had it exactly right when he wrote his ode:

The Immortal Jews

"If statistics are right, the Jews constitute but one per cent of the human race. It suggests a nebulous dim puff of star dust lost in the blaze of the Milky Way. Properly the Jew ought not to be heard of, but he is heard of, has always been heard of. He is as prominent on the planet as any other people, and his commercial importance is extravagantly out of proportion to the smallness of his bulk. His contributions to the world's list of great names in literature, science, art, music, finance, medicine, and abstruse learning are also way out of proportion to the weakness of his numbers. He has made a marvelous fight in this world, in all ages; and has done it with his hands tied behind him. He could be vain of himself, and excused for it. The Egyptian, the Babylonian, and the Persian rose, filled the planet with sound and splendor, then faded to dream-stuff and passed away; the Greek and the Roman followed, and made a vast noise, and they are gone; other peoples have sprung up and held their torch high for a time, but it burned out and they sit in twilight now, or have vanished. The Jew saw them all, beat them all, and is now what he always was, exhibiting no decadence, no infirmities of age, no weakening of his parts, no slowing of his energies, no dulling of his alert and aggressive mind. All things are mortal but the Jew; all other forces pass, but he remains. What is the secret of his immortality?"

The Crusades

Unlike the Jews, whose refusal to accept Jesus was solely a theological threat, the Muslims presented not just a doctrinal peril but a military one to Christians as well. By the eleventh century, Jews were being segregated in isolated *shtetls* and were almost totally powerless. The Muslims, however, were in their Golden Age and had far surpassed Christian Middle Age Europe, ostensibly "the Holy Roman Empire," in science, medicine, architecture, literature, classical learning, and other endeavors. Also, the Arabs were at least equal to the Europeans in military arts, and had used those skills to help spread Islam over an area larger than even Christendom. Islam, in many ways, was far more alien to Christianity than Judaism because Judaism was deeply interwoven with it via the Old Testament, which was part of the Christian Bible, whereas the Koran was completely unfamiliar and had no relevance in church services whatsoever. Christians, although hardly paragons of virtue in their dealings with Jews or even each other, were appalled when Muslims, led by Caliph Umar I, captured Jerusalem in 638 and slaughtered many of its predominantly Christian inhabitants. At the time, and especially during the first century after Muhammad, all Muslim lands were tightly united under the Caliph's political and religious authority. Umar I (534-644) had succeeded Abu Bakr (632-634), who had been chosen by Muhammad (570-632) as first caliph. The time period between Muhammad's death in 632 and the Muslim conquest of Jerusalem in 638 was so short — just six years — that many of the Arab soldiers who marched into the city with Umar had literally sat at the Prophet's feet, hearing his words, less than a decade before. Some had even fought at Muhammad's side and protected him in battle in the 620s against pagan Arab enemies. The point is that these Muslims were contemporaries of the Prophet himself, ablaze with fervor, intent on converting the world, and convinced they were right. Not since their conflicts with the pagan Romans, in the years before Constantine became emperor, had Christians experienced the emotion this new adversary wrought: *fear.* But Christianity was a fervent, young, powerful, and proselytizing religion itself with "Christendom" the solid membrane that embraced all Jesus's followers. This, despite the all-too-recurrent wars between the many Christian kingdoms and principalities and the rift that was rapidly deepening and would ultimately divide the Catholic Church in the West from the Greek Orthodox Church in the East. But when Muslims captured the very city where Christ was crucified, then resurrected, in fact where his body was buried and Christianity was born, a gaping, raw wound opened throughout the Christian world. Early on, the popes in Rome and the patriarchs in Constantinople resolved that Christendom would one day seize back the Holy Land from the detested Arab infidels and return it to much holier hands: *theirs.* That was not possible, however, in the seventh century, when Byzantium was barely able to hold the Arabs at bay, Charlemagne had not yet been born, and there was, as yet, no Holy Roman Empire.

Christendom bided its time. It had to. After Rome's fall, and with it the displacement, chaos, and economic decline wrought by the mass movement of Germanic and other tribes throughout Europe, the Dark Ages descended upon the West. Although in the East, Byzantium was a bright spot, alone it had no chance of defeating the Muslims and driving them from Jerusalem. So Christendom waited until slowly its Western European realm gathered strength and it felt powerful enough to send forth the Crusaders, i.e. *cross bearers,* in the late eleventh century. But even after the time of Charlemagne and the birth of the Holy Roman Empire in the 800s, it would take two-thirds of a millennium more for Renaissance enlightenment to arrive and lay the basis for Christendom to catch up with and eventually surpass the Umma in cultural and technological achievements. Even by the fifteenth century, however, the Byzantine Christians were still no match for the Ottoman Turks, and in 1453, Constantinople fell to them as had Rome to the Goths in 410, more than 1,000 years before. Constantinople (now Istanbul), however, unlike

Rome, has never again come under Christian control, except perhaps, as may eventually happen indirectly via an unexpected back door. If Turkey is admitted to the Common Market and its successor entity, the European Union, as eventually seems possible, Constantinople will once more be, politically, a formal part of Christian-dominated Europe. That would be a great blessing because it will be a much-needed gateway – symbolically, culturally, politically, and economically – to reconciliation between the Judeo-Christian and Muslim worlds. Almost needless to say, of all the Muslim countries worldwide, *Islamic and Democratic Turkey*, without any significant oil resources, unlike Saudi Arabia, Iran, and Iraq, is by most standards the most successful by far. Per-capita income, political rights, industrial production, and the status of women, for example, are considerably better there than in just about any other Muslim nation.

Before the arrival of the Renaissance, however, Pope Urban II, in the High Middle Ages, launched the First Crusade (1096-1099). He was flabbergasted by the vast numbers of common people, in addition to trained fighting men and knights, who answered his call. Most of the Orders of Knights who rallied to him were Frankish and had been around, at least in incipient form, since just after Charlemagne's death. They included the troops of Raymond of Gilles, the count of Toulouse in Southern France, of Godfrey of Bouillon, who led mostly northern French and Lorrainers, and of Hugh of Vermandois, the French king's brother. No wonder modern-day France considers itself among the greatest and most influential of nations. Although France's military and economic power no longer match its self-image, historically, from Charlemagne to Napoleon (1769-1821) and beyond, there is no doubt that France was the central country in the Western civilized world. But it was not a strictly French affair. The Franks were joined by thousands of Italians and Germans from all walks of life. The First Crusade's most notable personality, however, was French, a preacher called Peter the Hermit, who gathered around him throngs of the poor who, overcome by religious fervor, marched to Jerusalem believing their ascent to heaven assured if they retook the Holy Land and slaughtered as many infidels in the process as possible. Infidels, of course, included not only Muslims. On their way to Jerusalem, the Crusaders, as they marched through the Rhineland (region in Western Germany), murdered thousands of Jews. Thus did the Prince of Peace's followers demonstrate their piety.

Byzantium was shocked by the behavior of the Crusaders too. Byzantine Emperor Alexius I Comnenus (1081-1118) had expected they would provide crucial reinforcement for his own troops in the conflict with the Umma. Instead, when Peter the Hermit's hordes arrived, they wreaked havoc, quartering themselves in Byzantine villages, consuming huge amounts of livestock and produce, and intimidating the populace. Alexius I, therefore, just to get rid of them, eagerly re-provisioned these Crusaders and transported them from the Constantinople area on the European continent, across the Bosporus Strait to Anatolia, the Asia Minor part of Turkey proper. There, however, the Turks decimated them and Alexius had to help the survivors hurriedly escape and return to Western Europe. But, shortly afterward, the European lords with their retinues of knights and battalions of soldiers arrived. Alexius I, in exchange for his logistical and naval support, extracted a promise from these lords to cede control to him over any previously lost Byzantine lands they recaptured from the Muslims. All of them agreed but promptly reneged. In 1098, Godfrey of Bouillon's brother, Baldwin I, founded the first Crusader state of Edessa after conquering the city and its surrounding areas. Later that year, the Crusaders captured Antioch and established their second state under Lord Bohemond of Taranto. In 1099, Godfrey of Bouillon became ruler of the third and most important Crusader state, Jerusalem, taking the title "Defender of the Holy Sepulcher" when his troops encircled the city with 12,000 men, scaled its walls, and savaged the population. It would take ten more years for the fourth Crusader state to arise when Bertrand of Saint-Gilles conquered Tripoli in 1109. By then, the Crusaders had so alienated the Byzantines that they were detested by them almost as much as by the Muslims. The refusal of the lords to honor their pledge to Alexius, by failing to return even a small portion of the recaptured territory to him, resulted in his entering into military alliances with some of the local Muslim emirs against the Crusaders. This enabled him to grab back some of the formerly Byzantine territories with his own forces.

As mentioned, the Franks were the backbone of the Crusader enterprise. In fact, all four of the Crusader states established by the First Crusade were Frankish states with all but one having a Frankish ruler (Lord Bohemond). To survive, they depended on manpower reinforcements from other Germanic tribes (the Franks were Germanic), many of which had evolved into large principalities and kingdoms in Europe, as well as naval support, particularly from the Normans (also Germanic), who held sway in Northern Italy. When Godfrey died in 1100, his brother, Baldwin I, who already ruled Edessa, succeeded him and became King of Jerusalem. For nearly fifty years, these states, with only a few thousand fully armored knights, were able to keep at bay the much more numerous Muslim warriors. The first major blow came in 1144, when the Muslim leader, Zengi, emir of Mosul in Iraq, formed an alliance with the emir of Aleppo in Syria, and reconquered Edessa. That defeat triggered the Second Crusade (1147-1149). As before, but even more so, the vast majority of the Second Crusaders were French and their goal was to protect the remaining

Crusader states, re-take Edessa, and found as many new ones as possible. They were led by the French king himself, Louis VII, and with the knights of the kingdom of Jerusalem and some troops of Conrad III, the Holy Roman Emperor, he laid siege to the Muslim stronghold of Damascus in 1148. Meanwhile, the English (also Germanic), who had set out to join the Second Crusade in 1147, turned aside and instead, as their contribution to Christendom, liberated Lisbon from the Moors (as the Muslim invaders of Iberia were then called).

The siege of Damascus failed. Inspired by the success of Zengi, who in 1146 was succeeded by his son, Nureddin, the Muslims routed Louis VII and Conrad III's troops in 1148 and forced them to retreat home. Interestingly, after Zengi had recaptured Edessa in 1144, the Franks' local allies there, the Christian Armenians, revolted and, as punishment, Nureddin expelled them in 1147 and promptly replaced them with thousands of Jews, whom he considered far more dependable and loyal. Unlike the Franks, the Jews were a deeply embedded feature of the Arab/Turkish cultural landscape and were never considered foreigners. Over the next several years Nureddin united all Syria and became its principal leader. He was a constant threat to the remaining Crusader states, particularly Antioch, and they were repeatedly forced to cede chunks of territory to him. In time, Nureddin extended his authority into Iraq, what is now Jordan, and parts of Egypt. He was, by far, the most powerful Muslim leader of his day and the first to use the idea of *Jihad*, i.e. *Holy War*, to counter the religiously driven Crusades that, very obviously, were vicious Holy Wars themselves. Witness what the Crusaders did to all non-believers: Jews, Muslims, and at times, even their Christian co-religionists, the Greek Orthodox Byzantines as well!

When Nureddin died in 1174, his lieutenant in Egypt rose to power, whose name, Saladin (1138-1193), stirs the imagination like Charlemagne's and is the most renowned Muslim leader in history. Of Kurdish descent, Saladin became vizier of Egypt in 1167, defeated his rivals there, the Fatimid Caliphate, in 1171, united Egypt with the Abbasid Caliphate based in Baghdad the same year, and conquered Damascus in 1174. Pausing only briefly, he besieged the Assassins (from the Arabic word *Hashshashin* meaning *hash smokers*) at their Masyaf, Syria fortress in late 1176 after, fearful of his growing power, they made two attempts on his life, conquered Aleppo in Syria in 1183, and conquered Mosul in Iraq in 1186. By then he was accorded the title of *sultan*, which had been used for the first time 150 years before by a Turkic chieftain who ruled an empire encompassing large parts of what is now Iran, Pakistan, and Afghanistan. Much strengthened by his victories, in 1187, at the head of a 20,000-man army, Saladin attacked the kingdom of Jerusalem and at the Battle of Hattin near the Lake of Galilee, recaptured most of it from the Crusaders. Triumphant, Saladin gained the admiration of the entire world by preventing his men from slaughtering the city's populace, including the decimated Christian knights and soldiers. Instead, he permitted civilians and fighting men alike to pay ransoms in exchange for their lives. Apparently, Saladin's reputation as a magnanimous man was well-deserved, because there is evidence that he himself paid the ransoms of many of those who had no means to do so themselves.

Nonetheless, Christendom was horrified by Saladin's victories, and in 1189, at the behest of Pope Gregory VIII, it launched the Third Crusade. Led by the three most important European rulers of the time: Richard I, known better as Richard the Lionheart; Frederick Barbarossa of Germany, who was the Holy Roman Emperor; and Philip II, the King of France, the Third Crusaders arrived at the port of Acre in what is now Israel in 1191 and captured it from the Muslims. But seventy-year-old Frederick Barbarossa had drowned on the way and Philip II, ill and exhausted, returned to France almost immediately after the victory. Richard alone, with his decimated army, and some remnants of Frederick's and Philip's, was left to face Saladin and attempt to retake Jerusalem. Ill himself, and with barely enough forces to fend off attacks, Richard managed to negotiate a truce with Saladin that guaranteed Christians safe passage to and the right to worship in the Holy City. During the negotiations, Saladin, magnanimous again to a fault, provided Richard and his soldiers fresh water and food, without which most of them would have died from thirst or starvation. Having secured a favorable truce, which was scrupulously observed for many years, Richard headed home but, on the way, was captured and held for ransom in 1192 by his bitter enemy, Duke Leopold of Austria. The ransom was paid and finally, in 1194, Richard arrived back in England, where he was greeted by one of the staunchest defenders of his realm and most loyal supporters, Robert Fitzooth, the Earl of Huntington and Locksley, better known to history as Robin Hood.

There were five more Crusades. Most were abject failures. The Fourth Crusade (1202-1204) was initiated by Pope Innocent III because, despite the truce negotiated by Richard the Lionheart, Jerusalem was still under resented Muslim control. It ended in brutal fighting and bloodletting, not between Christendom and the Umma, but between the Latin West European Roman Catholics, nominally the "Holy Roman Empire," and the Greek Orthodox of the "Byzantine Empire." Beginning during the First Crusade in 1096, when Byzantium was forced to grant Western Europeans, particularly the Italians, one-sided and exorbitant trade deals to ensure their wholehearted commitment to the Crusades and their support, thereby, against the marauding Muslims who were threatening Constantinople, Byzantine hostility toward the Roman Catholics had steadily deepened. In 1187, in a vicious outburst of anger, the Byzantines massacred nearly all the Latins in Constantinople, including more than 500 Italians, many of whom were the hated merchants and traders who benefited from the one-sided trade arrangements. As revenge, the Venetians, in exchange for their providing sea transport for the Fourth Crusaders to the Holy Land, extracted a promise from them to detour to Constantinople and resecure Italian property and privileges there. The Crusaders ended up looting and ransacking the city, capturing it in 1204, and founding a Latin state there instead of in the Holy Land. Thus satisfied, they never even reached the Holy Land. The Greek Orthodox Byzantines, meanwhile, temporarily moved their capital to Nicaea in Anatolia, where they governed in exile until Byzantine Emperor Michael Paleologus VIII finally retook Constantinople in 1261 and drove out the Catholics

The Fifth Crusade (1217-1221) was also a disaster. The plan of the Crusaders, mostly Franks again, was to conquer important parts of Egypt and then barter them with the Umma for Jerusalem. In 1219, after a long battle, the Franks captured the large city of Damietta, causing the Egyptian Ayyubid Dynasty — which had been installed by Saladin — to become fearful of suffering even more devastating defeats and willing, therefore, to negotiate. They began to support the Franks' plan and urge the restoration of the Crusader Kingdom of Jerusalem so the Franks would quit Egypt and leave them in peace. Pope Honorius III, however, rejected the idea and urged the establishment of Crusader states not only in Jerusalem but throughout Egypt and elsewhere. That overreaching brought catastrophe. The Fifth Crusaders marched on Cairo in 1221 but were trounced, losing half their army. The same year, Damietta fell, with the Ayyubids inflicting heavy casualties on the Christians yet again and forcing them to retreat.

The Fifth Crusade would likely have been the last if not for the unintentional assistance Christian Europe derived from the onslaught of the fearful Mongol hordes of Genghis Khan (1167-1227) who swept through Asia in the early 1200s and in 1224 crushed the Muslim Empire of Khwarezm on the eastern shore of the Caspian Sea (which is bordered today by the Muslim states of Kazakhstan and Turkmenistan to the north and east, Iran to the south, and Azerbaijan to the west). The Holy Roman Emperor, Frederick II, observing this development on the international scene, realized that Khan had so terrorized and weakened the Islamic world that another Crusader enterprise might regain control of Jerusalem merely by using the threat of force and without engaging in any actual combat. He embarked, therefore, on the Sixth Crusade (1228-1229) in 1227 with an impressive-looking army but, due to illness, was forced to return home after only three days. This delay so infuriated Pope Gregory IX that he excommunicated Frederick and accused him of cowardice. In part, this was due to Pope Gregory's knowledge that Frederick intended to negotiate with the Muslims rather than put them, the hated heathens, to the sword. Unperturbed, Frederick set out again in 1228 and conducted his unusual Crusade almost entirely peacefully via consultations with the Egyptian Ayyubid Sultan. He recalled that these same Ayyubids, during the Fifth Crusade only a few years earlier, had actually supported for a while the Fifth Crusaders' demand that the kingdom of Jerusalem be restored to them in exchange for the Crusaders quitting Egypt. Then, it didn't work because of the papacy's greed in insisting upon re-securing not only the Crusader state of Jerusalem but new Crusader states in Egypt as well. Frederick did not make the same mistake. In 1229, he and Sultan al-Kamil signed the Treaty of Jaffa, which returned Jerusalem to the Christians and anointed Frederick its king, with the Muslims retaining control over the Dome of the Rock and the al-Asqa Mosque. The treaty lasted until 1244, when Sultan al-Kamil's successors, reinforced by Muslim soldiers from resurgent Khwarezm (which had been defeated by Ghengis khan), retook Jerusalem.

Despite Frederick II's spectacular success in regaining Christendom's holy sites without bloodshed, he was extremely unpopular in Europe due to the Church's unrelenting condemnation of him and its refusal to rescind his previous excommunication. Although he had resecured Jerusalem, which lasted for a period of fifteen years, the terms he'd agreed to, permitting the Muslims to retain control over portions of it, were unsatisfactory to the papacy as well as to most of the European populace. In 1245, Pope Innocent IV formally renewed Frederick II's prior excommunication, declared him deposed as Holy Roman Emperor, and threw his support to King Louis IX of France, who was in the midst of preparations for the Seventh Crusade (1248-1250). Interestingly, Pope Urban IV's deep loathing toward Frederick, which was fueled mostly by political considerations, was out of character from his usual broad-mindedness. To his everlasting credit, he was the pope who in 1247 publicly denounced the blood-libel charge that accused the Jews, ridiculously, of murdering Christian children to obtain blood for baking matzoh.

Louis IX, soon to be called Saint Louis for his efforts to defeat the Umma, arrived in Egypt, which had become the center of Islamic power, with a huge and well equipped army in 1249. Within a day, they captured Damietta. They next attacked Cairo but were surrounded and trapped by floods when the Egyptians opened sluice gates on the Nile. Louis surrendered, was taken prisoner, and after paying an enormous ransom and relinquishing Damietta, was freed, whereupon he sailed for Palestine, arriving in 1251. There he spent four years building fortifications to strengthen the defenses of the remaining Crusader states of Antioch, Tripoli, and the only portion of the kingdom of Jerusalem still under Christian control, the island of Cyprus.

Louis arrived home in 1254 and immediately set about organizing what would be the last of the Crusades. It took him fifteen years to marshal and equip sufficient forces, and in 1270, he set sail for the city of Tunis, where he felt the less numerous forces would be much easier adversaries than the Egyptians had been. The Eighth Crusade ended suddenly when Louis, fifty-six years old, died from natural causes only a few months after he'd landed in Tunisia. With the collapse of the Eighth Crusade, Muslim forces closed in until, in 1291, they overran the last Crusader fortress on the mainland in the city of Acre near Jerusalem. On the islands of Cyprus and Rhodes, however, a few Christian military/religious orders maintained garrisons for more than another two centuries.

After Louis IX's death, the papacy continued railing against the Muslims and exhorting Christendom to retake Jerusalem. But the fourteenth century was at hand, and with it, the start of the Renaissance (fourteenth to sixteenth centuries), a.k.a. *the rebirth*, which was destined to give rise to a new, much less religion-driven world vision, characterized by science, humanism, and logic. That new outlook would soon wrest control over the hearts and minds of Westerners from the iron grip of the Church. In short, by the late fourteenth century, other than the few garrisons in Cyprus and Rhodes, there were far fewer Christians willing to die fighting in the Holy Land than in the century before. For some reason, however, even though the fever to recapture Palestine from the Muslim infidels abated, probably due as much to the difficult logistics as to the new Renaissance thinking, hostility toward Jews reached a new crescendo.

Expulsions and the Inquisition

During the era of the Crusades (1096-1270), Jews, unlike in Christendom then and unlike in the Umma today, were respected, even admired throughout most of the Muslim world. The foremost example, Maimonides (1135-1204), who settled in Cairo in 1152, eventually became chief rabbi of Egypt and personal physician to Saladin, sultan of all Syria and Egypt, most of Jordan, and parts of Iraq. He was renowned among Muslim intellectuals for his vast learning in history, international affairs, and science, and considered the greatest medical doctor then living. Muslim commoners kneeled before him, acknowledging their esteem. Although Jewish physicians (and financial advisors) were often sought after by Christian sovereigns too, the Jewish masses in Europe were prohibited from doing many types of work, particularly types that would bring them into competition with the Christian masses. Jews in the Islamic countries, however, could buy land, rent it or sell it, or farm it. They could freely enter into trades and professions, set up businesses, even be teachers for non-Jews. The only major disadvantage they suffered was the requirement that they, as non-Muslims living in the Umma, pay a special tax over and above what Muslims paid. Nonetheless, they were able to fully participate in the Muslim economies, all while openly practicing their religion. They were seldom marked apart from the Muslim populace (although they lived in their own, segregated neighborhoods), by being forced to wear yellow stars or conical hats,[1] as happened in Europe beginning in 1215 due to laws enacted at the insistence of Pope Innocent III during the Fourth Lateran Council.

A partial chronological list of Christian mistreatment of Jews during the Crusader era is as follows: At the very outset of the First Crusade in 1096, thousands of Jews were murdered in the Rhineland by the advancing Crusader hordes of Peter the Hermit. In 1141, Bernard of Clairvaux, an extremely influential monk and founder of the Order of the Knights of the Templar, instructed Crusaders not to attack Jews, but reiterated that their degradation was justified. In 1144, Jews were accused of the ritual murder of a Christian boy in England, a blood libel that would be endlessly repeated until the early twentieth century. In 1215, at the Fourth Lateran Council, as above mentioned, laws were passed forbidding Jews to leave their homes without wearing yellow identification badges. In 1231, Pope Gregory IX greatly expanded the authority of Dominican and Franciscan courts in matters of heresy, which empowerment marked the start of the Inquisition. In 1242, King Louis IX of France (the same Louis who led the Seventh and Eighth Crusades) ordered the Talmud burned in Paris and other cities throughout his realm. Beginning the same year, James I, King of Aragon, herded Jews into churches, forced them to listen to conversion sermons and authorized friars to enter synagogues unannounced to monitor their activities. Later, in 1263, he required Nachmanides to publicly debate Dominican theologians, which debates became known as *disputations,* hoping thereby to humiliate him and other Jews everywhere. In 1260, Thomas Aquinas (1225-1274), considered one of the greatest Christian thinkers in history, condemned all Jews who refused to convert as "deliberately defiant" and therefore evil, instead of just "ignorant." The real horrors, however, would come after the last Crusade (1270) ended.

Perhaps, with the Muslims too distant to easily confront and having grown too numerous and powerful to subdue, "Christendom," thwarted in its efforts to retake the Holy Land, felt that Jews would be much easier and nearly defenseless targets.

At the turn of the fourteenth century, despite the wind of enlightenment beginning to blow across Europe with the dawn of the Renaissance, the situation of the Jews, bad as it already was, dramatically worsened. In part, this was due to advanced thinkers like Aquinas who tried to use Renaissance-type logic to argue that those who continued rejecting Christianity, particularly the Jews, whose own scriptures foretold Christ's coming, were deliberately ignoring the truth and intentionally following a depraved path. The theological differences that divided Christians and Jews were one thing, but there were other factors dividing them that had been in place for a millennium and had grown ever more obvious. After the Romans crushed the Bar Kochba rebellion in 136, Emperor Hadrian sent the Jews into exile, which marked the start of the Diaspora. Severed from the Holy Land, where they had resided since Joshua's time, the heyday of the Jews as farmers, toiling in *Sukkas* close to the land, and as journeymen in related professions like animal husbandry, blacksmithing, tool making, and carpentry, was over. Partly for that reason, there would be no more agricultural holidays added to the Jewish calendar, like *Sukkot, Shavuot,* and *Shemini Atzeret,* praying for rain or celebrating harvests. Scattered across the globe, with no homeland and no military forces to defend themselves, the highly educated Jews sought to become indispensable to the ruling classes wherever they settled. They accomplished this by becoming preeminent in fields like medicine, international trade, and finance. That Jews should gravitate toward medicine was a natural. From ancient times, they were reputed to be great healers, because it had not gone unnoticed that they seemed less susceptible to infections and diseases than other peoples. This was due to the Jewish purity laws concerning the preparation, preservation, and consumption of food which, intentionally or not, shielded them from harmful bacteria, food spoilage, and food poisoning. When plagues swept through Europe during the Dark Ages and again, in the 1300s, killing hundreds of thousands, the canard arose that Jews had brought on the Black Death by poisoning wells to intentionally kill Christians because, although huge numbers of Jews succumbed like everyone else, they were partially protected by their kosher practices and as a whole seemed healthier to an extent than Christians. Christian hysteria became so great that Pope Clement VI (1342-1362) investigated, publicly refuted the accusation, but still had to repeatedly quell anti-Jewish riots. Like Pope Clement VI, much of the Christian ruling classes and Christian intelligentsia realized that whatever health advantages the Jews enjoyed were due solely to their superior medicine and hygienics. A royal Christian court, therefore, without at least one Jewish doctor on its medical staff was in the minority. In this, the European courts chose wisely because the Jews had been living for centuries, not only among Christians but among Muslims during their still ongoing "Islamic Golden Age" (approx. 900-1400), and Muslim physicians, from whom the Jews learned, were by far the most skilled medical practitioners of the day.

The Jews' reputation as "the best-connected international traders in the world" was also based on reality. After Emperor Hadrian sent them into exile in 136, the Jews established communities across the globe often hundreds, sometimes thousands of miles apart from each other. They settled throughout Europe, including the British Isles, in Asia deep into Western Russia, all across North Africa and Asia Minor, and in the Orient in India and China. With no national territory or sovereign to hold them together, they remained united instead via their shared history extending back, even then, thousands of years, their common Hebrew language, spoken exclusively by Jews, their insular, non-proselytizing religion with its Torah and detailed set of laws, and by developing a complex, far-flung web of trade routes and international contacts, so as not to lose touch with one another. In an age before telephones, faxes, automobiles, and planes, communicating or traveling over distances — even relatively short distances by today's standards — was an extremely complicated and expensive affair. But the Jews managed it. It wasn't that their methods were so unique but they were scattered over such a vast area and their contacts with other Jews in distant places were so reliable and secure, that Christians of all nations – French, German, Italian, Spanish, English, Portuguese, Dutch – who were often warring with one another, could trust them to make deliveries of exports and receive deliveries of imports efficiently, at a reasonable price, and on time almost anywhere in the known world. One reason they were able to pull this off is that, unlike the Christian nations around them, the Jews in the Diaspora were never embroiled in civil wars, revolts, dynastic squabbles, wars of conquest, or interdenominational wars, and as a result, their international contacts remained incredibly stable for centuries.

Finance was the bedfellow of international trade. With the Jews firmly in control of a worldwide network of trade contacts, enviously admired for its efficiency, it was not long before Christian merchants and monarchs asked (more often, demanded) that the Jews finance the delivery of their goods to and from distant lands in addition to arranging all the logistics, including chartering the ships and caravans. The way this would work out practically is that the Jews would select which of their long-established trade routes to use, hire caravan drivers with pack animals, charter ships with crews, deliver European textiles to India, let's say, and then, usually retracing the same land and sea routes, return home with commodities like spices, perfumes, or silk. In Europe, these imported items could be sold for much more than it cost Christians to produce the textiles they'd exported. The Jews were paid from the profits. The reverse was also true; that is, the Indians could sell the European textiles in India for far more than it cost them to produce the things they exported. The payment the Jews received for this type of transaction consisted of two major components. The first was payment for the actual services they rendered, including use of their trade routes and contacts and arrangement for the transport of goods to their destinations, over what were then very great distances, and then transporting home the goods bartered or paid for. The second was payment, i.e. interest, on the loans the Jews advanced to pay for the ships, repairs, crews, dock workers, caravan drivers, pack animals, armed guards, tariffs, and other things that were necessary. Although the Bible, as Christians interpreted it, strictly prohibited them from charging other Christians interest, they usually had no qualms about having the Jews perform what they felt was the very unsavory yet essential role of "money lender." (The Old Testament only prohibits Jews from charging other Jews interest, not non-Jews.)

When the fourteenth century arrived, all the above pieces had long been in place and led Christians to accept the worst stereotypes about Jews. Instead of doing real work, Jews were, it was thought, "usurious money lenders" who took advantage of the non-prohibition in Judaism against charging non-Jews interest to financially subjugate Christians, "corrupt international traders" whose loyalty lay not with their fellow Englishmen, Frenchmen, or Spaniards, but with other Jews in distant places, and "practitioners of magic" who were somehow able to ward off the plague. Contributing to the idea that Jews didn't do real work was the fact that no one could remember the last time they had seen or heard of a Jewish farmer. Severed from their land for more than a millennium, there was much truth to this even then, and to the dismissive remark, therefore, of Henry Ford who quipped, centuries later, "I'll pay a reward of $1,000 to anyone who can show me a Jew who farms." In addition, and most damning, the Jews stubbornly refused to accept Jesus, the messiah foretold in their own scriptures, were suspected of killing Christian children to obtain blood to bake matzoh and were rumored to have caused the plague. All this proved their depravity. Mass expulsions of Jews from Christian-controlled lands – meaning most of Western Europe – would soon be at hand.

In 1290, at the urging of his advisors, King Edward I expelled the Jews from England after all debts to them had been cancelled. But this was merely the culmination of numerous local expulsion edicts that had banished the Jews from dozens of English towns beginning in 1190. A similar process took hold in French towns which climaxed with their expulsion from all France in 1306 and again, after some had drifted back, in 1394. Throughout the 1300s, the German principalities of the Holy Roman Empire repeatedly issued expulsion edicts, and most of the Jews were gone by 1450. Many of the Jewish refugees moved to Poland, where they prospered by becoming storekeepers, tanners, butchers, and tailors. Some became prominent merchants and later, bankers. The leap from money lender to banker was not great, the major difference being that instead of using their own money to finance trade expeditions, the Jews began using their depositors' money also and, in exchange, paid them a share of the profits.

Meanwhile, during the 1200s and early 1300s in southern Spain — which had been under Muslim control since 719 and parts of which would remain so until 1492 — the Jews were living in the "Islamic Golden Age" (approx. 635-1453)[2] which was still going strong there and throughout the Muslim world. In Spain, the Jews were persecuted only in the North, which was Christian territory. It is important to note that Charles Martel's defeat of the Moors in 732 had not driven them out of Europe but only out of France and the northernmost part of Spain. Only by increments did other Christian lords drive the Moors, as the Muslim invaders were then called, further into Spain, until by the mid 1300s, they occupied only the southernmost parts. During the period of Islamic overship, Moses de Leon, who lived in Castile, wrote the *Zohar*, the basic work of Jewish mysticism known as *Kabala*, which was published for the first time in 1280. It was also during those years that the Spanish Jews, a.k.a. Sephardim, fully developed the Jewish dialect called *Ladino* while those living in Poland and in German lands from which they had not been expelled, a.k.a. Ashkenazim, developed Yiddish. In Moorish Spain the Jews were considered so loyal and so integral a part of the landscape that their Muslim overlords entrusted the defense of Seville to them when the Christian forces of the Kingdom of Aragon attacked in 1248.

In 1483 — by which time Iberia was almost fully in Christian hands — the man who would become the most infamous monk in all history was appointed Inquisitor General of Castile by Pope Sixtus IV (1471-1484), and in 1487 Grand Inquisitor of all Spain by Pope Innocent VIII (1484-1492). Of the Dominican Order, Tomas De Torquemada (1420-1498) was directly responsible for burning some 2,000 people at the stake, most of them Jews, along with Moors, Christian apostates, and others, including bigamists, usurers, and homosexuals. On an unprecedented scale, he used techniques of almost unimaginable cruelty, even then, to inflict pain on the Inquisition's victims to extract confessions of heresy, witchcraft, and the like. Today, in every roadside "House of Horrors" at amusement parks throughout the world, there is almost always a sign, affixed above a glass-windowed exhibit depicting the unspeakable agonies suffered by *marranos* (secret Jews) and others, with the words *Tomas De Torquemada* printed upon it. That name, in Western thought and literature, has become synonymous with just one word: *torture*.

With the blessings of King Ferdinand and Queen Isabella, who considered Torquemada their protégé, Columbus set sail on August 3, 1492 and discovered the New World. But less than a week before, on July 30, they had issued their famous expulsion edict, driving all Jews, some 225,000 people, from Spain. As it turned out, that event was almost as much a disaster for the Spanish Kingdom as it was for the Spanish Jews. Those Jews had become such an important and integral part of the country's commerce, culture, and intellectual life — among them Don Isaac Abravanel (1437-1508), Ferdinand and Isabella's brilliant finance minister — that within two centuries of their expulsion, and as a direct result thereof, many would argue, Spain's influence and confidence markedly declined. It has still not fully recovered. Some of the Sephardim fled to neighboring Portugal, but in 1496 they, along with the native Portuguese Jews, were expelled from there also. The majority migrated to Turkey, North Africa, Holland, and the precious few other European countries where they were still welcome. From Holland, in the early 1500s, a group of Sephardim sailed for the Dutch-controlled city of Recife, Brazil, where they became the first openly practicing Jews to settle in the New World. But in 1654, when Portugal conquered Recife and the rest of Dutch-controlled Brazil, known as Surinam, the Inquisition drove the Jews from there too and they sailed north for New Amsterdam, which was still in Dutch hands. There, they joined up with a large group of Ashkenazim who had arrived just a few months earlier. Unexpectedly, the New Amsterdam governor, one-legged Peter Stuyvesant, tried to prevent them from settling in but was overruled by the Dutch West India Company that, along with the Dutch government, controlled the colony. In 1664, the British took over, renaming the colony New York, and the Jews, remembering the English expulsion edict of 1290, expected trouble. But they found instead that the British colonists were, for the most part, remarkably tolerant. In 1790, the year after English-born George Washington became first president of the United States, he issued the following statement, which launched the Jews' deep love affair with America:

"May the children of the Stock of Abraham who dwell in this land continue to merit and enjoy the good will of the other inhabitants while everyone shall sit in safety under his own vine and fig tree and there shall be none to make him afraid."

That statement, contained in a letter to the Jewish community of Rhode Island, was widely publicized at the time and helped set the tone that led James Madison, the framer of the Bill of Rights, enacted in 1791, to enshrine America's religious tolerance into this most remarkable of our founding documents. Even today, more than two centuries later, the First Amendment shouts out and inspires us:

"Congress shall make no law respecting an establishment of religion, or prohibiting the free exercise thereof; or abridging the freedom of speech, or of the press, or the right of the people peaceably to assemble, and to petition the Government for a redress of grievances."

In Europe, however, during the fourteenth to seventeenth centuries, despite the awakening brought on by the Renaissance and Protestant Reformation, the lot of the Jews continued to worsen.

Renaissance & Reformation

The Renaissance arose in Italy, the seat of the Vatican, first but it is difficult to single out any one overriding event as its birth. Many point to Florence as the place where it arose and to Florentine painter Giotto (1267-1337) and Florentine poet Dante (1265-1312), as the earliest Renaissance figures. Their works marked a radical departure from previous modes of expression and thought. As to the Jews, however, despite their high level of education and advanced culture, the new thinking had only minimal effect due to their near-total exclusion from the surrounding Christian society. It would take another 300 years before any Jewish writers or thinkers joined the ranks of notable Renaissance personalities like Giotto or Dante. Giotto's works, unlike his contemporaries', depicted human beings warmly and realistically, rather than two-dimensionally, with halos above their heads and almost always gazing toward heaven. His emphasis on realism and the individuality of his subjects was a stark break from the one theme, religious style of painting that dominated the Middle Ages. Dante, a towering figure in world literature, wrote with intensity unrivaled since classical times and possibly, some would say, ever since. Although he often emphasized religious devotion, his real concern was to describe human emotions, particularly the intense love for one another that humans are capable of. In his epic masterpiece, *The Divine Comedy*,

Dante presents in hundreds of pages of poetic verse his imaginary journey through hell, purgatory, and heaven, during which he encounters famous historical and mythological personalities. Each represents a particular fault or virtue, and is punished or rewarded accordingly. His guide through hell and purgatory is Virgil, the Roman poet, but his guide through paradise is Beatrice, the Florentine noblewoman he fell madly in love with. In turn, and as though in tribute to that intense human emotion, the poetry of Dante (and paintings of Giotto) triggered the deep love for theatre, music, sculpture, literature, architecture, and other artistic expression that would so characterize the Renaissance era.

The new emphasis on humanism, i.e., an attitude emphasizing the worth and dignity of each individual, soon spread into the political realm. Leonardo Bruni (1369-1444), another Florentine, and a diplomat and scholar, led an intellectual movement that looked to the pre-emperor, republican state of Rome as the ideal model for a representative form of government that would ensure its citizens fundamental rights. Albeit a long way from modern-day freedom and democracy, the system he envisioned placed much less focus on Church doctrine and the other-world of religion, and much more on the economic and social well-being of the Italian city-states in the here and now, and the burgeoning patriotism (good citizenship) of their people. Most important, Bruni and his followers felt that humanism had to become the governing philosophy of any regime that claimed to be just and legitimate.

As humanism took hold and the Renaissance deepened, broad segments of the European population, mostly Italian at first, but also French, Spanish, and Dutch, and later, German and English, began to seek new ways to make sense of the difficult world around them. Christianity, they realized, although overwhelmingly important, was not the sole prism by which to judge the value of things. At the Renaissance's start, to gain a fresh and less religious perspective, Europeans looked to their pre-Christian past and found, already available and accessible to many, the classical literature of the Greeks. This included works like Aesop's (620-560 B.C.E.) fables and the plays of Sophocles (496-406 B.C.E.), Euripides (480-406 B.C.E.), and Aeschylus (525-456 B.C.E.). Also, with Greece lying just to Italy's southeast, increasingly large numbers of Italians traveling there returned home with tales of some the most wondrous sculptures and architecture they'd ever seen. In addition, ruins of almost-as-magnificent Roman sculptures and architecture, based on the Greek, could be found in nearly every Italian town. The only other art they'd encountered, for most of their lives, was dominated by medieval Christian influence and included gothic-style churches, religious-themed paintings, or sermons of monks and priests. Surprisingly quickly, Europeans en masse became enamored of the Greeks and delighted in the beauty of classical art *"for its own sake"* rather than in terms of how it fit in with Christian doctrine. Along with the rediscovery of classical art came a rediscovery of classical learning, which was exemplified by, more than anything, the science and philosophy of Aristotle. When broad interest in his teachings took hold, and in those of other famous Greeks like the physician, Hippocrates, and the great rationalist-philosophers, like Socrates and Plato, a desire to understand the world via concrete sensory experience and logic, rather than via mysterious divine processes and faith, exploded on the European scene.

The new desire to sense the world as it really existed had a profound effect on artistic expression. Another Florentine, Donatello (1386-1466), one of the greatest stone shapers of all time, is considered the founder of modern sculpture. His most famous work, *David* (completed in 1435), was the first nude Renaissance statue and is remarkably and unabashedly lifelike. His contemporary, Paolo Uccello (1397-1495) – you guessed it, another Florentine – became famous for his innovations in perspective. He was among the first to create true-to-life action and authentic-looking depth in paintings. His three-paneled masterpiece, *The Battle of San Romano* (about 1456), makes use of the rhythmic pattern of the uplifted spears of mounted knights to organize the work and direct the viewer's attention. It is ablaze with activity and amazingly action-packed, even by today's standards. Of the same generation as Donatello and Uccello were at least two dozen other Italian, early Renaissance masters including Pisanello (1395-1455, Florence), a painter and medallion maker noted for his ornate style, Jacopo Bellini (1400-1470, Venice), whose paintings were unique for their complexity, and Piero della Francesca (1420-1492, Tuscany) whose paintings, although religious in nature, use color, light, and a style of arranging things that was original and extraordinarily three-dimensional.

Even the new Renaissance thinking, however, did not blunt Christian degradation of Jews. As noted in the previous section of this chapter they were expelled en masse from France for the second time in 1394, from virtually all the Germanic states of the Holy Roman Empire by 1450, from Spain in 1492, which was the same week Columbus set sail seeking new routes to the East, and from Portugal in 1496. The rise of Tomas de Torquemada, Inquisitor General of Castile and Grand Inquisitor of the entire Spanish Empire during the period from 1483 to 1498, in fact, actually coincided with and accompanied the arrival of the Renaissance. In part, these anti-Semitic developments, which were at odds with the new and supposedly enlightened Renaissance thinking, were due to the

Church having been put on the defensive by the deep appreciation of secular humanism and pre-Christian classical Greek culture that was starting to take hold throughout Europe. In response to the new thinking, the Church dug in and became more doctrinaire than ever. This included taking concrete actions against the "despicable Jews," the "murderers and rejecters of Jesus" – such as subjecting them to the mass expulsions and the Inquisition – who for far too long had escaped serious punishment for their "depravity and sins." In Italy, not surprisingly, which was the seat of the Holy See, but was also where the Renaissance took root most strongly, the Jews were treated better than just about anyplace else in Europe with the exception of Holland. Perhaps Church officials found it easier to mistreat Jews far away from home than in their own backyard, because in Italy, they were constantly confronted by the ideas of the numerous and increasingly influential Italian Renaissance personalities emerging on the scene.

By the 1500s, despite the Church's rigidity, the Renaissance kicked into full gear. Leonardo da Vinci (1452-1519), one of the most brilliant minds of all time, was a painter, sculptor, architect, engineer, researcher and inventor and he united art with science. He epitomized the raging curiosity about the natural world that was sweeping through Europe. He studied the moon and predicted its effect on tides, understood that fossils were the remains of living things preserved as stone, developed a theory of continent formation, developed the science of hydraulics, studied the circulation of blood and the workings of the human eye, and devised a workable system for the canalization of rivers. His inventions included an underwater diving suit, the hydrometer (device used to measure the specific gravity of liquid), and model flying machines that, although impractical, foreshadowed the modern science of aerodynamics. As to art, his paintings included *The Last Supper* (1497) and *Mona Lisa* (1506), works so famous, no description here is necessary. To list all his accomplishments would require a separate chapter. On the scientific front, da Vinci was not alone. The Polish astronomer, Copernicus (1473-1543), using careful observations and measurements, posited the revolutionary theory that the sun lay at the center of the universe, not the earth, and that our small planet was just one of the several revolving around it. Michelangelo (1475-1564), the undisputed master artist in all history, was a painter, sculptor, architect, and poet. His works included the sculpture *Pieta* (1500), showing Christ in his mother's lap, his renowned statue of *David* (1504), the paintings on the ceiling of the *Sistine Chapel* (1512) depicting in intricate detail the story of Genesis, and his masterpiece gigantic painting, *The Last Judgment* (1534). Of his contemporaries, besides da Vinci, Michelangelo's only near rival in artistic accomplishment and skill was Raphael (1483-1520) who produced dozens of stunning paintings including *The Knight's Dream* (1501) and his masterpiece fresco, *The School of Athens* (1511), portraying Plato, Aristotle, and other ancient philosophers, which some consider the greatest painting in history.

In the realm of philosophy, Erasmus (1466-1536) rejected rigid, overly God-centered belief systems and expounded the virtues of humanism and tolerance. He is often called the father of the Reformation, and advocated sweeping changes in Church doctrine. His works included *De Ratione Studii* (*On the Method of Study*, 1511), in which he criticized severe discipline and insisted on arousing the interest of students, and *De Libero Arbitrio* (*On the Freedom of Will*, 1524) wherein, along with his well-known assaults on the Catholic Church, he attacked Martin Luther (1483-1546). In 1517, that German theologian had launched the Protestant Reformation when he published his *Ninety-Five Theses* condemning the selling of indulgences to raise funds for the building of Saint Peter's Basilica in Rome. He detested the Church's injustices, including at first, its mistreatment of Jews, and gave every indication he would be their staunch ally and even, perhaps, protector. In his early career, he denounced the blood libel, argued that preachers had enormously exaggerated the Jews' transgressions against Christ, defended their right to resist conversion to Catholicism, and just the title of one of his earliest major treatises, *That Jesus Christ Was Born a Jew* (1523), was music to Jewish ears. Aside from his defense of the Jews, Luther had many doctrinal differences with the Roman Catholic hierarchy, and his criticisms were so severe that he, an ordained priest, was excommunicated in 1521. But twenty-two years later, Luther became the Haman of his day and laid the groundwork for the rise of Hitler in the twentieth century. (More about him in a moment.) In literature, Cervantes (1547-1616) wrote *Don Quixote* (Part I completed 1605, Part II 1615) and Shakespeare (1564-1616), whose accomplishments, like da Vinci's, are so numerous they would require a separate chapter, rose to prominence with the publication of his narrative poems, *Venus and Adonis* (1593) and *The Rape of Lucrece* (1594). Publication of his sonnets and plays would come later and establish him as the undisputed master English lyricist and most renowned playwright of all time.

If Martin Luther had adhered to his initial favorable impression of Jews, it might well have altered the course of history. With incredible renaissance ideas in the air – Greek classical art considered more meaningful than medieval church art, the sun at the center of the universe, not the earth and, most important, the new philosophy of humanism spreading through Europe and stressing the worth of each individual – many Christians would likely have followed Luther's lead and been willing to re-examine their hostile opinions about Jews or at least give them a fresh look. In the

1500s, the Church, it must be recalled, was in flux and very much on the defensive because of the new renaissance thinking as well as the cataclysmic assaults on Catholic doctrine contained in Luther's many works, like *On Christian Liberty* (1519), *To the Christian Nobility* (1520), *The Babylonian Captivity of the Church* (1520), *On the Bondage of the Will* (1525), and *Small Catechism* (1529). With all the turmoil he was causing, there's no telling how far he might have been able to transform Christian hostility toward Jews into Christian compassion, had he not turned decisively against them with the publication of his anti-Semitic rant, *On the Jews and Their Lies* (1543), three years before his death. What happened? In truth, simply put, Luther had never been willing to accept a Judaism that refused to acknowledge the divinity of Jesus. All along, it had been his hope that the Jews would eventually recognize his reformed Christianity – his Protestantism – as the true faith and come to see that Jesus was the Messiah. The Jews' rejection of what he considered his friendly overtures so enraged him that he turned vicious and began encouraging the burning of their synagogues, mass violence against them and, at times, their execution for praying to a false God. Luther's legacy, instead of opening an avenue of new understanding as at first seemed possible, deepened Christian hatred, particularly among his own Protestant followers, who, during the early years of Luther's career, had been the Christians most receptive to spiritual reconciliation. Luther's anti-Semitism was the major reason the lot of the Jews worsened during the Renaissance, despite the supposedly enlightened thinking that characterized the era. For a while, Catholic leaders, in an overreaction to Luther's assaults, vied with Protestant leaders as though competing in a contest, the winner of which would be the ones who adopted the policies most degrading to Jews. In such manner, some thought, it could be demonstrated which branch of Christianity was purer. On the Catholic side, Jews were ordered into the ghettos with the issuance of the bull *Cum Nimis Absurdum* (1555) by Pope Paul IV:

> Forasmuch as it is unreasonable and unseemly that the Jews, whom God has condemned to eternal slavery because of their guilt, should, under the pretense that Christian love cherishes them and endures their dwelling in our midst, show such ingratitude to the Christians as to render them insult........therefore do we feel constrained to issue the following ordinance......... Jews are to own no real estate, ...Jews are to hire no Christian servants. Jews' mercantile roles are to be strictly regulated. Jews' taxes are to be increased ....Jews are no longer to ignore the ancient requirements to wear distinctive clothing and badges. Jews are to refuse to be addressed as "sir" by Christians...... Jews are to live on

a single street, or in a distinctive quarter cut off from other sections of the town or city. This quarter is to have only one entrance.

On the Protestant side, the anti-Semitism of its founder became so further embedded in his homeland's psyche that German detestation of Jews, which had always been boiling just below the surface, erupted from time to time in massacres from the sixteenth to nineteenth centuries and exploded as the Holocaust in the twentieth. On a positive note, Jews in Protestant majority America, unlike in Europe, prospered. This was due in large part to the personalities and policies of George Washington and most of the other founding fathers (see previous section) which prevented anti-Semitism there from ever taking root. The whole Age of Exploration enterprise, in fact, which occurred contemporaneously with the Renaissance and unexpectedly found not only the New World in the Americas but new lands and trade routes around the planet, worked to severely undermine the Church's authority, particularly outside of Europe.

Nonetheless, Luther's viciously hostile attitude had a long-lasting effect on Christian opinion, Catholic as well as Protestant. During the 200 years immediately following publication of his book, *On the Jews and Their Lies*, not a single pope willing to speak in the Jews' defense came to power. Both before and after that period, however, although usually few and far between, there were at least some. The list below dramatically makes the point.

The Important Popes

As of the publication date of this book, 265 men have held the position of pope, not including the 39 rivals known as Antipopes, who claimed to be the real leaders of the Catholic Church despite the simultaneous reigns of the official popes chosen by the Roman canonical hierarchy. For a while, from 1309 to 1377, Avignon in France served as the official seat of the papacy, not Rome, and thereafter, from 1378 to 1408, was the residence of several of the Antipopes. From a Jewish perspective, some of the most important popes were as follows.

Peter (3 B.C.E.?- 67 C.E.) – Born a Jew, he was considered a Jewish-Christian by his Jewish contemporaries and the Romans. In around 50 C.E., he became the first bishop of Rome and, as such, is considered the first pope. Was one of the original twelve apostles of Christ, whose birth name, Simon, Jesus changed to Peter, meaning "the rock." Was such a threat to Roman authority that Nero, to make an example, had him crucified upside down.

Gregory I a.k.a. Gregory the Great (590-604) – Outlawed the mistreatment of Jews and, in particular, defended them against forced conversions. Was famous and beloved for using large portions of the Church's resources to provide for the poor. Introduced the Gregorian chant into Catholic services. Wrote fourteen books on historical, moral, and religious subjects.

Callixtus II (1119-1124) – Issued the papal bull *Sicut Judaeis* meaning *In Defense of the Jews*. Outspoken advocate of Church reform. He opposed Henry V who insisted that kings, like himself, had the right to make church appointments. This conflict, known as the investiture controversy, led to the establishment by Henry of the Anglican Church in England and its split from the Roman Catholic Church on the continent.

Innocent IV (1243-1254) – In 1247, he promulgated the first papal bull refuting the ritual-murder charge, a.k.a. blood libel, which alleged that Jews murdered Christian children to obtain blood for use in the ritual baking of matzoh.

Clement VI (1342-1362) – Protected Jews against the ridiculous accusation that they caused the plague, and ordered his bishops to instruct Christians never to attack them. On several occasions, he quelled anti-Jewish riots, putting his authority and himself at risk. He pointed out that the Jews were dying like everyone else and said, "That they have provided the occasion or the cause for such a crime has no plausibility."

Martin V (1417-1431) – Prohibited and made illegal the baptism of Jewish children without their parents' uncoerced consent. Instituted many other reforms concerning the treatment of Jews and ordered that "every Christian treat the Jews with a humane kindness."

Nicholas V (1447-1455) – Condemned the Statute of Toledo, issued by that city's council in 1449, which prohibited anyone with Jewish blood from holding public office. One of the most learned popes, he was called the Great Humanist.

Alexander VI (1492-1503) – Although his reign was marred by corruption and bribery, he welcomed Jews to Rome after they were forcibly expelled from Spain in 1492. His notorious daughter, Lucrezia Borgia (1480-1519), was a renowned patron of the arts.

** After Alexander VI, who died just before Martin Luther's rise to prominence, it would be nearly two and a half centuries before another pope favorable to Jews held office. **

Michael Grossman

Benedict XIV (1740-1758) – Appointed Cardinal Lorenzo Ganganelli, who later became Pope Clement IV, to investigate the ritual-murder charge. Ganganelli's report totally exonerated the Jews and asserted, in effect, 'the blood libel has no basis whatsoever.' Benedict XIV strongly supported the teaching of science and founded the chairs of physics, chemistry, and mathematics at the University of Rome.

Leo XIII (1878-1903) – Loudly condemned all forms of anti-Semitism. Spoke in defense of Captain Alfred Dreyfus, the French Jewish officer who was framed by a superior, Major Charles Esterhazy, the real spy, and accused of treason in 1894. Although Dreyfus was initially convicted and sent to Devil's Island for five years, he was ultimately exonerated.

Pius X (1903-1914) – Although extremely conservative, and an opponent of modernism, he denounced the blood libel accusation when it was used against Melvin Beilis, a Russian Jew, during the most famous ritual-murder trial of modern times. In 1911, Beilis was arrested by Czar Nicholas II's secret police, charged with the murder of a Christian boy, Andreu Yutchinsky, and of desecrating his body by using his blood to bake matzoh. He was imprisoned for nearly one and a half years in medieval-like conditions, but in 1913 was acquitted by an all-Christian jury.

Benedict XV (1914-1922) – In 1916, responding to a petition of American Jews protesting anti-Semitism in Poland, he said, "The Supreme Pontiff… as Head of the Catholic Church, which, faithful to its divine doctrines and its most glorious traditions, considers all men as brothers and teaches them to love one another, he never ceases to indicate among individuals, as well as among peoples, the observance of the principles of the natural law, and to condemn everything that violates them. This law must be observed and respected in the case of the children of Israel, as well as of all others, because it would not be conformable to justice or to religion itself to derogate from it solely on account of divergence of religious confessions."

Pius XI (1922-1939) – Issued an encyclical in 1937 called *Mit Brenneder Sorge* (With Searing Anxiety) that condemned the Nazis for their anti-Semitism. It was smuggled into Germany and read from most Catholic pulpits. In 1938 Pius said: "Mark well that in the Catholic Mass, Abraham is our Patriarch and forefather. Anti-Semitism is incompatible with the lofty thought that fact expresses. It is a movement with which we Christians can have nothing to do. No, no, I say it is impossible for a Christian to take part in anti-Semitism. It is inadmissible. Through Christ and in Christ we are the spiritual progeny of Abraham. Spiritually, we are all Semites."

John XXIII (1958-1963) – Born Angelo Giuseppe (Joseph) Roncolli, he greeted a visiting Jewish delegation in 1960 with words that have become legendary. "Welcome," he said, "I am *Joseph*, your brother." Convened the Second Vatican Council in 1962, which issued a declaration of new Church policy called *Nostra Aetate* (In Our Time) that repudiated 2,000 years of previous church teachings blaming the Jews for Jesus's crucifixion and condemning them to eternal damnation. Played a major role in rescuing Jews from Nazi-controlled countries, particularly Hungary, during World War II.

Pope Paul VI (1963-1978) – Passionately embraced the new policy toward Jews and opened his arms to "especially the Jews, of whom we ought never to disapprove and whom we ought never mistrust, but to whom we must show reverence and love ..."   Reached an agreement in 1965 with the Patriarch of the Greek Orthodox Church in Constantinople to nullify the mutual excommunications of the Western and Eastern Churches of 1054.

John Paul II (1978-2005) – Openly acknowledged the Church's repeated failures with respect to its treatment of the Jews. Repeatedly condemned "the hatreds, the persecutions, and all manifestations of anti-Semitism directed against the Jews of any time by whomever." Led the Vatican to formal recognition of the State of Israel in 1994 and, during a visit to Jerusalem in 2000, prayed at the Wailing Wall and at *Yad Vashem*, the Holocaust memorial. He said, "I have come to *Yad Vashem* to pay homage to the millions of Jewish people who, stripped of everything, especially their human dignity, were murdered in the Holocaust. More than half a century has passed but the memories remain. No one can forget or ignore what happened. No one can diminish its scale. We wish to remember. But we wish to remember for a purpose, namely to ensure that never again will evil prevail as it did for the millions of innocent victims of Nazism. As Bishop of Rome and successor of the Apostle Peter, I assure the Jewish people that the Catholic Church, motivated by the gospel law of truth and by no political considerations, is deeply saddened by the hatred, acts of persecution, and displays of anti-Semitism directed against the Jews by Christians at any time and in any place."

Benedict XVI (2005-   ) – Too early to tell, but all indications are that he will follow the path of John Paul II. As a German, who lived through the Nazis and World War II, it is likely he will make huge efforts to demonstrate respect and support for Jews and Israel.

Baptists, Jesuits, Methodists, More

Let's detour now for a moment. If you don't know a Methodist from a Baptist or a Jesuit from a Dominican, this section's for you. The huge number of Christian groups make the four major Jewish divisions – Reform, Conservative, Orthodox (which includes the Hasidim), and Recontructionist – seem simple in comparison. So very briefly, we'll take a look at some of the most important Catholic and Protestant orders, sects, denominations, and movements with large followings worldwide.

The *Franciscans* or *Friars Minor* is a religious order of the Roman Catholic Church founded by Saint Francis of Assisi in 1208. Their ideal is to live modestly, even in poverty, as a means of demonstrating that worldly possessions are unimportant, since devotion to God will earn the true believer entry into heaven. They are known for their charitable work and proselytizing.

The *Dominicans* or *Friars Preachers,* founded by Saint Dominic in 1214, is another Roman Catholic order. Their goal was to stamp out the many heresies that threatened Church doctrine at the time. They were so resistant to departure from orthodox theology that many of its members became leaders of the Inquisition. One them, Tomas De Torquemada, became Grand Inquisitor of Spain in the fourteenth century and one of the most reviled men in history. On a more positive note, Dominicans are credited with having produced some of the most beautiful church art and most influential Christian writers, although some of them, like St. Thomas Aquinas, were deeply anti-Semitic. They are similar to Franciscans in their devotion to modest living.

The *Jesuits* or *Society of Jesus,* also a religious order of the Roman Catholic Church, was founded by Saint Ignatius of Loyola in 1534. Its goal is to spread the teachings of the Church throughout the world, including Protestant and Islamic countries. Their constitution binds them to serve as missionaries wherever they are directed by the Pope. At times, they have been so aggressive in demanding loyalty to the Vatican that they've been expelled by national leaders; particularly leaders of Roman Catholic countries who, until recently, found the Jesuits' allegiance to Rome a threat to their own authority.

Lutheranism emphasizes the ultimate authority of the Word of God as found in the Bible in all matters of faith, unfiltered by a corrupt priesthood, and the life of Jesus as the key to understanding the Bible. Founded in the sixteenth century by Martin Luther, who was excommunicated by the pope, it holds that salvation does not depend on worthiness or merit but is a gift of God's sovereign grace. Thus the slogan "salvation by faith alone." To criticism that this position does not do justice to Christian responsibility to do good works, Lutherans reply that true faith means actively loving others and that good works, i.e., good deeds toward others, will always follow love.

Presbyterian is from the Greek word *presbyteros,* meaning "elder," and church government by elders, who may be men or women, laypeople or clergy, characterizes Presbyterianism. This democratic arrangement permeates all Presbyterian practices and is credited with having helped shape the American political structure with its system of checks and balances, separation of powers, and constitutional limits on authority. Their theology is derived in large part from the teachings of John Calvin (1509-1564), an older contemporary of Martin Luther, who led the Protestant Reformation in Geneva. Although Presbyterians regard the Bible as the supreme authority for the church and individual believer, they issue frequent "confessionals" or "guides to worship" that continually revise and update practices.

Baptists are Protestants who have incorporated some distinctive, non-traditional beliefs into their theology. Founded in Amsterdam in 1609 by John Smyth, they now number 44 million worldwide and are more than one-third of all Protestants in the United States. The sacrament of Baptism *by total immersion during teenage years* rather than by sprinkling in infancy, is central to their ritual. They feel that infants have no understanding of faith, and only individuals with some maturity can make a conscious, meaningful decision to accept Jesus. Those who do, that is, who have a personal experience with Christ, are considered members of the Baptist *gathered church,* as opposed to other churches in which everyone born in a particular geographic region and who receives certain sacraments are members.

Methodism was founded by John Wesley and his brother, Charles, in 1729 in England. Their theology leaned heavily on Arminianism (a seventeenth-century Christian doctrine that says free will can exist without limiting belief in God or contradicting the Bible) and rejected predestination (the teaching that a person's ultimate destiny is predetermined by God). When a group of students at Oxford became the Wesleys' followers, and would assemble for worship, their fellow students called them "methodists," alluding to the methodical manner in which they went about performing rituals. John Wesley's activities among the poor, and his charismatic personality encouraged a social consciousness that became the hallmark of Methodism.

The *Episcopal Church*, organized in Philadelphia in 1789, is almost identical in theology to the Anglican Church of England, which leans heavily toward Roman Catholic traditions, as opposed to Reform Protestant and Evangelical traditions. Of the seven Christian sacraments, the Episcopalians, like the Anglicans and Lutherans, accept only two[3] – Baptism and the Eucharist (bread and wine are consumed as the body and blood of Jesus) – as having been instituted by Christ. But the Episcopalians are aggressively ecumenical and hope to join together with other Protestant denominations and create a United Christian Church worldwide. Most of the signers of the Declaration of Independence were Episcopalian, as is Trinity Church in New York City, where Alexander Hamilton is buried.

Mormonism and the *Church of Latter-Day Saints* was established by its prophet, Joseph Smith, in 1830 and has grown to some 13 million members. It is now one of the world's major and most dynamic religions. It is a Christian faith but has its own holy book, *The Book of Mormon*, that sets forth doctrines sharply at odds with Catholic or Protestant theology. Mormons believe that traditional Christianity became corrupt and God, therefore, presented a new revelation to Joseph Smith, setting forth His original teachings in purer form. Although the traditional Bible is one of the Mormons' scriptures, their interpretation of it is radically new. They hold, for example, that God, the Father, and Jesus are three entirely separate beings, but are united in purpose as the Trinity. Commendably, however, Mormons are religiously tolerant and teach that all faiths contain at least some good. On the other hand, women are not ordained nor permitted to be clergy.

The Church of the Seventh Day Adventists is a Protestant denomination founded in 1844 that believes in the imminent second coming of Christ. They are fundamentalist in their insistence that the prophecies in the Bible will all come to pass. Adventists believe that the human body is the temple of the Holy Spirit, place great importance on good health, and most are vegetarians. Interestingly, they observe the Sabbath on Saturdays like Jews.

Evangelicalism, from the word *evangelical*, Greek for *Good News*, is a movement within most branches of modern Protestantism that emphasizes the supreme authority of the Bible and absolute commitment to Christ. Evangelicals believe that "spiritual rebirth" and right living can come only after an encounter with Jesus and a personal conversion experience. All of the television preachers are Evangelicals, and include Oral Roberts, Billy Graham, Jimmy Swaggart, Benny Hin, and Joel Osteen, to name a few. Their missionary reach and charitable fundraising abilities are truly astonishing.

With that short detour out of the way, let's return to the Renaissance and see fully how it reshaped European thinking, brought on the Enlightenment, and transported Christianity into modern times.

The Enlightenment and Modern Times

Whereas the giants in Renaissance humanities painted, sculpted, and wrote primarily during the 250-year period from the late fourteenth to early seventeenth centuries, and in doing so, along with the explorers, opened people's imaginations to exciting new vistas, most of the greats in Renaissance science rose to prominence later, beginning with Galileo in the early 1600s. By then, it was as if European minds, stirred by the incredible visions of Renaissance artists, were at last ready to find out if those visions could be made real. Not by praying, not in the afterlife, but in the here and now by human logic, inventions, ingenuity, and machines. The impact of Galileo (1564-1642) in hastening the already-declining influence of the Church — which we discussed at length at the end of the previous chapter — cannot be overstated. For the prelates to have threatened him for insisting that the earth revolved around the sun, as posited earlier by Copernicus (1473-1543), not vice versa, was an incredible misjudgment. Instead of enhancing the Church's authority that action made it an object of ridicule and scorn in many European quarters. The Church had no rationale arguments with which to counter Galileo's, in fact not even scripturally based arguments, and thereafter science and religion would often be perceived as two entirely separate, mutually exclusive, and frequently at odds magesteria. The religious realm got the worst of it, by far, and came to be thought of as an obstinate enemy of knowledge and no longer the sole or even a reliable repository of truth.[4]

Science rushed headlong to the fore. And with the perfection of the printing press in the seventeenth centuary — the first model of which was built by Johannes Gutenberg in 1450 — the new scientific truths became widely disseminated. Galileo's contemporary, the English physician William Harvey (1578-1657), studied human anatomy in meticulous detail and discovered that blood, pumped by the heart, circulated through the body via arteries and veins. He performed hundreds of dissections, recording and publishing his findings, and set a standard for biological research. He theorized the existence of capillaries, although there were as yet no microscopes to observe them, and studied the mating process, the reproductive system, and the development of embryos. His best known works include *Anatomical Essay on the Motion of the Heart and Blood in Animals* (1628) and later, *Essays on the Generation of Animals*. Like Galileo, the Church considered him a threat, particularly because his studies indicated that the physiologies of humans and animals were incredibly similar. In the realm of physical science, another Galileo contemporary, the German mathematician and astronomer, Johannes Kepler (1578-1670), furthered Copernican theory and formulated several famous laws of planetary motion including: (1) The planets move in elliptical orbits with the sun at one focus, (2) The sun emits a force which diminishes proportionally with distance and pushes the planets around it (precursor to Isaac Newton's theory of gravity) and, (3) The closer a planet comes to the sun, the more rapidly it moves – all amazingly accurate. He also formulated a system of mathematics that was the forerunner of calculus. Despite the frequent illogic of the Church, however, he saw no conflict between his Christian religious devotion and his scientific theories. He felt that the simplicity of the Copernican system had to have been God's plan.

Sir Isaac Newton (1642-1727), arguably the most important scientist in history, was a physicist, astronomer, mathematician, and philosopher. He formulated the laws of gravitation and motion, developed the science of optics, explained the phenomena of light and color, built the first reflecting telescope, and invented calculus. His singular contribution was to give the world a non-religious, all encompassing and unifying theory, *gravitation*, that explained many seemingly diverse natural phenomena: the tides, the motion of the moon and planets, the speed of falling objects, the trajectory of cannonballs, etc. Newton's most famous works were his treatises *Philosophiae Naturales Principia Mathematica* (1687), setting forth his laws of forces, motion and gravity, and *Opticks* (1704), explaining his theories of color and light. He was also active politically and emerged as the chief defender of intellectual freedom at Cambridge University when King James II, in an attempt to re-establish Roman Catholicism in England, ordered that a certain Benedictine monk be given preferential academic treatment and accorded a professorial seat without fulfilling Cambridge's rigorous requirements. Ultimately, Newton and his allies prevailed and James II was overthrown in the Glorious Revolution of 1688. In addition to his scientific treatises, Newton wrote numerous forward-thinking theologies and is considered one of the foremost figures of the Age of Enlightenment. His theory of gravitation, repeatedly confirmed by experiments, coupled with his non-dogmatic theology, and the ideas of the emerging rationalist philosophers, so altered people's everyday perception of the universe (even more so than Einstein's relativity theory, which deals with the slowing of time and other phenomena that occur only at very high speeds beyond people's daily experience) that religious explanations came to seem naive and even, perhaps, unfounded. The religious explanations, certainly, could not be verified by scientific experiments, as could Newton's. The glimmerings of doubt about Christianity's worldview, which first took hold during the early Renaissance and grew firmer over the next two centuries, became widespread and fashionable.

The names on the roster of Enlightenment philosophers, like the names of the Enlightenment scientists, are at least vaguely familiar to anyone who has attended college. Their revolutionary ideas, even if just subconsciously, are deeply embedded in our twenty-first-century Western thinking. The roster is lengthy. Thomas Hobbes (1588-1679), argued that there must be a clear distinction between knowledge and faith. Rene Descartes (1596-1650), said *"I think, therefore I am"* and insisted that true knowledge comes not from faith but from human reason alone. Baruch Spinoza (1632-1677), a Jew who rose to prominence in the Christian world, believed man can be free and that only a free man, *exercising his reason*, is happy. John Locke (1632-1704), attacked the *divine right of kings,* insisting that sovereignty resides with the people, and founded the doctrine of *empiricism* which holds that all knowledge must be based on what we learn through our senses, not faith. Charles Montesquieu (1689-1755), argued that a government must be structured with a *separation of powers* to prevent any part of it from becoming dictatorial and infringing on individual rights and freedom. Voltaire (penname for Francois Marie Arouet, 1694-1778), fought against tyranny, intolerance, and superstition in his vast body of writings and attacked any religion, particularly his own Christianity, that persecuted non-adherents. Benjamin Franklin (1706-1790), one of the two or three most famous men in the world in his day, was a printer, author, inventor, statesman, and philosopher who helped draft the Declaration of Independence and Constitution, urged religious tolerance for all and the abolition of slavery. Jean Jacques Rousseau (1712-1778), vehemently supported individual rights, particularly freedom of expression, but was out of synch with many of the other Enlightenment thinkers with his argument that the civilized state, permeated by science and art, was corrupt and inferior to the primitive, natural state in which he believed people were freer and happier. Immanuel Kant (1724-1804), insisted that the welfare of each individual be an end in itself and the ultimate goal of society but that knowledge had limits and concepts like freedom and happiness could not be understood via only logic and reason. Thomas Jefferson (1743-1826), who, among his many accomplishments, wrote in the Declaration of Independence: *"We hold these truths to be self evident, that all men are created equal, that they are endowed by their Creator with unalienable rights, that among these are Life, Liberty, and the pursuit of Happiness"* and successfully urged James Madison to add a Bill of Rights to the Constitution guaranteeing freedom of religion, freedom of the press, protection against standing armies, restrictions on monopolies, the unremitting force of the habeas corpus laws, and trial by jury.

With the arrival of Enlightenment philosophers — and there were dozens more in addition to the above — *modernity*, as we understand it in the West today, began. Of note, the names of those philosophers were predominantly French, just as the names of the Crusaders and their leaders were predominantly French, centuries earlier. And centuries earlier still, it was the Franks led by Charlemagne who established the political entity that lifted Europe out of the Dark Ages (from 410 C.E., the sack of Rome, to 800 C.E., the crowning of Charlemagne) and became the Holy Roman Empire. One begins to understand why, despite their no longer first-rate economy and nearly non-existent military, the French, having always been at the center of world affairs, think it inarguable they are a great nation and rightfully entitled to a large voice on the international stage. During the lifetimes of Voltaire, Franklin, Rousseau, Kant, and Jefferson, the death knell for the *divine rights of kings* in the Western world, which doctrine had been clinging desperately to legitimacy, began loudly tolling when the Americans, backed by French military support, revolted against Britain and King George III in 1775 and the French revolted against Louis XVI in 1789. The Americans declared independence in 1776, the British retreated in 1779, and Louis was guillotined in 1793. Both the newly enacted U.S. Bill of Rights (first ten amendments to the Constitution) and the French Declaration of the Rights of Man and Citizens (preamble to their Constitution) guaranteed freedom of religion and thereby outlawed the persecution of Jews and other minorities. In 1789, Washington issued his famous letter to the Jewish community of Rhode Island: *"May the children of the stock of Abraham who dwell in this land continue to merit and enjoy the good will of the other inhabitants while everyone shall sit in safety under his own vine and fig tree and there shall be none to make him afraid."* And in 1799, Napoleon broke down ghetto walls throughout Europe. There were horrific setbacks along the way, like the numerous Eastern European pogroms, the Russian pale of settlement, the Dreyfus affair, and Hitler's concentration camps, but the formerly impenetrable wall of Christian hatred toward Jews was crumbling, and by the late twentieth century, nearly gone. Today, fundamentalist Christians are among the Jews' and Israel's strongest supporters.

Thus has Christianity metamorphosed over the millennia; blinding doctrinal hatred of Jews has receded and Christian compassion has ascended. Likewise, many modern Jews are able to accept that Jesus, although himself not God, was an extraordinary prophet and leader and divinely inspired.

In the twenty-first century mainstream Jews and Christians "feel" the world with a remarkably similar mindset. That cannot be said, however, with regard to how most Muslims view the world. The frequent acts of anti-Semitism in Europe we read about are most often committed by angry members of their communities, not Christians. The Islamic mindset and history are briefly explored in the next chapter.

Chapter Fifteen - My Brother-In-Law The Muslim

About five months after 9/11, I was visiting my brother-in-law, who is Muslim, in Lafayette, Louisiana, where he is a highly regarded and extraordinarily successful cardiologist. Basketball player Shaquille O'Neal would now be his next-door neighbor there, but the deal fell through at the last moment. At a Cajun crawfish and crab boil my brother-in-law was hosting (he doesn't eat shellfish himself as it is non-Kosher), he began speaking to me, and some Hindu and Christian friends, about the suffering that afflicts huge parts of the Islamic world and, in his opinion, fuels their anger toward the West. He said, "In the U.S., where we are all employed, free to vote, well-fed, schooled, sheltered, and medically cared for, with enough money left over to entertain ourselves, we can't even begin to conceive of the hopelessness experienced by the majority of Muslims."

He was about to try to defend Islam against the accusations from some quarters that it is an intrinsically violent religion but, before he could finish even a sentence, one of the Hindu men shouted, "Don't tell me again what a beautiful religion Islam is. If that's what you see, you're intentionally blind. What I see are gangs of murderers yelling 'Allah' and rejoicing as they slaughter as many non-Muslims as they can." To which one of the Christian men added, "And I don't see supposedly peaceful Muslim leaders moving against them either. It was only after the U.S. threatened Pakistan, within an inch of its economic life, that its dictator took the first steps in fifty years to control its fundamentalist animals. Until then, he craved their support. The support, Doctor, of the animals who slit Daniel Pearl's throat because he was Jewish and amuse themselves by blowing up churches to maim and kill Christians."

I nodded my head in total agreement.

Now, my brother-in-law is no idiot and, confronted with the above hostility, he knew this was not the time to argue with a Hindu, a Christian, and a Jew about what he thought were the underlying reasons for Islamic terrorism. The mood had changed dramatically since my previous visit with him, about a year before 9/11. This time, one of us would have punched him.

But the truth is that my brother-in-law and his entire family — which includes my wife's sister, to whom he is married, and my nephew — are horrified and deeply wounded by the actions of the terrorists. They are deeply wounded because, as practicing Muslims, they now face an impossible situation, to wit: With each sickening terrorist act, the religion they love, as much as you and I love Judaism, is becoming ever more discredited and despised in the Judeo-Christian world. That is not the Islam they know and practice.

About three years before 9/11, my brother-in-law and his wife took into their home their son's fourteen-year-old Jewish friend whose parents, for whatever reason, could not care for him. *In loco parentis,* they provided for him financially, emotionally, and spiritually. For three years, even as they attended mosque, they insisted he attend synagogue, do Shabbat services, celebrate the Jewish holidays, and take pride in his heritage. If they didn't know what one of the Jewish holidays meant, they called me, learned what it meant, and explained it to him. Can you believe it? That's more than many Jewish families do. When this Jewish boy, raised for three years by Muslims, graduated from high school in June 2001, he was presented with the school's highest award for excellence in computer science, and received substantial scholarship money. His real parents, who attended the graduation, approached my brother-in-law and said, "Doctor, you and your wife did for him what we couldn't do. With you, he made something of himself. You taught him morality. You gave him love. Thank you for helping our son and thank you for helping us."

The above behavior is typical for my brother-in-law's family. To them, Islam is a system of beliefs and ethics in which the virtues of kindness toward, peace with, and love for others are not optional. They are sacred commands and, therefore, absolute requirements. And not just as regards other Muslims. The Islam they know values all human life.

But no matter how admirable their private deeds, my brother-in-law and his family, as I mentioned, find themselves in an impossible situation. How dare they claim Islam's teachings are beautiful when some Muslims, with the support, it seems, of many others, take perverted delight in slaughtering everyone else? They have begun to notice the suspicious looks of some of their neighbors. They have become concerned for their own safety. And they are devastated by the hatred the fundamentalist murderers have brought upon Islam. I can tell you, unequivocally, that although my brother-in-law and his family sympathize with the suffering of oppressed Muslims, and may feel U.S. policy contributes to that suffering, they do not sympathize with terrorists. They are as horrified by and as afraid of them as the rest of us. To them, the terrorists are Islam's worst enemies.

What is the moral of this story? Well, I find that I am so angered by the terrorists – whether here, in Israel, Europe, India, Pakistan, or Iraq – that

I'm often beset by feelings of intense loathing toward the religion they say justifies their actions. I suspect that most Jews, Christians, and Hindus are beset by those feelings too. But when it comes to terrorists, millions upon millions of Muslims feel exactly as my brother-in-law's family does. And just maybe, a good number of those Muslims are as kind in their private deeds as my brother-in-law and his family have always been in theirs. By the way, that Jewish boy, he was bar mitzvahed in Iyar 5763 (May 2003). Guess who was there in front-row seats?

Given the tenor of the times, and my deep respect for my brother-in-law and his family, I've become interested in the life of Muhammad as a means of gaining insight into the mindset of his more than 1 billion modern-day followers. Surpassed only by Christianity, which has 2,000,200,000 adherents, Islam is the world's second-largest religion. We Jews, by comparison, number only 15 million. In the Islamic world, hatred of Jews (and Christians) has become widespread, and in many places, deeply imbedded, but that was not always so.

Muhammad was born in 570 C.E. on the Arabian Peninsula in Mecca, in an era when the Arabs were organized into dozens of tribes and clans. One thousand years after the age of Jewish prophets ended, and almost six centuries after Jesus's crucifixion, nearly all the Arabs were still pagans, although a few Jewish Arab and Christian Arab tribes lived alongside them. Muhammad, a pagan, began his spiritual journey to monotheism in adulthood and it was not until he was forty that he came to believe he was a prophet of the One God. Throughout his adult life, Muhammad taught that the One God was first revealed to the Jews, via the Torah, and then to the Christians, via the Gospels. In his early career, he did not denigrate Jews and Christians, but rather admired and was somewhat jealous of them for their superior, universal systems of ethics. He looked upon the concept of One Ethical God as an idea that could unify and bring justice to all humankind. But first, he had to unite the diverse Arab tribes, which were economically and socially backward and constantly raiding, and often slaughtering one another.

For generations, the Arab pagans, including Muhammad, believed that the temple of **Al-Llah**, "The God," was the **K'aba** in Mecca. That cube-shaped shrine had existed for many centuries and may have been a place of worship even before the Hebrews became monotheists. In the Arab scheme, Al-Llah was the highest, but only one of a pantheon of deities. To make the transition from paganism to monotheism appealing to his fellow Arabs, Muhammad taught that Abraham and his son, Ishmael, by the concubine, Hagar, had traveled together to Mecca and built the K'aba before Isaac was born. This was after God had instructed Abraham to journey to the Promised Land and become a great nation. The great nation to Muhammad, of course, was the Arab nation he was going to build. Thus, Abraham, through his son, Isaac, and grandson, Jacob, was not only the father of the Jews but, through his eldest son, Ishmael, the father of the Arabs as well. Muhammad believed that everything he taught had been revealed to him by the same One God that had revealed Himself to the Jews and Christians earlier. The teachings received by Muhammad were written down by his contemporary disciples and became the **Koran**. The One God had at last revealed himself to the Arabs and given them their own sacred scripture.

As Muhammad's ideas took root, the entrenched tribal chieftains became hostile and he, and many of his followers, were forced to emigrate from Mecca and other parts of the Arabian Peninsula to the city that would become the prophet's power base, Medina. That journey was called the *Hijra* (emigration). The converts to Islam were required at least once in their lifetimes to visit Mecca to worship at the K'aba. That journey was called the *Hajj* (pilgrimage). In 630 C.E., when Muhammad's army peacefully forced the surrender of Mecca, which had been controlled by the tribe into which he had been born but no longer accepted him as a member, **the Quarysh** (which is apparently derived from the same root as Quran a.k.a. Koran, meaning "reading" or "recitation"), it was clear to everyone that Islam was on the verge of total triumph over paganism. All Muslims could now make the Hajj unopposed by any power. The prophet, at the height of his power, died unexpectedly two years later at the age of sixty-two.

Muhammad's closest followers in Medina chose the Prophet's aging father-in-law, Abu Bakr, to succeed him as supreme leader of the triumphant Muslim community. Bakr took for himself the title *Khalifat Rasul Allah*, meaning *Successor of the Messenger of God*, which gave rise to the term *caliph (successor)*. Conceptually, and in many ways in actuality, the caliph was to Islam what the pope was to Christendom as both exercised not only spiritual but extensive secular authority. When Bakr died in 634, after a very brief reign, his designated successor, Umar I, father of Muhammad's third wife, became the second caliph. Umar added the title *Amir al mum Imim*, meaning *Commander of the Believers*, to that of caliph and managed to extend the reach of Islam into the Byzantine Empire and beyond. His generals took Jerusalem in 638. He died in 644, at which time Muhammad's son-in-law, Uthman Ibn Affan, became the third caliph. After continuing the territorial expansion of Islam, although not as successfully as Umar, he was assassinated in 656 and succeeded by Ali, another son-in-law as well as cousin of Muhammad.

With Uthman's assassination and Ali's ascension to caliph, the split between the Sunni Muslims and Shia Muslims began. The *Sunnis*, from *Sunna* meaning *the way* or *example*, believed and still believe that Muhammad intended that the Muslim community choose by consensus successors to lead the theocracy he created. The *Shias*, meaning *partisans*, on the other hand, believed and continue to believe that Muhammad chose his son-in-law, Ali, as successor, and only the descendents of Ali and his wife, Fatima, Muhammad's daughter, were entitled to rule the Muslim community. To the Shias, the three caliphs before Ali – Abu Bakr, Umar I, and Uthman Ibn Affan – and all caliphs after him who were not his or his wife's descendents were illegitimate usurpers. Today, the divide between Sunnis and Shias, which in Iraq has turned depressingly vicious, is as real as the divide between Catholics and Protestants, but much rawer, and is based more on the question of succession than on ideology.

To the Arabs, for whom life was even more difficult and brutal than for most in the seventh century, Muhammad's teachings promised the beginning of a new society in which each person would be equal before the Lord, including women and slaves. Muhammad taught that freeing slaves and giving alms to the poor were among the holiest of deeds. Furthermore, he dramatically improved the lot of women. It is a mistake to think that Islam, as taught by Muhammad, mistreats women. To him, women were equally holy before Al-Llah and had to be treated with respect and affection. During his life Muhammad took many wives and records of his dealings with them show that he was generous, kind, and forgiving to them all. Moreover, some were close advisors and confidants without whose guidance and support he might not have succeeded. The treatment of women by the Taliban in Afghanistan was a gross perversion of Muhammad's teachings and his own documented behavior.

If, for a moment, we could look upon Muhammad as we would at any of the world's important historical figures, we would immediately realize the enormity of his accomplishments. He unified and brought peace to dozens of Arab tribes, the peace raised the standard of living of all Arabia's inhabitants, and he founded a religion that taught that all humankind should follow the same just God, an ethic that is certainly to be found in Judaism. That he used raw military force to dominate recalcitrant tribes, including the execution of nearly every member of a Jewish tribe, should not blind us to his vision of holiness. We need only remember the frequent brutality of Moses toward non-believers, and the repeated attacks by Joshua on the Canaanites, to put Muhammad's conquests in perspective.

The hatred toward the Judeo-Christian world that infests Islam in many places today is a late development, largely unknown to Muhammad and his early followers, in its present virulent form, despite savage conflicts with some Jewish tribes during his rise to power.[1] It stems, in great part, from the failure of Islam as a modern system of governing, as compared to the secular West, which predominates culturally, politically, economically, and militarily. The Muslims are acutely aware of their present-day weakness, and recall the seventh to thirteenth centuries, when the Islamic world was ascendant and Europe was in the Dark and Middle Ages. At the very moment when Europe emerged into the Renaissance and became incredibly strong, the Islamic world began to decline, dramatically. It has never recovered. Even now, the Industrial Revolution and Enlightenment have yet to arrive in vast areas governed by Islam. Their desperation is further intensified by our refusal to acknowledge that the Muslims are heirs to a religious revelation equivalent to our own, whereas the Islamic world, from its beginning, always accepted the validity of the earlier revelations to the Jews and Christians. This perceived arrogance fuels their animosity toward the West like nothing else. In fact, aside from blind ignorance, it's the main reason some Muslim societies have outlawed the open practice of Judaism and Christianity and prohibit the construction of new churches or synagogues.

There is no easy way out. Common sense tells us that it simply cannot be that all the good in today's world resides within the Jews and Christians, and all of the evil within the Muslims. Learning about Muhammad forces us to see that the Muslims possess a vision of universal justice and righteousness as all-encompassing and powerful as our own. The terrorists who prey upon us, and on peaceful Muslims as well, are an abomination. We should not allow these mass murderers and their supporters to prevent our acknowledging the humanity of hundreds of millions of Muhammad's present-day followers, and their suffering. There is a beautiful prayer by British social reformer, philosopher, and theologian, Annie Besant (1847-1933),[2] now making the rounds in Universalist circles, that reminds us of what is perhaps the most basic teaching of all the monotheistic religions:

> *O hidden life, vibrant in every atom,*
> *O hidden light, shining in every creature,*
> *O hidden love, embracing all in oneness,*
> *May all who feel themselves as one with Thee*
> *Know they are therefore one with every other.*

May the One God help us all in our quest for peace.

Chapter Sixteen - Hindu Homeboys

In Louisiana, where my in-laws live, there are a lot of homeboys. They're called Cajuns, who have a vibrant local culture with an exquisite cuisine that exists no place else. My wife's mother, her two brothers, her sister Audrey, and her sister's husband – the wonderful Dr. Patel, our two nephews, two of her first cousins, and two of her aunts all live in Acadiana Parish alongside them. Her brother Leslie's wife, Sheila, is Cajun as are her brother Michael's wife, Mary, and her cousin Barbara's husband, Brian. The Cajuns I've met are all great people, but over the years, although I've been to Louisiana at least a dozen times, I've only spoken with and gotten to know a handful. You see, when I go to Louisiana, and when I go I stay for a week at least, I hang out almost exclusively with my Indian in-laws (my wife is ethnically Indian with a little Chinese thrown in to make her even more exotic) and their large circle of Indian friends. Many are doctors, some successful businessmen, and a couple are helicopter or small-plane pilots for oil companies in the Gulf. Surprisingly, although Dr. Patel and Audrey are mosque-going Muslims, almost all of their Indian friends are Hindus. Like the doctor, they were all born in India, but they are very *Americanized*, even *Cajunized* Hindus, and I never tire of teasing by calling them *Hindu Homeboys*.

Whenever I go down there with my family, or alone as has happened occasionally, Audrey and Dr. Patel, whom we've nicknamed Pepe, treat me as if I was a visiting head of state. And not just me. My father's visited and had the same experience. So have cousins of mine from California and some New York friends who I e-mailed Audrey might stop by. But the even more remarkable thing is that all of Pepe and Audrey's Hindu friends, whom I've grown to know quite well, treat me and my family that way too. It's incredible, but when it comes to hospitality, it's difficult for even Pepe to outdo them. And that got me to thinking. Is there something in their culture, upbringing, and religion – their Hinduism – that makes them such an amazingly welcoming group? Or is it something even broader than Hinduism, something about Indians in general that's responsible?

In 1988, about three years after I married Phyllis, she brought me and our little daughter, Aly, to Louisiana for our first visit to the new in-laws on their home turf. At the time, just Audrey and Pepe, their son Faizel, and her brother Michael, were living there. The rest of her family moved from New York to Acadiana later. Pepe picked us up at the airport and, when he stopped for gas, I pulled out some money to help pay because he'd misplaced his credit card. He said, "Look, do me a favor, don't do that.

Keep your wallet in your pocket and please don't take it out the whole time you're here. Everything's taken care of. Okay?" I was a little surprised but figured he was just being overly hospitable.

We arrived at his home, close by the Lafayette airport, in about fifteen minutes. It was spectacular: huge rooms, high ceilings, beautifully furnished, elegant decorations, gorgeous landscaping, and comfortable. I noticed there were several mosaics and paintings on the walls almost all with *Indian* motifs: the Taj Mahal (tomb of the wife of Muslim emperor, Shah Jahan, in Agra, India, erected 1643), Bengali warriors mounted on elephants (West Bengal[1] is an Indian state, and Bengali is one of the eighteen languages officially recognized in the Indian constitution), ornate palaces, portraits of maharajas, and pages of scripture in Sanskrit or Arabic. There were also shelves of books that included the Koran, treatises on Islam and Hinduism, histories of India and even a few on Buddhists, Christians, and Jews. Their home, in a word, was sensational, and enveloped by a spiritual aura that was unlike what I was used to in the mostly suburban-type homes I'd been to in New York.

Audrey was waiting in their gargantuan kitchen, twenty by twenty-five feet at least, to greet us. It was about 5:00 PM, and she had prepared tons of Indian food for dinner. I soon realized, however, it wasn't just for us. Guests arrived, including Miss Mildred, their sixty-year-old neighbor, a Cajun; Dr. Surinder, an anesthesiologist, with Shashi, his wife, both Hindus; Dr. Akshay, a gastroenterologist, and Neelam, also Hindus; Subhash, a small-plane pilot, with Usha, Hindus again; and about a half dozen others. All Hindus. And then, through the front door, to my delight, came someone I knew. I recognized her immediately because she was a relative of my first cousin Bruce's wife, Sumona, who is Hindu, and I'd met her before. Her name was Meetu and she too, like virtually all the other guests, was Hindu. Both Sumona and Meetu were from California, but somehow, Meetu had moved to Lafayette like my in-laws.

My wife, my daughter, and I were staying the week with Pepe and Audrey in guest rooms that were almost a separate wing of the house and, after the Cajun guests left, their Indian friends remained to play cards. As I was to find out, it was a big deal and each of us had to purchase a minimum $50.00 of chips to buy into the game. It was three-card poker, very fast-paced and, after we anted up and the betting began, the pots always grew to over $150.00. There were nine of us playing and, since I wasn't used to the rules and made bad bets, was down about $100.00 after just four hands. Three hands later, I had started to work my way back, but got nailed by Surinder when he called me and raked in a pot of almost $300.00, a third of it my money, by beating me with three kings against my three sixes. That put me down $165.00. When the game finally ended at 11:30 PM, I was down even more, but everyone was reluctant to take my money. Surinder, the night's big winner, said, "You're new to this, it wasn't fair," and tried to give me back a hundred. I wouldn't take it, so he slipped it to Pepe, who sneaked it into my wallet later. Before we returned to New York, Audrey organized another game. This time I won big, over $225.00, but when I tried to reciprocate by giving back some of my winnings, my new Hindu poker partners wouldn't hear of it. They outright refused.

That was just the beginning. For the entire week, my wife and I were wined and dined like we really were heads of state. Each night, Pepe's Hindu friends took turns taking us to fancy restaurants or hosting lavish dinner affairs at their homes – for us. Pepe was working that week and, since Audrey assisted him in the office, he let us use one of his cars so we could get around and see the sights. When it broke down, one of the Hindu men immediately showed up with one of *his* cars and loaned it to us so we wouldn't be stranded. Also, since Pepe and most of his Indian friends were doctors, that week I got what was unquestionably the most thorough set of physical exams I've ever had. Free! I went from office to office for X-rays, CAT scans, EKGs, diabetes tests, blood tests, stress tests, allergy tests, flu shots, nuclear cardiograms and more. They refused my offer to pay up front, give me a bill, and let me be reimbursed from my HMO. They refused my offer to fill out all the insurance forms myself so they wouldn't be bothered and would just have to sign them. They categorically refused to take my health insurance. When one of them wrote me prescriptions, he outright refused to let me pay the pharmacy. He charged them to his own account instead. They all absolutely refused to let me pay a red cent for anything.

Finally, on the night before we were scheduled to fly home to New York, an opportunity arose for me to reciprocate for their incredibly gracious hospitality; – I thought! Pepe and Surinder had made dinner reservations for about twenty-four people at a Cajun restaurant in town. This included my family, my in-laws, three of Pepe's nephews and nieces, and nearly the entire group of Hindus I'd met. When the check arrived – the food had been exceptional but pricey – I grabbed it knowing the tab was going to be at least $1,750 plus tips, but was determined to pay for everyone. But, as I pulled out my wallet, I suddenly felt my arm being grabbed, firmly twisted, my fingers pried open, and my wallet removed from my hand and shoved back in my pocket. Subhash, the pilot, saw what was happening and yelled, "Forget it, Michael, we won't let you do it. Don't even try." I turned quickly and saw behind me one of the guys from that first night's poker game. I knew him, of all the Hindus, the least. When I faced him, he grabbed the check out of my hands too. I couldn't remember his name but only that he wasn't a doctor but a food or clothing store owner. "Listen," he said, "I felt bad that you lost big when we played poker, so this is on me." I protested... loudly. He said, "Sit down, please, and finish your drink. We're all going to my house for dessert."

This all happened while Phyllis and I were living in an apartment in Queens, more than three years before we moved to upstate Warwick in Orange County, New York and seven years before we joined Jewish Community Centre of Greenwood Lake. At the time, I had no real thoughts about religion, including Judaism, other than that I was hostile to it, and the extent of my thinking about Hinduism was that its adherents didn't eat beef – they considered cows holy – and the women often wore dazzling, brilliantly colored saris with gold jewelry so dark and rich that it had to be not just fourteen but twenty-four-carat. But my experiences with Pepe and Audrey's friends that first time I went to Louisiana, and every time I went there afterwards, whetted my appetite as to *"Who were these Hindus?"* When it came to religion, I wanted to know what was important to these *Hindu Homeboys* and to Hindus in general. Also, running into my cousin's wife Sumona's relative, Meetu, reminded me that some of my own family members were Hindu, including a few of Phyllis's relatives, whereas she and I were Jewish (she'd converted to Judaism before we met and is very spiritual, being a total vegetarian), I had two cousins who were rabbis, Audrey and Pepe were Muslim, and the rest of my wife's family were Christian. What a mixture!

"What a mixture indeed!" one might exclaim, in trying to describe Hinduism itself. Dozens of deities, the concept of *Karma,* scriptures older than Torah, meditation, mantras, the caste system, reincarnation, Hare Krishnas, nirvana, gurus, and yoga; Hinduism is the third most widely practiced religion on the planet. The vast majority of its now nearly 1 billion followers have always lived in India, with large communities in Southeast Asia, particularly Cambodia, Nepal, and Sri Lanka, and more recently in South and East Africa and England and America. Unlike Christianity, Judaism, and Islam, Hinduism does not insist on a faith-based belief in or worship of a single divine entity. At core it is a polytheistic religion with a large diversity of divine entities from which the devout Hindu selects his chosen god while simultaneously recognizing the importance of other gods. Each divinity represents a different aspect of the holy and are all philosophically united in one "supreme principle" called *Isvara* which means *"Concept of God."* In essence, Hinduism attempts to create "approaches" to the spiritual way of life and teach "maintenance" of the right path. Selection of a particular god, to whom to pay special devotion, out of the large number in the Hindu panoply, is but one of the many "approaches" Hinduism offers.

The word "Hindu" is derived from the Sanskrit word *sindhu*, which means "river," and more specifically, the Indus, from which the name of the whole subcontinent arose. The river was a god. The forest on its shores was a god. The crocodiles in its waters were gods. The sun, the wind, the rain, the tsunami were gods. The whole land of India was awash in the holy. Vishnu, Shiva, and a group of goddesses: Kali, Uma, and Durga, all different manifestations of Devi, the supreme goddess, became the most venerated among them. Vishnu never sleeps but rests on a coiled serpent, Shesha, and is attended by Lakshmi, his consort. He has four arms which hold a lotus flower, a conch shell, a mace, and a discus, all divine symbols.[2] He is the protector and preserver of creation and the embodiment of mercy and goodness. The Ganges River flows from his feet. He maintains the cosmic order. Whereas Vishnu protects, Shiva destroys. He rules over demons, evil, death, and fear, and is himself fearsome. He is the god of destruction, death, and asceticism. But he is good. He is also the god of procreation, salvation, and the arts. He appears on earth in several forms, animal, plant, and human and, like Vishnu, has multiple arms. Devi, in some Hindu mythology, is the primal universal force and commands the male gods to create or destroy. She too is fearsome. As Dirga, she defeats the great demon, Mahisha, and as Kali, she appears adorned with the still dripping skulls of enemies she has killed in battle. But as Uma (a.k.a. Parvati), she is gentle and kind. She is a healer. On a lower order is Ganesha, god of wisdom and intelligence. He appears with the head of an elephant. He is the sun. There is also Ganga, goddess of India's most sacred river, the Ganges, who is daughter of the mountain god, Himalaya. Hindus believe, like Jews on *Tashlich* throwing bread crumbs into moving water,[3] that bathing in the Ganges washes away sins. And there are many other – scores of other – Hindu deities as well.

Belief in the sacredness of the Ganges is based on passages contained in the earliest of India's sacred literature. Written in ancient Sanskrit, the Four *Vedas* are to Hindus what the Five Books of Moses are to Jews. They are the highest canonical authority and considered "not of human origin." Portions of the oldest of them, the *Rig-Veda*, meaning *Hymns-Knowledge* (or Hymns of Knowledge) were composed about 1500 B.C.E., more than a millennium before the Torah began to take final form. It is a ritual and ceremonial handbook and consists of over 1,000 prayers, hymns, and formulas. The *Brahmanas* (approx. 1000-800 B.C.E.), meaning *Divine Powers*, were written next and are commentaries attached to the Vedas, similar to the Mishna and Gemara of the Talmud, which clarify and interpret the Torah. After the Brahmanas, the *Aranyakas* (approx. 800-500 B.C.E.), meaning *Forest Treatises*, were composed. Meant to supplement the Brahmanas, they were written by sages in the seclusion of deep forests where they could contemplate the divine. The final books of the Aranyakas are the *Upanishads* which expound a philosophy called *Vedanta* that explores the purpose of our existence, the nature of the universe, and the identity of our innermost souls. Next, there are the *Sutras* (approx. 500 B.C.E.-current era) meaning *thread or string of rules*. They set forth the requirements for marriages, funerals, and other events, and are the basis of most Hindu law. There are several other sacred Hindu writings, the most famous of which is an epic poem, the *Bhagavad-Gita* (approx. 300 B.C.E.), meaning *Song of the Lord*, that by means of a dialogue between the god *Krishna* (an incarnation of Vishnu) and a noble warrior, Arjuna, conveys the most important ethics in Hinduism. In this respect, it is somewhat similar to the *Pirkei Avot*, meaning *Ethics of the Fathers*, which is the last book of the Mishna and sets forth the most important moral insights of the Jewish rabbinic sages. *Krishna's followers*, by the way, are the *Hare Krishnas*, the popular name for the International Society for Consciousness meaning *Divine Energy* (Hare) of *God* (Krishna).

Hindu law, which developed in large part from the Sutras, is troublesome for Westerners because it legitimizes the caste system, an arrangement perceived by us as a denial of basic human rights and akin to apartheid. But it is based on the Hindu belief in reincarnation, which holds that all people, regardless of the lowly caste they may have been born into, have a chance to be born into higher castes in future lives if they are moral and just in this one. Due largely to the efforts of Mahatma Gandhi (1869-1948) the Indian Constitution, enacted into law shortly after his death, contains this clause: "Untouchability is abolished and its practice in any form is prohibited." Nonetheless, there is today still widespread discrimination against the lower castes throughout India. Most of the "untouchables," however, attribute their lowly status to *Karma* (which literally means *action* but conceptually is the sum total of one's behavior, good and bad, in this and all previous lives) and hope that, via reincarnation, their present situation will be only temporary.

Another man who rebelled against the Caste System was Siddhartha Gautama (approx. 563-483 B.C.E.), a.k.a. *Buddha*, meaning *Enlightened One*. He was born into Hindu surroundings but founded an entirely new religion, and in this regard was similar to Jesus, who, although born a Jew, gave rise to Christianity. Legend holds that Siddhartha experienced a life-changing revelation when he encountered an old man, a sick man, and a dead man all on the same day in short order. He realized then that the thing all humankind shared, more than anything, was intense suffering. This led him to renounce family ties, wealth, and power, and embark on a quest to discover "an eternal truth" that would ease mankind's torment. In around 528 B.C.E., while meditating under a tree, he experienced Nirvana (the Great Enlightenment) and learned how to escape pain. Nirvana, however, is actually a Hindu religious concept which Siddhartha perfected, and it thus became more closely associated with Buddhism than Hinduism. *Nirvana* is a Sanskrit word that means *extinguishing* or *cooling off*. The idea is that only by extinguishing cruelty, prejudice, ignorance, greed, and lust will we ever experience transcendence from the pain of our existence. Strangely, beginning in the eighth century C.E., Buddhism started to die out in India, so much so that it migrated almost completely off the Indian subcontinent into China, Tibet, Thailand, Myanmar, Korea, and Japan. It remains, however, the world's fourth largest religion, behind only Christianity, Islam, and Hinduism in that order, and is rapidly growing.

One way to experience Nirvana is by the practice of *yoga*, Sanskrit for *yoke (as in "yoked together" or "unison")*. It is one of the six systems of Hindu philosophy, another of which is *Vedanta* which explores the purpose of our existence as I mentioned above. Through seemingly impossible bodily control, yogis attempt to liberate themselves from the limitations of our fragile human forms and thus from the illusions of our senses and everyday thoughts. By doing so, they hope to achieve ultimate spiritual knowledge. The yoga pathway to such knowledge involves eight steps, most of them familiar: (1) Extreme self-control, (2) Religious observance or, for agnostics and atheists, recognition of a universal truth, (3) Postures, (4) Regulation of breathing, (5) Restraint of the senses, (6) Steadying of the mind, (7) Meditation, and (8) Deep contemplation. This system of discipline, after years of intensive training, enables accomplished yoga practitioners to perform incredible physical and mental feats such as insensitivity to heat, cold, and pain; the chanting mantras with total focus on one thought and complete detachment from all distractions nonstop for weeks; and the documented ability to emerge unharmed after being buried alive for days or submerged in water for record-breaking stretches of time. Thus do yogis try to achieve self-illumination, the ecstasy of true knowledge and thereby reach Nirvana.

As for me, attaining Nirvana would be great and yoga may work for some, but when I tried to get into the lotus position, instructed by one of Pepe's friends from the card games, I got cramps. Phyllis and Pepe's seven-year-old niece did better but got bored after five minutes. In Hinduism, fortunately, in addition to yoga and Vedanta, there are four other recognized philosophies,[4] all of which try to teach us how to live spiritual lives. Together, they provide several approaches to spirituality in addition to worship of one or more of the many Hindu deities. That, I think, is Hinduism's great attraction. It provides so many ways to be religious – worship of a deity or deities, gods and goddesses, Nirvana via faith *or philosophy*, the teachings of respected gurus, high castes, low castes, karma and reincarnation – there is a place for every Hindu to fit in. Also, like Judaism, Hinduism's roots and traditions stretch back at least four millennia, and its adherents feel a strong sense of cultural cohesiveness and continuity, regardless of the depth of their belief or level of observance. They all feel they *belong*.

So too do Indians who are Sikh, Buddhist, Jain, and Muslim, or even Christian. Although Hindus make up 80.5 percent of India's nearly 1.1 billion people, there are more than 25 million Christians, 21 million Sikhs, 6 million Buddhists, and some 5 million Jains. There are also 150 million Muslims, the largest religious group by far after the Hindus. There are even a few thousand Jews, many of whom claim to be descendents of the ten lost tribes. The Christian presence in Indian society is not as ancient as most of the other groups, but is of long standing and dates from before the time of British rule (1774-1947), when it expanded enormously and solidified. Unfortunately, they have often been the targets of brutal acts of violence, not by Muslims, although that's happened occasionally, but by Hindu fundamentalists still resentful over Britain's former colonial rule. The Buddhists, however, are the home-bred remnants of the followers of Siddhartha Gautama, a.k.a. Buddha, who founded his new religion in Northern India, after which it spread throughout the country, winning millions of converts, before ebbing and migrating to the Orient. Similar to Buddhism is the religion of the Jains, in that it relegates belief in a divine entity to minimal importance and totally rejects violence. Its founder and Buddha's contemporary, Nataputta Mahavira (599-527 B.C.E.), taught that most of our everyday thoughts and actions lead to enslavement of our souls, which can be freed only by right knowledge and right conduct. To Jains, fulfillment of the following five vows is much more important than worship: refusal to inflict injury, total honesty, refusal to steal, refusal to accept unnecessary or extravagant gifts, and sexual restraint. Jainism's emphasis on total pacifism had a significant impact on Mahatma Gandhi, who elevated peaceful protest into an effective means of political resistance when confronting the British. In India, somewhat like Jews in the U.S., Jains exert influence far beyond their small numbers. As for the Muslims, despite the ongoing Muslim-Hindu violence concerning disputed Kashmir, many of them are loyal to the Indian nation, support its egalitarianism, and are a rock-solid part of its culture.[5] But the savage conflict between Muslims intent on separating the state of Kashmir from India, supported by Pakistan on the one side, and opposed by the overwhelming Hindu Indian majority on the other, has taken more than 50,000 lives since 1948. From all I've read, however, when thinking of India, it is important to keep separate in one's mind the brutally militant politics from the all-encompassing culture. Muslims and Hindus, for example, dine on basically the same, to us, exotic Indian cuisine, look upon the Taj Mahal as a national symbol and one of their greatest treasures, revere Mahatma Gandhi as nearly a saint, and most Indian women wear the same brightly colored saris and distinctively Indian rich and dark gold jewelry.

The Sikhs, for me, are the most interesting group, because their creed blends elements from Hinduism and Islam into one religion, and therefore serves as a sort of theological bridge between the two giant and often warring super-faiths. Extremists on both sides regard them as heretics, but the moderate majority, for the most part, holds them in high esteem. Sikhs embrace the Hindu ideas of deep meditation, karma, and transmigration of souls, i.e., rebirths into new forms in future lives, but reject the caste system and multiple deities. From Islam they embrace the concept of the oneness and unity of a personal god as well as prohibitions against idol worship and alcohol. Their founder and most revered *guru*, the Hindu word for *teacher*, was Nanak (1469-1539), who preached, like Jews, that the true God transcends all religious distinctions and is the same for everyone. Historically, unlike the pacifist Jains, the Sikhs have garnered a reputation as relentless fighters who are more than capable of defending themselves. In 1966, after unremitting armed confrontations, the Indian government agreed to divide the greater Punjab state into a Sikh-dominated one which continued to be called Punjab, with the Sikh language of Punjabi its primary tongue, and a smaller, Hindi-speaking state called Haryana. In 1984, on a much more disquieting note, after Indian government forces seized the Golden Temple in Amritsar from Sikh terrorists who were agitating for further expansion of their portion of Punjab, Prime Minister Indira Gandhi was assassinated by her own Sikh bodyguards. Eventually, an accord was reached; the government withdrew from the Golden Temple and the radicals toned down their demands. There is virtually no Sikh terrorism today.

Despite all the interfaith squabbles, much too frequent and much too violent, there is a majority consensus among Indians that their country always remain multi-ethnic, multi-religious, and multi-lingual, with the rights of minorities protected and equality enshrined into law. That has happened in India, more so than most other places in Asia, with the exceptions of some of the Oriental countries and, believe it or not, Russia. It has happened obviously due mostly to the overriding influence of the

Hindus. Their religion does not aggressively proselytize, in stark contrast to Islam and Christianity and to a much, much lesser extent, Judaism. Hinduism wants converts but doesn't insist. You are free to take it or leave it. You won't hear Hindus calling non-believers in Vishnu or Shiva or Dirga or Ganesha or Ganga *sinners, unworthy,* and *infidels.* In fact, the Hindu belief in the existence of multiple deities creates a built-in theological tolerance for, even acceptance of, the Yahweh, Jesus, and Allah of the three Abraham-based monotheistic faiths. But can you imagine for a moment what things might be like if militant Islamists controlled India? None but they would have full rights and citizenship. The Jews and Christians, as "Peoples of the Book" and monotheists, would have some rights but secondary citizenship at best. The Sikhs might fit into that category too. But the Hindus, under Islamic Law a.k.a. *Sharia,* would be considered detested idol worshippers, and the Buddhists and Jains far worse — atheists! That is what happened in Afghanistan when the fanatical Taliban ruled (1996-2001), one of their first actions being the destruction of two-millennia-old Buddhist statues; and that is what is happening now in Iran with the recent call by its Muslim fundamentalist president, Mahmoud Ahmadinejad, for "the total annihilation of Israel" and, by implication, "the mass killing of Jews." Ask yourselves, would Hindus preach that?[6]

Now, there comes a point when, by trying to make an argument too often or to strongly, it begins to lose some validity. So I won't do that concerning my high regard for the open-mindedness of Hindus by saying, more than once more, that I believe the theologically built-in tolerance of Hinduism toward the practices and beliefs of other faiths accounts, in large part, for the amazingly friendly reception I receive whenever I visit my brother-in-law Pepe's Louisiana friends, those Cajunized *Hindu Homeboys.* That Pepe treats me, a close relative, well is one thing, but for his Hindu friends to treat me, a total outsider, and Pepe himself for that matter, a Muslim and potential foe that way too is another. Their attitude toward religion reminds me of the attitude of some secularized Jews I've often noticed — like me! It's inside them, buried somewhere, but they're embarrassed by too strong a belief in rebirths, rituals, or miracles. They don't buy into all the hoopla about divine entities or prayers. But, just as Judaism is as much the story of the 4,000-year-old Jewish people, as it is a distinct religion, with the Jews' insistence that acts of justice are more important than a belief in God, Hinduism is the story of the ethical values of the vast majority of the even older Indian people as much as it is the story of India's primary religion. Remember, too, that from Hinduism arose Buddhism, as did Jainism and, in part, Sikhism. Together, those four religions are the faiths of more than 85 percent of the Indian population. And what are Hinduism's ethical values? A philosophic, sort of laid-back attitude toward life, embodied by the idea of *karma;* tolerance and pacifism, more so than Islam and Christianity, certainly; a realization that each of the many gods in the Hindu panoply, and by extension the non-Hindu gods of other faiths, represent different aspects of the divine and are all worthy of respect; embracement of many, at least six including yoga and Vedanta, philosophical paths to the discovery of "truth"; and ongoing efforts to abolish the caste system via enforcement of a famous clause in the Indian constitution, quoted above, that was inserted at the insistence of Mahatma Gandhi. And in Hindu culture, there is also an unmistakable joyfulness, as though life can and should be an endless festival. If you've ever attended a Hindu wedding, you'd have to have been dead to have missed what I mean. I know because in 1995, I was invited by an old friend, Shri, to attend hers at a Hindu temple in New Brunswick, New Jersey. Actually, she and her groom had to rent a huge outdoor hall in nearby Somerset because her temple couldn't accommodate their 2,000 guests. "Members of my temple always do that," she explained. "And my wedding is pretty modest." I almost fell for that, despite her being dressed head to foot in gold, surrounded by two dozen bridesmaids similarly dressed, as she sat upon a solid golden throne, awaiting her groom. That is, until the groom and his entourage finally arrived, *mounted on live elephants,* the animals themselves covered with spectacularly jeweled silver, platinum, and gold ornaments. That's a lot of gold, and that was one incredibly joyous wedding, the likes of which I'd never seen. But I've been to many Hindu weddings since, and even the most *truly* modest of them was several times more celebratory than the most elaborate bar mitzvah I've ever been to. And most bar mitzvahs, as you know, including all the ones I've attended, are no five-and-dime affairs.

Since that long-ago week of visiting my in-laws in Louisiana for the first time, I've been back there more times than I can remember. About two months after I'd made a visit in 1999, I received a letter from Dr. Akshay, one of Pepe's closest friends and one of the Hindu poker players I'd met at that first card game years before, explaining that he and his family had been planning to be in New York the next week but couldn't make it due to a family emergency. Inside the envelope were four tickets to *The Scarlet Pimpernel,* a popular Broadway show that had just opened and they weren't going to be able to use. I made a mental note to call and thank him after we'd seen the show, to let him know we'd had a great time, no matter how good or bad it really was.

When the night for the show arrived, Phyllis and I were expecting, no matter what, that she, Alyson, Zack, and I were in for a tremendously enjoyable evening, but none of us were at all prepared for how overwhelmingly sensational it turned out to be. We arrived at the theater about three minutes before curtain time and, after fumbling around in my pockets for a while, I produced the tickets and presented them to an impatient usher. He stared at them and then at me, and then at my kids. Of the four of us only Phyllis was slightly more than casual and appropriately dressed. He said, "Sir, I don't know if you realize where you're sitting, but please follow me." I thought, "Just great, we're probably gonna be in the last row of the first or even second balcony." I wished fervently I had brought binoculars. So without getting our hopes up, we all followed him. To our amazement, he didn't stop at the first flight of steps we passed to hand our tickets to another usher who'd take us upstairs. Nor at the second. He kept right on walking, with us sheepishly following, to the front of the orchestra section, fifth row. Now, if you've ever been to Broadway, you'll know that orchestra section, about fourth to about eighth rows, are usually a theater's best seats. Anything closer, the actors are on top of you and the music is deafening. Further back in orchestra, the seats are still great but not out-of-this-world great like those fourth to eighth rows. But then, way to my right, I saw four empty seats, which were the very last seats in row five and up against the wall. From there we'd have to crane are necks so much to see anything we'd probably all need heating pads the next day. But, as I stepped in that direction, the usher said, "No, those aren't your seats, sir. Yours are there." I turned to look where he was pointing. "There!" For a moment I almost didn't comprehend. But, as I realized where they were and started toward them, I actually became giddy. They were fifth row all right and DEAD CENTER. Not a little to the left; not a little to the right; ABSOLUTELY DEAD CENTER, FIFTH ROW, ORCHESTRA! The usher handed us our playbills. He said, "Enjoy the show. I don't know how you got these tickets. You must have ordered them a year in advance and paid a fortune because, sir, YOU'VE GOT THE BEST SEATS IN THE HOUSE." I found out later the tickets cost Dr. Akshay over $200 each.

That episode is just one of the many kindnesses I've grown accustomed to from my *Hindu Homeboy* friends down in Cajun Country. The next time I went down there, in spring 2000, partly on business for my Manhattan based law practice, Audrey and Pepe couldn't put me up because they had sold their old home and were living temporarily in an apartment while their new house was being built. At Pepe's request, one of the Hindu guys I had become acquainted with from the now scores of three-card poker games I'd participated in, drove me to a small hotel he was part owner of, and got me a room. I stayed for nearly a week. When the time came to check out and I requested the bill, it was suspiciously low. In fact, the only charges on it were for three meals I'd had in a restaurant on the premises which was independent from the hotel and separately owned. And, at my

Hindu friend's request, even those charges had been slashed. All in all, for the five days and nights I stayed, including the meals, I paid a whopping $32 plus maids' tips. There was no rental car fee either. One of the other Hindu guys lent me his.

By spring 2000, the year I stayed at my Cajun Hindu friend's hotel for a week – for free – I had already served, to my dismay to this day, nearly a year as president of the Jewish Community Centre of Greenwood Lake. The kindness and ethics of my Muslim Indian relatives and their Hindu friends has made me see that religion, *real religion,* tries to make us "just" and "moral" and need not nor must ever be used to divide people into separate, hostile camps. Those who use religion for that purpose are in no way "religious" at all; they're angry, self-righteous bigots. Also, Hinduism's laid-back and deeply contemplative approach to comprehending the universe and discovering "truth," I've never forgotten. When thinking about my own congregation and Judaism, sometimes, I feel sweeping over me, to my endless delight, *Karma.* I feel it now.

* * *

In India, sandwiched between Bangladesh and Burma in the small state of Mizoram, there is an interesting town. Mizoram is majority Christian, bordered to the east by states home to millions of Hindus, but there is an unusual community in that town which consists of 2,000 people. They are indistinguishable in appearance, language, and dress from the 5,000 other Indians there, and the hundreds of thousands of others in neighboring towns, except that they worship differently because virtually all 2,000 of them are Jews. What's more, if their local historians can be believed, they appear to have been living there undisturbed, albeit practicing Judaism again only recently, for some 2,600 years. They claim they are the descendents of the lost tribe of *Menasseh* and, even if we don't believe it, they do. Amazingly, although there is no way to be sure, there is credible evidence that their claim may be true. Their oral history, for example, passed down through the millennia, includes poems describing their crossing the Red Sea and being led by a pillar of fire. They also point to a huge stone upon which, they say, are imprints of Elijah's chariot ascending to heaven, etched by their ancient ancestors. DNA testing has been inconclusive but suggests a genetic link, of the females at least, with Middle Eastern, Semitic people. Also, while still outwardly Christian until the 1960s, they've practiced circumcision and observed the Sabbath – on Saturdays, like Jews – for as long as they can collectively recall. There is circumstantial historical evidence as well.

In 722 B.C.E., just over 2,700 years ago, Assyria conquered the northern Kingdom of Israel, exiled its ten Hebrew tribes, including *Menasseh,* and dispersed them throughout its massive empire They were all, it was thought, slowly absorbed into the surrounding non-Hebrew populations until they completely disappeared. At the height of its territorial expansion (699-627 B.C.E.) the Assyrian Empire's eastern border extended toward India into what is today western Iran, but what was then lands shared by Medes and Persians. The distance from there to the Jewish community in Mizoram is well over 2,000 miles; a huge trek in ancient times to be sure, but doable, especially over a generation or so along the "Silk Road" to the Orient. Also, during the eighth to seventh centuries B.C.E., the years when the trek would have been made, Jesus and Muhammad had not yet been born, no Christians or Muslims were on the scene, and the small band of Menassehites would not have been worried about those potential enemies on the way. It was also centuries before the hostile Romans and Greeks, who were just beginning to attain influence, arose destined to build their own massive empires. Moreover, it was a century and a quarter before the Babylonians rampaged through Jerusalem and conquered Judah in 586 B.C.E. The incipient power on the eastern edge of the Assyrian Empire in 722 B.C.E., although still dominated by the Medes, was Persia, just beyond which lay India. And the Persians, of all ancient peoples were, more often than not, the friendliest to Jews. There may have been good reason for this in that the Persian religious prophet, Zoroaster (650?-540 B.C.E.?), who founded *Zoroastrianism* and lived about the time when the Menassehites might still have been trekking through Persia, preached that there is but One God, like Jews. In fact, some of Zoroaster's ideas so deeply influenced Judaism that they were recorded, but not attributed to him, in the Dead Sea Scrolls. He was still alive when Cyrus became king of Persia in 550 B.C.E. and died just a few years before Cyrus, who by then had become known as Cyrus the Great, allowed the Jews exiled in Babylon to return to the Promised Land.

If the Menassehites arrived in India within a hundred years from the date of the Assyrian conquest in 722 B.C.E., that would have been only five to six centuries after the death of Moses (approx. 1230 B.C.E.) and they would not have been practicing Judaism as modern Jews do, since the Hebrew Bible was not completed, at the earliest, until 300 B.C.E. and the Talmud not until 600 years later. Thus, even after the Menassehites in Mizoram forgot their Jewish roots and became animists (who believe all creatures are spiritual beings with souls), and later, when they converted to Christianity in the 1800s, their traditions and style of worship continued to bear striking resemblances to ancient Judaism. So striking that beginning in the 1960s, several of these *Lost Menassehites* took note, started openly practicing Judaism again, and in 2005, the state of Israel accepted their claim to be descendents of the tribe of Menasseh as legitimate, and dispatched its chief rabbi to perform formal conversion rituals. So far, more than a thousand of these Mizoram *Menassehites* have officially converted and are considered, even by the Orthodox, to be Jews. This has all happened in India – home to Hindus, Muslims, Sikhs, Jains, Buddhists, Christians, and incredibly, lost Jews. It is the land of my *Hindu Homeboy* friends, and is truly drenched in the holy.

Chapter Seventeen - The Gift Shop

On Old Dutch Hollow Road, there stands, behind a crooked board fence, a quiet old building. Faded paint, crumbling plaster, loose steps, and splintered wood, it is unchanged from the time, nearly fifty years ago, when it was transformed from a dance club and bar into Jewish Community Centre of Greenwood Lake, now known as Congregation B'nai Torah. Except then, it was newer and the paint must have been brighter, the plaster fresher, and the steps and wood in much better condition. But when you walk through the front doors, you are transformed no less dramatically than when the building itself was transformed from a discotheque into a place of worship.

Once inside, upon looking up, you can see that there is still hanging, from the highest spot on the wood-paneled, soaring arched ceiling, a huge, no-longer-working discotheque light fixture with more than a dozen, decades-ago burned-out, multi-colored bulbs. There was a time when that fixture cast wildly colored, gyrating beams of light onto the dance floor below in perfect synchrony with the music of live bands that performed on the stage directly across from the front entrance. The dance floor is now the congregation's sanctuary and the stage our *Bimah* where, in the ark, are the synagogue's treasured Torahs.

You will also notice that on the inside, like its exterior, the building is run-down and, in many places, the old wooden floors are weak and sunken by age, the ancient plumbing rusted and leaking, and a few of the half-century-old stained-glass windows are cracked and ajar. But that is not what you will remember, not what will imprint itself into your mind. Instead, what will certainly captivate you is the incredible friendliness and warmth of the place, and its enchanting beauty. You will be puzzled because there is nothing in particular, no one or two things you can point to, to explain why the building should affect people so. There are no unusual or especially attractive paintings on the walls; in fact, no notable art at all. There is no expensive or fancy furniture, only a bent metal rack with ordinary *Tallit* on it, for example, and only the usual prayer books and *Mahzor*, and not even an especially imposing ark or Torah or *Ner Tamid*. Nonetheless, the place is impressive. Its charm envelops you.

After stepping through the front doors, you find yourself in a small foyer. Along a wood-paneled wall, at right angles and immediately to your left, is the door to the president's cramped office. It is very tiny, five and a half by four and a half feet at most and, amazingly, it serves as the Hebrew school and treasurer's office as well. At right angles to your right is another paneled wall with a door to another equally tiny room. In there, a Boy Scout troop, which meets at the synagogue once every month, stores its equipment. There is also a twisted old coat rack in it for the use of our congregants and guests. And a few steps in front of you is the double-door-size entrance to our sanctuary, with the old discotheque light fixture hanging high overhead. As you enter the sanctuary, to your left is the bent metal *Tallit* rack and, next to it, an antique oak table piled high with pamphlets, newsletters, and papers. Beyond that table are several similar oak tables that are used by one of our Hebrew school classes. Directly ahead of you, fifty feet across from the sanctuary entrance, is the old live-band stage, renovated by the congregation's founding members to be our *Bimah*, with the Hebrew words "Know Before Whom You Stand" emblazoned above it. In front of the *Bimah*, on the sanctuary floor, are seventy high-backed, antique chairs, which match the old oak tables, arranged in neat rows. Only during the High Holidays and at our annual dinner dances do they ever fill up. Usually, just the first row, and occasionally the second, are needed.

As you stand at the threshold to the sanctuary and look in the other direction, to your right, there is another paneled wall fifteen feet away. Close to that wall, standing alone, is an odd, multi-level counter with a glass front and glass top. It is wood framed and inside, has four warped wooden shelves. It is seven feet long, four feet high, and two feet deep. It is illuminated by only a single fluorescent bulb but attracts your attention at once, like an oasis. On the two highest wood shelves are a half dozen dazzling, brightly colored yarmulkes, assorted matzo covers, and several books on Jewish history and worship. On the lower two shelves are Seder plates, menorahs, and Havdalah candles. And on the glass countertop itself, below which sit the wooden shelves, there are discount coupon books, *mezuzot*, and Sabbath cups. You will notice that all of these items, every last one of them, are for purchase because this small, odd little counter is Congregation B'nai Torah's proudly open-for-business – but only on Sundays and on Fridays before services begin – Judaica Gift Shop. Jokingly, we advertise it as by far, the biggest and best-stocked Judaica shop anywhere in Greater Greenwood Lake. In truth, it is, because it's the one and only Judaica shop, in this century or any other, that's ever been there.

I headed to the counter and could see that Sheri Fistal, our gift shop manager, was busily, almost lovingly, polishing the glass front and top and placing new inventory on the shelves. Without Sheri, the shop would never have reopened and would still be as dark and unused as it had been for the nearly ten years before she and her husband, Mayer, became members of the congregation in 1999.

"Boy, Sheri everything looks great. Let me take a look at that electric menorah over there in the corner. Maybe I'll get it as a Chanukah gift for Matt and Bonnie Kessler. What'll it cost me?"

"We're having a special," she said, handing it to me. "For you, $35. And if you buy other items, 10 percent off on each. You may as well buy all of your Chanukah presents now, before the special ends. Why don't you buy a second menorah for yourself or as a gift for Pat Weisslander? I'll give it to you for $31.50. And, as you well know Mr. President, we're non-profit so there's no tax."

Not only had she been able to get the shop up and running, but she was actually making a few sales now and then and starting to generate some extra money for the congregation. To do it, she was always running specials. So when she told me the electric menorah was on sale, I well knew her shtick and had to chuckle because her specials, in truth, never ended. I said, "Sheri, if there was no special, what would you charge?"

Looking at a catalogue, she answered, "Let me see, the suggested retail price is $42.50, but even at $31.50 we still make a small profit. I'd rather get what I can and move the stuff off the shelves instead of just letting things sit around unsold. I worked out a deal, you know, with our suppliers to give us our inventory on consignment so we don't have to pay them until after I make sales."

I looked at some of the other new inventory. "I like that Chanukah book and those two Sabbath candle holders." I made it a point to be a regular customer because I desperately wanted the shop to succeed and all of Sheri's time and effort running it worthwhile. "How much are they?"

"The book is $11.95 and with 10 percent off comes to $10.75. The candlesticks are $20 and with the 10 percent discount, $18."

"I'll take them, Sheri, and one of the menorahs too. And by the way, how did the shop do this month?"

"Well, with the things you just bought, we actually made a profit of around $500, but a lot of that was from the twenty-five or so discount coupon books I sold. I wish we could make that kind of profit every month. Usually, we're lucky if we clear $125. I know that's not much but, believe me, I'm trying."

"Listen," I said, "every dollar you bring in helps. Just having the gift shop open and brightly lit boosts everyone's morale. It makes people feel things are happening around here."

Just then, Mayer Fistal, who was a member of the synagogue's finance committee, walked over. He was also the chairman of our advertising and publicity committee and his wife's assistant at the gift shop. Like me, he was worried about our money situation and trying to come up with some effective fundraising ideas. He said, "If you were depending on the gift shop to pull us out of the red, forget about it. It's helping a little but we're going to have to do something else drastic and soon. For years, this place has been spending thousands more than we take in. Technically, we're broke."

"I know, Mayer. In fact, I've been going over our books with Sylvia Levy and things are even worse than you think. In 1998, we ran a deficit of over $12,000 and this year it'll probably be much more. We have at least $11,000 to $12,000 of repairs to do on the roof alone that can't wait. Sylvia's been treasurer around here for longer than anyone can remember and, as soon as I became president, she warned me that if things don't change dramatically, and soon, we'll go under."

"Well, I have a couple of ideas but have you come up with anything since we last spoke?"

"Yes," I said, "but no one thing is going to save us. First of all, at our next board of trustees meeting, I'm going to propose that we immediately raise our dues. Can you believe that for an annual family membership here, dues are still only $300? And for a single, $150? That's idiotic. We have about fifty-five families and five singles, so if we raise the family dues $100, to $400, and the singles $50, to $200, it'll bring in an additional $5,750 right away and before the end of the year. That's still ridiculously low, so next year I want to raise the family dues to $500 and the singles another $50, to $250. That'll bring in another $5,750. All in all that's $11,500 more in annual dues than we're taking in right now."

Mayer asked, "How many of those families and singles are active and actually do things around here?"

"Maybe a quarter," I said. "You know the routine. The others show up on the High Holidays or for *Yizkor* and Mourner's Kaddish for their relatives. That's it."

"Mike, I know we have to raise dues but some of the *schneurers* we have for members are in arrears, even on the $300. If we raise them, they won't pay anything toward what they owe, and may leave."

"Who cares?" I said. "They're not paying anyhow, so if they leave, we're not losing a thing. But I'm certain most will stay and won't complain much. At any other synagogue in the area, they'd be paying at least $950 in dues and a hefty building maintenance fee on top of that. Also, where are they going to go for the High Holidays? Other synagogues will charge them at least $75 per person to get in the door. And if they stop being JCC members, there's no way we're going to let them in here for free anymore. There's just no place else for them to go."

"I hope you're right."

"Me too," I said. "But if I'm not, and a lot of the *schneurers* disappear, it'll be a blessing. People looking for a synagogue to join know that you get what you pay for, so once we raise our dues, maybe we'll start attracting the kind of members we want. You know, *mensches*."

"Yeah," Mayer said, "*Menshes* with money".

However, Mayer didn't sound that confident and frankly, I didn't either.

But I had something up my sleeve. Nothing that original, but it hadn't been tried for so long that only the oldest members hadn't forgotten that our synagogue, in its golden days, had done it almost every year. I'd been looking through some old papers in one of the mildewed boxes in our closets when I came across a stack of yellowing Dinner Dance Journals, each filled with pages of advertisements from local businesses, personal announcements from JCC members, and also, pages of messages with words of congratulations from the family and friends of the Annual Dinner Dance honorees. I found almost twenty journals, the earliest from the 1950s and the most recent one from 1983, with the following words printed on the cover:

29th Anniversary
Year 5744 Dinner Dance
Honoring
David Goldstein
September 30, 1983

Apparently, 1983 had been the last year JCC's membership had been able to muster sufficient energy to solicit contributions for a Dinner Journal, or for any fundraiser, for that matter. By 2000, the year after I took office, no one could remember how to do it anymore. Even so, although it hadn't been tried in seventeen years, I was determined to give it a shot. And I had a bit of a head start. In 1999, just after Susan Lobel stepped down as president, the congregation had thrown a huge dinner party for her right at the synagogue. It wasn't a fundraiser because no one had thought to put together an Ad/Announcement Journal, and we actually lost money on the affair because the money we collected for tickets wasn't enough to cover the cost of the caterer. Nonetheless, the food had been good, I still had the caterer's phone number, and if my own energy level held up along with just a little help and enthusiasm from our congregants, I was sure I could raise thousands of dollars. I had a lot of professional contacts and was confident they'd come through when I asked them to buy space for ads and announcements. If only two or three other members had similar connections, we'd be home free. Moreover, I had already decided who the year 2000 honoree was going to be, and knew the board of trustees would go along. The person I had in mind was so popular in fact, that if I hadn't suggested her name, the board undoubtedly would have suggested her on its own. She was so popular in the Greenwood Lake community, both Jewish and non-Jewish, that when people found out she was being honored, contributions would start flowing in. Our honoree, I decided, was going to be JCC's longest-serving member, in fact, one of our last still-living founding members, well up into her eighties, and the wife of the now-deceased 1983 honoree, Mrs. Jessie Goldstein. I was excited about the opportunity her affair would give us to raise enough money to pull us back from the financial brink, and was chomping at the bit to start putting her Journal together. Also, and probably more important, morale at the synagogue was very low and I felt that if people saw a successful fundraising drive taking shape, their mood would change, perhaps dramatically. I was planning to bring up my Dinner Journal idea at the next board meeting, along with my proposal to raise our annual dues, but before I did, there was something very basic and very troubling about our membership's low morale that was holding us back like an iron ball and chain. I wanted to address *that* right away, before I got too involved with anything else. The thing that was bothering me was that our morale was not just very low, it was virtually non-existent. In truth, it stunk. It was abysmal. It could hardly be worse. We were moribund. There was so much frustration, complaining, bickering, and backstabbing that, as a congregation, we were almost dysfunctional.

Before I became president, even during the two years I was serving as second vice president, I hadn't been fully aware of just how cynical the synagogue's leadership and general membership had become when it came to trying to accomplish anything positive. I knew I had to do something to improve the morale around here fast, and I tried to do it, at least in part, with a series of articles I wrote for JCC's newsletter, *From the Lakeside*, and by constantly repeating what I had written whenever I addressed the congregation. Although our success at the "Jewpardy" competition in 1999 had given us a big shot in the arm, almost everyone felt it was an aberration, and it only lifted our spirits temporarily. Without a big, permanent boost in morale, my efforts to raise money for Jessie's Dinner Journal would fall miserably short. With our morale as low as it was, i.e., virtually non-existent, I was worried that there would be no way I could get enough members to help out. I hoped that my own unbounded and genuine excitement about our synagogue's potential, as expressed in my articles, would be catching and motivate the congregation to realize just how much we could do and the great congregation we could become if we really wanted to.

Chapter Eighteen - Spreading the Word

From the President – May 2000
Getting New Members

We all know the line "I would never join a club that would want me as a member." It's supposed to be, and is, funny because the sentiment expressed, "I'm not qualified to belong to something really good," is the type of self-deprecating humor everyone enjoys. But for some reason, many of us here at JCC truly believe that we somehow don't have the credentials for membership in the club or group – that is, the synagogue – we really want to be part of. Maybe it's that we don't think we have enough knowledge of Hebrew language, synagogue rituals, the holidays, or Jewish history? Maybe it's that, for whatever reason, we don't think we can socialize in a way that will be enjoyed by other members? Or is it, maybe, that we don't think we can afford, financially, to belong to a top-notch congregation?

Let me tell you, if you're among those who feel that way, **you need to break through that mindset immediately.** If we're going to attract more than a trickle of new members, we, the existing membership, need to take much more pride in each other, our accomplishments together, our spirituality, and our one-of-a-kind building. Don't worry about your Jewish history or Hebrew language knowledge, or even your finances. Our biggest selling point is that we welcome all Jews, regardless of their level of observance, affiliation, knowledge, or income. As a congregation we must want people to know that we're a unique synagogue filled with excitement, energy, activity, and joy. **We must want to be a great congregation.** Only then will we be able to bring in the kind of new members that each of us would want to be with in any club we might join.

To put it another way, if we ourselves are not joyful and excited about our congregation, why should anyone else be? Only if we take genuine pleasure in and are really excited about being members of JCC will other Jews feel our joy and excitement and want to be with us. We must change the mindset that says "How good can this synagogue be if I'm a member?" to "I'm a member of a unique synagogue infused with energy and spirituality; I want everyone to know about us because I believe we are becoming a great congregation." This change of mindset is the crucial first step that we need to take to expand our membership.

Of course, feeling good about ourselves, by itself, can only go so far. There are a number of other things we should do. In speaking with friends and acquaintances in Warwick, Monroe, West Milford, and other neighboring communities, I've learned that, aside from Greenwood Lake residents, not many people know we exist. Part of the reason is that the entrance to our property is on a very lightly traveled road, so very few persons – persons who might be interested in joining a synagogue – ever notice our building. Fortunately, there is a solution. The northwestern boundary of our property abuts busy and heavily traveled Lakes Road and, insofar as I have been able to determine, there is no serious legal obstacle preventing us from cutting a driveway from Lakes Road into our parking lot. Building the new driveway will cost several thousand dollars and we'll have to comply with village and town codes, but the end result will be a brand-new entrance from a major roadway that will make us visible to hundreds of motorists on a daily basis. And we'll be able to erect a large, attractive sign on Lakes Road as well.

This is something we can and should do soon. Hand in hand with cutting the new entranceway, our building needs a paint job, our parking lot needs re-graveling, and our property needs some serious landscaping. When motorists on Lakes Road start to notice our synagogue, we want to be sure it looks great.

To put all this together, I need two or three members to help me out. I just can't make the arrangements by myself. Any member interested in working on the plans for this new entranceway project (along with the new paint job, re-graveling of our parking area, and landscaping) please call me at 212 406-36XX.

Finally, an additional step toward attracting new members will be continued improvement and invigoration of our Hebrew school, which is the very heart of our congregation. Rabbi Modek, Director Joanne Birnberg, Eli Mermelstein (a terrific teacher who will be back next year), me, and a few parents have been meeting regularly and putting together some new plans and ideas. Remember, each new student we enroll will usually bring with him or her an entire family of new members. The efforts we are making to better our curriculum and increase our enrollment will be the subject of another newsletter article.

From the President – June 2000
Getting New Members II

In my article entitled "Getting New Members" in last month's newsletter, I stressed the importance of changing our thinking from "How good can this synagogue be if I'm a member?" to "I'm a member of a unique synagogue infused with energy and spirituality; I want everyone to know about us because I believe we are becoming a great synagogue." This kind of stuff is catching. If we believe it and feel it, so will other Jews, and they'll want to join us. Think of it this way. If your child wanted to become a Boy/Girl Scout, would you have him or her join Troop F, let's say, that met half-heartedly once a week, rarely went camping, almost never had a member reach the rank of Eagle, and could never raise enough money to keep itself in the black? Or, would you have him or her join Troop AAA, bursting with energy, filled with activity, confident, and always able to finance itself? I'm saying, "LET'S BE TROOP TRIPLE A!"

In last month's newsletter, I described the benefits of constructing a new entranceway from busy Lakes Road into our parking lot. It'll make us visible to hundreds of motorists on a daily basis. In fact, this is something we can probably do soon, because a great deal of preliminary planning has already been done by immediate past president Susan Lobel, and we're not starting from scratch. As soon as we get town approval, which should be in a month or two, we'll start cutting our new entranceway. Also, the board and I have been trying to raise money for a new paint job, for re-graveling our parking lot and doing some landscaping. When motorists on Lakes Road start to notice our synagogue, we want them to be impressed.

An additional step in attracting new members will be continued improvement and invigoration of our Hebrew school, which is the very heart of our congregation. Toward that end, I am pleased to announce that member Debra Bloom, whose son, Steven, was bar mitzvahed on May 20, will be our new Hebrew school director beginning in September. She is enthusiastic and talented, and I look forward to working with her. Debra, Rabbi Modek, Cantor Weinberg, outgoing director Joanne Birnberg, Ellie Mermelstein, me, and a few parents have been meeting and putting together some new plans and ideas. We hope to create a hip, enjoyable program that kids will want to attend.

JCC'S MONTHLY FRIDAY NIGHT COMMUNITY DINNERS
The Fantastic Potluck Smorgasbord

Every month JCC hosts a Friday Night Community Dinner at which people of all backgrounds and faiths are welcome. JCC members and their guests, and anyone who comes after reading about us in the local press or flyers we circulate, are asked to bring a dinner dish or dessert to contribute to our *fantastic potluck smorgasbord*. We invite speakers or performers of interest and are making these dinners real social shebangs. They are informal, entertaining, educational, and fun. They give all of us the opportunity to deepen friendships, meet new people, and learn. On Community Dinner nights, Rabbi Modek and Cantor Weinberg conduct a short service, followed by dinner, then the guest speaker's presentation and afterwards, discussion with the congregation. To finish things off, Rabbi Modek leads us in "Table Shabbat" during which everyone joins in songs in English, in Hebrew, and in Aramaic. Don't be intimidated by the Aramaic. I know very little Hebrew, let alone Aramaic, but the song that gets everyone up, pounding the table and stomping their feet, "D'ror Yikra" ("Give Us Freedom"), *is partly Aramaic*. During the speaker's discussion with the congregation, coffee and dessert are served.

Since Rosh Hashanah 5761, our guests have included: modern dancers and choreographers Art Bridgman and Myrna Packer, performing numbers from their show *"Partners in Life, Partners in Dance"*; Dr. Steven Rubinsky, a distinguished member of the Orange County Jewish Federation Board of Directors, who spoke about the surprising programs they offer, like counseling for stress from divorce, discord at home, or death in the family; JCC members Joanne and Gary Birnberg, with a beautiful presentation concerning their trip to historic Jewish communities in Poland; and Leana Wild, a talented rabbinic student and teacher at Manhattan's Congregation B'nei Jeshrun, which draws two thousand people to its Friday night services. Last year, during 5760, some of our guests were Jim and Linda Meyer and members of their church with a multimedia presentation of their adventures helping orphans in Africa; an American Muslim woman, Rabia Terri Harris, of the Istanbul-based Jerrahi order who led a discussion on the Islamic religion; JCC member and art professor, Judith Peck, whose works have been exhibited internationally; and an extremely informative presentation by a member of JACS – Jewish Alcoholics, Chemically Dependent Persons and Significant Others.

Just as we have worked hard to make JCC's Hebrew school – "The New Jewish Learning Experience" – the most innovative and exciting in the county, we want to make JCC's Monthly Friday Night Community Dinners among the most interesting and entertaining events around. Up here in the country, other than going to the mall or driving *your* kids to *other* kids' houses, there's not much to do weekend evenings. Think of our Community Dinners as something to really look forward to – spiritually, intellectually, and gastronomically. We've been running them for a couple of years, everything's in place, and they are truly worthwhile. All that is needed is your support and participation. Join Us!!

Bring as many friends and neighbors as you like. You'll be surprised how satisfying and enjoyable the evening will be. The dinner speakers who are scheduled for the next several months are: Attorney Robert W. Abrams, specializing in criminal law, whose topic will be Jewish Ethics and Biblical Law as Embodied in the U.S. Constitution, Project Presentations by our Hebrew school students, an Islamic speaker on Jewish/Moslem relations, a Christian speaker on Jewish/Christian relations, and Michael Grosso, a local writer and philosopher of note.

Special thanks to Bonnie Kessler, our Dinner Coordinator, and to Rabbi Reuben Modek, who lines up most of our speakers and performers. Thanks also to Irving and Sydell Fishman for arranging for Steve Rubinsky and family to be with us as guest speaker(s) on 1/19/01.

Remember to call Bonnie Kessler before each dinner to let her know what dish or dessert you want to bring. If you know someone you think could be an interesting speaker or performer, call Rabbi Modek or me and we'll contact that person.

The Silver Shofar Award

Everyone knows that the very heart of a congregation is its young people. With this in mind, immediate past president Susan Lobel started the Jewish Community Centre of Greenwood Lake Hebrew School in 1993. It began as a Sunday-morning meeting of members' children of all ages who would gather around then-Rabbi Harris Goldstein, and hear him tell Bible stories, sing Jewish songs, and demonstrate Sabbath and holiday rituals. In 1995, Rabbi Goldstein moved to California and, under the congregation's new religious leader, Mark Blazer, our Hebrew school became more organized. Mark's wife, Tracy, took charge of the younger students while Mark and Cantor Brenda Weinberg shared teaching the older students. On alternate Sundays, Rabbi Blazer conducted adult education classes, which were a huge success.

Then, in August 1998, Rabbi Reuben Modek joined us and, with his arrival, member Joanne Birnberg became our Hebrew school director. Under their guidance, the school has been running efficiently and effectively. We have separate classes for the youngest, middle, and oldest students, and for adults, that meet Sunday mornings from 10:00 to 12:30.

Our Hebrew school is fast becoming something we can all be proud of. It needs to be pointed out, however, that although nearly all of our students perform well in class and go on to be bar or bat mitzvahed, very few feel any deep connection to our congregation. With some notable exceptions, most, after their bar or bat mitzvahs, disappear never to be heard from or seen again. Synagogues everywhere face this problem because of the incredible number of activities that compete for our children's attention in our technological society. Years ago, as a Scoutmaster, my Boy Scout troop faced the same problem: how to retain the interest of kids whose opportunities for entertainment and learning elsewhere are almost limitless. One way the Scouts dealt with and still deal with this is by presenting their kids with merit badges and rank badges at public ceremonies, from Tenderfoot all the way up to Eagle, in recognition of their achievements. This recognition lets the Scouts know just how much their accomplishments are admired and respected. We should let our children know how admired their learning and accomplishments are as well. Not only will the kids appreciate and be proud of the public recognition, they deserve it!

The board of trustees has decided that once every year, the congregation will present to our most deserving young member, currently enrolled or a graduate of our Hebrew school, an award which we will call The Silver Shofar. It will be presented to the young person who best exemplifies Jewish ethics, spirituality, and learning, as determined by majority vote of the board, our rabbi and cantor, and our Hebrew school director. This will be an important, prestigious honor, and I hope it will give our kids a goal to reach for. We will, in addition, continue to present certificates and gifts to our students and young people in recognition of specific accomplishments, such as proficiency in Hebrew, exceptional knowledge of events in Jewish history, and acts of *Tzedakah*. In awarding The Silver Shofar, we will look for all of these qualities and more.

The Jewish Community Centre of Greenwood Lake Silver Shofar will be presented this year sometime in the spring at a special Oneg Shabbat celebration. For the young person chosen and his or her family, it will truly be a special occasion. We already have candidates in mind and are looking forward to bestowing the honor for the first time.

To all of our children, from your parents and congregation, may God bless you as He blessed Ephraim and Mannasseh, and Sarah, Rebecca, Rachel, and Leah.

Chapter Nineteen - The Jerahhi Connection

Attracting new members turned out to be much, much harder – hundreds of times harder – than I thought it would be. I had made the mistake of thinking that simply because I had become passionately interested in learning about Judaism and, therefore, deeply involved in my synagogue, there had to be thousands of other Jews out there just waiting for someone like me to turn them on to it too. There *were* thousands of Jews out there – even in such a non-Jewish place as Greenwood Lake, New York, – that is, if you counted in at least seven of the nearby towns and villages in Orange County, New York, along with two or three in neighboring New Jersey. But the majority of them had not the slightest interest in Judaism, while the majority of those who did were already loyal congregants at other synagogues. Thank God I hadn't been expecting that my wonderful personality was going to attract scores of new members; I'd have taken it personally. Actually, I did think my personality would attract at least some new members, and did take it personally, very personally, when only two of my friends reluctantly agreed to join, paid partial dues to appease me, and then never showed up again. But attract new members we did; not a flood, not a river, not even a slow-moving stream. It was more like a weak little gully or creek that several times a season completely dried up. Over time, even that little flow, on average four new families each year, would have been enough to steadily increase JCC's total membership, except for one obvious thing: we always lost members each year too. A few died, some grew old and too frail to remain active, some moved away, and some just didn't like the way things were done at JCC, and quit to become congregants elsewhere. Given these dynamics, we counted ourselves lucky, very lucky, if we could show a net membership gain of one or two families per year and maybe one single.

In 2001 and 2002, Rabbi Modek's avant-garde Hebrew school program, "The New Jewish Learning Experience at JCC," really took off and started paying dividends by giving us a big but temporary surge in new membership sign-ups over and above our usual, very small, annual net gain. During the second year of the program, we packed the school with more than two dozen brand-new students, with total enrollment peaking at around twenty-eight. But, as these students grew older, as many as one or two would be bar or bat mitzvahed every other month and graduate. When that happened, they and their families often disappeared and were never heard from again. We found that just to keep even, we had to enroll at least ten new students each semester. Nevertheless, "The New Jewish Learning Experience" ultimately enlarged our overall dues-paying membership

The Reluctant Jew

significantly, from about fifty-five families to sixty-four before leveling off. Even more importantly, the new members it brought in included several people with fresh ideas and fresh energy, who became very active in synagogue affairs. Among them were Barbara Martus who eventually became our recording secretary, Annual Dinner Dance coordinator, and a Hebrew school teacher; Carol Louer, who became a trustee and fundraiser; and Carla Koenig, who was always available to help out.

Even sixty-four dues-paying families, however, even after JCC raised the annual dues from $300 all the way up to $500, were not enough to lift the synagogue out of its dire financial straits. And try as I might, I just couldn't expand the membership much further. In 2002, for a while, we had sixty-five families but, by the end of the year, families we lost balanced that out, and we were back down to sixty. Nonetheless, although Rabbi Modek and I grew very concerned, we were having such a good time running JCC, we never became too discouraged. Nor did the group of members who made up the core activists at the synagogue – Gary Birnberg, jack of all trades and future treasurer; Joanne Birnberg, former Hebrew school director who would serve in that capacity again; Mayer Fistal, advertising and publicity committee chairman and future financial secretary; Sheri Fistal, gift shop manager and doer of innumerable other jobs; Al Levy, trustee and former president of the congregation; Sylvia Levy, treasurer, assistant newsletter editor, and doer of so many other tasks, they're impossible to list here; Richard Gedzelman, newsletter editor, choir director, synagogue photographer, and Hebrew school music instructor as well; Pat Weisslander, corresponding secretary, future bingo manager, and future congregation president; Mark Weisslander, Pat's loyal and tireless helper and supporter; Bonnie Kessler, my closest friend at JCC, as well as Community Dinner coordinator, second vice president, future first vice president, and future president; Debra Bloom, current director of "The New Jewish Learning Experience at JCC"; Irving Fishman, finance committee chairman; Sydell Fishman, annual Dinner Dance coordinator and former second vice president; Estelle Cohen, recording secretary and future corresponding secretary; Barbara Martus, future Dinner Dance coordinator, future recording secretary, and future Hebrew school teacher; and Nancy Deangelo, sometimes attorney for JCC and one of my most loyal backers on the board of trustees – to name a few.

Since I was having so much difficulty increasing JCC's membership further, I stopped worrying about it for a while, and turned my attention to trying to make the existing membership as happy and satisfied and, at the same time, as productive as possible. Reuben and I figured that the way to do that, in addition to always having exceptionally stimulating and uplifting services Friday nights and on the holidays, was to put in place a whole panoply of social and educational activities so people would feel that things were really starting to happen around here. Besides, if the existing members began to look forward to and enjoy those events, and to socializing with one another, they might become as determined as Reuben and I were to keep our membership growing, so the synagogue would remain viable. They'd want those events to continue and they knew, in order to do so, we needed dues and donations from new members to keep JCC's doors open. If the events were impressive enough, they'd want to show us off to their Jewish neighbors and friends, whether or not they already belonged to other congregations, and maybe, try to steal them away from whatever synagogues they'd been accustomed to attending. That actually happened more than a few times. Some of our most devoted new members were refugees from other temples. As to making people more productive, that was the easy part. Since our core group of active members was so small, I started being very careful not to overload anyone with too much to do, so that whatever synagogue projects they were working on, in the little spare time they had left after family commitments and toiling at their jobs all day, would actually get done. We were, after all, with the exception of the rabbi, cantor, and Hebrew school teachers, all volunteers. When I saw that someone was too tired or struggling to finish something, I always tried to get a less-involved member to help out and, if I couldn't, I'd step in and help do it myself. Eventually, however, I found it was not that difficult to persuade a lot of those "less-involved" members to become much more active. I found, a little to my dismay, that being the president of the congregation gave me a lot of respect in the eyes of most of the congregants, especially for some reason in the eyes of those who didn't know me that well, and I was seldom turned down by anyone when I told them I really needed their help. All I had to do, I found, was ask. And when I realized that, I started asking a lot of people and often. You know, most people want to feel that they're doing something useful and important. They usually want to help and like feeling needed. The more I asked for help, the more that sunk in, and it wasn't long before some of those less-involved members were doing so much work around the synagogue that they became part of the group of core activists.

Now, having explained all of this, what on earth is the Jerahhi connection? Well, for starters, it was one of the most stimulating and uplifting, most provocative educational and spiritual events we ever organized, i.e., Rabbi Modek organized, in an effort to demonstrate that exciting things were really beginning to happen at JCC. In fact, aside from our second-place finish at the Jewpardy competition in 1999, it was probably the most amazing thing JCC experienced during my entire tenure as president. Rabbi Modek planned it when he saw the incredible popularity of the monthly Community Dinners JCC had started running shortly after he became religious director. When we held a Community Dinner, anywhere from thirty to sixty people showed up, so at least on those Friday nights, we had no trouble getting a *Minyan*. Reuben, Community Dinner coordinator Bonnie Kessler, and I made sure that every month, we lined up an interesting, sometimes charismatic speaker, performer, or educator, and heavily publicized it. We asked each member who planned to attend to invite non-member friends and guests and bring a large dinner dish or dessert to contribute to the smorgasbord. Once a year, we set aside one of those Community Dinner nights for the presentation of the Silver Shofar Award, the honor given annually to JCC's most deserving young person, and that dinner was usually the most heavily attended of all. Later, after Rabbi Modek departed and Cantor Weinberg took charge as rabbi, we began designating another of the Community Dinner nights as our annual "Shabbat Across America Celebration." The first time we did it, more than ninety-five people showed up, and a quarter of them were curious visitors from nearly a half dozen other synagogues. A couple of times a year also, we invited representatives of different religions to speak to us, and those interfaith events were very heavily attended too. The first Islamic speaker we had was an extremely intelligent, formerly Jewish representative from The Mosque of the Jerrahi Order of Dervishes in Chestnut Ridge, New York. The mosque's spiritual leader, Sheik Bayrak, had sent us a Jewish convert to Islam to demonstrate that there was no built-in animus between the faiths. When I asked her privately, to my surprise, she admitted that there were instances, although extremely rare, of Muslims having converted to Judaism too. Her presentation was completely non-political, and she spoke instead about Islam's spiritual teachings and, in particular, how Muslims *were commanded* to treat Jews, the People of the Book and the first people to whom God revealed himself, as moral and ethical equals if they obeyed His laws. It turned out she was able to recite passages from the Koran that, in the edited form she quoted, supported her contention:

> "If the People of the Book accept the true faith and keep from evil, We will pardon them their sins and admit them to the gardens of delight. If they observe the Torah and the Gospel and what has been revealed to them from their Lord, they shall enjoy abundance from above and from beneath." Sura 5:65

> "Believers, Jews, Sabaeans [inhabitants of the ancient kingdom of Sheba in what is now Yemen] and Christians – whoever believes in God and the Last Day and does what is right – shall have nothing to fear or regret." Sura 5:69.

"Be courteous when you argue with the People of the Book, except with those among them who do evil. Say: 'We believe in that which has been revealed to us and which was revealed to you. Our God and your God is one. To Him we submit.'" Sura 19:46

"We have revealed the Koran in clear verses. God gives guidance to whom He will...
As for the true believers, the Jews, the Sabaeans, the Christians, the Magians [priestly class in ancient Persia who were followers of Zoroaster], and the pagans, God will judge them on the Day of Resurrection, God is the witness of all things." Sura 22:18

I very much liked this woman. She was not preaching or proselytizing, and she steered way clear of anything having to do with Israel or the Middle East, so as to avoid contention. She made it clear that her sole purpose in coming was as an ambassador of good will to promote mutual respect and deepen understanding between Judaism and Islam. On the other hand, I had studied the Koran and knew that the portions she had quoted, to say the least, gave an incomplete, even false picture. She had given us only the politically correct version. The whole thrust of what Muhammad had really dictated to his scribes about Jews – which dictations, with hundreds of pages of his other dictations that had nothing to do with Jews, comprise the Koran – was an accusation that we and the Christians had repeatedly disobeyed God's commandments, enthusiastically sinned, corrupted his Scriptures, and were, except for a few, extraordinarily evil. The Muslim Holy Book is replete with passages venomously contemptuous toward Jews:

"Believers, take neither Jews nor Christians for your friends. They are friends with one another. Whoever of you who seeks their friendship shall become one of their number and God does not guide the wrongdoers." Sura 5:51

"Because of their iniquity, We forbade the Jews wholesome things which were formerly allowed them, because time after time they have debarred others from the path of God; because they practice usury – although they were forbidden it – and cheat others of their possessions. ......" Sura 4:159

"Believers, do not seek the friendship of the infidels and those who were given the Book before you, who have made of your religion a jest and a diversion. When you call them to pray, they treat their prayers as a jest and a diversion. This is because they are devoid of understanding. "Say: 'People of the Book, is it not that you hate us only because we believe in

God and in what has been revealed to us and others before, and because most of you are evil-doers?" Sura 5:57

> "You will find that the most implacable of men in their enmity to the faithful are the Jews and the pagans, and that the nearest in affection to them are those who say: 'We are Christians.'........." Sura 5:82

> "Some Jews take words out of their context and say: 'We hear, but disobey. May you be bereft of hearing! Ra'ina [Look at us]!' Thus distorting the phrase with their tongues and reviling the true faith. But if they said: 'We hear and obey: hear us and Unzuma,' [Regard us],' it would be better and more proper for them. God has cursed them in their disbelief. They have no faith except for a very few." Sura 4:46

> "But because they broke their covenant We laid on them Our curse and hardened their hearts. They have tampered with words out of their context and forgotten much of what they were enjoined. You will ever find them deceitful, except for a few. But pardon them and bear with them. God loves those who do good." Sura 5:13.

There's more, much more, but the above is a fair sampling. Upon reflection, however, I recollected that the Torah was no paradigm of tolerance toward those whom Moses felt were non-believers either. There are sections of the Torah, in fact, which on nearly every page call for the slaughter of those who refuse to accept the one God. At least Muhammad, in Sura 5:13, did not advocate the wholesale murder of Jews "but to pardon them and bear with them." Moses extended no such mercy:

> "Moses saw that the people were out of control – since Aaron had let them get out of control [by allowing them to worship the Golden Calf] – so they were a menace to anyone who might oppose them. Moses stood up in the gate of the camp and said, 'Whoever is for the Lord, come here!' And all the Levites rallied to him. He said to them: 'Thus says the Lord, the God of Israel: Each of you put sword on thigh, go back and forth from gate to gate throughout the camp, and slay brother, neighbor, and kin.' The Levites did as Moses had bidden; and some three thousand of the people fell that day." Exodus 32:25-28.

And seldom did Yahweh himself:

"And the Lord spoke to Moses: Say further to the Israelite people: Any man among the Israelites, or among the strangers residing in Israel, who gives any of his offspring to Molech [pagan god], shall be put to death; the people of the land shall pelt him with stones." Leviticus 20:1-2

"But, if despite this, you disobey Me and remain hostile to Me, I will act against you in wrathful hostility; I, for My part, will discipline you sevenfold for your sins. You shall eat the flesh of your sons and the flesh of your daughters. I will destroy your cult places and cut down your incense stands, and I will heap your carcasses upon your lifeless fetishes." Leviticus 26:27-30

And we haven't even gotten to the really good stuff yet. Here's Moses again:

"Sihon with all his men took to the field against us at Jahaz, and the Lord our God delivered him to us and we defeated him and his sons and all his men. At the same time we captured all his towns – men, women, children – leaving no survivor." Deuteronomy 2:32-34

"So the Lord our God delivered into our power Og king of Bashan, also, with all his men, and we dealt them such a blow that no survivor was left...We doomed them as we had done in the case of Sihon king of Heshbon, annihilating every town – men, women, children – but retaining as booty all the cattle and the spoil of the towns." Deuteronomy 3:3, 6

"When you approach a town to attack it, you shall offer it terms of peace. If it responds peaceably and lets you in, all the people present there shall serve you as forced labor. If it does not surrender to you, but would join battle with delivers it into your hand, you shall put all its males to the sword. You may, however, take as your booty the women, the children, the livestock, and every which the Lord your God gives you.
Thus shall you deal with all towns that lie far from you, towns thatdo not belong to nations hereabout. In the towns of the latter people, however, which the Lord your God is giving you as a heritage, you shalt not let a soul remain alive. No, you must proscribe them – the Hittites and the Amorites, the Canaanites and the Perizzites, the Hivites and the Jebusites – as the Lord your God has commanded you, lest they mislead you into doing all the

abhorrent things that they have done for their gods and you stand guilty before the Lord your God." Deuteronomy 20:10-18[1]

I often wonder whether the Torah and other books of the Jewish Bible, if they had been written not before but after the Koran was composed and Islam came on the scene, would have been as merciful toward and forgiving of Muslims as Muhammad was of the Jews. Given the Jewish holy books' attitude toward Amalekites, Canaanites, Hittites, Amorites, Perizzites, unfaithful Jews, and other non-believers what do you think? The answer seems crystal clear: Not likely; in fact, not a chance! Their slaughter would have been self-righteously, even enthusiastically, called for too.

In April, 2000 Rabbi Reuben Modek, spiritual leader of The Jewish Community Centre of Greenwood Lake, accepted the invitation of Sheik Tosun Bayrak, spiritual leader of The Mosque of the Jerrahi Order of Dervishes in Chestnut Ridge, for our members to be guests at one of his congregation's community dinners on the Muslim holy day. And it was on that Friday evening the Jerrahi spiritual connection with JCC came into being.

I arrived right on time, parked my car in the street, removed the CD I'd been listening to, and opened the door. As I was getting out, Gary and Joanne Birnberg pulled up and parked five cars behind me. As we started to walk together toward the mosque, Pat Weisslander drove by and honked for us to wait while she tried to find a spot on the next street. Two minutes later, she joined us and, as we approached the gate to the Jerrahi's property, we recognized several cars owned by other JCC members parked very close to it. They had to have arrived very early to have found such good spots because, within two blocks around, every street was packed with scores of other cars – the cars, we knew, that belonged to the Dervishes.

We walked through the gate, and once inside, saw not just the mosque but a whole compound of buildings with dozens of people about. Two or three seemed to immediately know who we were, greeted us warmly, and led us to the mosque's front door. In some ways, it reminded me of JCC's building; incredibly friendly and welcoming, rustic and quaint, but it was freshly painted, much better maintained, and the grounds beautifully landscaped. We could tell straight away that The Mosque of the Jerrahi Order of Dervishes was a very large and very prosperous congregation. There was a line to get in because the people ahead of us, as they entered, paused in the vestibule to remove their shoes and place them in bins that were there for that purpose. I had been in mosques before, with my brother-in-law in Louisiana, and well knew the etiquette. As we waited, I started removing my shoes too. But in this mosque, right away, I sensed a mood that was wonderfully different; almost overwhelmingly gracious and inviting.

A Pakistani man in the vestibule who'd been expecting us approached me and asked, "Are you Mr. Grossman, president of the Greenwood Lake Jewish Centre?" He must have recognized my Bukharin yarmulke.

When I answered that I was, his eyes sparkled, he smiled and grasped my hand. Not letting go, he said, "Mr. Grossman, we are honored and delighted that you and your congregation could come. If there's anything you need, anything at all, or if you have any questions, tell me at once and I'll do everything I can to help you."

I smiled back and told him I was fine.

Then he said, "Please follow me inside. Sheik Tosun Bayrak wants to meet you."

The place was gorgeous; plush, richly dyed carpets on the floors, oak-paneled ceilings arching higher than even JCC's, odd corners and passageways, and a huge main room with doors leading to other large rooms, and a library. Including the JCC contingent, there must have been more than one hundred people there, many dressed in dazzlingly colored Indian or Arab-style clothing. There were three levels. The main room was the sanctuary where the men began seating themselves cross-legged on the plush, rich carpeting. Sunken a few steps below it and separated by a low banister was an area like a synagogue's *Bimah*, a pulpit, known in Arabic as a *minbar*, where the sheik and others would perform the Islamic religious rituals. On the floor in that area, fifteen of the men had seated themselves in a tight circle and were chanting. Above the main room was a spacious balcony that extended nearly halfway toward the *minbar*. I could see it was for women only, many of whom were already waiting there for the other women present to join them.

Pat said, "I'm not used to this. Are they going to make me sit up there, in the back too?"

I said, "Pat, come on! We're guests here. Your view from the balcony will be better than from anyplace else, so don't say anything to offend anyone." But I started to smirk; I couldn't help it. "Besides," I kidded, "whose idea was it to treat women as equals at JCC and let them sit with the men in the first place? I like the way they do things here better. I think women belong in the back at JCC too."

She said, "You're lucky Bonnie, your Temple Wife's not here. If she was, you'd be missing three teeth by now. And if your wife was here, you'd be missing all of them." She grabbed Joanne and headed upstairs.

I knew Rabbi Modek had planned to arrive early but I couldn't find him. I asked Gary Birnberg, "Have you seen Reuben? He was supposed to be here already."

He said, pointing to the ritual area, "He's right there, Mike. Look!"

I did but I couldn't pick him out. All I saw and all I heard were the Dervishes chanting!

Actually, they were doing more than chanting. Their bodies swayed. Their eyes were shut. There was joy, no, rapture etched on their faces. They were in the throes, I could see, of some sort of intense ecstasy. They were One! Their mantra had taken them to a spiritual level that their souls, I imagined, in their circle could touch, but we on the outside could only guess about. "Look where?" I said to Gary.

"There," he answered, "he's right in front of you."

I scanned the ritual area again but still didn't see him.

All fifteen of the chanting men were dressed with Middle Eastern-type prayer caps pulled down on their heads. These head coverings were deeper and covered much more area than the traditional Jewish yarmulkes. But in size, in shape, and in style, they looked almost the same as the Bukharin yarmulkes we had taken to wearing at JCC; except for their color: they were all dazzling pure white. That is, all but one of them, and that one, I was sure, I had seen hundreds of times before. As my eyes scanned the circle, finally they stopped, and I found myself staring at a cap that was multi-colored and bright. It was patterned with red, blue, gold, and purple. It was almost identical to the one I was wearing. The one that had been given to me *by* ... And then, all at once, I recognized who was wearing it. – I saw!

But what I saw, I couldn't believe, and that's why earlier, it just hadn't registered. He was *with* them. He was *at one* with them. His chants were *theirs* and their chants were *his*. They swayed *together*. They *felt* together. They were *in ecstasy together*. I had thought he was another Dervish praying – that is, chanting – with the others. But now there was no mistaking it. The man who I saw, the man wearing the yarmulke that was red, blue, purple, and gold, was my friend, JCC's religious leader, Rabbi Reuben Modek. Of course, he couldn't see me; he was in another place, on another level. He had connected with the Dervishes and they, along with him, had connected with something transcendent, the unknowable – With God? I thought to myself, "I'd been right about Reuben all along." From the moment I'd met him I'd known he was truly a spiritual man.

I watched him, watched all of them for a couple minutes, fascinated. But, before they were done, the Pakistani man who had spoken to me earlier tapped my shoulder and said, "Let's go see Sheik Bayrak now. He wants to speak with you for a while before the formal services begin." Without Reuben to accompany me, I was a little nervous. I hoped to God the sheik wasn't going to start in with a discussion of the Middle East and the folly of the U.S. continuing to support Israel. And that was a real possibility. I knew he was Turkish and, when younger, had vehemently resisted, politically, the Israelis in the 1950s. But I hoped, even more, he wasn't going to insist that I start chanting with him. The Pakistani man brought me to a small and modest, but when I looked inside, elegant office. He showed me in.

"Welcome, Mr. Grossman. May Allah smile upon you, always. How wonderful for you and your congregation to come. I feel that I already know the Greenwood Lake Synagogue a little because Rabbi Modek speaks of it so often and so warmly. And of its members and you." His accent was heavy but it didn't matter. Here, I could tell, was another spiritual man.

I wasn't sure if it was appropriate, but I extended my hand. He grasped it and shook it strongly.

I said, "Sheik Bayrak, I've been looking forward to this visit for a long time. It is an honor to meet you. I can't wait to observe the services here. If they're anything like what I've already seen, it's going to be quite an experience."

"Observe?" he said. "I hope you'll do much more. I hope you'll feel comfortable enough to participate, like your wonderful rabbi."

I replied, "Well, this is going to be quite a learning experience for me. I've been in mosques before, but I'm still not familiar with the Islamic prayers and rituals."

He said, "I have a feeling you may know a lot more than you think. Come, we'll talk some more later. But now, I'm being signaled that they're ready to begin."

And with that, he and I, accompanied by two of his assistants, went back to the main room. The sheik joined the chanting men in the ritual area but he, with his assistants, sat on a platform raised slightly above and forward of them. I headed to the sanctuary and sat, as comfortably as I could, cross-legged with the other men from JCC on the thick, soft carpeting. There were no chairs. The Dervish men surrounded us. The women looked on from above.

Respectfully, Reuben withdrew from the ritual area and circle of chanting men. And then, seamlessly, almost unnoticed, the chanting grew softer. Then softer. The sheik chanted too, still softer. I tensed. I knew they were building to something, preparing us for something. But what? The chants grew softer. Even softer. Then suddenly, simultaneously with the chanting, sheik Bayrak began singing, *began calling*, in Arabic verses while all of the Dervishes threw themselves onto hands and knees and leaned forward to touch the rich carpeting with their faces. They were so ardent that Gary and I were almost swept up with them and had to resist positioning ourselves that way too; even though we knew, as non-Muslims and Jews, no one expected us nor were we, even inside the mosque, required to. Although a little alien to us, the mood and the ardor were not, contrary to what I had anticipated, the least bit frightening or threatening. We got used to the Jerrahis' intensity and, as we did, the melodic Arabic verses became soothing and comforting, almost hypnotic. As I looked at the faces around the room, I noticed, for the first time, that a good third of them were not Arab, Indian, or Pakistani, but white. Almost all of those, I realized, had to be former Christians or Jews and, at the churches and synagogues I had visited, including my own, I'd seldom seen worshipers with as much passion and fervor as these. My attitude toward religion was not nearly as zealous. I had learned and was still learning a great deal from religion, and I had never read so much history, philosophy, and theology in my life. But I never got lost in religion, that is, gave myself to it, as these people did. I couldn't. I was too skeptical, too unconvinced to let myself go.

Even so, I knew what they were feeling and could appreciate it. The mood in the mosque was *releasing* and *healing*. It was almost trancelike. As they chanted, the Jerrahi were being *liberated* and *refreshed*. I couldn't and just didn't want to completely join in but the mood was so irresistible that some of it reached me, an outsider, and I felt *drawn* to and *compelled* by it too. So did all of us from JCC; strangers, but as the People of the Book, as close to their tradition – without actually being part of it – as any possibly could. The entire service, if that's what it was, was like that. It didn't seem structured; it flowed as the sheik called verse after verse. Occasionally, when he paused, one of his assistants would call a verse for him and the mood would continue unbroken. And then, after about thirty minutes, the chanting grew so soft it was a whisper. Then, slowly softer. There was silence. We had to shake ourselves to stir our minds and bodies from the dream like spell that had filled the room. As if to help, one of the sheik's assistants called out, "The evening meal is now being served." And with that, all the Jerrahi rose to their feet, waited graciously until everyone from JCC had risen too, and escorted us into the dining room.

I tell you, the moment we stepped into that room, every one of us from JCC was treated at least like a foreign dignitary, and Reuben and I like visiting prime ministers. They sat us in places of honor, on plush cushions at long, low tables, with Sheik Bayrak between Reuben and me and the mosque's other leaders alongside us. Prayers were said, food and non-alcoholic drinks were served, and they made sure our plates were filled before anyone else's. Before we began eating, I remembered that I had recognized one of the Jerrahi woman, the one who was formerly Jewish, had converted to Islam, and been our guest speaker at JCC months ago, in the sanctuary on the balcony. I looked around for her in the dining room because I wanted to say hello and pick up our conversation where we had left off. But when I spotted her, I realized that, like in the sanctuary, the men and women just didn't mix, and there was a separate area designated for only women to dine in. It wasn't exactly roped or curtained off from where the men were, but the moment I glanced in her direction and turned as though to take a step toward her, I was stopped, not by words, but by the entire Jerrahi congregation's body language. It was simply not customary and would have been totally inappropriate for a male to socialize with any Jerrahi woman in the mosque unless he was married to her. Also, for me to have left my seat of honor next to the sheik to speak to anyone, especially a woman, would most likely have been taken as extremely rude and an insult by him. So the second I rose, I had the good sense to sit right back down. It sunk in that I wasn't at a social or mixer that just happened to be taking place in a mosque, but at an important inter-religious event at which, as president of JCC, aside from Rabbi Modek, I was the most visible representative of my congregation.

I turned to Sheik Bayrak, who was speaking intently with Reuben. As I remember, their conversation went something like this:

The Sheik said, "You know, Reuben, the struggle in the Middle East is about land more than religion or ideology. The area shared by the Palestinians and the Israelis is so tiny that every hundred yards, no matter how barren, is significant and valuable. Although there are many cultural differences, and dangerous religious fanatics on both sides, mainstream Islam and Judaism are so similar as spiritual and ethical systems in mood and outlook, there is no reason, philosophically, for them to be at odds with one another."

Sheik Bayrak was in his seventies, old enough to be Rabbi Modek's father. Therefore, he called the rabbi "Reuben," whereas Reuben, out of genuine respect, always addressed him as "Sheik Bayrak."

"Sheik Bayrak," Reuben said, "I agree. It is about land, at least partly. But whether it's about land or ideology doesn't make it any less bloody. How can Arafat keep rejecting Clinton and Ehud Barak's proposals which will give the Palestinians 95 percent of the West Bank and half of Jerusalem?"

"It's those few hundred yards here and few hundred yards there," the sheik said. "Like the Israelis, the Palestinians believe they are fighting for their very lives and need every inch of land they can get for their survival. They feel that the Jews have already taken the best land, will never give any of it back, and that the settlers are taking still more. With nearly 2 million Palestinian refugees out there, many of whom want to be repatriated, the Palestinian leadership has to get enough land to make room for them."

"I know. But most of those settlements can and, I bet, will be dismantled if Arafat would only do something to convince the Israelis that the Palestinians are prepared to live alongside them in real peace. Instead, Barak makes a proposal, Arafat says 'No.' Barak makes another proposal and Arafat still says 'No.' Barak makes more proposals and Arafat says 'No' again and again and winks approval when there are new suicide bombings. Where's his toning down of the rhetoric of murder? Where are his counter-proposals? When will he stop inciting mass hatred? Where's his plan to dismantle the terrorist groups? Where's his map of an Israel, of one even much smaller than exists today, with defensible borders? I tell you, Sheik Bayrak, if Arafat offered real peace, the Israelis would have to close down the settlements and turn over East Jerusalem, like it or not. America would force them to...."

And so the discussion went. Like the conflict itself, it seemed their debate might go on forever. But at least it was open and honest and, most important, never angry or personal. Legitimate points had been raised on both sides and the two religious leaders did not, even for a moment, lose respect for one another or stop trying to view the conflict through the other's eyes. And they were in total agreement on at least one very crucial thing: The conflict had to be resolved peacefully; there was simply no other way. The cycle of attacks and counter-attacks was accomplishing nothing other than increasing the misery and desperation of both peoples.

Michael Grossman

In Jewish eyes, devastating military responses to suicide bombings were almost always justified even when, unintentionally on occasion, innocent civilians were killed along with their terrorist targets. Not surprisingly, the Palestinian Arabs saw it differently. In their eyes, suicide bombings, being the only effective weapon they have against the much more powerful Israelis, were a justified means of driving a militarily superior occupier from their lands. And the occupiers to them were not only the Israeli army but also Israeli civilians. On the other hand, of course, the Jews didn't just appear by magic one day and dispossess every Arab in sight. Six million Jews had been murdered by the Nazis and their collaborators during World War II, while the world watched and did nothing. In fact, one out of every three then living Jews died in the concentration camps. So as soon as hostilities ceased, they began fleeing Europe – atrocities had been committed not only by Germans, but by Poles, Austrians, and to a lesser extent Russians and French – for their ancient homeland in a last-ditch effort to preserve, they believed, their very existence. The Jews living in Palestine before 1948, the year World War II ended and when it was still a British mandate, had agreed to accept a homeland less than three-quarters the size of what Israel is today, much of the territory for which they had purchased or were negotiating for. And the territory they agreed to accept entirely excluded Jerusalem, which was supposed to become an "international city" under United Nations control. The Jews, however, were rebuffed by the entire Arab world. Every surrounding Arab nation, all five of which coveted the territory of Palestine for themselves, declared war on Israel the same day it declared independence, May 14, 1948, in an effort to grab chunks of land by force so they could extend their own borders. - Not just at the expense of the few hundred thousand Jews at the time but at the expense of *the 2 million Palestinians!*

The sheik and Rabbi Modek would have kept talking all night, except for the fact that the last dinner dish, dessert, and cup of coffee had been served and consumed. Dinner was over and people were starting to clear the tables, fold up the chairs, and put away the tablecloths. As that was happening, an official of the mosque went from table to table and began guiding each guest from JCC into a large adjoining room, where Sheik Bayrak was going to speak about the shared origins and monotheistic spiritual vision of Islam and Judaism. All the Muslim men took places cross-legged on the thickly carpeted floor, facing the sheik while he, alone among the Jerrahi, sat in front of them on an elaborate, deeply cushioned, mahogany chair at one end of the long, rectangular room. The women sat behind the men, although the Jewish ones were provided with low benches. The mosque official who had escorted us from the dining area then seated Rabbi Modek in a wooden chair alongside the sheik's, and the rest of the men from JCC in similar chairs, in a row alongside Reuben's. The room became silent. The sheik began.

His talk was not really a talk but a sermon consisting of quotations from the Koran, and some from the Tanach, arranged to tell a parable about how to live righteously, with his own observations woven in. His sermon was compelling but often confusing and very difficult to follow – not the least because he frequently switched from English to Arabic and forgot, seemingly, to switch back until one of his assistants gently reminded him. It was a good thing for everyone that the assistants were on their toes and kept it mostly in English, because it was apparent that the majority of the Jerrahi congregants were not that Arabic-fluent, just as the majority of congregants at JCC were not that Hebrew-fluent. Arabic, the language of Muhammad, occupies the same place in the Islamic world that Hebrew occupies in the Judaic world: it is the holy language and everyone takes a stab at trying to master it. In fact, while the sheik was delivering his sermon, I noticed that more than a few of the Jerrahi were making an effort to carefully follow along using Korans printed in Arabic with English transliterations for each *sura* printed below. And there were full English translations on the opposite pages. Sound familiar? That's sure how my Hebrew *siddur* looks.

Sheik Bayrak spoke for some forty-five minutes and concluded his sermon, compassionately, by honoring his Jewish guests with the same beautiful blessing he had greeted me with soon after I had entered the mosque and met him in his elegant little office. He said, first looking to his right to take in all the JCC men seated on the wooden chairs, and then straight ahead over the cross-legged Jerrahi on the plush carpeting, to take in the Jewish women seated on the low benches in the back, "To our Jewish brothers and sisters, we are deeply honored by your presence. May Allah smile upon you. Always."

And with that, the president of the Jerrahi Mosque, David Gulali, introduced Rabbi Reuben Modek to the assemblage. It was now Reuben's turn to speak, but before he said a single word, the whole Jerrahi audience, almost in unison, smiled up at him, remembering how he had joined the circle of fifteen chanting Dervishes in the ritual area and become spiritually *at one* with them, *in ecstasy* with them and, through those fifteen, *at one* with the entire Jerrahi congregation. Reuben smiled back, equally warmly, and began.

I can't write down here accurately exactly what Rabbi Modek said, because for some reason, surprisingly, I just can't remember his words very well. Even more surprisingly, neither can Reuben. I've asked him. The reason, I think, is because it wasn't precisely what he said that so impressed everyone, but how what he said was received. Having so intimately connected with the Jerrahi earlier, via the circle of chanting men, Reuben found himself addressing an audience so favorably disposed toward him, so spiritually linked with him, that they would have wildly approved of just about anything he had to say, as long as it wasn't too political. Reuben knew that and when he spoke, he hit a perfect home run. The gist of what he said really was simply a plea for deeper understanding between religions, a hope for justice between Muslin and Jew, and an unmistakable declaration of respect for our Muslim co-monotheists. He began by introducing himself as a fellow truth-seeker during the few years' journey each of us is granted on earth, and he ended with the thundering words of Amos: "…Let justice rush down like waters, and righteousness like a mighty stream."

The audience, if they had been able, would have applauded and cheered wildly for all they were worth. As it was, given the etiquette required at a mosque, they beamed up their esteem for Rabbi Modek by the admiring and respectful expressions on their faces instead. And on some faces there were tears of joy. Somehow, Reuben had reached across the built-in political divide between Muslim and Jew, particularly between Arab-Muslim and Jew, to the very core of what the religions of our shared forefather, Abraham, are really about: "that every human life must be considered sacred because a spark of the divine dwells in each of us." And that was the mood in the place when Rabbi Modek finished. People were so enthralled with it that no one wanted to be the first to get up and break the spell. Finally, people began to stir. The Pakistani man who had greeted me when I first entered the mosque – it seemed like a week ago – approached me and said, "However you define God, Mr. Grossman, the purpose of religion I think is to make that divine spark Rabbi Modek spoke about glow brightly. Don't you agree?"

I did. And that mutual realization is what I've come to call "The Jerrahi spiritual connection with JCC."

There was only one discordant note. As we were saying goodbyes to the Jerrahi and thanking them, in particular Sheik Tosun Bayrak, I warmly shook his hand and said, "Thank you, Sheik Bayrak, for your hospitality and making us feel so welcome. If it's okay, I'd like to speak to your president, Mr. Gulali, and try to schedule a date for your congregation to come visit us at JCC, so we can return the favor."

He said, "Please do. That will be a wonderful and much-looked-forward-to event, and I'm sure many of our members will want to attend."

I replied, "I hope your members will come away from our synagogue with as favorable an impression of Judaism as we have of Islam, due to your hospitality and kind words."

He said, "I hope so too."

But then he added, "But, you know, I think all people are Muslims at heart, only some just don't know it yet."

That didn't sit right at all. It made me realize that maybe he didn't think Judaism was as equally valid as Islam. The Koran in fact says as much. I could only imagine how he would have reacted if I had said, "You know, all people are Jews at heart, only some don't understand that yet." I'm sure he'd have resented it and been offended, deeply.

Nevertheless, the overall experience with the Jerrahi, including and especially with Sheik Bayrak, had been so positive and so enlightening that I walked away from their mosque with newfound faith in the morality and good intentions of the human race.

Chapter Twenty - We Already Live in the Promised Land

When I think of God's promises to Abraham, Jacob, Isaac, and Moses, I think of a place that could only come true in a dream:

> The Lord said to Abram, "Go forth from your native land and
> from your father's house to a land that I will show you.
> I will make of you a great nation,
> And I will bless you;
> I will make your name great,
> And you shall be a blessing:
> I will bless those who bless you,
> And curse him that curses you;
> All the families of the earth
> Shall bless themselves by you." Genesis 12:1-3

And the Lord said to Abram..
"Raise your eyes and look out from where you are, to the north and the south, to the east and the west, for I give all the land that you see to you and your offspring forever. I will make your offspring as the dust of the earth, so that if one can count the dust of the earth, then your offspring too can be counted. Up, walk about the land, through its length and its breadth, for I give it to you." Genesis 13:14-17

The Lord had appeared [to Isaac] and said,
"Reside in this land, and I will be with you and bless you; I will give these lands to you and your offspring, fulfilling the oath that I swore to your father Abraham. I will make your descendents as numerous as the stars of heaven, and give to your descendents all these lands, so that all the nations of the earth shall bless themselves by your offspring - …." Genesis 26:2-4

And the Lord stood beside Jacob and said, "I am the Lord, the God of your father Abraham and the God of Isaac: the ground on which you are lying I will give to you and your offspring.
Remember, I am with you: I will protect you wherever you go and will bring you back to this land. I will not leave you until I have done what I promised you." Genesis 28:13, 15

God said to him,
"You whose name is Jacob,
You shall be called Jacob no more.

But Israel shall be your name."
And God said to him,
"I am El Shaddai [Almighty God].
Be fertile and increase;
A nation, yea an assembly of nations,
Shall descend from you;
Kings shall issue from your loins." Genesis 35:10-11

God called out to him from the bush: "Moses! Moses!"
He answered, "Here I am."
And God said, "Do not come closer. Remove your sandals from your feet, for the place on which you stand is holy ground.
"I am," He said, "the God of your fathers, the God of Abraham, the God of Isaac, and the God of Jacob."
And Moses hid his face, for he was afraid to look at God.
And the Lord continued, "I have marked well the plight of My people in Egypt and have heeded their outcry because of their taskmasters; yes, I am mindful of their sufferings. I have come down to rescue them from the Egyptians and to bring them out of that land to a good and spacious land, a land flowing with milk and honey......" Exodus 3:4-8

A place like the one described in the scriptures and promised to our forefathers, with borders reaching out to the horizons – "Raise your eyes and look out from where you are …I give all the land that you see to you and your offspring forever"; led by rulers destined to be righteous – "A nation, yea, an assembly of nations shall descend from you; Kings shall issue from your loins"; fabulously rich and prosperous – "….a land flowing with milk and honey"; and forever divinely blessed – "Remember I am with you. I will protect you wherever you go…" is not just some dreamlike paradise – a non-existent Eden – like the one described in Genesis. Nor is it a mere fantasy that has dwelled in the human imagination as a forlorn hope since we first began living together in groups because we were desperate for comfort and companionship. Such a place really exists, right now, and has been, since its founding, a "light unto nations." And, no, I'm not talking about Israel.

It is a country that is not based on religion, race, national origins, or ethnicity. To become a citizen there, those things are irrelevant. Its inhabitants practice all religions. Nor are they predominantly Scandinavian, Polish, Hispanic, Russian, Indian, Italian, Oriental, Hungarian, African, or even English. Its people come from everywhere. America, rather, is an idea. – An idea so wonderful and so powerful, but also so radical and against the grain of history that it must be vigorously and vigilantly guarded, with our very lives if necessary, by each generation. It is an idea that must be continuously emblazoned into America's institutions and the hearts and minds of its citizens or the force that holds us together, as the mightiest, wealthiest, freest, and most creative society ever to arise on the planet will shatter. In a word, that idea, that force, is simply this: *tolerance*. Not tolerance meaning just a grudging, hostile acknowledgement of different peoples, their lifestyles, and opinions, but tolerance meaning a genuine acceptance, heartfelt respect for, even admiration for those differences – in fact, a celebration of and rejoicing in them. In truth, if America has a national religion, it is not Christianity or Judaism or some Judeo-Christian combination of the two, but the very idea of "freedom to always do and be what we please," that is, of *tolerance* itself. Unlike huge tracts of our planet, America, thank God, does not preach hatred toward those who are different, but instead has built a civil society dedicated to protecting them. George Washington, considered by many as the single most important individual in American history, perhaps put it best when he wrote, in 1790, to the Jewish community in Newport, Rhode Island:

> "May the children of the stock of Abraham continue to merit and enjoy the good will of the other inhabitants of this land, while everyone shall sit in safety under his own vine and fig tree, and there shall be none to make him afraid."

Of all the countries in the world, America was the first to have recognized Jews under its laws as absolute equals with all other citizens. Moreover, we didn't have to fight for that recognition. Here, it was freely and unreservedly given. At the time of the American Revolution, there were only 2,000 Jews living in the colonies, the vast majority of whom were descendents of Jews who had been part of the Spanish Expulsion in 1492, with a large community of them having settled in Newport, Rhode Island. The collective memory of that community was of having been cruelly set upon by their Spanish countrymen and ultimately of being brought before the Inquisition and forcibly converted or, if they refused, executed or expelled. But in America, Washington hoped that he could establish "a government...which gives bigotry no sanction ... persecution no assistance, and requires only that they who live under its protection should demean themselves as good citizens." With that type of government in the making, for Jews and oppressed minorities everywhere, America was indeed the Promised Land. What Washington wrote was part of his reply to a letter he received from the Newport Jewish community that said: "Deprived as we heretofore have been of the individual rights of free citizens, . . . we now behold a Government erected by the majesty of the people . . .whose basis is philanthropy, mutual confidence, and public virtue." If only Washington's largesse from the outset had extended to blacks and Native Americans as well, the scar of our nation's mistreatment of those groups might not weigh so heavily upon us. It is only in the last decade or so that the wound seems to have healed a bit and at last begun to fade. Despite any shortcomings, however, it is undeniable that the principle that animates America is "equal rights for all and everyone," regardless of who they are, where they come from, or what they believe. The only right that all do not have is to deprive any of their right to equality; that is, Americans may be anything but intolerant.

The first openly practicing Jews in the New World arrived in South America in the early 1500s. They were descendents of refugees from the expulsions from England in 1290, from France in 1306 and 1394, from Spain in 1492, and from Portugal in 1496. Prior to coming to the New World, those refugees had settled peaceably for a while in Poland, Germany, and Italy but were, starting in the late 1200s, being segregated into ghettoes, although that word would not come into use until the sixteenth century. From the ghettoes and the few still-tolerable enclaves in the Netherlands, a small group gathered in London, where they leased a ship which transported them to Recife, Brazil. Recife was first settled about 1535, captured by the English in 1595, and occupied by the Dutch in 1630. In Recife, the Jews prospered and were safe until Portugal began expelling its Jewish citizens in 1496 and the Portuguese sovereigns decided to extend their anti-Semitic policies and the Inquisition to the New World. When Portugal took control of Brazil in 1654, the Recife Jews hung on for a while but, by the end of that year, many saw the handwriting on the wall and twenty-three persuaded a French ship to bring them to the Dutch town of New Amsterdam, which would soon become New York. One of the passengers was Asser Levy, their leader, and after disembarking, he was confronted by the New Amsterdam governor, none other than one-legged Peter Stuyvesant, who vehemently protested to the Dutch West India Company against permitting the Jews to remain. He called them "a deceitful race" whose "abominable religion" worshipped at the "the feet of mammon." The relatively enlightened Dutch government, however, and the Dutch West India Company, heavily dependent on Jewish investors in Europe, blocked him due largely to Levy's skillful negotiations. The Jews were, nonetheless, denied citizenship and forbidden to build a synagogue. But when the British seized New Amsterdam in 1664 and it became New York, the new regime, whose policies were later confirmed by King Charles II, decided to grant Jews all the rights of citizenship "so long as they demean themselves peaceably and quietly, with due obedience to His Majesty's laws and without scandal to his government." Despite this auspicious start, some of the earliest colonial statutes, while stressing religious liberty, granted full equality only "to those who profess Christianity." Fortunately, those laws were never actually enforced, and the Jews simply blended into the populace, enjoyed rights, voted, ran for office, sometimes won, and prospered like everyone else.

In the New World, in at least one respect, the Jews had an advantage. They never made the assumption — often made by the Christian majority — that there was an absolute distinction between the high ethics set forth in the Bible on the one hand and the much-less-lofty ethics that frequently characterized business bookkeeping and business practices on the other. Rabbinical Judaism said things about business – "profits are to be shared with those who earn them," "workers are always to be paid promptly and in full," "their health is to be safeguarded," "they are to be treated with dignity and honor," and "they [and even animals] shall not work on the Sabbath," for example – which all sensible men knew to be true and just, but which convention and outright hypocrisy normally excluded from the realm of everyday business discourse. The Jews, however, tried to practice in their business dealings what they preached in their synagogues, though that attitude was not entirely selfless. Due to their minute minority and, therefore, very vulnerable status, the New World Jews felt their business ethics had to be above question, lest their undeserved Old World reputation as "dishonest moneylenders" and "unscrupulous international traders" envelop them in the New World too. Jews, therefore, were in a frame of mind that made them extraordinarily well-prepared psychologically to take honest advantage of the vast growth in the world economy which marked the sixteenth century. Indeed, in view of their brutal expulsion from the Spanish peninsula and their mistreatment in Reformation and Counter-Reformation Europe, they had no alternative but to push the Diaspora as far into the New World as possible so they could seek new opportunities there for their business skills wherever they'd be accepted. They had no intention of "cheating around the edges" and blowing their chances. They were incredibly successful, and Columbus's voyages to the West were not the only ones which had a Jewish background in business ethics, practices, finance, and technology. That many of Columbus's crew were Marranos or Conversos, by the way, is well known and beyond question. Expelled Jews voyaged to all the Americas – North, Central, and South – and were among the earliest merchants to flourish and prosper. Spanish laws forbidding them to immigrate to the colonies proved ineffective and were repealed in 1577. They set up successful factories, stores, and trading posts everywhere they landed. In St. Thomas, for instance, they became the first large-scale plantation owners. Jews and Marranos were particularly active in settling Brazil; the first governor-general in fact, Thomas de Souza, sent there in 1549, was of Jewish origin. They owned many of the sugar plantations in South America and the West Indies, they controlled the trade in precious and semi-precious stones, and Jews expelled from Brazil in 1654 helped to create the sugar industry in Barbados and Jamaica. In particular, the British colonies in the New World welcomed them. The governor of Jamaica, rejecting a petition for their expulsion in 1671, wrote he was of the opinion that "His Majesty could not have more profitable subjects than Jews and the Hollanders (Dutch); they had great stocks and correspondence." The governor in Surinam pronounced: "We have found the Hebrew nation ...have ... proved themselves useful and beneficial to the colony."

One of the reasons religious tolerance, *not intolerance*, was rampant in the New World was that many of the earliest pilgrims were themselves Puritan refugees escaping religious persecution in England and other countries back in Europe. Many viewed their emigration from England as a virtual reenactment of the Jewish exodus from Egypt. The Atlantic was their Red Sea and the Indians their ancient Canaanite enemies. They believed themselves to be the new Israelites, entering a new covenant with God, in a new Promised Land. As devout Christians, they probably had no great affection for Jews, but the analogy of Jewish history to their own experience in "escaping" from England was so close that it prevented rampant anti-Semitism from taking root. Wrote Gabriel Sivan in *The Bible and Civilization:*

> No Christian community in history identified more with the People of the Book than did the early settlers of Massachusetts Bay Colony, who believed their own lives to be a literal reenactment of the Hebrew nation...these émigré Puritans dramatized their own situation as the righteous remnant of the Church corrupted by the "Babylonian woe," and saw themselves as instruments of Divine Providence, a people chosen to build their new Commonwealth on the Covenant entered into at Mount Sinai.

In 1655, the New Haven legislators adopted a legal code which contained seventy-nine statutes, half of which contained biblical references, virtually all from the Hebrew Bible. The Plymouth Colony had a similar law code, as did the Massachusetts assembly, which in 1641 adopted the so-called "Capitall Lawes of New England" based almost entirely on Mosaic Law. Thanksgiving, first celebrated in 1621, the year after the *Mayflower* landed, was initially conceived as a day parallel to Yom Kippur, the Jewish Day of Atonement. It was to be a time for fasting, introspection, and prayer. Even today, it retains some of its original mood – looking inward, counting our blessings, remembering friends and loved ones – and remains, by far, the most popular of American holidays. Just think of some of the others, Presidents' Day, Labor Day, Veterans' Day etc.; there's no comparison. It is, however, no longer nearly as serious a holiday as Yom Kippur has always has been.

Interestingly, the "vine and fig tree" reference by Washington, in his letter to the Jewish community of Rhode Island, comes from the Hebrew prophet, Micah, as he foretells a messianic utopia:

> "And he shall judge between many peoples, and shall decide concerning far away strong nations; and they shall beat their swords into plowshares, and their spears into pruning hooks; nation shall not lift up sword against nation, nor shall they learn war anymore [note here that Prophet Micah is using the famous phrase attributed to Prophet First Isaiah, who was his contemporary]. But they *shall sit every man under his vine and fig tree; and none shall make them afraid;* for the mouth of the Lord of hosts has spoken it." Micah 4: 3-4

The choice of these words on the part of Washington was not surprising in light of the enormous influence that the Hebrew Bible had on the Pilgrims and on the Founding Fathers of the new nation.

In 1776, fourteen years before Washington took office, the Jews' contribution to the Revolution was vital, though, as mentioned, only 2,000 of them were living in America. In Charleston, South Carolina, virtually every adult Jewish male fought on the side of freedom, and many lost their lives or suffered grievous wounds in battle. In Georgia, the first patriot to be killed was a Jew named Francis Salvador. The Jews also provided significant financing for the patriots, way out of proportion to their numbers. The most important of the financiers – Jewish and non-Jewish – was Haym Salomon, who lent the Continental Congress a fortune and then, in the last days of the war, advanced the American government $200,000 more which, back then, was an incredible sum. He was never paid back and died bankrupt. President Washington remembered the Jewish contribution when the first synagogue in America – the Sephardic Touro synagogue – opened in 1790 in Newport, Rhode Island, and he sent the congregation his famous letter.

In America, Jews were not the only group that found safe haven. Due to the protections against persecution enshrined in the Constitution via the First Amendment – *"Congress shall make no law respecting an establishment of religion, or prohibiting the free exercise thereof…"* – a diversity of denominations, offshoot sects, and religious practices spread like wildfire in the new nation. The depth and breadth of that religious diversity has been unrivaled anywhere else on Earth, with the possible exception of India. Catholic groupings, of course, and an avalanche of Protestant denominations arose first but, as the years passed, totally non-Western and non-Christian Baha'i, Buddhist, Hindu, Sikh, and Muslim congregations took root too. As has often happened throughout history, but not in the U.S., many of the most vicious religious conflicts involved schisms within the same faith. Wars between *Sunni* and *Shia* and Catholics and Protestants immediately come to mind. But here, even drastic and heretical deviations from mainstream Christianity, that is, attacks against the prevailing religious dogma from within by other Christians, have been abided including *Shakers*, who practiced total celibacy and "shook" in religious ecstasy, some say, to relieve their sexual tension; *Oneida Perfectionists*, who encouraged the abolition of marriage and urged frequent sexual encounters for both men and women as a means of "transcending the secret adultery of our hearts;" and *Mormons*, who are flourishing today and, during the first sixty years after Joseph Smith founded the Church of Latter Day Saints, practiced polygamy,[1] as did the ancient Hebrew patriarchs, in the hope of reviving the age of miracles and prophecy. One of the most interesting religious groups to flourish here and, I might add, the Christian sect closest in doctrine to Judaism, is the *Watch Tower Bible and Tract Society of Pennsylvania*, better known as *Jehovah's Witnesses*. I have firsthand, personal experience with the Witnesses, positive experience, and in the next chapter, we take a closer look at this notable group who, like the Jews, found a Promised Land in America.

Chapter Twenty One - Jumpin' Jehovahs

"No," I said. I found out that her name was Nelsy later. "I'm not interested in discussing 'Judgment Day' or anything else with you right now." It was summer 1994, about six months after my family and I had joined JCC.

She was with another Jehovah's Witness, very tall and very blonde, who put a copy of "Watchtower" in my mailbox anyway. She introduced herself, "I'm Julie."

I said, "You guys are relentless." I was at the top of my driveway, trying to apply asphalt sealant to some cracks. "Can't you see I'm busy?" I was covered with the stuff.

"You know, Mr. Grossman ..." Nelsy said. There was only a street number on my mailbox, and I was surprised she knew my name. "I know your wife pretty well. I run into her at the gym in town all the time. How is she?"

"Fine," I answered.

"Is she home?"

"No. In fact, I think she's at the gym right now."

"Well, please say hello for me and tell her my daughter, Melissa, can baby-sit for you tomorrow."

I remembered. "Wait a minute," I said. "I didn't know your daughter is Melissa. My kids are crazy about her. She's an absolute doll. She babysat for us a month ago also. Right?"

"No, that was Lauren, my younger daughter. Melissa babysat for you the month before that."

I could picture both sisters well. My kids, Aly and Zack, who were eight and five years old, couldn't stop talking about them. They had told me that the two girls not only took care of them but *loved them* – enveloped them with it. They could feel their kindness and, because of my kids, I could too. They read great stories to them, played all kinds of games with them, tickled and wrestled with them, even sang to them, before softly holding and tenderly kissing them, and then tucking them in, *dreaming*. From the way they spoke, I could tell that they weren't just crazy about Nelsy's daughters but loved them back, passionately. *That's why*, I realized, my kids had started to look forward so much to the nights Phyllis and I went out.

"Your daughters," I said, "are the most wonderful teenagers I've ever met. And now that I'm thinking, I remember meeting your husband when he dropped them off. Dave, right?"

"Yes. He and my girls say your kids are wonderful too. In fact, Lauren and Melissa were arguing last night over which one of them would get to baby-sit tomorrow. They both wanted to."

I wiped the tar from my hands and extended my right one. "I'm Mike. It's great to meet you."

"I'm Nelsy Ool. It's great to meet you too."

"You know, Nelsy, it's a good thing that Dave came by two weeks ago. I was in the foyer trying to hang a large painting but I couldn't hold it, stand on the ladder, and adjust the hook at the same time. Your husband said, 'You're gonna fall. That ladder's no good. Let me do it.' So he did. Except he didn't need a ladder. He's huge. How tall is he anyway?"

"Oh, he's a big boy. He's about 6'6" in his socks. In his work boots he's almost 6'8". I'm 5'4" so when I stand next to him it's like David and Goliath."

"Well, no wonder he could reach up there. And I think he was wearing those work boots when I saw him too. Tell Dave I said 'thank you' again. Okay?"

"I will, but I don't know if your wife told you, Dave and I are going to be here all day next Sunday to repaint Aly and Zack's bedrooms and hang your new wallpaper in the kitchen, bathrooms, and mud room. Phyllis hired us. We do that kind of work for a living and any other household maintenance or repair job you can think of. Melissa and Lauren will be with us to help. So if I forget, you can thank Dave then yourself."

I was impressed. Until that moment, I hadn't been sure whether Jehovah's Witnesses did anything really except try to preach to people in their driveways.

"Do you seal driveways?" I joked. I was still dripping tar.

"As a matter of fact," Nelsy said, "we do. We have the right equipment and can do the whole job in about twenty minutes. The way you're doing it, you'll be here for hours. Why don't you let us do it when we come by on Sunday?"

I was so relieved I didn't even ask her 'How much?' "It's a deal," I said.

Julie interjected, "We should let him get cleaned up before that stuff dries on him, Nelsy. You know, Mr. Grossman, it's in your hair and all over your face too. I think I see some in your mouth. It can't be good for you."

I said, tasting the tar on my lips, "Yeah. Thanks. I'd better get inside."

Julie said, "But the next time I make the rounds with Nelsy or other Witnesses, maybe you'll have time for some Bible discussion? Okay? See you later."

"Yeah," I said. "Later." But to myself I was thinking, "Yeah. Much later!"

It turned out that Nelsy and Dave's work was so professional and well-priced that we started using them whenever we needed anything done around the house. Once in a while, they brought Julie along to work with them. Over the years, after they finished wallpapering and painting the kids' bedrooms the first time, they painted Aly and Zack's bedrooms again, painted our bedroom and the guest room, painted the living room, family room, dining room, foyer, and the entire finished basement downstairs. In addition, they installed light fixtures, hung shelves, resealed and retiled the bathrooms, repaired cracked walls, and even replaced a large portion of the second-floor ceiling after I fell through it while I was in the attic and stepped off a beam onto the unsupported plasterboard. As I got to know Nelsy better, I found that she was one of the most genuinely kind, honest, and well-intentioned persons I had ever met. She took being a Jehovah's Witness very seriously and, in accordance with its teachings as she understood them, tried to be actively good. – By God's commandments, she felt, she was required to be good to everyone. For example, whenever she did a job for us, she always ended up doing way more than we had bargained for without complaint and without ever asking for more money. Sometimes she stopped by just to see if there was anything she could help us with. If there was, and it wasn't too big a deal, she would do it right then and there. No charge! She was tireless and very skilled. In truth, she did *Tzedakah* much more than I – a soon-to-be president of a synagogue – did. Her husband and daughters were very much like her. They were all overwhelmingly kind, helpful, and respectful. As we became friendlier and they got to know more about me, in particular my devotion to my synagogue, they even stopped preaching to me. Except, that is, on the few occasions when they just couldn't help themselves. For Jehovah's Witnesses, that was extremely hard to do.

Like almost all Witnesses, Nelsy, Dave, their friend Julie — and Melissa and Lauren to a much lesser extent — regarded themselves as ministers of their creed, and door-to-door and street-corner preaching as the most important mechanism by which to spread their teachings. They cherished prayer; they loved religious discussion; they rejoiced in being able to quote biblical passages apropos to almost any situation. But above all, they loved sermonizing. If they didn't or couldn't make time to preach, and often, and try to persuade some outsider or non-believer to join their Kingdom Hall, they felt almost as though they were sinning, and grew noticeably dejected. In fact, sometimes, when Nelsy and Dave were in my presence, I could see discouragement on their faces, because very early in our relationship, they realized I would not be receptive to their proselytizing and it still disappointed them. Their deep, core need to constantly try to win converts, as opposed to my much less ideological, yet intense interest in Judaism and Jewish history, created a distance between us that prevented our becoming really close or entirely at ease with each other. Nonetheless, we always held one another's point of view in high regard and, unexpectedly, shared more than a few interesting, exciting and, for me, eye-opening experiences together.

In June 1997, Julie invited Phyllis and me to attend her wedding at the Jehovah's Witness Kingdom Hall in Warwick. We arrived late and, as soon as we entered, sensed right away that we were the only non-Witnesses there. After taking a few steps through the front entrance, we found ourselves standing outside the main sanctuary, which was packed with people, in a medium-sized room immediately adjacent to and connected to it by large double doors. In there, we were alone with the bride and groom, the members of the wedding entourage, and a couple of ushers. One of the ushers told us to remain with the entourage and not to take seats in the sanctuary just yet, because the ceremony was going to begin in seconds and he didn't want us to get in the way of the procession. Everyone was waiting for the wedding music to begin, which would be the signal for the entourage to start marching into the sanctuary and the bride and groom up to the altar. Phyllis and I felt quite awkward because everyone else in the room, including the ushers, were relatives or extremely close friends of the groom or bride, and every single one of them was, it was obvious, a Jehovah's Witness. I was on my guard because, in the back of my mind, I had never been able to shake off, despite my friendship with Nelsy and my kids' affection for her daughters, my lifelong impression that the Witnesses were, in essence, just an oddball, overzealous cult. Our awkwardness was even greater because, not being part of the wedding entourage, we weren't even supposed to be in that room in the first place. We tried mightily to keep out from under foot, and hide, by pressing ourselves tightly up against a wall. The only spot available, however, was very close to, almost next to, Julie and her husband-to-be. Like almost anyone about to walk down the aisle, Julie, I could tell, had the jitters, and to relieve her tension, she began making small talk, not with her relatives or close friends, but with me. To my surprise, I was able to banter back and forth with her, comfortably, and succeeded, I think, in calming her nerves. – This woman who three years before had insisted on pushing a copy of "Watchtower" into my mailbox, despite my protests, and preaching to me. But I very much liked Julie. Phyllis and I were flattered that she had invited us.

The wedding music started. As the entire entourage took their places in the sanctuary, and as Julie and her groom made their way to the altar to stand before the Service Elder (minister), Phyllis and I, following behind them, at last found seats. We were careful to follow way, way behind them so that no one could possibly think we were part of the entourage. The ceremony began. It was incredibly contemporary and common-sensical, and had much less religious content than I'd expected. The minister was young, in his mid-forties at most, and 95 percent of what he said was advice about how to have a successful marriage, and not at all about Jehovah's Witness dogma, or any religious dogma, for that matter. In fact, the ceremony was so modern and unburdened by ritual that it moved along very quickly and, almost before we knew it, the vows were exchanged and Julie and her groom were pronounced husband and wife. Phyllis and I relaxed a bit. Our defensiveness about possibly being unwelcomely proselytized to began to ease. Then, someone announced, "Let's eat," and we all moved into a large adjoining room.

Very long lines formed at the buffet carts at once, even though more than half the guests had opted to wait out the first crowded rush of people for food, by immediately seating themselves at the dozen or so, ten-person tables that had been set up, instead of joining the lines right away. In fifteen minutes, after that first rush, the lines would be much shorter. Since Phyllis and I didn't know anybody, other than Julie, Nelsy, Dave, Melissa, and Lauren, and they weren't around for the moment, we decided to kill time by waiting in the longest of the lines, rather than attempting to strike up conversations with total strangers at one of the tables. The man standing in front of me, however, caught my eye. He looked vaguely familiar and I was pretty sure I had seen him around town a couple of times, probably preaching or handing out literature with Nelsy or Julie. He turned and introduced himself. It was obvious that he thought he recognized me too.

He said, "My name is Bob Wilson. I don't think I've seen you at this Temple before, but I know you're from around here, right?"

"Yes," I replied, "we live in Horizon Farms out near Pine Island. My name's Michael Grossman and this is my wife, Phyllis."

"Hello Phyllis," he said, "I know that neighborhood. I've been through there once or twice with Nelsy and David Ool. I saw you talking to them before as we were all leaving the sanctuary. Mr. Grossman, you and your wife look very familiar. Have we met?"

"I don't think so, but we know Dave and Nelsy well. In fact, that's why we're here. Nelsy is the one who introduced us to Julie about two years after we moved to Warwick, from the City, in 1992. And Nelsy and Dave, along with Julie once in a while, have been doing a lot of work around our house lately."

Bob said, "That's why you look so familiar. I don't remember exactly when but about two or three months ago I dropped Nelsy off where you live. She needed a ride because Dave had driven to your place way before her and arrived much earlier. We must have said hello to each other then."

Phyllis said, "Yes, I think I remember. That was the day Nelsy came over with five or six rolls of new wallpaper to hang. She brought them in your trunk."

Suddenly, the man standing in line behind me said, good-naturedly, "Hey, Bob, would you please move up. I love to talk too, but people have been cutting in front of us while you've been blabbing. And I'm hungry."

He continued, "Mr. and Mrs. Grossman – I overheard your names when you introduced yourselves to Bob – I'm William Kohler. I saw you listed on Julie's guest register. Other than some of the bride and groom's family members, you're the only people here I don't think I've met before. It's a pleasure. Which Kingdom Hall do you belong to? The one in Jersey? The one down in Rockland?"

I hesitated a little. But then, "Actually," I said, "we're not Witnesses. Phyllis and I are Jewish and we're members of the Jewish Community Centre Synagogue in Greenwood Lake. But Nelsy and Dave discuss religion with us all the time when they're working over at our house and, as a result, I've learned a great deal about The Watchtower Bible and Tract Society of Pennsylvania." Without hesitating for a breath, I reeled off, "It's the legal governing body of the Jehovah's Witnesses worldwide, and was founded in 1872 by Charles Taze Russell. The Society, as you know, was formally incorporated in 1884."

I wanted him to be aware that I was no easy mark and that I already knew a good deal about his religion. I was purposely trying to take away his thunder by showing off the knowledge I'd acquired, so as to back him off a bit if his intention was to start preaching at me to make me consider converting. And I anticipated that William Kohler or Bob Wilson might do just that. – Because that, bottom line, seemed to me to be the goal of every committed Witness. They wanted you to join up. If you gave them the slightest opening, they'd start preaching Bible to you till they completely wore you out. On the other hand, I remembered that Nelsy and Dave had basically given up trying with me, yet we still remained good friends. And their daughters, who never tried preaching to me, were two of the kindest and most gracious teenagers I had ever met. By their example – through actions, not words – they were the best advertisement for Jehovah's Witnesses I had ever seen. "Nelsy and Dave," I thought, "must be doing something right" and I never tired of telling them that.

So in my mind, I had bumped up against a conundrum. The problem was this: Were the Jehovah's Witnesses the fanatic cult I had always suspected them of being, based on their seemingly single-minded desire and incredibly organized campaign to convert everyone they encountered to their point of view? Or were they regular people, like almost all the rest of us, to whom religion was important – perhaps to Witnesses extraordinarily important – but not an all-consuming endeavor that made it impossible for them to accept other faiths as equally valid? The answer is, "I don't know." Sometimes, I feel that their tribal mentality rivals or exceeds even that of the Hasidim and makes it almost impossible for them to comfortably socialize with or relate to anyone except other Witnesses or with those who they feel are receptive to converting. And vice-versa, making it impossible for any non-Witness to comfortably socialize with or relate to them. In truth, I just don't know what their end game really is. But despite their tribalness, i.e., extreme cultishness, almost frightening intensity of purpose, and a number of unusual beliefs and practices, I can definitively say this: As a group, Jehovah's Witnesses are completely non-violent and, to the last man or woman, uncommonly gentle and kind.

Let's start with the unusual beliefs and practices. Jehovah's Witnesses consider the world and all its governments, as they currently exist, to be controlled by Satan and, therefore, do not run for public office, salute the flag, join the Armed Forces, or vote in elections. They do not celebrate their birthdays or any "worldly" holidays including Thanksgiving, July 4th, Veterans' Day, Memorial Day, Halloween, or even Christmas, and the penalty for doing so is disfellowship, i.e., excommunication. They are also, unquestionably, an extremely fundamentalist, conservative group and, as such, a sexist organization that does not treat women as equals. They regard only their version of the Bible as the infallible, revealed word of God, but their translation, called New World Translation of the Holy Scriptures, has been widely criticized by scholars, who charge that it distorts the original Hebrew and Greek texts to more closely match Jehovah's Witness theology. They demand that their members devote enormous amounts of their personal resources and thousands upon thousands of hours of their time to Kingdom Hall activities and Watchtower learning. Those who do not are visited by and disciplined by Elders. If they refuse to mend their ways, they are ultimately disfellowshipped and then shunned. There is no such thing as a Jehovah's Witness who, like so many of my Jewish friends, only shows up for the "High Holidays." On the medical side, they urge their members to refuse blood transfusions and not permit them for their children. They are also urged to discontinue chemotherapy treatments for Witness cancer patients when blood platelet transfusions become needed, and disapprove of the storing of one's own blood for later auto-transfusions. This is all based on biblical passages such as the following, which Witnesses interpret as prohibiting not only the eating of blood but the taking of it into their bodies in any way: "But flesh with...blood...ye shall not eat" (Genesis 9:4). "...No soul of you shall eat blood...whosoever eateth it shall be cut off" (Leviticus 17:12-14). Until 1952, based on these same passages, members were prohibited from getting vaccinations for polio, smallpox, mumps, measles, or any disease. It was believed that a vaccination was a violation of God's laws forbidding the taking of bloodlike fluids into the system. Even the Witnesses, however, backed off on that one. As to what's in store for the world in the future, Witnesses believe that very soon the battle of Armageddon will begin and Jesus, under Jehovah's divine rage, will exact vengeance upon the rest of Christendom and the followers of all other religions. Witnesses refer to other religions, including Judaism, as "Babylon the Great" or "The World Empire of False Religion." After much suffering and massive human extermination, the world will be purified of non-believers and God's Kingdom, a theocracy, will be established for 1,000 years. And also, as to the U.S. judicial system, Jehovah's Witnesses refuse to serve on juries, because they believe only God, not men, may judge human behavior. For this reason, although they must answer jury duty summonses like everyone else, they are invariably excused by the lawyers the moment they identify themselves as Witnesses.

So out of mainstream Christianity are the beliefs and practices of Jehovah's Witnesses that in many Christian circles there is controversy as to whether they are really part of Christendom at all or should be considered a separate, disapproved-of, religion. For example, they reject the Trinity concept of God and embrace an absolute monotheism. In this, they are closer to Judaism than they are to most Protestant denominations and, certainly, than they are to Catholicism. To Witnesses, God is Jehovah, the one and only Supreme Being, and they accept Jesus, not as God or an aspect of God, but as the Archangel Michael who, in his pre-human form, was God's son. Eventually, Michael took the form of a man and came to earth as Christ. As do most Christian churches, they teach that Satan constantly prowls the earth attempting to turn people against Jehovah, but they totally reject the traditional Christian view of hell. They believe that hell is just the common grave of mankind where people go when they die, not a pit of fire. People are not conscious there and experience no pain. Unbelievers simply cease to exist at death. Again, some of this is closer to Jewish thinking than to Christian. Witnesses do not have a Sabbath; all days are regarded as equally holy. They do not observe any of the traditional Christian holidays and recognize only one day of celebration: the Memorial of Christ's Death. And Jehovah's Witnesses outright reject the cross as a symbol of their religion, and the wearing of one is strictly forbidden. They base this on their translation of the Greek word from New Testament Scriptures, *stauros,* as "torture stake," and believe Jesus was crucified on a single upright wooden post with no cross beam.

On the other hand, many Jehovah's Witness practices and beliefs are not at all strange or extreme but overtly loving, kind, and admired, or at the very least, respected by nearly everyone. They are taught, for example, that racism and cruelty are unforgivable sins. In their relations with each other and with outsiders also, they strive mightily to be just and good. You know what I'm talking about because, like me, you've encountered them in your driveways or on street corners. You know how they are. They can be maddeningly persistent and annoying, but never impatient or rude. Their voices are invariably friendly, soft, and warm. Also, they are immensely charitable and generous, and will assist almost any needy person who asks – especially if he or she lets them preach to him or her a little. In addition, Jehovah's Witnesses, as a result of their own struggle for self-preservation, have contributed tremendously to the protection of religious freedom throughout the U.S. and, therefore, to the preservation of the civil rights of everyone. In fact, between 1938 and 1955, they won thirty-six out of forty-five religiously based cases in the U.S. Supreme Court and dozens more since then in lower courts around the country. But above all, the thing Jehovah's Witnesses are known for most is their total non-violence. Due to their basic pacifism and belief that all worldly governments are unjust, they will not voluntarily serve in the armed forces, nor assist in the war efforts of any country. If drafted, and thereby compelled to join the military, they are taught to go but to seek non-combat roles; in particular, as medics, cooks, secretaries, or counselors. Their resistance to military service and anti-war attitude crosses into their private lives. It is a rare day indeed when you will read that a practicing Jehovah's Witness has been arrested for any violent act. And, like the vast majority of Jews, they do not hunt. They will not spill the blood of any of God's creatures.

These thoughts about Witnesses filled my mind but, as I stood with them, try as I might, I couldn't completely relax. I couldn't help, despite my basically positive attitude toward them, being a little wary of their intentions.

After having waited in the food line for more than ten minutes, we finally reached the buffet carts. Bob, William, and I piled food high on our plates: roast beef, chicken, pasta, cheese, you name it. My wife, a health nut, took only salad and fruit. She looked over at what was on my plate and nearly fainted. She wasn't kosher but, in an effort to get me to eat healthier, zinged me by saying, "Boy, you say you're so interested in the synagogue and Judaism, but you don't watch what you eat at all. You're eating dairy and meat together and that's a no-no, it's not kosher. If you ate salads and fruits once in a while, you wouldn't have to worry about that. Fruits and vegetables are always kosher. And they're better for you anyway." To make her happy I laid some pineapple chunks on the side of my plate; but that was in addition to all the other stuff, although Phyllis forced me to put the cheese back and some of the meat.

I don't know what Bob and William thought about that exchange with my wife. All I know for sure is that they were amused by it. William said, as if to comfort me, "It's a good thing my wife's not here. If she was, she wouldn't let me eat half this stuff either."

Bob added, "Yeah, well, my wife is here, and if she sees anything on my plate other than very lean meat, fish, or vegetables, she'll make me stand on this line all over again. So I'm not taking any chances."

He decided to put everything fatty back except one large piece of Swiss cheese. And after thinking about it for a moment, he put that back too.

We spotted Nelsy and Dave sitting at a table off to the side. William, Phyllis, and I walked over to join them. Melissa and Lauren were there, as well as three others: a young, engaged couple who had been Witnesses all their lives but had moved to Pine Island, close to where Phyllis and I lived, and joined the Warwick Kingdom Hall only last month; and a woman in her mid-forties who, it turned out, had just very recently joined the Hall too. Before converting, she had been Lutheran, but so removed from any religious involvement, for so long, that she didn't know what being Lutheran meant anymore. She had been divorced for about a year, and her youngest son, her twenty-four-year-old, had finally moved out of the house four months ago and was gone. When that happened, she had been worried and scared. She was alone. A tight-knit, well-organized, and highly motivated group like the Jehovah's Witnesses was perfect for her. With them, she had found a new home and was glowing with excitement among her newfound "family."

Nelsy motioned for us to sit down. I ended up next to Barbara, the former Lutheran, with Nelsy sitting on the other side of her and Phyllis on the other side of me. On the other side of Nelsy was the engaged couple, with Dave and his daughters on the other side of them. On the other side of Phyllis was William Kohler, ten of us altogether. Barbara was addressing the group excitedly about some big building project the Jehovah's Witnesses were going to begin in nearby Middletown in a few months. I noticed that she assumed at once that Phyllis and I were Witnesses like everyone else, even though we were complete strangers to her and hadn't been introduced yet.

She said, "I can't wait for the new Kingdom Hall in Middletown to be finished. I love it here in Warwick, but that one will be only a five-minute drive from my house. I'll probably end up spending a lot of time there. Maybe as much as I do here."

Nelsy said to William, "Did you know that Barbara is an experienced house painter? She'll be able to help out when construction begins. Dave, me, and our girls are going to do some of the painting and a lot of the heavy carpentry work."

Roberta, the young wife, spoke up. "My husband, Doug, is an electrician for Warwick Valley Telephone and I think he's going to ..."

"Yes," Doug said, "the building committee has already asked me. I'll be in charge of the crew that's going to run all the wiring and install the fixtures."

The Reluctant Jew

Bob Wilson and his wife, Janice, walked over from the table they had been sitting at. He said, "Nelsy, I think this time Janice and I are going to volunteer for kitchen duty, the evening and late shifts. We're going to keep that kitchen going twenty-four hours a day and we'll probably get the whole building up in three weeks, as usual. Remember how fast we put up the Kingdom Hall in Jersey two years ago? We had the entire thing done and open for business in twenty-three days."

As I was listening, I said to myself, "Are they kidding? They can't build a full-size Kingdom Hall in three weeks. A professional construction crew couldn't do it that fast. The one they put up in Jersey must be tiny. It couldn't be the size of the Kingdom Hall I was sitting in now. Impossible!"

Nelsy continued, "They want to start work in Middletown in August so the warm weather will still be here and the kids will still be out of school on summer vacation. A lot of them, like my daughters, are going to be very involved in the construction. Melissa, didn't you tell me that your friends Amy, Louis, and their parents are going to do the tiling and grouting in the bathrooms and kitchen? Their dad does brickwork for a living, right?"

Melissa answered, "Yes, Mom. And Louis just finished masonry trade school. He gets his license this month."

Bob Wilson said, "The Middletown Kingdom Hall is going to be one of the largest around here. I've seen the plans. It'll be at least 25 percent bigger than ours."

As they continued talking it dawned on me that they weren't exaggerating. They were deadly serious and they all, except for Barbara, the new convert, had plenty of previous experience in erecting Kingdom Halls. But it was Barbara who turned to me and said, "Sir, I haven't had the pleasure. I'm Barbara Collins. What's your name?" I told her and introduced Phyllis.

"Mr. Grossman, we've all given ourselves jobs for this project. Maybe you and your wife will be available and would like to help too. You know how it works. You don't need any experience or training. Just give the building committee your name, tell them what you think you can do, and they'll assign you to one of the work crews. That's what Nelsy tells me they're going to do with me. But you've probably been through all this before and know that. So if I'm talking too much just tell me to be quiet. How long have you been Witnesses, anyway? I joined up just two months ago."

Nelsy said, "Well, Barbara, you know Michael and Phyllis are our friends but they aren't…"

I broke in, "Yes, Barbara, we're not Witnesses, We're Julie's friends and her guests. We're Jewish."

"Oh, I didn't realize…… I just assumed that… that everyone here… Uh, sorry."

"That's okay," I said. "When we walked in, Phyllis and I assumed that everyone here, except for us, were Witnesses too. I guess we were right."

"Well, I didn't mean to launch off on a discussion that you two couldn't be part of. Forgive me."

"No problem," I said. "And we didn't feel excluded. In fact, we're amazed by all this."

Barbara leaned over and said, "Between you and me, Michael, so am I. I'm dying to see how a bunch of mostly volunteers and amateurs are going to get that building up in only three weeks. And they're not just talking 'up.' They're talking up, completely finished, and ready for use on the twenty-first day after the work starts. It doesn't sound possible."

Nelsy said, "I wouldn't bet on that! Michael and Phyllis, I'm going to call to let you know when work starts, so you can come visit the Middletown work site as our guests. Food is served continuously, so no matter what time you stop by, you'll be able to get a free meal. Bring your kids. They'll be able to hang out with Lauren and Melissa."

We accepted the invitation unhesitatingly. Observing the goings-on at the work site, we anticipated, would be a very out-of-the-ordinary experience. And we were flattered by the invitation, just as we had been by Julie's wedding invitation. But in the depths of my consciousness, I couldn't stop a disquieting thought from taking form: *Maybe the reason Nelsy's inviting us – maybe the only reason – is because she feels there's still a chance we'll convert. Maybe that's the real reason why Julie invited us to her wedding too.*

I tried to quickly submerge those thoughts. But then Nelsy added, "When you come to the work site and see how we operate, I think you'll be impressed. – Real impressed."

Impressed doesn't cover it. Not nearly so. Nor does amazed, astonished, or flabbergasted. In truth, we were staggered. We arrived on August 20, exactly two weeks after the first shovelful of earth had been dug. They were way ahead of schedule. They were, except for some interior walls, plumbing, wiring, painting, and decorating, done. In four more days, they expected the furniture to be delivered, and the day after that, to open the doors for a first combination service and celebration that would be attended by as many as a thousand Witnesses. In other words, the whole job, from start to finish, was going to take them only an incredible nineteen days. Almost immediately, as we were taking this in, several people who had been at Julie's wedding started to recognize us and nodded hellos in our direction. Some strangers from Kingdom Halls outside of Warwick, who Nelsy must have told we were coming, seemed to know who we were too. No one gave us literature, no one preached to us, no one said, "Have you thought maybe about attending one of our services and joining us?" Instead, a tall man, Tom, who seemed to be one of the top work supervisors, asked if we were hungry, and offered us food. The twenty-four-hour kitchen, as promised, was in operation round the clock. And that, in part, is how they built the Middletown Kingdom Hall in record-breaking speed. There were four work crews, each of which worked about six hours straight and then broke to eat and go home to rest. The moment one crew finished its shift, the next crew took over and picked up where the previous one left off. That's how the Witnesses accomplished, in less than three weeks, work that would have taken any professional construction company at least four months. "The only organization that might be able to compete with them, *maybe*," I thought, "was the Army Corps of Engineers."

Watching them, I was overwhelmed with admiration but a little frightened at the same time. Their astonishing determination and incredibly disciplined effort to get the job done was like nothing I could remember having experienced at JCC, and seldom, if ever, anywhere else. At one point, I even picked up some tools and helped Dave cut and nail some plasterboard into place. I worked alongside him for nearly two hours. In the end, the Witnesses' mind-boggling motivation taught me something I haven't forgotten. It was a lesson that several years later, eight months after my term as our congregation's president ended, would help JCC overcome the most serious crisis – a catastrophe actually – in its history. But, as I worked with Dave at the Middletown Kingdom Hall in summer 1995, that catastrophe was still almost a decade away, and I'll talk about that in a later chapter.

In the meantime, though, a smaller catastrophe was in the works at the synagogue. Reuben Modek had graduated from rabbinical school, was about to be ordained, and was seeking full-time employment with a commensurate salary. That was something JCC couldn't offer. "Who," I wondered, "would replace him?" When I had found Reuben to take Mark Blazer's place years before – after almost having to settle for a far less qualified candidate – it had been a miracle. "Now what?"

Chapter Twenty Two - The Singing Rabbi

In early June 2002, the JCC Board of Trustees convened its last meeting of the Jewish year to wrap up some unfinished business. We would not meet again until after Rosh Hashanah in September. Sylvia Levy said, "Fire codes, gentlemen. We have to do something already. You know, the day school we rent space to downstairs has been notified that they'll be closed down by the County Education Department unless we comply with the new codes within thirty days." None of us was surprised. On the interior, our building was constructed entirely of wood, which would ignite like an old barn if a candle, accidentally and unnoticed, was knocked over or maybe, even if just a fuse blew and sparked. David Weinberg and I volunteered to look into it and, over the course of the next few weeks, we reached an agreement with the school to share the $8,000 cost of installing new smoke detectors, high-tech alarms, new fire extinguishers, lighted exit signs, push bars on all exterior doors, as well as a new, fire-resistant heating unit and a twenty-four-hour hookup of our alarm system to the fire departments in Warwick and Greenwood Lake. As best we could, we got the problem solved and, eventually, passed inspection.

But the business that was most on everyone's mind was "Who would be our new rabbi?"

Reuben Modek's contract with JCC ran out in August 2002, and at about the same time, he graduated from the Academy for Jewish Religion in Manhattan. Although he offered to stay on, not as our rabbi if we couldn't afford him, but as our new Hebrew school director, with his declared intention being transformation of "The New Jewish Learning Experience at JCC" into the most exciting and well-attended Hebrew program in the county, it became clear, unfortunately, that it was time for him to move on. While attending rabbinical school, he had been our religious director for four spiritually uplifting, event-filled years, but now had completed his studies and would be ordained in May 2004. A small congregation like ours simply couldn't afford the salary he'd be entitled to as an ordained rabbi, nor even the lesser salary he'd require to become our new Hebrew school director because, on top of that, we'd have to pay a salary to another rabbinical student to be religious director in his place. So, frantically, we made other plans. It occurred to me, and simultaneously to everyone else on the board, that the perfect person to take over would be Cantor Brenda Weinberg. Her years of service as cantor nearly spanned the tenures of three religious directors – Reuben's, Mark Blazer's, and part of Harris Goldstein's – a period of almost a decade, and her skills equaled and, in some areas, even surpassed theirs. There was no question that she was superbly qualified. Also, her singing remained consistently beautiful and professional and she'd be able to continue as cantor while simultaneously assuming the duties of rabbi. That would save us a separate cantor's salary and ease our increasingly desperate financial situation. It was a perfect solution, except for one thing: We had to talk Brenda into it before we got too excited.

Unlike Reuben Modek or Mark Blazer, when they became JCC's religious directors, Brenda was not looking for part-time work to hone her skills as an adjunct to formal rabbinical studies. She was not a rabbinical student. She had a demanding, full-time real-estate job in the City and was the mother of a young daughter. Serving as cantor, in a support role for our religious directors over the years, had been one thing, but agreeing to become our rabbi would be something else and on entirely different level. And she knew it. For starters, the "rabbi" was always and by far, by a huge margin, the single most important personality in the congregation, and everything that went on revolved around him. "Maybe soon," I hoped, "if all went as planned, I would be saying "around 'her'." Whoever was "rabbi," for example, had wide discretion to conduct services on Sabbaths and all holidays as he or she deemed fit, institute new synagogue programs and activities, commit the congregation's time and resources to participation in various community events like interfaith services or charity fundraisers, and had an enormous influence on the type and quality of instruction that went on at our Hebrew school. While serving as cantor, Brenda had also served as one of our Hebrew school teachers for years, but she hadn't had any responsibility for designing or running the program. However, along with our school director, overall responsibility for running the school was part, a gargantuan part, of the rabbi's job. To give you an idea as to just how much we expected of our "rabbi" it's instructive to take a look at the contract we insisted he or she agree to. And remember, JCC employed only a part-time "rabbi," paid only a part-time salary, yet the responsibilities could still be daunting. Especially for someone like Brenda, who had to commute to the City every day to earn her real paycheck at her real job in Midtown. The contract appended at the end of this chapter is a simple, widely used format, and can be adapted, obviously, to suit the particular needs of any congregation. I invite anyone interested to make use of it.

It turned out that I was much more worried about Brenda being able to take over as "rabbi" than she was. In fact, she approached me about it way before I made up my mind to approach her. I had hesitated because I'd thought that her job demands in the City would make it impossible for her to devote the huge amount of time that would be necessary to function effectively as our spiritual leader. But she very much wanted and was committed to doing it. As she explained, "I've wanted to do something like this all my life and I'm ready."

After speaking to Brenda repeatedly, the board and I were finally convinced that she could free up enough time from her career and family obligations to successfully perform as religious leader. When I showed her the contract she had to sign, after a little squabbling and negotiating about days off, sick days, and things like what exactly was meant by "In addition to the duties set forth above Religious Director shall perform such other reasonable work as may be required of her by JCC….", we had a deal. Brenda Weinberg was about to become the first female "rabbi" in Congregation B'nai Torah/JCC's forty-eight-year history.

She radiated satisfaction and pride. She intended to direct all the energy she could muster into raising the synagogue to a new level. But at the outset, she had some major concerns. Chief among them was, since she wasn't an ordained rabbi, nor a rabbinical student for that matter, whether she would have the legal authority to solemnize major life-cycle events such as baby namings, bar/bat mitzvahs and, particularly, whether she could legally perform weddings. During my tenure as president, the question hadn't come up before because Reuben Modek had always operated under the supervision of the ordained rabbis at his rabbinical school. So when he officiated at a wedding, it was legal, I assumed, because he was functioning as their agent under their authority. But, as I researched the question in an effort to allay Brenda's worries, I discovered that there was another, much more reassuring reason why any weddings Reuben had performed, and any weddings Brenda might perform in the future would be 100 percent valid, enforceable, and binding.

The law of the State of New York that deals with marriages – the Domestic Relations Law – provides that marriages my be solemnized, i.e., legally performed, by all of the following persons: mayors of villages and cities, former mayors, county executives, local magistrates, county recorders, clerks of counties wholly within cities having a population of 1 million or more, federal and state judges, judges of the Civil and Housing Courts of the City of New York, and retired judges. But it also provides in relevant *italicized* part as follows:

Domestic Relations Law

§ 11. By whom a marriage must be solemnized.

No marriage shall be valid unless solemnized by either:

1. *A clergyman or minister of any religion,* or by the senior leader, or any of the other leaders, of The Society for Ethical Culture in the city of New York, having its principal office in the borough of Manhattan, or by the leader of The Brooklyn Society for Ethical Culture, in the borough of Brooklyn of the city of New York, or of the Westchester Ethical Society, having its principal office in Westchester county, or of the Ethical Culture Society of Long Island, having its principal office in Nassau county, or of the Riverdale-Yonkers Ethical Society having its principal office in Bronx county, or by the leader of any other Ethical Culture Society affiliated with the American Ethical Union.

2-6. (These sections set forth the circumstances under which village mayors, city clerks, judges etc. may perform marriages. Except for federal and state judges, all the other officials may only perform marriages in the jurisdictions that elected or appointed them.)

Forget about the language above concerning the authority of leaders of Ethical Culture Societies to perform marriages. That stuff's completely irrelevant to our discussion and besides, I've never met anyone who was married by an Ethical Culture Society leader anyhow. We know, however, from the very first sentence of Section 11-1 that one of the ways a marriage can be solemnized is "... *by a clergyman or minister of any religion.*" So the next question has to be "What makes someone a clergyman or minister?" The answer is found partly in Domestic Relations Law Section 11-7 which states:

7. *The term "clergyman" or "minister" when used in this article shall include those defined in section two of the religious corporations law.* The word "magistrate," when so used, includes any person referred to in the second or third subdivision.

So we have to look still further, at Section 2 of the Religious Corporations Law. Now, the Religious Corporations Law has nothing to do with marriages per se but deals rather with how such corporations are to be structured and governed, and it limits and regulates their authority. JCC, in fact, like most congregations – Jewish, Christian or otherwise – is a New York Religious Corporation and has been since 1955. That's why our legal name is Jewish Community Centre of Greenwood Lake, N.Y. *Inc.* But the Religious Corporation Law also tells us, unequivocally, that the terms "clergyman" and "minister" include not only ordained pastors, rectors, priests, and rabbis but *any person having authority from his congregation to preside over and direct his church's or synagogue's spiritual affairs* (my paraphrasing). The exact language is in Section 2 as follows:

Religious Corporations Law

§ 2. Definitions

The term "clergyman" and the term "minister" include a duly authorized pastor, rector, priest, rabbi, and a person having authority from, or in accordance with, the rules and regulations of the governing ecclesiastical body of the denomination or order, if any, to which the church belongs, or otherwise from the church or synagogue to preside over and direct the spiritual affairs of the church or synagogue.

And there you have it. In short, a "clergyman" or "minister" is anyone chosen by a religious organization to run its spiritual affairs, and once chosen, that person can perform marriages. Incredible at first glance maybe, but legal. But upon reflection, in a free country like ours, what other rule would make sense? Prior to enactment of the laws discussed above, New York had on its books a statutory provision that actually limited the authority to solemnize marriages to only those ministers affiliated with religions listed in something called the "federal census of religious organizations." In striking down that provision as unconstitutional, a New York court held, "The constitutional guarantee of freedom of religious worship includes the right to have a marriage solemnized by a minister of one's own faith. While the state may act to prevent marriages from being solemnized by mere philanderers purporting to officiate under the guise of a pseudo-religious faith, it may not interdict marriage ceremonies having a reverent character performed by a person having ecclesiastical sanction." *O'Neill v. Hubbard*, 180 Misc. 214, 40 N.Y.S.2d 202 (Sup. Ct. Kings County, 1943). Also, and particularly relevant to Congregation B'nai Torah/JCC, which is a congregation unaffiliated with any parent organization, and to our part-time, unordained religious directors, is *Matter of Silverstein's Estate*, 190 Misc. 745, 75 N.Y.S.2d 144 (Surr. Ct. Bronx County, 1947). In that case, the court ruled, "To have authority to solemnize marriages, there is no requirement that the church, synagogue, or other religious congregation over which the clergyman presides be affiliated with any denomination or order. Nor is there any requirement that its clergy have received formal sanctioning authority from a governing board of a denomination or order or even from the church, synagogue or congregation itself. Thus, where the proof showed that the clergyman who performed the marriage ceremony had regularly conducted services in a synagogue attended by some twenty five congregants, there was sufficient evidence that the clergyman was recognized by his congregants as their spiritual leader and was, in that capacity, legally empowered to solemnize marriages." So, on the question of whether "Rabbi" Brenda Weinberg would have authority to perform marriages, there's your answer: Yes; emphatically. Case closed!

With that worry aside, after a short time, Brenda came into her own. As we watched her conduct the services, not in a supporting role as cantor anymore but now as the center of attention, it became apparent, just as everyone expected, that her talents were at least equivalent to and often superior to her predecessors'. She had learned from each of them, absorbed their best qualities, and brought her own style and insights to the table as well. It took her a few weeks to completely relax and get comfortable but, once she did, her services and sermons were outstanding. When I observed Brenda at her lectern or on the *Bimah*, I could sometimes actually pick out the portions of her presentations she had adapted, probably unconsciously, by her tone of voice maybe or mannerisms, from previous presentations given by Reuben Modek or Mark Blazer. I had known Reuben and Mark well, been very close to both of them, and remembered their "auras." Sometimes Brenda could be very erudite and learned and turn a large part of the Friday night service into a fascinating Jewish history lesson. When she did that, she was Rabbi Mark. Other times, she could be so uplifting, inspirational, and deeply meditative that she transformed the services into an intense, Kabala-type spiritual experience. When she did that, she was Rabbi Reuben. And sometimes she was such a superb storyteller that she completely captivated the Sabbath audience. When she did that, she was Rabbi Harris Goldstein. But when she sang, she was always Brenda – Cantor Brenda.

Aside from her singing, one of Brenda's biggest strengths is that she was an exceptionally effective teacher. I had known that firsthand well before she became "rabbi." For one thing, about eight months before Reuben left, she invited all the JCC adults who had never been bar or bat mitzvahed to begin intensive monthly Torah classes at her home. I was among them along with Bonnie Kessler, Pat Weisslander, and Joanne Birnberg. Her goal was to have us all ready to read from the Torah – in Hebrew if possible – and become B'nai Mitzvah at a joint celebration and service by June 2002. At our first class, however, in October 2001, I was so Hebrew illiterate that I thought to myself, "This is ridiculous; none of us understand more than a few words of Hebrew; we barely know the *aleph-bet*; we can't – at least I couldn't – follow more than two or three lines in the prayer book on Friday nights; and we certainly didn't have much time to devote to this insanity, since we all worked like slaves five days a week and looked desperately forward to our little time off. And now we were going to have to spend part of a sixth day – a few hours early Sunday mornings – worrying about this gobbledygook because we didn't want to embarrass

The Reluctant Jew

ourselves in front of the entire congregation come June, the planned date of our B'nai Mitzvah ceremony. Why, I couldn't even read the English transliterations of what Brenda expected me to read in Hebrew without so mispronouncing everything that it must have seemed like I suffered from a congenital speech impediment."

But Brenda got us through it. She was patient, she gave us tapes, she demonstrated the pronunciation, and she came up with her own, original transliterations that made it easier to follow the Hebrew. And no matter how badly we mangled the words, she never laughed or grew frustrated with us. She said, "Your kids got through it and, I promise, so will you," like there was never a doubt. A month before June 2, however, I – the president of the congregation, no less – had a lot of doubt. I was afraid to tell her, but I wanted to call it off. I was buried in work at my office, my daughter was applying to colleges and driving me nuts, and my son had injured himself like he had the year before and couldn't try out for the baseball team again. I had to take care of all kinds of pressing synagogue business and, most discouraging of all, I still couldn't read or properly pronounce the very tiny Torah portion Brenda had assigned to me, not even the transliterated English version. The only thing that gave me some comfort was that Bonnie, my Temple Wife, was doing almost as badly with the Hebrew as I was. Pat and Joanne were way ahead of us both. But Bonnie said, "Even though I'm terrified I'll blow the Hebrew, I just made up my mind. Mike, no matter what happens, I'm going through with this."

I said, "Well, think of an excuse for me, because as bad as you may think your Hebrew is, I guarantee mine's worse. I haven't listened to the tapes in three months. I just can't get to it."

I was about to panic. Big time.

After the last bar mitzvah class on the last Sunday in May, I waited for Bonnie, Pat, and Joanne to leave, because I was desperate to speak to Brenda alone. I had gotten a ride to her house that morning from Pat, who lived not far from me in Warwick, because my car wouldn't start and I couldn't use my wife's either because she needed it to take Zack somewhere. Pat said, "What are you waiting for, Mike? Come on. I've got to get to the synagogue to give Sylvia stuff for the newsletter that I've been carrying around with me all week. Sylvia told me she's got to have it by 9:30 or it won't get published. Let's go! I know you have things to do there too."

I did but I was frantic to speak to Brenda privately for a while to decide on some face-saving way out of my having to show up for my bar mitzvah in two weeks. I said, "Don't worry about me, Pat. I'll catch a ride with Brenda. She needs to be at the synagogue by 10:00 to teach Hebrew school classes."

The second she left I turned to Brenda and said, "I hope you'll understand and won't feel let down but there's no way I can get myself ready to do this bar mitzvah the week after next. I haven't been able to make time to learn my Torah portion, and it'll be better if we just put it off. Maybe I can give it a try next year."

Brenda looked at me. "I've got bad news. Joanne has already sent out the invitations, and your name's on them. At least sixty people will be coming plus *your* family and friends."

I said to myself, "Is she kidding? I wasn't planning to invite my family, and certainly not any friends – to see me embarrass myself up there – even if a miracle happened and suddenly I was persuaded to go through with it."

"Besides," she said, "you are ready. You could do it today. The problem is that when you practice alone, with only yourself for an audience, you get impatient and start rushing and fumbling your words. Everyone who's not Hebrew fluent has that problem. I know because I see it happen all the time. Do you think you're the only guy around here who's come up to me at the last minute and wanted to back out?"

My stomach churned. She was going to argue with me. She was determined not to let me get out of it. I was so miserable that for a moment I couldn't speak, not even English.

"Look," she said, "I'll give you all the extra help you need. Why don't you stop by Thursday night this week? We'll practice together until you get it. I won't let you down."

I said, "Brenda, as president I have to maintain a little dignity in front of the congregation, and I'm afraid when they see me up there, everyone will realize just how Hebrew illiterate I really am."

She said, "Please stop worrying. You, of all people, have never had trouble speaking in front of an audience. And remember, no one expects you to speak perfect Hebrew, because no one, except maybe Rich Gedzelman, Gil Goetz, and the Hebrew school teachers can either. All you have to do is give it your best shot. I'm sure you'll have the Hebrew down by next week and do great."

I was glad she thought so. My stomach churned harder; worse than before.

She added, "Have a good week. I'll see you on Thursday."

I was so miserable and my stomach so upset that I walked out the front door, forgetting for a moment that I needed a ride from Brenda to get to the synagogue. I turned back.

We got in her car. During the five-minute ride to the synagogue, she went to work on me. She said, "Okay, let's take your Torah portion from the top. Repeat after me, *'Heenaye mahtove ooo meenaiyeem...'*"

And, somehow, during those five minutes, I actually made progress.

No, I didn't invite my family or any friends. And only my wife, when my family found out, insisted on coming. But, as the four of us – me, Pat, Bonnie, and Joanne – stood at the *Bimah* reciting some preliminary prayers together seconds before we would be called upon to read our individual Torah and Haftorah portions, I noticed to my surprise that my pronunciation was off only a little. So little, in fact, that aside from me, there was a chance that no one else would pick up on it. Rabbi Modek and Brenda, who was still cantor in June 2002, and would not take over as "rabbi" until August, stood beside us. She had warned me I was going to be called to read first. I started gasping for air. I took deep breaths. As I got ready to walk to the center of the stage to stand at the *Bimah*, with the Torah unrolled directly in front of me, Reuben whispered, "Do you remember that night when you had to give that lecture on Jewish history for me in Nyack? You were about to pass out then too but it came off great. You spoke for almost an hour. This will be much easier. In six or seven minutes, you'll be done."

Brenda said, "And you know your *parsha* portion cold. You've memorized it. You don't even need your notes. Just do it! You're up."

And I did. With a few long, nervous pauses for sure, but not a single mispronunciation.

Michael Grossman

* * *

CONTRACT BETWEEN CONGREGATION B'NAI TORAH/ JEWISH COMMUNITY CENTRE OF GREENWOOD LAKE, INC. AND RELIGIOUS DIRECTOR

AGREEMENT made this__ day of _____, 200__ between Congregation B'nai Torah / Jewish Community Centre of Greenwood Lake, Inc. having its principal place of business at 21 Old Dutch Hollow Road, Greenwood Lake, N.Y. and 'Jane Doe' residing at xxxxxxxxxxxxxxx xxxxxxxxx, Greenwood Lake, N.Y., WITNESSETH:

1. 'Jane Doe' hereby agrees to perform the following duties as Religious Director for Congregation B'nai Torah/Jewish Community Centre of Greenwood Lake, Inc. (JCC):

   a) Religious Director shall plan, run and perform all Friday Night Services.

   b) Religious Director shall plan, run, and perform services on all Festival Jewish Holidays and other major Jewish Holidays. The Board of Trustees shall determine which of the Jewish Holidays are major Jewish Holidays for purposes of this agreement.

   c) Religious Director shall serve as Co-Director of JCC's Hebrew School and shall be responsible, along with her Co-Director, for planning and running the entire program and supervising all classes including Adult Education.

   d) Religious Director shall teach Hebrew School classes, which includes Adult Education, Sunday mornings. She shall teach said classes and be present at the Synagogue premises during the hours 10:00am until 12:30pm each Sunday on which Hebrew School is scheduled except on days off, during illness, or due to dire personal emergency or extremely urgent business obligations. Religious Director shall use her best efforts to schedule any and all business meetings, appointments, etc. for dates other than Hebrew School Sunday mornings during the hours 10:00am to 12:30pm.

e) Religious Director shall officiate at, run, supervise, and perform Bar/Bat Mitzvah Services for all graduates of JCC's Hebrew School.

f) Religious Director shall participate in community events, as required by the Board of Trustees, including but not limited to Memorial Day celebrations, Flag Day Celebrations, Ecumenical/Interdenominational services, Community Charity events, and as JCC's representative at affairs/dinners/ceremonies to which she or our congregation is invited by other local congregations, non-profit organizations, and the like such as the American Legion and Greenwood Lake Police/Fire Fighting Departments. It is understood that Religious Director shall not engage in fundraising on Shabbat except for Tzedakah.

g) Religious Director shall use her best efforts to increase the membership of JCC and enrollment at our Hebrew School and shall participate in Membership Committee meetings, Hebrew School meetings and other activities in connection with same as requested by the President of the Congregation.

h) In addition to the duties set forth above Religious Director shall perform such other reasonable work as may be required of her by JCC under and subject to its instruction, direction, and control. It is anticipated, for example, that Religious Director will plan, perform, and run Saturday morning services from time to time. It is understood that no Saturday morning services, except for Bar/Bat Mitzvah and/or Baby Naming and/or Wedding and/or Funeral services scheduled by congregants/members with Religious Director, will be held during the summer months of July and August.

2. For the duties performed by Religious Director as above required JCC shall compensate Religious Director as follows:

a) $xxxx per year in equal monthly installments of $xxxx payable on the 1st day of each month during the term of this agreement.

b) The term of this agreement shall be xxxx, 200_ through xxxx, 200_.

c) Religious Director shall be entitled to three (3) weeks vacation per year (meaning three week ends: Friday, Saturday, Sunday) and shall give JCC 30 days notice of her vacation schedule.

d) In addition to vacation time, Religious Director shall be entitled to three (3) paid personal days during each year of the term of this agreement. Personal days include days missed due to illness or due to personal business.

3. If Religious Director, due to illness, injury or other reason cannot perform the duties required by this Agreement for an "extended period of time" JCC shall have the right to terminate this Agreement. The Board of Trustees shall determine what constitutes an "extended period of time" but in no event shall an "extended period of time" be anything less than three (3) consecutive weeks.

4. By this Agreement JCC authorizes Brenda Weinberg to perform all life cycle events and/or services, within the County of Orange, on behalf of JCC members and/or congregants including but not limited to Baby Namings, Weddings, Bar/Bat Mitzvahs, and Funerals.

5. In the event Religious Director violates any provision of this Agreement or performs any act by which JCC shall incur liability or cannot perform her duties for an "extended period of time" as set forth in paragraph 3 then, JCC may terminate this Agreement upon 10 days written notice to Religious Director at her home address and shall be under no obligation to Religious Director except to pay her for services as may have been performed up to the date of termination of this Agreement.

6. Religious Director will cooperate with and shall follow the instructions and directions of the President of the Congregation or, in the event of his/her absence or unavailability, the Vice President(s) of the Congregation.

7. During the term of this Agreement Religious Director shall arrive timely at all services, classes, and events and earlier, if necessary, for planning, preparation and set up; shall make herself available to congregants for conversation, questions, and spiritual counseling; and shall at all times devote her best efforts to advance the interests of JCC.

IN WITNESS THEREOF the parties have set their hands and seals the day and year first above written.

In presence of:

_____

Congregation B'nai Torah/Jewish Community Centre of Greenwood Lake Inc

_____

'Jane Doe'

Chapter Twenty Three - At Ease With The Baha'i

Brenda, thank God, had been a patient, skilled, and incredibly dedicated teacher. I knew also she was going to be an incredibly dedicated religious director, but expected that in that capacity, as our "rabbi," she would be much more inflexible and conservative than ever Mark or Reuben had been. I felt that way because Brenda had been raised in an orthodox household, and I figured some of that had to have rubbed off on her. Her mother, who lived in Haifa, Israel, was so ultra-orthodox that Brenda had avoided telling her, for the last nearly ten years, that she'd been serving as JCC's cantor. Brenda's mother would have strenuously objected to any female, including her own daughter, being cantor at any synagogue, and probably would have collapsed if she'd been told that Brenda was going to become our "rabbi." On one occasion, I remembered, when Brenda introduced her mother to my wife, who is ethnically Indian-Oriental and slightly dark-skinned, she immediately asked, "Why, Phylees, I hear your husband's president of the congregation. You must be Seefardeek. Right?

My wife is actually from a Protestant-Hindu family and converted to Judaism years before we met.

Before my wife could answer and blow her cover, Brenda broke in, "Yeah, Mom, she's Sephardic. Let's go, Phyllis. We'll see you later mom. Bye." And they escaped.

I was wrong about Brenda's conservative bent. Despite her old-school upbringing and, to me, traditionalist aura, she was not so entrenched in any of the conventional branches of Judaism – Orthodox, Conservative, or otherwise – that she could not open her heart and mind to everyone who walked through our doors, no matter what their background or level of Judaic knowledge. For certain, she was not Reform, but nevertheless, was extremely liberal when it came to considering and sometimes even accepting opposing arguments. She wanted people to enjoy and be inspired by Judaism, not ideologized by it. She wanted JCC's congregants to come to their own conclusions about spirituality and God, not impose her theology or any particular theology on them or on anybody.

I found these qualities of Brenda's to be admirable: her projecting a stern, somewhat austere, establishment image but in fact having a very inquisitive nature, being exceptionally broad-minded, and genuinely receptive of everyone, no matter the depth or shallowness of their Judaism and no matter, it turned out, whether they were Jewish at all, Christian, Muslim, Hindu, or even followers of Baha'u'llah.

The Reluctant Jew

In September, 2002 Brenda had been "rabbi" only two months when she came up to me and said, "Michael, I've got a great speaker lined up for October's community dinner which is happening in just two weeks. As a matter of fact, I should say 'speakers,' because on that evening, most of the Baha'i congregation from Middletown will be joining us. You've heard of the Baha'i and Baha'u'llah, right?"

For a long moment, I looked at her, blankly. I couldn't remember if the Baha'i was some exotic Jewish sect or a separate religion altogether. And Baha'u'llah? Yeah, I knew as much about him as I did about advanced string theory or Cambodian calligraphy. Absolutely nada!

"Baha'i?" Baha'u' *whatchamacall it?*

"Yes," she said. "You know. Remember Melinda, who used to teach music lessons at the synagogue on Tuesday nights? *'Melinda's Music'?* For kids? Well, she became Baha'i a few years ago. From what she tells me, they are a progressive and extraordinarily tolerant group. Will you put an announcement in the newsletter right away, telling everyone that they're going to be here? And please, be sure to send an e-mail out or telephone all our congregants a few days before, reminding them to come. I want there to be a really big turnout."

I said, trying to sound as though I knew what she was talking about, "Yeah. Sounds good, Brenda. The Baha'i are, – are, um, interesting, uh, extremely interesting and, yeah, very tolerant. I'll get an announcement together and bring it over to Richie Gedzelman tomorrow. That'll give him just enough time to get it into the October issue, which comes out next week." By October 2002, Richie had replaced Sylvia Levy as newsletter editor.

When I got home, I pulled out the *Encyclopedia Britannica*, looked up Baha'i, and came up with this:

TO ALL MEMBERS AND FRIENDS:

JOIN US THIS FRIDAY EVENING, OCTOBER 11 FOR CONGREGATION B'NAI TORAH'S MONTHLY COMMUNITY DINNER. OUR GUESTS AND SPEAKERS WILL BE MEMBERS OF THE BAHA'I CONGREGATION FROM MIDDLETOWN, N.Y. BAHA'ISM WAS FOUNDED BY BAHA'U'LLAH (1817-1892) IN THE LATE NINETEENTH CENTURY AS A BREAKAWAY SECT FROM IRANIAN STYLE SHIA ISLAM. ITS MAIN TEACHING IS THAT ALL HUMANITY IS A SINGLE RACE AND EVERY PERSON, MEN AND WOMEN ALIKE, AND ALL RELIGIONS ARE EQUAL. BAHA'ISM SAYS MOSES, ZOROASTER, BUDDHA,

Michael Grossman

KRISHNA, JESUS, AND MUHAMMAD WERE ALL GOD'S HOLY MESSENGERS, EACH BUILDING ON THE TEACHINGS OF THE PREVIOUS ONES AND BRINGING NEW INSIGHTS INTO THE WORLD AS TO HOW TO DO JUSTICE. MAN'S UNDERSTANDING OF GOD IS CONTINUALLY EVOLVING AND BAHA'U'LLAH IS BUT THE LATEST OF GOD'S PROPHETS. THERE WILL BE A TIME WHEN ANOTHER GREAT PROPHET ARRIVES, FURTHER EXPANDING AND PERFECTING OUR UNDERSTANDING OF WHAT GOD EXPECTS OF US.

PLEASE JOIN US THIS FRIDAY AND REMEMBER TO CALL BONNIE KESSLER TO LET HER KNOW WHAT DINNER DISH YOU'LL BE BRINGING AND HOW MANY WILL BE IN YOUR PARTY. SERVICES WILL BEGIN AT 7:00, FOLLOWED BY DINNER, THEN DISCUSSIONS WITH OUR GUESTS, AND DESSERT.

On my own, I read further: Because of its emphasis on the equality of all religions, Baha'ism is an amazingly tolerant faith. In fact, to become Baha'i, there is no requirement that one discard his or her previous religious identity. The overwhelming majority of adherents in the U.S. are Christian-Baha'i, many of whom continue to attend church. They insist that religion must never be used to separate or divide people, but always to unite them. Although Baha'ism was first established in Iran, its adherents were forced to flee from there when the Shiite religious authorities outlawed it. Today, the Baha'i world headquarters is located — as should come as no surprise — in the most tolerant country in the Middle East, in Israel, in the city of Haifa.

Two weeks went by and, from the little I'd read, my interest piqued and I looked forward to meeting and learning a lot more about Baha'ism. I was hoping and expecting the turnout for them would be good.

Fourteen of the Baha'i walked through JCC's doors en masse at about 6:50. That was a wonderfully large showing, but I was little embarrassed because, so far, only twelve of our own members had shown up. I was surprised because in response to my e-mail I had received immediate replies from at least ten congregants saying they would be at the Community Dinner without fail, along with their children and spouses. That meant at least twenty people at bare minimum and, with an initial response like that, I figured word would get out and maybe fifty or more JCC members would actually come.

While anxiously waiting for more JCC members to arrive, I greeted Linda, the Baha'i leader, but after talking with her a while, realized that one of their practices was to rotate leadership responsibilities frequently. She was serving as the Baha'i president and spokeswoman that night, but in a few weeks, those duties would pass to someone else. Slowly, the synagogue filled up and, by 7:30, thirty JCC congregants had arrived.

Linda began. "We are the newest of the monotheistic religions. While Judaism is nearly 4,000 years old, Christianity and Jesus some 2,000 years old, and Islam with Muhammad 1,400 years old, we Baha'i have just arrived. In 1844, Mizra Ali Muhammad of Shiraz, Persia, known as *the Bab*,[1] Arabic for *'the gate,'* prophesized that the Universal God would manifest himself in a divine figure on earth in nineteen years. Then, in 1863, exactly on schedule, Mizra Husayn Ali of Nur, known as *Baha'u'llah*, meaning *the glory of God*, proclaimed himself to be that manifestation. His followers believed he was the latest in a series of divine messengers, including Moses, Zoroaster, Jesus, and Muhammad, and that his purpose was to bring a new revelation to humanity. That new revelation, Baha'ism teaches, does not denigrate or demean the revelations of other religions, nor reject or claim to replace them. It adds to and builds upon them. Worldwide, Baha'ism has 7 million adherents, thousands of whom are Jewish-Baha'i and tens of thousands Christian-Baha'i. There is no conflict in that, because all religions seek truth, and all humanity is but one race bound together in that pursuit.

"What is this new revelation? In essence, it's the emphatic realization that we are all equal before God. Baha'ism's teachings and its scriptures, which in their entirety consist of the writings of the Bab, Baha'u'llah, and his eldest son, Abd ul-Baha, urge the abolition of religious and racial discrimination, total equality of the sexes, universal education, an international language, a democratic world government, and a universal religion based on the conviction that all the great faiths are pathways to the same truth. In line with Baha'ism's insistence that all are equal, there is no priesthood; lay persons take turns leading discussions and prayers and, in stark contrast to Judaism, Christianity, and Islam, there is no fixed body of rites. If there was, a class of professional priests would arise to oversee and administer them because only they would have the requisite training and knowledge.

"A 'Spiritual Assembly,' loosely similar to a *Minyan*," Linda said, "can be formed whenever nine or more Baha'i are gathered together. Each Assembly selects delegates who, in the United States, meet annually at a National Spiritual Assembly at the Baha'i national headquarters in Wilmette, Illinois."

As she spoke, I noticed she was wearing a bright purple sweater. In itself, that color meant nothing, but it caught my eye because, for the first time, I was wearing the bright purple Bukharin yarmulke I'd bought at a Judaic shop in Manhattan the week before.

"There are," she continued, "more similarities among the world's religions than differences."

As I listened, I thought, "Baha'ism, boy, is some religion." Unlike a lot of Jews, Christians, and Muslims, the Baha'i don't smugly dwell on doctrinal distinctions. Instead, they celebrate the ethical insights all faiths offer and repeatedly emphasize their essential identity with one another. That's why you can be Jewish and Baha'i, or Christian and Baha'i, or whatever and Baha'i at the same time. It's like a spiritual supplement.

Linda kept going. "But in the fundamentalist Shiite world of Iran, where Baha'ism arose, the claim that a new prophet, Baha'u'llah, had brought the world religious insights equivalent to Muhammad's, was heresy. The Baha'i were outlawed, persecuted, and thousands slaughtered. Prior to that, as many as 20,000 followers of the Bab, who had predicted Baha'u'llah's coming, had been slaughtered too. Nonetheless, at least 325,000 Baha'i still reside there and have no intention of leaving. They hope that the rule of the Mullahs ends soon and some semblance of democratic government takes root. In the meantime, they are free and welcome in Haifa, Israel, where we have established our world headquarters and built a shrine to the Bab."

She took questions. And there were many. When she couldn't answer, another of the Baha'i would stand up and answer for her. To my surprise, a couple of JCC's congregants were a bit resentful. Linda and the Baha'i had gone over so well that these resentful few, in whispers to me, accused them of proselytizing. But I and the majority did not react that way at all. We felt we had forged a close and valuable bond with another religious community and looked forward to their visiting again. Melinda, of *Melinda's Music,* incidentally, who Rabbi Weinberg had reminded me was a former member of our congregation who'd become Baha'i, was among Linda's visiting entourage. But it turned out that Melinda wasn't a *former* member of Congregation B'nai Torah but was still a current, paid-up member. She was proof that a person could embrace Baha'ism without abandoning Judaism. Neither the Bab nor Baha'u'llah, after all, claimed to be the messiah. Melinda, by the way, showed up for services at the synagogue the next Friday.

At the evening's end, I walked to the podium and, to thank the Baha'i, said, "Linda, your presentation was wonderful. Most of us here had no idea what Baha'ism was about until now. We'd like to show you our appreciation so, from the world's oldest monotheistic religion to the world's newest, I hope you'll accept this gift."

And I handed her my purple Bukharin yarmulke.

Chapter Twenty Four - A Concept of God a Modern Can Live With

What is God? An eye-opener for me was that during my adventures as a synagogue president, I discovered that even those who profess to be the most religious among us don't know. I've asked that question, repeatedly, not only of the most observant Jews at Congregation B'nai Torah, including our rabbis and cantors, but of devout Christian, Muslim, Hindu, and Baha'i friends as well. My question is always the same and directly to the point: "Would you please tell me exactly what it is you believe in when you say you believe in God?" When asked that, the people I address almost always become, at a minimum, defensive, and on occasion, offended. And sometimes, just by my posing the question, they react as if I was challenging their core value system or intentionally disparaging their self-professed piety. But, in truth, it's a simple and honest question; a question to which you'd think people who regularly attend churches, synagogues, or other places of worship would have complete, consistent, and well-thought-out answers. In fact, however, the answers I get are almost never satisfactory, not to me and not, surprisingly, even to the persons giving them. And they are seldom consistent, not even among followers of the same religion. Usually I get different, remarkably incoherent answers from any random group of people I talk to. What's going on here? What are people who have serious doubts about God's existence, like me, supposed to make of it when those who say they have no doubts whatsoever can't tell us – in plain English – what they're talking about?

And I want to know what they're talking about – badly. So, although not overly helpful, here's a partial list of, to me, the woefully inadequate answers I've received. They've shed only a few rays of light on the subject and, as often as not, have confused rather than enlightened. At the very most, they hint at, not give, explanations. The question again: "Would you please tell me exactly what it is you believe in when you say you believe in God?" or, simply, "What is God?"

1. God is ineffable and cannot be described in words. (I don't even know what ineffable means. Do You? For the record, it means: inexpressible or unutterable.)

2. God is unknowable and must be accepted on faith. (That's great. What is any thinking person supposed to do with this definition or the one above?)

3. God is the divine force that's everywhere; in everything we do, think, and feel. (Doesn't really say anything: What's God? It's the divine force. But what's the divine force?)

4. God is love. (Better, but still not much. Is God just a feeling? An emotion?)

5. God is the force that watches over and guides us. (Sorry, but in all my life, I've never felt any outside presence watching over or guiding me.)

6. God is our conscience. (More than I like to admit, this one appeals to me because I have, well, a conscience. For some reason, I care whether I'm doing good and not evil. And so, I know, do most others.)

7. God is our creator and made us in his image. (This one raises more questions than it answers. Before God created us who or what created God? We all know the pat response, 'God was always here before the universe, before time.' So we're back to where we started: Who or what is God and where did God come from?)

8. God is the divine spark of goodness in each of us: our souls. (Not terrible. It's similar to 6 above. There dwells within most human beings, many would agree, at least some good: if you will, 'a divine spark'.)

9. The human mind has limitations and one of them is its inability to fully understand God. One manifestation of God, however, is the force that exists in the world that causes us to attempt to be righteous. (To an extent, I like this one. It's similar to 6 and 8 and, in addition, reminds us to be humble and realize that there are some things human minds simply cannot grasp. Just as pigeons, for example, cannot grasp the concepts of language and calculus, there are many concepts that our minds, because of the way we're constructed, can't grasp either. But just because we can't understand everything does that mean, logically, that those things are to be considered divine and be worshipped as God? Is calculus God to pigeons simply because it's beyond their conprehension, unknowable to them, and for that reason shomehow divine?)

10. God is our sovereign, our king and ruler of the universe. (Save for the person who gave me this answer and a very few others, I know hardly a soul who accepts this one anymore. This idea is the

main reason why I feel so uncomfortable with the prayers of Rosh Hashanah. Most of them endlessly and, to me, meaninglessly, praise God as our 'Sovereign ruler forever and ever.')

11. God is the Father, the Son, and the Holy Spirit. (I can relate to the Holy Spirit part because it's generally understood, according to Christian teachings, to mean the ever-present goodness and love in the world that emanates from the divine. That part of this answer is similar to 6, 8, and 9.)

12. God is One. (This, the mantra of the Jewish faith, describes the extraordinary truth about God Jews believe they were the first to have discovered: *That God is one for everyone.* It's the idea that transformed Yawehism from the tribal cult of the ancient Hebrews into Judaism, the first worldwide, monotheistic religion. This definition too, however, is insufficient: God may be One, but One what?)

13. God is the being that regulates all existence and gives it meaning. (I don't particularly like this idea because if a righteous God is regulating everything why is it that the world is filled with such horrendous suffering and misery? Some God.)

14. God is the ultimate spiritual being. He is everywhere, transcending time, space, and nature, and knowing all. (I like the "ultimate spiritual being" part. Since I, and many of you I suspect, will probably never be able to understand, by means of logic, what people believe when they say they believe in God, an attempt at a spiritual understanding may be the only way to have a meaningful conversation. Also, by directing our mental energy into the spiritual realm, we may at least gain better insights into ourselves and what's really important to us, apart from any religious insights we might discover. When I try to comprehend what people mean by God through logic, I usually end up with a headache.)

15. God is mercy, justice, forgiveness, kindness, compassion, and love. God is everything and everywhere, and we must absolutely submit ourselves to His will. (This idea is the sine qua non of *Islam* which, in fact, means *submission*. But to whom or what exactly does Islam want us to submit? If God is an amalgam of everything good in the world, like justice, kindness, etc., I 'm all for it. However, the question remains: God is a merciful, just, forgiving, kind, compassionate, and loving what? Or whom? Is God just a collection of beautiful ideas, or a real entity with whom

you and I are supposed to be communicating? Please tell me already.)

For myself, believe it or not, not in spite of, but directly because of the mostly disappointing and unrevealing answers I'd grown accustomed to, I've found a solution that even I, a very secular, twenty-first-century modern can live with. As president of Congregation B'nai Torah, I'd tried so long and hard to grasp what it meant to be religious – let alone to be religious myself – that when a solution finally dawned on me, I was stunned I hadn't figured it out sooner and embarrassed at how naïve my thinking had been. First, I belatedly realized that there is no, and can never be, an all-encompassing answer to a question like "What is God?" Any answer you or I or anyone else offers is equally legitimate. And no single answer can ever come close to being complete. God has been invested with so many different qualities, by so many different people, from so many different backgrounds that no definition could cover it all. It's like trying to insist upon the same answer from everyone to "What is the best-tasting food?" or "What is the most beautiful music?" There are no wrong answers to questions like those, because every answer is correct to someone. Second, having belatedly realized this, I stopped looking for the "correct" answer and started, instead, looking for my own. And one evening, as I tried once again to come up with a concept that felt right and fit, it finally came to me: *It's the struggling to understand God that counts more than anything.* And with this concept, I knew – biblically speaking – I was in good company.

In Genesis, you may recall, Jacob fled his parents' house in Beer-Sheba because he feared that Esau, his older twin by a split second, would kill him when he found out that he, the younger brother, had tricked their father, Isaac, into bestowing on him the blessing that should rightfully have been bestowed on Esau as the firstborn. In the ancient world, such blessings were of enormous importance because they confirmed the eldest son's birthright and could mean the inheritance of substantial wealth and privilege, as opposed to the mere pittances, in comparison, younger sons usually received. Although years earlier, Jacob had persuaded Esau to outright trade him his birthright in exchange, unbelievably, for only a hot meal, it seems likely that Esau did not feel bound by such a ridiculous bargain and considered the whole episode as a kind of joke. However, when the nearly blind Isaac bestowed his deathbed blessing upon Jacob, even though when he did so he had been duped into believing Jacob was Esau, there was no undoing it. Once bestowed, the blessing could not be withdrawn. Going back to an even earlier time in the twins' lives, when they were still in Rebecca's womb, the two brothers had struggled for possession of the birthright too. Esau prevailed then and emerged first, but with Jacob hanging tightly onto his heel. Jacob, however, in his mind's eye, never let go until years later when, as a young adult, he succeeded in stealing Esau's birthright and making it his.

Rebecca favored Jacob over Esau. In fact, it was she who had encouraged Jacob to disguise himself as Esau and obtain Isaac's blessing under false pretenses. But she too became fearful of what Esau might do when he learned of Jacob's deceit and instructed Jacob to stay with his uncle, her brother Laban, in the town of Haran, until Esau's fury subsided. In Haran, however, Jacob met Rachel, Laban's daughter, and fell deeply in love with her — so much in love that he agreed to serve his uncle seven years in exchange for her hand in marriage. His love was so great that the seven years seemed like only days to him. The date of the marriage arrived, but Laban sent Leah, his eldest daughter, to Jacob's tent instead of Rachel. In the dark, they cohabited. When he arose, Jacob immediately realized what Laban had done, but his uncle curtly explained that it was the custom to marry off *the eldest daughter first, not the younger.* At that moment, Jacob must have remembered back to the cruel hoax he had perpetrated to steal his father's blessing and deprive Esau of his birthright, full well knowing that by custom and law the blessing should have gone to *the eldest son first, not the younger.* The bitter irony of Laban having pulled a cruel switch too could not have escaped Jacob's notice. Jacob must have realized he had more than earned that punishment.

Laban required Jacob to serve him another seven years before finally allowing him to take Rachel as his second wife, whom he continued to love above Leah. After toiling for Laban twenty years and siring many children, six by Leah, two by Rachel's maid, Bilhah, two by Leah's maid, Zilpah, and two by Rachel herself, Jacob told Laban the time had come for him to return to the lands of his father, Isaac, in Beer-Sheba. Jacob, by his excellent work, had made Laban a very rich man and as payment, after much haggling, was given flocks of goats, sheep, asses, camels and cattle numbering several thousand. With his entire entourage, Jacob set off. But in the wilderness, his old fear of Esau, who now led a fighting force of 400 men, returned with a vengeance. Desperately, in an effort to appease his brother, Jacob sent messengers ahead with gifts of goats, rams, cows, camels, and other livestock. He also sent all his material possessions, family members, and followers ahead reasoning that the advance gifts and advance entourage of people would buy him time and might so impress Esau that his anger would dissipate.

Jacob was temporarily left alone to fend for himself and the stage was at last set for one of the most extraordinary events, among the many extraordinary events, presented in the Bible. As evening descended and Jacob prepared to sleep an imposing stranger approached who refused to identify himself. To back him off, Jacob began wrestling with him but could not prevail. More surprisingly, neither could the stranger who seemed possessed of remarkable strength and stamina. Jacob's tenacity must have seemed as incredible to the stranger as did the stranger's to Jacob, because they continued to struggle, with neither showing any sign of weakening, throughout the night. At daybreak, frustrated, the stranger wrenched Jacob's hip with such force that he permanently crippled him. From then onward, Jacob walked with a limp. But, before he departed, the stranger's conversation with Jacob, as recorded in Genesis, was this:

He said, "Let me go now, for dawn is breaking."

Jacob, however, although badly injured, finally began to realize the man's true identity and answered, "I will not let you go, unless you bless me."

Surprised, the stranger asked, "What is your name?"

He replied, "I am Jacob."

To which the man, if he was a man, said, "Your name shall no longer be Jacob, but *Israel*, for you have *struggled with God*, and with men, and have prevailed."

Jacob asked, "Pray tell me your name."

But he said, "You must not ask me my name."

And with that, the man took leave of him. But Jacob knew that the stranger had been no man but a divine being; an angel perhaps, or maybe the Lord himself. So Jacob named the place Peniel (the face of God), meaning "I have seen a divine being face to face, yet my life has been preserved."[1]

So *Israel*, it turns out, and incredibly, means *to struggle with God.* – Not "to believe in" or "to worship God," not "to champion God," but "to struggle with Him." And Jacob, whose twelve sons became the twelve tribes of Israel, struggled with God face-to-face, as none other; not Abraham before him nor even Moses afterward. To be an Israelite then, i.e. to be Jewish, has to mean at least in part "to be someone who struggles with God." How does someone struggle with God? Not physically, of course – Jacob, I believe, did so metaphorically – but with the concept of God. That is, by struggling to come to grips with the very question we started with, "What is God?" and all its derivatives like, Does God really exist? If so, where is He? If so, why is there so much suffering? etc. In other words, being an Israelite and being Jewish means doing exactly what I'd been doing from the moment I joined JCC: *struggling with the meaning and existence of God*. And, like most people — except those who have completely given up — I'm still struggling. It's often been argued and may well be true that we humans, in our imaginations, created God – at first, at the dawn of human history, because we had no science to account for mysteries like the change of seasons, the death of loved ones, and why the sun rose every day – but now, in a world totally immersed in science and technology, as a kind of collective dream and longing plea for the way things ought to be; and not the other way around. That is, God didn't create us, we created Him. As a secularist, I lean toward that point of view. As secular as I am, however, I want, almost need, to believe that our bodies are more than just collections of complicated organic molecules, our emotions more than mere chemical reactions, whole human beings more than just somewhat intelligent, naked apes, and our existence, therefore, not meaningless. But my disquiet, in large part, is the very essence of what it means to be a Jew.[2] *It's the struggle to understand that counts more than anything.*

Chapter Twenty Five - Why the Resentment?

For more than two millennia, Jews have been subjected from nearly all quarters to an almost unrelenting rampage of hate. But why, in the twenty-first century, throughout much of the world, are Jews still regarded with such disdain? I'm not talking about ignorant anti-Semitism typified by attitudes like: Jews are greedy, money-hungry usurers (the truth is that some Jews became prominent in banking because it was among the few lucrative professions Christendom did not forbid them, and the only interest rates they could charge were those permitted by their Christian overlords); Jews intend to take over and rule the world (an absurd belief based on a Czarist forgery dating from 1905, *The Protocols of the Elders of Zion*, purporting to be transcripts from a secret World Zionist Congress); Jews are unrepentant killers of the Son of God (but Jesus, whose real name was *Joshua*, was a Jewish rabbi and considered himself such all his life; moreover, it was the Romans who crucified Christ, who had both Jewish detractors and Jewish supporters, along with thousands of other Jews whose bodies could often be seen rotting on crosses lining the roads leading to Rome); and Jews murder non-Jewish children to obtain their blood for use in religious rites (a ridiculous accusation known as "The Blood Libel" which arose for the first recorded time in Norwich, England in 1144 when a Christian boy was found dead and Jews were blamed for it). This type of extreme hatred, based on a total disregard for facts and the deliberate dissemination of falsehoods, is rampant throughout the Arab and Muslim worlds, where school curricula are heavily infused with religious teachings, extremely limited as to sciences and the objective histories of other civilizations and, in more than a few places, purposely designed to indoctrinate students with a loathing toward Israel, Jews and, as often as not, all other non-Muslims as well.

What I'm talking about is the extraordinary dislike and resentment of Jews that has begun to take root among the intelligentsia in the non-Muslim world, including throughout much of the West, particularly on the extreme left of the political spectrum. When large numbers of faculty and students at many universities across the United States demand that the schools they teach at or attend disinvest from Israel — the only free and democratic country in the Middle East — and not from a single Arab or Muslim country, nearly all of which are brutal dictatorships, there is cause for great concern among Jews. When Israel tries to make peace with the Palestinians by offering 95 percent of the West Bank, half of Jerusalem, mega-billions in development money, and indicates it will negotiate further, yet is blamed by a majority at the United Nations for the breakdown of talks when Arafat walks away from the table with no counteroffer and, instead, renews terrorist attacks that kill and maim hundreds, half of whom are women and children, there is cause for great concern among Jews.[1] When attacks on synagogues, Jewish people, and their property dramatically increase in Europe, along with frequent media characterizations of Israel as a 'vicious and murderous regime' or 'the most dangerous country in the world' (comparable to even North Korea or Iran,[2] that's right, postage-stamp-size Israel), particularly in France, Germany, and Russia, as has happened since 9/11, there is cause for great concern among Jews. When the Malaysian prime minister, leader of one of the most economically and politically successful countries in Southeast Asia and supposedly a highly educated man, announces at a meeting of Muslim heads of state that "the Jews invented socialism, communism, human rights, and democracy so that persecuting them would appear wrong...."[3] and receives a standing ovation, there is cause for great concern among Jews, and any Jew who is not concerned, frankly – it can't be said otherwise – is a moron.

So what accounts for – it can't honestly be described as anything else – this venomous hate? What is it about Israel and the Jews, whose actions are at least as moral as any other state or people, and in many cases much more so, that still makes them the targets of such unremitting enmity? Where does it come from and why, it seems, won't it end? What keeps feeding it? The historical reasons, I think, contrary to what you may have read elsewhere, are obvious. We Jews have been around for so long and in so many places, retaining nearly unchanged our thousands-of-years-old traditions and attitudes, that through the centuries we've presented to others a stark, well-defined stereotype that, like a young, only few-millennia-old mountain range, remains craggy and steep and has barely eroded. The hostile attitudes that developed in the ancient world have simply not chipped away. During the several centuries before Christ, when Greek influence was at it height, and long before the Romans rose to power, the Jews, as a people, were the only group that presented a serious, often antagonistic alternative to the prevailing cultural outlook. To Greeks, in fact, the Jews were an obstacle to their near-total cultural domination. But the clash that developed between their dominant, pleasure-seeking culture and the much-less-powerful, God-seeking Jews was a great deal more threatening to the latter. Greek culture, in truth, was so appealing that it succeeded in persuading huge numbers of Jews, as well as huge numbers of other peoples, to abandon their ancient ways and adopt Greek language, attitudes, and social mores. Put another way, Greek culture won millions of converts throughout the Mediterranean world and beyond while the numbers of Greeks who converted to Judaism were so minuscule as to be virtually non-existent. Nevertheless, a significant majority of the Jews fiercely resisted the prevailing culture and, although impressed by and very willing to learn from Greek scientific and artistic accomplishments, refused to assimilate. They insisted on keeping their concept of God – the One God of Abraham, Isaac, and Jacob – the central focus of their lives. Jews were disturbed by many things about Greek culture, in particular the open homosexuality of Greek society, its veneration of nudity, its seemingly total abandon to the pursuit of pleasure, its widespread slavery (although mild and humane in comparison to the slavery that would soon be practiced by the Romans), and instances of pagan human sacrifice which, although becoming extraordinarily rare, was still practiced. The Greeks, for their part, although aware of the nearly universal literacy, high education levels, scientific achievements, and vast historical knowledge of the Jews, were troubled by many Jewish practices, particularly circumcision, which they considered brutal and barbaric, the kosher dietary restrictions, which they perceived as condescending and silly, and the constant Jewish denigration of Greek and pagan deities.

Greece stood, in relation to the ancient cultural, political, economic, and military landscape, in much the same way America stands today in relation to the modern landscape. In a word, the influence and appeal of Greece, like that of twentieth and twenty-first century America, was so overwhelmingly attractive as to be irresistible to most. The Jews alone, however, stubbornly set themselves apart with their self-image as the "Chosen People" in possession of a unique and special relationship with God. Gradually, Greek anger at Jewish inflexibility and perceived condensation toward others progressively heightened, and the earliest documented instances of anti-Semitism arose. In about 315 B.C.E., the Greek scholar, Hecataeus of Abdera, wrote that Jewish society was "an inhospitable and anti-human form of living." In around 250 B.C.E., the Greek-speaking and Greek-acculturated Manetho, an Egyptian priest, posited that "the Exodus was not a miraculous escape cruelly resisted by Pharaoh, but the expulsion of a dangerous leper colony." Greece's resentment came to a head in 175 B.C.E. after Antiochus Epiphanies became king of the Syrian portion of Alexander the Great's Hellenist empire, the territory of which included Judea, when he installed statues of Greek gods in the Jerusalem temple and outlawed, upon penalty of death, many of the most important Jewish practices. These conditions were unacceptable to most Jews, and beginning in 167 B.C.E., led by Mattathias of the Hasmonean family and his son, Judah the Maccabee, they revolted. Eventually, they wore down the Syrian-Greek troops and, in 147 B.C.E., proclaimed total victory when they succeeded in re-establishing control over most of their biblical homeland. The area they ruled became known as the Hasmonean Kingdom where, to the Jews' discredit, given their recent persecution by Antiochus, the Hasmonean sovereigns methodically, and at times brutally, suppressed pagan worship which had become extensive during the period of Greek control. That, of course, contributed to and hardened anti-Jewish attitudes. The Jews' newfound freedom, however, lasted less than a century. By 100 B.C.E., Greek political, military and economic influence was in dramatic decline, as Rome began to rapidly replace Greece as the paramount power, and became ascendant. Greek cultural influence, on the other hand, if anything, became even more widespread, because the Romans incorporated it, in only slightly modified form, into their own vast empire which, as a cohesive unit, far exceeded that of the Greeks. In 63 B.C.E., the Roman General, Pompey, deposed Hyrcanus II, the last of the Hasmonean kings, and Judea became a Roman province. At first, the Romans, who had never before been in such close contact with the Jews, were extremely tolerant and permitted them a great deal of freedom and self-government. After only a quarter of a century, however, they became painfully aware, as had the Greeks before them, of the incredible, religiously driven Jewish opposition to even minimal assimilation. Whereas the majority of the peoples over whom the Romans held sway welcomed the peace, stability, rule of law, roadway and public building infrastructure, and opportunities for economic prosperity their empire offered, the Jews fiercely resisted. As a result, Rome's attitude toward its disruptive Jewish subjects soon became as negative as that of the Greeks. In 45 C.E., Emperor Claudius, for example, warned them that if they continued to be intolerant, they would be treated as a people who intentionally spread "a general plague throughout the world." And a bit later, in around 100 C.E., the Roman historian Tacitus wrote, "The Jews regard as profane all that we hold sacred; on the other hand, they permit all that we abhor," and "...customs of the Jews are debased and abominable and owe their persistence to their depravity...," and also, "...the Jews are extremely loyal to one another and always ready to show compassion, but toward every other people they feel only hate and enmity."

Greek and Roman feelings, although extreme, were not entirely baseless. How else could they have reacted to the Jews' insistence that the Greek/Roman gods were debased and profane and only the One God of Abraham was valid and virtuous? In modern times, it has become fashionable in many synagogues for rabbis to teach that Jews are the "Chosen People," not because they are intrinsically special or were selected by God above all others to do his work, but because the Jews were the first people to have chosen, of their own volition, to obey the one, universal God's laws – including "Do not kill," "Do not steal," and "Be kind to strangers" – and thereby try to build a better world for everyone. This teaching, obviously, is far less offensive and condescending to non-Jews than the traditional formulation. This teaching, however, if it existed at all during the few centuries before and after the start of the Common Era, was not, putting it mildly, prevalent among the ancient Jews. What the Greeks and Romans perceived themselves to be confronting was an arrogant, insular, and self-righteous tribe, fanatically hostile to every religion but their own, who refused to break bread with others because of their incomprehensible kosher rules and who practiced – universally among all their males, not a single one having escaped the *mohel* – the barbaric rite of circumcision. Given that perception and the relative inflexibility of the Jews in comparison to all other peoples the Greeks and Romans had contact with, it is not surprising that they ultimately became deeply anti-Semitic. As uncomfortable as it may be for anyone who values his Jewish identity to search for reasons, like the above, that from some perspectives may logically – even warrantedly – have given rise to anti-Jewish feelings, I think the only way to understand anti-Semitism is to try to "feel it" through the mindsets of those who practiced, and in some cases, were consumed by it.

The Romans' distaste for their Jewish subjects, like the Greeks', did not subside and, due to numerous armed confrontations and brutal crackdowns because of the unrelenting pressure by Rome to assimilate, the Jews ultimately rose up and launched a full-scale rebellion in 66 C.E.. It was a massive uprising but, unlike two and a third centuries earlier, when they rose against the Syrian-Greeks and re-established an independent kingdom, this time they were decimated. This time, they not only failed to win independence, but General Titus burned the Second Temple to the ground and his father, Emperor Vespasian, enslaved the Jewish populace. Nevertheless, less than a century later in 131 C.E., under the leadership of Shimon Bar Kochba, still defiant and unbowed, the Jews again revolted and for a few years regained control over most of Judea. But in 135 C.E., they were trounced, Bar Kochba executed, and most of the Jews expelled from Jerusalem. Thus began the Diaspora, which did not end until nearly two millennia later with the re-establishment of independent modern Israel in 1948. But back in 136 C.E., as a final nail in the coffin, Emperor Hadrian (117 – 138 C.E.) pointedly completed construction of a huge shrine to Jupiter he had broken ground for just before the revolt, on the exact site of the destroyed Second Temple. As it was to turn out, however, even the deep enmity toward Jews prevalent among the ancient Greeks and Romans paled and was nothing as compared to the coming anti-Semitism of Christendom.

Between the date of Jesus's crucifixion in 33 and the revolt in 66, and for decades afterward, nearly all persons who identified themselves as Christian were still viewed by the Romans, and often by themselves, as adherents of the Jewish faith. There was good reason for this, because virtually everyone who became Christian in the few years immediately following Jesus's crucifixion was Jewish. Even a quarter of a century after his death, the first Gospel had not yet been written and, despite the widely disseminated epistles of Paul, Christian theology was centuries from being fully developed. The fact is that even after Paul's execution by Emperor Nero (37 – 68 C.E.) in 66 C.E., although he had succeeded in winning thousands of Christian converts from the pagan masses, the Romans continued to describe the man Paul believed to be God's son, derogatorily, as the "King of the Jews." In Roman eyes at the time, Jesus was just a rebellious, fanatically religious rabbi, and they did not look upon him as the originator of a new religion. More so, because the early Christians had no separate holy book of their own, and they used the Hebrew Bible or, more often, its Greek translation, the Septuagint, just like the Jews. Paul's epistles and the writings of some other early Christians, Jesus's brother James, for example, would not be elevated to the level of scripture for decades to come, the four Gospels not finished until the second century, and the New Testament not rendered in final form for another two hundred years. Christianity was still at its very beginning. Moreover, at no time during the first century after Christ's birth did more than a few handfuls of the Roman citizen-elite, unlike the non-citizen masses, ever accept that he was a divine being. The Roman citizen-elite was as much anti-Christian as it was anti-Semitic, because to them, the Christians were just a breakaway Jewish sect.

That would change dramatically after Constantine succeeded his father, Constantius, and became emperor of the Western Roman Empire in 306; defeated his rival for the throne there, Maxentius, in 312, attributing the victory to the intervention of Christ; outlawed the persecution of Christians in 313; reunited and became sole emperor of the Western and Eastern (Byzantine) empires in 324; installed Christianity as the official religion of the united Roman Empire in 325; and was himself baptized, shortly before his death, in 337. Constantine, who began life as a pagan sun worshipper and at first strongly supported laws that were hostile to Christians, ended up as one of the four most important people in all Christian history. The other three are Paul, Augustine, and Jesus himself. Whereas Augustine, by far the greatest of Christian philosophers, would in the next century solidify Christianity's heavenly infrastructure, i.e., its theology, Constantine solidified its worldly infrastructure, i.e., its institutions of power in the here and now on earth and, like Paul before him, propelled Christianity along its way to becoming the most widely practiced religion on the planet. Under Constantine, the governing organs of the Roman Empire endowed the Church with special legal rights, enthusiastically supported its seminaries and teachings, aggressively participated in its theological development, encouraged its proselytizing, massively funded it and, with the Roman army, guarded it against all enemies. The Roman Empire, therefore, really was, in fact not theory, the edifice that enabled Christianity to exert influence over millions and explosively grow. Constantine was the first emperor, and for that matter, the first sovereign anywhere, to reign in the name of Christ. After him, all Roman emperors, with the single exception of Julian the Apostate (361 – 363 C.E.), ruled as Christians, culminating in the establishment of the Holy Roman Empire by Charlemagne's successors in 960. Even after the collapse of the Holy Roman Empire in 1648, which had never been that cohesive and, according to Voltaire, "never really holy, Roman, nor an empire," all European sovereigns, whether Catholic or Protestant, continued to justify their rule by claiming "the divine rights of Christian Kings." In contrast, Jewish kings never claimed such "divine rights"; God was the only true King, all human beings were made in his image, and the Jews, as a people, had been chosen as his messengers with the task of being, by their example, "a light unto nations."

By the time Constantine took power in the early 300s, Christianity had totally separated from Judaism and the collective Christian memory that the earliest of them – like Paul, Peter, and James – were all originally Jews was fast fading. Think of it this way: The timeframe between the crucifixion of Jesus in 33 C.E. and the installation by Constantine of Christianity as the official religion of the Roman Empire in 325 C.E. was 292 years, more than a half-century *longer* than the period between the American Revolution in 1776 and the 2006 publication date of this book, a relatively short interval of only 232 years. Yet shockingly few of us today, despite all the sources of information available to us, have detailed knowledge about or meaningfully identify with any of the revolutionary personages like Washington, Hamilton, Paine, Adams, Nathan Hale, etc. Except for a very small percentage of us, Americans are no longer a people of predominantly British ancestry like we were when the Declaration of Independence, Constitution, and Bill of Rights were written. Rather, we are now overwhelmingly non-British immigrants or the children of non-British immigrant parents. The ancient Christians of Constantine's time, without the benefit of legions of historical researchers, computers, the Internet, vast libraries, compulsory public education, nor even printing presses and newspapers, would have had even less knowledge, apart from what they were taught in church, about their Jewish predecessors, *292 years earlier*, and would all but have forgotten Christianity's Jewish roots. The vast majority of new Christians in 325 were the children of Christian parents or recent pagan converts. They had no allegiance whatsoever to any previous Jewish identity. The period during which large numbers of Jews voluntarily converted to Christianity which, for the most part, was the two decades or so immediately after Jesus's death, was long over. Therefore, the only perspective on Jews the Christians of Constantine's time had — as opposed to the early Christians, who had once themselves been Jews — was the theology they learned from their priests. And what did their priests teach? Backed by all the institutions of power of the Roman Empire, they continually proclaimed: "Christians are the new Chosen People and have replaced the Jews who grievously sinned, continue to sin, and refuse to repent." What was the Jews' sin? They murdered the Son of God. Never mind that Jesus had been Jewish and considered himself such all his life. Never mind that all of Jesus's teachings were based on the Hebrew Bible, which consisted of the five books of Moses, the writings of the Hebrew prophets, and other Hebrew writings like the psalms of King David and the proverbs of his son, King Solomon. Never mind that the Romans, not the Jews, executed Jesus, albeit he certainly had Jewish theological opponents, some of whom may not have regretted his passing. Never mind that but for Judaism, upon which Christianity is entirely based, there would be no Christianity. Never mind that as to basic ethics, Jewish and Christian teachings, both of which derive from the Ten Commandments, are virtually identical. Jesus's instruction "Do unto others as you would have them do unto you" is exactly the same as that of Rabbi Hillel, who died just a few years before Christ's birth, having said: "What is hateful unto you do not do unto your neighbors." In fact, Jewish Jesus likely knew of and reworded Jewish Hillel's earlier instruction so as to make it, more powerfully expressed, his own.

So if at bedrock, Christian ethical teachings are virtually the same as Jewish, what happened? The answer is primarily and obviously what it has always been, *this*: The Jews refused to accept Jesus as the true God, descended from David himself, the very messiah foretold by their own scriptures. To Christians, Jesus was the pathway to the Father, to wisdom, to love, to righteousness, to heaven, to life everlasting, but the Jews, seemingly on purpose, tried to block their way. They laughed at Christians, sneered at them, looked upon them as inferiors, less intelligent, unrighteous, as *goyim*. Yet it was the Christians whose message attracted tens of millions, not Jews; the Christians who had converted and now governed the Roman Empire, not Jews; the Christians whose religion was so uplifting that it explosively grew, not Jews; and the Christians whose bishops' influence and power rivaled and often exceeded that of kings and emperors, not Jews. Who were the Jews to sneer? Who were they to condescend? How dare they continue to proclaim: "We, and only we, are the Chosen People"? Defeated, exiled, scattered, unsettled, dwindling in numbers, weak and growing pathetically weaker still. Some Chosen People! And why were they weak? Why were they suffering? It couldn't be clearer: They had brought it upon themselves because they rejected, and still rejected, Jesus, the one true God. And not only that, unlike any other group that refused Him, the accursed Jews murdered Him. He, who was the Father, the Son, the Holy Spirit and everything else good all at once. Couldn't the Jews see that? No! Whatever the Jews once were, they were no longer. They had become evil and refused to repent. *They* were inferior; *they* were less intelligent; *they* were unrighteous. No longer were they the "Chosen"; God's grace had obviously passed from them to the Christians. Let the Jews' heavy suffering bear witness to the punishment that, deservedly, the Almighty hurled down upon this contemptible people who refused to convert.

Unlike Christendom, Greece and pre-Christian Rome had not cared what gods or God the Jews, or any of the peoples they ruled over, believed in, as long as the constituent peoples of their empires obeyed the law, paid taxes, did not interfere in the general prosperity, and accepted, at least ceremonially, the supreme sovereignty of the Greek and Roman emperors. Primarily, their anti-Semitism had arisen from the perceived arrogance and condensation of the people called Jews, and definitely not from their refusal to worship pagan deities. Greece and Rome, for the most part, simply did not proselytize. They were perfectly willing to permit the practice of whatever faiths their subject peoples deemed fit. Even Antiochus Epiphanies might not have outlawed Judaism had his Jewish subjects been willing to acknowledge Greek religion as at least somewhat legitimate, if only outwardly and no matter how disingenuously, the same as he at first had been willing to acknowledge Judaism. The Jews, however, were not only unwilling to acknowledge Greek deities, or Roman, but instead were almost literally, continuously "on the warpath" against them. In the Hebrew Bible, the prohibition against idolatry is the *second* of the Ten Commandments – *"You shall not make for yourself an idol, whether in the form of anything that is in heaven above, or is on the earth beneath, or that is in the water under the earth, You shall not bow down to them or worship them; for I the LORD your God am a jealous God, punishing children for the iniquity of parents, to the third and fourth generations of those who reject me ..."* – and it ranks way above even the prohibition against murder, which is the Sixth Commandment or the prohibition against "bearing false witness" (lying), which is the ninth. The First Commandment also drives the point home: *"I am the Lord your God, who brought you out of the land of Egypt, out of the house of slavery; you shall have no other gods before me."* It was this theology that it made it impossible for the Jews to accept pagan Greek and Roman religious practice as in any way legitimate, although that was not the case not the other way around. That is, there was nothing in pagan theology preventing the Greeks and Romans from accepting the legitimacy of Jewish practice. In fact, they preferred to think of Yahweh, the Jewish God, as just another of the many deities worshipped throughout their empires. The Jews, however, could never permit that and insisted their God was the only God and all others were false.

Christianity's take on Jews was much different. First and foremost, their hatred of Jews, as opposed to Greek and Roman, *was* theological and only later became ethnic. The Jews, since they believed in one God, were clearly not pagans, but to Christians, they were considerably worse. To Christians, the God the Jews believed in was false; they had arrogantly rejected the true one and, most damning of all, they, not pagans, not the Romans, had murdered him. Among even the most educated, it became accepted fact: "True, the Romans nailed Christ to the cross but the Jews had instigated and encouraged it." It simply did not occur to most Christians, looking back, that Jewish Jesus was executed for the most obvious of reasons: The ideas he espoused were dangerously disruptive and Rome decided to eliminate him before the forces of revolution coalesced and he led an uprising. And if not him, then before the movement he created caused one. The feared uprising was forestalled, but less than a generation after the crucifixion, while eyewitnesses to Jesus's life were still alive, and in the very year Paul was executed, 66 C.E., a massive, full-scale rebellion began. This was a Jewish, not Christian, uprising that included virtually all Jewish-Christians. In 66, Christianity had not yet totally split from Judaism and was still, primarily, just a Jewish sect. Christians were so closely associated with Jews, in their own minds and in Jewish ones, that when Jesus's brother James, who other than Paul was the most prominent Jewish-Christian of his day, was assassinated in 62 by the Romans, it so angered the Jews that it was one of the major events that triggered the revolt.

By the time of Augustine, Christian theological hatred of Jewish beliefs, i.e., of Judaism, had become a hatred of Jewish people; a magnified echo of the Greek/Roman hatred of the "arrogant," "insular," and "condescending" Jewish tribe. In very large part, this had to do with the fact that the Jews, the descendents of the tribe of Judah, were a racial/ethnic group in addition to being adherents of the religion called Judaism. Prior to and during Augustine's life (354-430 C.E.), and for centuries afterward, virtually all practitioners of Judaism, except for a few handfuls of pagan converts from time to time, were ethnically Hebrews. Even as early as about the third century B.C.E., the only surviving and identifiable Hebrews, i.e., descendents of the twelve tribes of Israel, were the progeny of the tribe of Judah. Ten of the other tribes had disappeared from history when they were dispersed after Assyria conquered Israel, the Northern Hebrew Kingdom, in 722 B.C.E. Of the remaining two tribes, Benjamin also disappeared because it was so small that it had been totally incorporated into and absorbed by Judah, the largest of the tribes and the name of the Southern Kingdom. Thus, all of the last surviving Hebrews were descendents of the tribe of Judah, called Ju's a.k.a. Jews, and they were the only group that practiced Judaism.[4] Christianity ended that ethnic group's claim to sole ownership of the ethical teachings of the Old Testament and brought them to the world at large unencumbered by circumcision, kosher rules, and other impenetrable Jewish rituals. In other words, Christianity cut Judaism away from the ethnic group that founded it – the remnant of the Hebrews known as Jews – and made it, in its revised Christian form, a system of morality and beliefs that actively sought out and welcomed converts, regardless of their ethnicity. Moreover, Christianity claimed that, far from being hostile to Judaism, it was actually its fulfillment because Jesus was the long-awaited messiah foretold in the Old Testament. Yet the Jews, just as they had resisted Greek and Roman practices, ferociously resisted Christianity. They were one of the few ethnic groups in the ancient Western world to so completely reject it. That rejection triggered intense loathing among Christians because, on top of the Greek and Roman ethnically centered Jew hatred that was already in place — they are a people with "an inhospitable and inhuman form of living" (Hecataeus) and they "spread a general plague throughout the world" (Claudius), Christianity added the heretofore non-existent theological dimension: The Jews, who had once been the Lord's Chosen People, now turned their back on Him and refused accept Jesus, the true God. That loathing, which turned ever more virulent through the centuries, became so deep-seated that all people with Jewish blood – even those who voluntarily converted to and embraced Christianity – were enveloped by it. Often, for example, it didn't matter to the Inquisition that many accused *conversos*[5] had been practicing Christians for generations. They were all suspect, and in the vast majority of cases doomed, because ethnically, they were still Jews. It didn't help that a Christian accuser, upon a converso's conviction for the crime of backsliding to Judaism, was awarded half the victim's property. Accusers, therefore, appeared by the thousands. And the truth or falsity of a converso's backsliding, in the minds of the Inquisitors, had little bearing; his or her Jewish blood was enough to merit imprisonment, torture or, in many cases, death by burning at the stake.

Today, in the third millennium, six centuries after the end of the Inquisition, the ethnic purity of Jews has been greatly diluted by several generations of intermarriage. That was not the situation, however, during the time of Constantine or Augustine in the fourth and early fifth centuries, nor even much later during the years of the Spanish Inquisition (approx. 1478-1834). Then, the Jews were still, much more so than now, a genetically distinct group. That situation had not changed during the Dark Ages (approx. 400-800 C.E.) nor Middle Ages (approx. 800-1450 C.E.), because those were years when the Jews were forced into segregated areas and lived apart and away from the general populations of the countries where they resided. They virtually never married outside their own or neighboring villages, let alone outside their own people, except in extremely rare instances. Moreover, that was the state of affairs not only in the Christian world, but everywhere. In the Islamic realms also, beginning in the seventh century, virtually every city had a separate Jewish section, and Jews were strictly prohibited from living elsewhere. For many centuries, however, the Jews were not subject to the same level of physical intimidation in the Islamic countries as they were in Europe. In fact, in Dark and Middle Age Christian Europe, since Jews were universally detested and unwelcome, they often *wanted* to live in their own walled-off villages, to protect themselves from their neighbors. – And not just from physical attack, but also from contamination by what they considered "unkosher" practices. The word *ghetto*, however, was not used to describe "an area where Jews were compelled to live by law" until 1516, when by government decree, one was established on an island in Venice upon the site of an old iron foundry; *ghetto* being the Venetian word for foundry. Soon other ghettos were set up in Italy and throughout most of Europe. They were surrounded by walls, their gates locked at night, and the Jews required to wear identifying insignia, like yellow stars or conical hats, when they ventured out. The ghettoes lasted all through the Renaissance (approx. 1450-1700 C.E.) and did not disappear until the late 1800s. But the Pale of Settlement in Russia, which was a large area consisting of twenty-five Western provinces, was not even established until 1812, and not eliminated until a half century after the last ghetto disappeared; i.e., several years after the Russian Revolution in 1917 and the overthrow of the Czars. Within the Pale Jews were prohibited from engaging in most trades and therefore driven into extreme poverty, required nonetheless to pay exorbitant taxes and fees and thereby often forced into indentured servitude and, among many other injustices, subjected to conscription into the Russian army way out of proportion to their small numbers. They were virtual prisoners and unable to travel, even within the Pale, without special passes the fees for which were, along with the required bribes on top, astronomical. They were also the victims of repeated pogroms by Poles, Ukrainians, Cossacks, and other groups who had intentionally been incited into pitched anti-Semitic anger by the Czarist regimes to deflect attention from their own misgovernance. It was during the Pale period, in 1905, that the Czarist forgery, *The Protocols of the Elders of Zion,* was published. In Western Europe proper, meanwhile, the last legally compulsory ghetto, in Rome, was abolished in 1870. Only then did intermarriage really begin, becoming widespread starting in the early 1900s; especially in America, where the Jews had begun settling in large numbers after World War I. But for millennia prior thereto, the Jews possessed not only a separate religion, separate language, and a separate history, but were, in fact, an ethnically separate people with a very segregated gene pool.

That made them easy targets, although many Jews, like the *Marranos*,[6] were not so different in appearance from their neighbors that they were unable to conceal themselves and hide, undetected, within the general populations for years. Beginning around the time of Constantine and Augustine, however, with the Jews being in reality a distinct ethnic group and when the memory that the earliest Christians had all been Jews was just about gone, it was almost inevitable that Christian enmity toward Jewish people became as much racial as theological. Christendom's frustration and anger at the Jews' refusal to see the light, i.e., to convert, had been growing steadily ever since Paul's missionary travels. Christian minds began to search for reasons to explain why first thousands, then millions, then tens of millions accepted Jesus, but only the Jews stubbornly refused. "It must be," Christians thought, "something depraved deep within their basic make-up," and when that idea took root Christendom's hatred of Jewish religion rapidly transformed into a hatred also of anyone with Jewish blood – even of those who no longer practiced Judaism and had converted. Increasingly, Christians took note of their ascendancy and increasing prosperity in comparison to the rapid decline and growing poverty of the no-longer-numerous Jews. And they attributed the Jews' miserable and wretched lot to their depravity as a race. In fact, Christendom began to measure its self-perceived righteousness in direct inverse proportion to the Jews' suffering. The worse off the Jews, it seemed, the better off the Christians. To them, the worse the Jews suffered meant the more Christians had obviously earned God's favor since they, not the Jews, were prospering. The Jews' suffering demonstrated, they thought, for all to see, that the Christians were righteous and right about God. It made sense: God made the Jews suffer because they were "wrong" and the Christians prosper because they were "right." The more the Jews rejected Jesus, the more they suffered. The more Christians believed in Him, the more in comparison they prospered. It was Augustine himself who taught that *(paraphrased)* 'the suffering of the Jews is a permanent reminder to all of the fate that befell the followers of a religion that no longer taught the truth; they deserved to suffer and had brought it upon themselves.'

But Augustine was several notches above most Christian thinkers and did not believe that the Jews, because of their race, were beyond redemption. In this regard, he opposed, unlike many of his contemporaries, racially based anti-Semitism. He wrote: "Let us preach to the Jews, whenever we can, in a spirit of love... It is not for us to boast over them as branches broken off... We shall be able to say to them without exulting over them ...'Come, let us walk in the light of the Lord.'" But even Augustine could not hold back the coming, viciously hateful, anti-Semitic tide that would reverberate through the centuries and culminate in the twentieth with the greatest catastrophe to ever befall the Jews: Adolph Hitler's sadistic and nearly successful attempt to exterminate them.

Kristallnacht, the Night of Broken Glass, began in the early evening on November 9, 1938. When it was over, some twenty-four hours later, 7,500 Jewish stores and businesses had been ransacked, 267 synagogues set ablaze, 76 completely destroyed, and 91 Jews lay dead on streets in Germany and Austria. What started as basically a horrendous pogrom, but of the kind the Jews had seen and survived many times before, ended as the largest mass murder in history. In the concentration camps, more than 8 million people, 6 million of them Jews, amounting to approximately one-fourth of all Jews then living, perished. But what scares me, as much as if not more than the Holocaust itself, are the modern Holocaust deniers. Their efforts to rewrite history are obscene, but if previous efforts to spread falsehoods about Jews are any guide, some very successful like the Deicide charge, the Blood Libel, and the Protocols of the Elders of Zion, it is not at all clear that they will fail. Who is to say that 250 years from now, when all Holocaust survivors are long gone – as well as their children, grandchildren, great-grandchildren, and even great-great-grandchildren – that the historical evidence will still be persuasive and hold up? After all, even today the deniers allege that at most a few hundred thousand Jews were killed in the camps, the claim that millions were gassed is scientifically and logically ludicrous, the photographs are fakes, and the incessant mourning and whining of the Jews is just a Zionist effort to gain sympathy so as to enable them to control Palestine. Sometimes, they liken the claim that 6 million Jews were gassed to the biblical claim that Moses led 600,000 Jews out of Egypt and wandered the desert forty years: "Nonsense!" they say. "Absurd!" And millions if not tens of millions believe them. In the future, with the passage of time and the absence of living eyewitnesses, there is really no telling what historians may think. "Maybe," they may conclude, "the Holocaust actually happened but was grossly and shamefully exaggerated for political reasons." Remember, the evidence they will have in front of them and consider will be not only the Nuremberg trial transcripts and allegedly fake photographs but the literature and propaganda of the deniers. Recall for a moment the London court trial beginning in January 2000 involving British historian and notorious denier, David Irving. For years he'd been averring that the Jews were perpetrating a massive fraud; the gas chambers were never used to kill people but only to delouse clothing and blankets and dispose of the bodies of prisoners who had died from overwork, starvation, or natural causes. He took issue when author, Deborah Lipstadt, wrote about him disparagingly in her 1993 book, *Denying the Holocaust*, in which she called him anti-Semitic and racist, and he, get this, sued *her*, not the other way around. He claimed Lipstadt had libeled him and damaged his reputation. Throughout the proceedings, the numerous courtroom reporters and observers were never totally confident of the outcome and, as evidenced by their worried newspaper articles and interviews, fearful he could win. His arguments were sometimes strangely persuasive: 'I have the right to free speech,' he said, 'and in my opinion,' he continued, in sum and substance, 'the claim that millions of Jews were murdered is simply not supported by the reliable facts. It's just my opinion mind you, and that of some others, but here's what I base it on....'

And he proceeded to reel off a list of reasons that on their surface, God help us, often didn't seem insane or even irrational. Like "it was logistically impossible to have killed 6 million people," or, "given the huge reparations and compensation Jews insist they're entitled to, evidence has been distorted or manufactured," or "some Nazi criminals, acting without direct orders from above, maybe did carry out liquidations of certain groups, including Jews and gypsies, but the allied bombing of Dresden was much worse." At other times he ranted. At on point he addressed the judge as "Mien Fuhrer." Along the way, for good measure, he exhorted the Jews to "ask themselves why most people have hated them for 3,000 years." He – the denier sine qua non – lost, thank God; at least that time. Irving was ordered to pay Lipstadt $250,000 in legal fees and costs. But in the future there will be other denier trials, maybe not in courts of law but in the courts of public opinion, and I'm not going to bet my house on their outcome.[7]

When an event like what was perpetrated by Hitler on the Jews has befallen any other group, although it's nearly impossible to call to mind any other event as horrific as the Holocaust, legions of deniers and total revisionists do not rise up. The few who do are looked upon as what they are: ignorant, idiotic, and racist. Take, for example, the slavery of blacks in America. When's the last time you heard anyone try to deny it? When's the last time anyone claimed it was only 100,000 blacks, not millions? When's the last time you read a serious book trying to justify it? When's the last time someone said they deserved it? To be honest and accurate, contemptible ideas about blacks are out there, but consider who espouses them. The sources are almost invariably Klansmen or other white supremacist groups, not purportedly serious researchers and scholars, as is the case with the Jews. The only recent exception I can think of are authors Richard J. Hernstein and Charles Murray who co-wrote *The Bell Curve* in 1994. It purported to be a scientific study of why, genetically, blacks could not compete intellectually with whites, Asians, and some other groups. It was completely and totally discredited and never gained traction anywhere. The point is that hateful attitudes about blacks are clearly on the decline, whereas the same attitudes about Jews, if anything, seem to be on the rise. Or consider the experience of Native Americans, scores of thousands of whom were slaughtered during the seventeenth through nineteenth centuries by Europeans, and those few who survived herded onto reservations. No one says it didn't happen. No one denies our responsibility for bringing them to near extinction. And no one, from any quarter, says it was the right thing to do. We are today almost unanimously ashamed of it. True, there exists some resentment against Native Americans because of the special privileges they've been given, on their reservations, as a kind of attempt to make amends. They don't have to pay taxes; they can sell cigarettes and liquor at bargain-basement prices; they can run casinos. "Why should a tribe of a few thousand Sioux or Cherokee be given the means to become fabulously wealthy while the most the majority of us can ever hope for, by killing ourselves at our jobs every day, is a one-week vacation at Best Western or, if we're lucky, at the Marriott once a year?" That sentiment is fairly common and extremely widespread, but the pique that exists has nothing to do with racism. Most of us reluctantly accept that in order to bring Native Americans up to speed with the rest of us, economically, they deserve a few breaks. Until recently, most Americans accepted "affirmative action" as regards blacks for the same reason. That a sizable majority of whites are now opposed to affirmative action is a testament, I believe, to realization of the astonishing fact that incredibly large numbers of blacks, as compared to only a few years ago, have finally become bona fide members of the middle class. Most Native Americans, however, still live in extreme poverty on desolate reservations in the Southwest.

Where does all this leave the Jews? For starters, it is surely obvious that the inkling of resentment Americans feel at affirmative action for blacks or special privileges for Native Americans is quite mild as compared, for a recent example, to the resentment of modern Europeans at having been forced to pay Jews reparations for allying themselves with or collaborating with the Nazis. In particular, the seething bitterness of the Swiss, French, and others, caught red-handed with hundreds of millions in unpaid life insurance policies and hidden bank accounts they hoped would never be claimed, but belonged to Jews who perished during the Holocaust, is palpable. Their resentment has translated into irrational anger toward Israel – a nation of Jews – way out of proportion to its policies which have nearly always been designed with an eye toward achieving peaceful and mutually beneficial relations with its Arab neighbors – without, however, destroying itself in the process. That is, the vast majority of Israelis are willing give back land, lots of it, but insist that they retain enough to defend themselves. They will not be persuaded to sign their own death warrant. Recall that former Israeli Prime Minister Ehud Barak was willing, in sum and substance, to withdraw to the pre-1967 borders, just as the Palestinian leadership had always demanded, but when he made that proposal, Arafat withdrew from peace talks with no counteroffer and renewed terrorist attacks instead. That, despite the willingness of the Israelis and international community, as mentioned elsewhere in this book, to not only withdraw from territory but pay mega-billions in development money so that any Palestinian state would become economically viable. The truth is that the fanatics on the Jewish side can be controlled and forced, kicking and screaming if necessary, to go along with the majority of their countrymen. The fanatics on the Arab side, however, are so numerous and venomously hateful that they cannot be controlled by Israel, their own leadership, or anybody. In the Palestinian areas, in fact, the Arab fanatics, a.k.a. the recently elected Hamas, *are the leadership*. Their goal, which they have never denied but, indeed, repeatedly and proudly declare is to kill, exile, or rule over every Jew in Palestine. They want to "drive them all into the sea." To be fair, however, see the endnote indicated here, [8] because, according to some, it's Israeli Zionist policy that has nearly driven the *Arabs* into the sea. Nevertheless, even though that may be partly true, whenever the opportunity has arisen, the extremists have been willing to indiscriminately slaughter Jewish men, women, and children. They've been willing to slaughter Americans. They've been willing to slaughter any Arab who disagrees with them. They have dedicated their lives to fanatic resistance against all efforts to find a peaceful solution. Nor does the relatively mild inkling of resentment that Americans feel as regards Native American privileges or black affirmative action compare to the two millennia of Christendom's virulent hatred toward Jews for rejecting and allegedly murdering Jesus. That hatred brought on the Inquisition, the ghettoes, pogroms, and the Holocaust. Nor does it compare either, in its mild magnitude, to the intense ancient Greek and Roman anger at the "insular", "arrogant", and "condescending" Jewish tribe. This unrelenting anger and David Irving's taunt, "ask yourselves why most people have hated you for 3,000 years?" reverberates painfully in the minds and hearts of the Jewish people. First the Greeks, then the Romans, then Christendom, then the Arabs and Muslims and now, even many modern, enlightened, and highly educated Europeans. Why? Why the Jews?

This chapter, at least to some extent I hope, has answered that question by outlining the historical events that have shaped world opinion, much too often negatively, as regards the Jewish people. But there is a final, important piece to the puzzle which ties things together. In addition to Greek/Roman anger at the "arrogant" and "condescending" tribe, in addition to Christendom's anger at the rejecters and supposed murderers of the Son of God, in addition to the Islamic/Arab anger at the infidel usurpers of Muslim holy lands, and in addition to modern European resentment at having been forced to pay Jews reparations, we Jews have always occupied a place on the world stage absurdly out of proportion to our numbers. Throughout history, much more so than any other people, we've somehow often played starring roles and had vast impact in societies other than our own. We continue to do so. In the eyes of others, that has made us seem overly loud, overly visible, and forever front-and-center in their faces like an annoying prima donna. It could hardly be otherwise because we Jews claim to be the first people to whom God revealed Himself and the one people whom He selected, above all others, to enter with Him upon an unbreakable covenant. Judaism's daughter religions, Christianity and Islam, base their very legitimacy on the truth of that revelation. Both religions acknowledge that Moses received the law tablets and God spoke to the assembled Jewish nation in the desert at the foot of Mount Sinai. God had never before and has never again spoken to an *entire people*, and that experience was central to the Jews' self-perception as the Chosen People. Christians know that God spoke to Jesus, in fact was Jesus, but He did not speak as or through Jesus to an entire assembled people as He had spoken to the *entire* Jewish nation. And Muslims know that God revealed himself and spoke to Muhammad, whose scribes wrote down His words in the Koran, but He did not speak directly to the rest of them. Nevertheless, because of those new revelations – which were revelations to only single persons, not to entire nations – Christians and Muslims believed that the Jews had lost their way, lost God's favor, and thereby lost His covenant which He transferred to them. Because the Jews sinned by rejecting Jesus, the Christians supposedly became the new Chosen People and after them, according to Islam, the Muslims. But even so, despite their always small numbers, which became proportionately still smaller due to the explosively increasing numbers of Christians and Muslims, the Jews refused to leave the stage. That's made us, no question, like a very disturbing, very persistent, overwhelmingly loud sound, that many non-Jews wish they could just shut off and silence. In fact, that's the key to it; it's the secret of Jewish survival. We just won't exit the stage because to us, our role in the world is unfinished. We live on, still intact as the same people we were in ancient times, having outlasted the Egyptians, Assyrians, Babylonians, Persians, ancient Greeks, ancient Romans, and Dark and Middle Age Christendom because we believed then and still believe there remains ahead much for us to do. Our persistence dismays everybody. The command of our sages to "complete God's work by being a light unto nations" still inspires us. To us, our ancient history is no legend, no myth. It remains what it has always been: *real* and the sine qua non of our self-image as the "Chosen." It's our unbroken history that makes us immortal. South African novelist and social activist, Olive Schreiner (1855-1920),[9] may have put it best when in 1906 she wrote:

A Letter on the Jew
(Revised and Updated Posthumously)

"Indeed it is difficult for all other nations of the world to live in the presence of the Jews. It is irritating and most uncomfortable. The Jews embarrass the world as they have done things which are beyond the imaginable. They have become moral strangers since the day their forefather, Abraham, introduced the world to high ethical standards. They brought the world the Ten Commandments, which many nations prefer to defy. They violated the rules of history by staying alive, totally at odds with common sense and historical evidence. They outlived all their former enemies, including vast empires such as the Romans and the Greeks. They angered the world with their return to their homeland after 2000 years of exile and after the murder of six million of their brothers and sisters.

"They aggravated mankind by building, in the wink of an eye, a democratic State which others were not able to create in even hundreds of years. They built living monuments such as the duty to be holy and the privilege to serve others.

"They had their hands in every human progressive endeavor, whether in science, medicine, psychology or any other discipline, while totally out of proportion to their actual numbers. They gave the world the Bible and even their "savior."

"Jews taught the world not to accept the world as it is, but to transform it, yet only a few nations wanted to listen. Moreover, the Jews introduced the world to one God, yet only a minority wanted to draw the moral consequences. So the nations of the world realize that they would have been lost without the Jews. And while their subconscious tries to remind

them of how much of Western civilization is framed in terms of concepts first articulated by the Jews they do anything to suppress it.

"They deny that Jews remind them of a higher purpose of life and the need to be honorable, and do anything to escape its consequences. It is simply too much to handle for them, too embarrassing to admit and above all, to difficult to live by.

"So the nations of the world decided once again to go out of 'their' way in order to find a stick to hit the Jews. The goal: to prove that Jews are as immoral and guilty of massacre and genocide as some of they themselves are.

"All this in order to hide and justify their own failure to even protest when six million Jews were brought to the slaughterhouses of Auschwitz and Dachau; so as to wipe out the moral conscience of which the Jews remind them, and they found a stick.

"Nothing could be more gratifying for them than to find the Jews in a struggle with another people (who are completely terrorized by their own leaders) against whom the Jews, against their best wishes, have to defend themselves in order to survive. With great satisfaction, the world allows and initiates the rewriting of history so as to fuel the rage of yet another people against the Jews. This in spite of the fact that the nations understand very well that peace between the parties could have come a long time ago, if only the Jews would have had a fair chance.

"Instead, they happily jumped on the wagon of hate so as to justify their jealousy of the Jews and their incompetence to deal with their own moral issues. When Jews look at the bizarre play taking place in The Hague, they can only smile as this artificial game once more proves how the world paradoxically admits the Jews uniqueness. It is in their need to undermine the Jews that they actually raise them.

"The study of history of Europe during the past centuries teaches us one uniform lesson: That the nations which received and in any way dealt fairly and mercifully with the Jew have prospered; and that the nations that have tortured and oppressed them have written out their own curse."

The above is not at all an exact rendition of what Schreiner actually wrote. It's been embellished and updated several times since her death in 1920. She could not have known, for example, about Aushwitz or Dachau and the slaughter of millions of Jews there during World War II. Nor could she have known about the Jews' return to their homeland in 1948 with the re-establishment of Israel as an independent nation. Nonetheless, like Mark Twain, she viewed the Jews' accomplishments as incredible, as "beyond the imaginable," as "embarrass[ing] the world." Her insights as to why the Jews have been and are still so resented remain unrivaled by anyone.

Chapter Twenty Six - The Reluctant Jew

It was over. I stepped down as president of my beloved congregation in June 2003. Looking back, I knew that, far and away, the most important tasks I had accomplished were having infused the congregation with newfound energy, enormous enthusiasm and, most important, an unexpected but desperately needed high level of confidence about our future. Some of my own excitement about Judaism and the adventures of the Jewish people had clearly rubbed off. That amazed me because, despite all my reading and voracious appetite to learn Jewish history, I had always felt, in my role as president, that maybe I was just play-acting. How could I, a doubter and hardcore agnostic, a man who could barely read or pronounce a Hebrew word, ever have realistically expected to effectively lead an established, conservative-leaning congregation? Giving myself the benefit of every doubt, I was still, when my tenure ended, and had always been, from the moment I joined JCC, only a very amateur and reluctant Jew at best. Proof of this was that even after serving four long years as president, I was still embarrassed to talk about religion with my family or non-synagogue friends too much, because I feared doing so would create a distance between us and might drive them away. Sometimes, a close friend who knew me from the years before I joined JCC, or close family member who had known me all my life, would ask "Do you really believe all that nonsense?" or even "What's happened to you? How can you believe such crap?" What they didn't realize but I always reminded them was that my transformation was far from complete. Although I no longer considered most rabbis, ministers, and other religious leaders unthinking, medieval dogmatists, I was still beset with serious misgivings and deep bouts of cynicism. A Supreme Being? A righteous and caring God? Come on! Trying to force that down the throats of secularly raised, secularly educated, Woodstock generation people like me, or my circle of pre-synagogue friends, or my non-religious immediate family was well-nigh impossible. Especially against the background of the Holocaust, unremitting Middle East conflict, 9/11 terrorist attack, resurgent anti-Semitism, and other religiously driven horrors. A just God who cares about humanity? Yeah, right! Call Him Yahweh, Jesus, Allah, Vishnu, or whatever you want. If God exists, where is He already? Why won't He intervene?

And yet, it is undeniable we all have free will. Jewish teaching is that God left it to us try to complete His Creation work by building an earthly paradise – a holy community in the here and now – *by acts of loving kindness performed, not by God's compulsion, but of our own free wills*. That was part of the deal. That is, Jewish tradition teaches that God created us in His image by placing a divine spark in each of us, but He gave us the freedom to think and do whatever we please. He resolved not to control our minds or actions. He thus made us capable of doing great good or great evil, but we have to choose which path to follow on our own. Therefore, the argument goes, the horrors in the world are of human making, not God's. In accord with these ideas, I think the majority would agree that although many of us have done horrendous evil, most of us do both good and evil during our lives and, moreover, aspire to do good as often as possible. Both impulses, therefore, reside in everyone, and the struggle for each person is which will prevail. And what do we consider good? Making money? Acquiring power? Becoming famous? Having successful careers? Each of these objectives is much sought after by just about everyone, but they are clearly not what we mean by "the quality of being good." To most of us, that quality means nothing more than being kind to, caring about, and helping others. How rich, powerful, famous, or successful we are does not correlate with whether we are good. Which brings us to this question: If God does not exist, why do most of us seem to care so much that we all behave justly toward one another? Why do we measure our own goodness and the goodness of the societies in which we live as a function of how the minorities and most needy among us are treated? Why, in fact, do we define the very essence of goodness in terms of how well or poorly we treat other people? Maybe human beings are just born that way? But that's no real answer, because we're left with another question: Why are we born that way? Perhaps it's in our chemical make-up?. But again: Why is it in our chemical make-up? So we're back to where we started: If God doesn't exist, what is it that seems to so compel us to care about trying to do good and, to boot, to define the essence of being "good" as "how well we treat others"?

One answer is this: God – i.e., the force that makes us capable of doing great good – does exist, if not in scientific reality, as is believed by the orthodox, then certainly in our collective spiritual imagination, as is true for many of the non-orthodox rest of us. For the most religious and orthodox, God is a concrete, tangible, and undoubtedly existent entity. They sense His divine presence in everything. For the less religious, God is a hoped-for possibility. They want him, sometimes need him to be real, but are not certain. They long for the reassurance of an ordered world watched over by a righteous force or being. For agnostics, God probably does not exist, and more likely is a creation of the human mind, residing only in the imagination. They acknowledge they could be wrong, but feel the evidence is overwhelmingly in their favor. For them, goodness stems not from God but from the minds and hearts of human beings. And for atheists "Religion," in the words of Karl Marx, "...is the opium of the people."[1] There is and never has been a God, miracles and prayers are nonsense, and the only sources of morality are man's sometimes base instincts and not-to-be-trusted intentions, which must be harnessed and controlled for the greater good. On this scale, I am closest to the agnostics, and that's why I describe myself as a reluctant Jew. It's only with great skepticism that I can even entertain the possibility that a Supreme Entity might exist, although somehow my mind has become open to it. My assessment that such a possibility is extremely remote is also the reason I am still only an amateur Jew. If a person only half-heartedly believes there might be an *Elohim*, like me, why should he or she bother mastering the prayers and rituals religious tradition says are necessary to communicate with Him? If you just mindlessly mouth the words and disinterestedly do the rituals, you never learn them. They have to become important to you and mean something before you can internalize them. I'm still trying, but am not up to "How does God want me to pray?" and will always be working on, "Does He really exist at all?"

In Judaism, fortunately, belief in God is important, but not everything. There are millions of secular, agnostic/atheist Jews around who, nonetheless, treasure their Jewish identities. Being Jewish, i.e., *"an Israelite,"* means being *"a struggler with God,"* as was Jacob, who wrestled all night with an angel and was crippled in the process, but does not require blind acceptance of every article of faith. All but the ultra-Orthodox, in fact, make room in the Jewish house for almost every opinion and for almost everyone, including amateur Jews and reluctant ones. Jacob, you'll recall, was unable to defeat the angel, but even more important, metaphorically, and very surprisingly, the angel could not defeat him. That is, the angel could not *force* Jacob to believe he was confronting a divine entity. After their all-night wrestling match, the angel, exasperated, withdrew and God renamed Jacob *"Israel,"* thus honoring him. God must have looked approvingly upon Jacob's refusal to unthinkingly accept the angel's pretensions of holiness, i.e., his airs of being a divine being, and then, disgusted at the angel's refusal to identify himself, physically grappling with him in an effort to chase him off. Thus, a struggler with God can mean not only one who struggles with God physically, or one who struggles with what God wants us to do, or how He wants us to do it, but also one who struggles with whether He really exists at all. Thank God it's a big and welcoming house, or someone like me would never have been invited to enter it.

But, despite all my doubts and misgivings, and despite my being only an amateur and very reluctant Jew, I managed to do a reasonably good job of leading Congregation B'nai Torah/JCC from the brink of disaster to the brink of success. If, after I left office, just a few more things fell into place, we might really cross the Rubicon and become something special.

There were, however, some very serious problems. When I left office, notwithstanding all my efforts, the synagogue's membership was still quite small, although holding steady, and its financial situation still frighteningly tenuous, although profitable fundraisers were in place. Just as Susan Lobel had designated me, more or less, to be her successor four years earlier, it now fell upon me, with much-needed input from the board of trustees, to search for someone suitable to become my own successor. And the next president no doubt was going to have her hands full.

But there was hope and solid reason to believe things would continue to improve. First of all, the Annual Dinner Dances we had been running, beginning with the affair we held for Jesse Goldstein, our longest-serving active member, shortly after I took office – the first Dinner Dance the congregation had put together in more than fifteen years – were all tremendously successful fundraisers. Jesse's dinner brought in what was for us a phenomenal sum of money. The next year's dinner dance, honoring Al and Sylvia Levy, was also hugely profitable. Al had been president of the congregation before Susan Lobel – that is, ten years before the date my term ended – and Sylvia had been treasurer starting way before even that and continued in the position until my successor took office. They were both extremely well-known and liked, not only among the congregation, but in the community at large. They were also my personal, very favorite people at the synagogue. I loved them. For that reason, I twisted all our congregants' and all my business associates' arms so hard that most of them felt compelled to place ads or announcements in their Dinner Journal. With that, and money coming in from ads placed by local stores and businesses, we again collected, what was for us, a ton of money. The next year, we honored Frank and Lillian Hilowitz, another couple who had been active in synagogue affairs for longer than almost anyone could remember. Frank had been on the board of trustees and Lillian had been our financial secretary for — get this — almost two decades. But you know, there comes a point where you can't keep asking the same people you asked in previous years to make yet another generous donation. They begin to resent your assumption and expectation that they can always be called upon to willingly fork over a few hundred or even a few thousand dollars. That began to happen. My business associates, whom I had tapped for contributions for the Dinner Journals in the two prior years, didn't want to be bothered anymore. They didn't answer my letters and they ignored my calls. As a result, it was very difficult to fill up Frank and Lillian's Journal with a sufficiently large number of ads but, nevertheless, we managed. Lo and behold, we were able to raise a respectable amount of money. That is not to say that the Dinner Dance being planned to honor me and my wife, after I left office, would be a disaster. However, I was worried because that time around, since I was the honoree, it would be inappropriate for me to be out there aggressively soliciting money for my own Dinner Journal like I had always done for the previous honorees. I just wasn't sure that anyone else on the Dinner Dance Committee would be willing to be nearly as aggressive as I had been. Given that our usual donors were becoming resistant, I felt there was real cause for concern. And, brother, calling myself aggressive when it came to fundraising doesn't begin to cover it. Once, for example, for Jesse Goldstein's Dinner Journal, I visited one of the large local supermarkets in our area and insisted upon seeing the manager. After a few minutes, I was shown into his office.

I said, "My name is Michael Grossman and I'm the president of Congregation B'nai Torah on Old Dutch Hollow Road. We're a small synagogue and I've been visiting local businesses to ask that you help us stay open by placing advertisements in our Dinner Journal. Here's one of our previous journals and, as you can see, many merchants around here helped us out. You know a lot of our congregants patronize your store, and we'd really appreciate it if you'd take a half-page or even full-page ad this year."

He replied, "Well, it's good to meet you, Mr. Grossman, but unfortunately, company policy is that we just aren't permitted to make contributions like that. I'll put in a request, but I'm certain I won't get approval. They never okay those requests. Sorry."

I said, "Really. That's very strange, because I asked around before I decided to come see you, and have with me three journals in which your store placed ads last year. Look, this one is the Lutheran Church's Journal, this one's the Methodists', and this one's the Presbyterians'. In fact, Minister Jervin is a friend of mine and he told me to see you personally."

The manager, so help me, actually began to perspire. A bit shaken, he said, "Hmmm. I didn't realize, uh, let me make a call. Can you stop back in half an hour or so?"

I said, "Sure. Here's the price sheet. And since you took out half-page ads in the church journals, please be fair and do at least the same for us."

When I returned, the manager handed me an envelope. I opened it. Inside was a check for 600 bucks, exactly enough for a full *silver* page ad. He said, "They approved it right away. Sorry for the misunderstanding."

I said, "No problem. See you next year."

And I did.

There were other instances like that. I had been very good on the practical front when it came to things like fundraising, organizing events, completing projects, and thinking of the right things to say when called upon to make speeches at affairs like bar mitzvahs or community dinners. In other words, I was good at getting things done. Where I was weak was in my commitment to the whole "God enterprise." As I had told Susan Lobel when she asked me to become second vice president of the synagogue years earlier, "You can't be serious, Susan. You know I have absolutely no religious training or background. You know I don't speak or read Hebrew, that I can barely follow the services, and I was never even bar mitzvahed. And you've heard me try to speak Yiddish and know that I mispronounce every word. My accent, in fact, is a joke around here. Not only that, I don't even think there's a God. How can I possibly be part of the leadership of this, a Conservative synagogue, or any synagogue? Why don't you ask Pat or Gary Birnberg? Or even Warren? You'd be better off with him."

As it turned out, although Susan Lobel and most of the members of the board of trustees and congregation were far more religious than I, they didn't hold it against me. In fact, it didn't even faze them. They seemed to welcome my evolving, albeit skeptical commitment to Judaism and even more, my intense determination to make the synagogue an ongoing success. That's why the Dinner Dance in my – the Reluctant Jew's – and Phyllis's honor, that was held a few months after I left office, was extremely successful; not so much financially, but as a rallying point for the even bigger accomplishments we hoped to achieve under the leadership of the next president.

Chapter Twenty Seven - The Dinner Dance

Although Pat Weisslander had officially taken my place as president in June, it didn't fully sink in until my wife and I walked through the synagogue's doors on November 1, 2003 as Congregation B'nai Torah's Annual Dinner Dance honorees. Most of my family, my closest friends, and the congregation's membership turned out. I had stood before them many times during the past four years, and talked much too long, but this time I knew would be the last before people's attention turned fully to the new leadership, and the only permanent reminder of my once having been at the center of things would be my name affixed to the plaque of former synagogue presidents that hung on the wall. As much as I was glad to be unburdened, I already sorely missed the fun, challenge, and excitement of being the key figure in trying to transform JCC into a great congregation. I had so enjoyed and become so accustomed to that role, it was difficult for me to believe it was over. JCC's Constitution, however — wisely, I thought — prohibited the president from serving more than two consecutive two-year terms and thus, even when many in the congregation urged me to stay on and suggested we vote to amend the constitution, I strongly felt that was a bad idea. Despite my inner wish that my term hadn't ended, I firmly believe that periodic new leadership is essential to any organization. After a while, existing leaders often become overly complacent, grow too comfortable with their routines, and start to lose their edge. With fresh leadership comes fresh energy and fresh ideas, and that, I knew, was what Pat Weisslander could offer. She had, for example, already put in place increasingly successful weekly Sunday night bingo games, which were at last starting to show a profit and become a much-needed source of revenue. To Pat, as well as to her son, Todd, and her father, Norman, the congregation was perhaps the central thing in her life. That had been demonstrated by her nearly 100-percent attendance at every synagogue event, including community dinners, all holidays, inter-religious services, adult ed., Hebrew school activities, and all outings; her long and indefatigable service as our corresponding secretary; her volunteering to help with virtually every project going on at JCC; and by, believe it or not, being the record holder for the most consecutive Friday night services ever attended by anyone, including rabbis and cantors. Pat was so knowledgeable about the services, in fact, that when our rabbi wasn't around, she'd step in and run them instead. There's no telling how far Pat might have been able to push Congregation B'nai along the path of success, were we not staggered by a disaster that, as of the date of my dinner dance, hadn't yet struck, but would on February 23, 2004, only eight months into her term as president. That calamity, from which we slowly and painfully recovered, we'll talk more about later.

In the meantime, though, things were looking up. As Phyllis and I walked to our table, people warmly greeted us and extended congratulations. The mayor of Greenwood Lake was there. Our Orange County assemblyman was there. The minister from the Greenwood Lake Church of the Good Shepherd was there, and the priest from the local Holy Rosary Roman Catholic Church was there. A candidate running for Orange County judge was there. My friend, our former rabbi, Reuben Modek, was there. My kids and my dad were there. And all those JCC members who had worked with me through thick and thin and formed, in essence, the heart of the congregation, were there. I didn't cry but I wanted to. Every moment I'd served as president had been an almost doctoral education in Jewish and world history, an amazing spiritual adventure, and a phenomenal blessing and honor. That most members thought I had done good job, despite some horrific gaffes, was in itself an honor. The worst of those gaffes was my having forgotten to tell Rabbi Modek that one of our longest-serving members had died, after her daughter-in-law called me with the bad news in my office on a late Thursday afternoon. As a result, when the family sat *shiva* during the next several days, virtually no one from the congregation joined them. I've never been able to fully forgive myself for that but, as I looked around the room, I noticed that the deceased's son, daughter-in-law and many of her other family members were there anyway. Although I couldn't forgive myself, they apparently were ready to at least try. Thank you, Robert, Wendy, Allison, and Michael Dembeck, and thank you, Carole Zove. And during Yom Kippur a year later, in 2004, after the *Al Khet* prayer, meaning *For Sins (We've Committed)*, I finally gathered the courage to approach them and ask their forgiveness face-to-face.

I realized, however, that the good turnout was almost as much a show of support for the synagogue's new leadership as it was a kind of goodbye party for me. That was important because, although I had succeeded in holding the place together pretty well, by organizing some very successful fundraisers, by significantly increasing Hebrew school enrollment, by reopening our long-defunct Judaica shop, and by, in general, instilling a lot of new excitement and energy, we had only just started to turn the corner. We still had a very long way to go, and the new leadership was going to need all the support it could get. We had, for example, a lot riding on Pat's increasingly successful bingo games, and on the profitable annual dinner dances I'd instituted, with their accompanying Dinner Journals filled with paid for ads and announcements, but, even together, they weren't going to be enough to save us financially. We were still deep in the red and had to do something fast to make ends meet. My dinner dance, which brought in a few thousand much-needed dollars in profit, was going to be, hopefully, the launching pad for the new administration.

The same three-man non-Jewish band that had performed at the four previous dinner dances began playing. The youngest of them had to have been at least over seventy-five. They weren't Jewish, but might as well have been. After about twenty minutes, the oldest said, "We're taking a break now. If we're not back soon, call 911." While they'd been playing, our congregants had been devouring everthing at the hors d'oeuvres table. As the guests of honor, my wife and I tried to show some restraint and decorum, but that didn't stop us from elbowing our way to the whole, huge whitefish at the center of the table and attacking it. After the band returned and played for another half hour, the caterer's helpers started ushering us to our seats for the kosher sit-down dinner. As these affairs go, the food wasn't bad, and compared to some of the previous caterers we'd used, it was an absolute banquet. While we ate, speakers presented awards to the outgoing leaders, who included not only me but First Vice President David Weinberg, Treasurer Sylvia Levy, Financial Secretary Lillian Hilowitz, Hebrew School Director Joanne Birnberg, and three of our twelve trustees. Then Mayer Fistal, Lillian's replacement as financial secretary and one of my closest synagogue friends, walked to the podium. He told a few jokes, all involving something I'd said or done as the punch line but, mercifully, didn't roast me as badly as he might have. Nonetheless, there was a list of lawyer jokes he couldn't resist telling.

"As you all know Mike doesn't run a synagogue full time, though he'd probably like to. He actually earns a living as an attorney so, I thought I'd share with you some of his best legal gems, straight from his private case files. (Actually, Mayer found these on-line and they are questions and answers from real court cases that were most recently published in a 2006 issue of the Massachusetts Bar Association Lawyers Journal. The author swears they are true):

"Mike's Q: 'So the date of conception, madam, was August 8, correct?'"
Witness A: 'Yes.'
Mike's Q: 'And what were you doing at that time?'"

"Q. 'How was your first marriage terminated, sir?'"
"A. 'By death.'"
"Q. 'And by whose death was it terminated?'"

"Q. 'Now Doctor, isn't it true that when a person dies in his sleep, he doesn't know about it until the next morning?'"

"Q. 'Can you describe the individual?'"
"A. 'He was about medium height and had a beard.'"
"Q. 'Was this a male, or a female?'"

"Q. 'Were you present when your picture was taken?'"

Or my favorite,

"Q. 'All of your answers have to be oral, O.K.? What school did you go to?'"
"A. 'Oral.'"

Then Mayer said, "Now, I don't always like lawyers but, all kidding aside, I've always liked Mike and I want to thank him for making this congregation a great place to belong to."

Inside, I hoped he realized the feeling was mutual.

Next, Susan Lobel spoke. She had been my erstwhile mentor and immediate predecessor as president. Her prodding is what got me to join JCC in the first place and agree to become its second vice president six years ago. Without her encouragement, it's likely I'd never have joined JCC, or any synagogue, let alone eventually try to fill her shoes. And they were big, big shoes. She said, "I've always been a good judge of character, and when I met Michael I thought, 'Here's a guy who with a little help might make a difference around here.' I wasn't wrong. As his term ends, the synagogue is in better shape than in a long time. We have fundraisers in place, annual dinner dances, some new members, monthly community dinners, a good Hebrew school, trips and outings and, more important than anything, hope for a bright future. He's been a great president and friend. I'm going to miss him and his enthusiastic leadership and devotion." – Now, I didn't make notes as Susan was talking, and I don't remember every word exactly, but she really did say something like that and I can still *feel* her compliments and smile.

It was time for me to speak. I was excited. It was as if the entire past four years were preparation for this moment. Those years had been unique, exhilarating, and incredibly rewarding. During them, I had learned more than during my entire university and post-university educations. And I wasn't finished. The taste of history and spirituality I'd absorbed, having read hundreds of books on the subjects during that time, made me want more. I looked at the audience, the congregation and guests. I looked at my dad. My eyes met theirs. I looked at Susan Lobel, Pat Weisslander, Mayer Fistal, Sylvia Levy, Gary Birnberg, Bonnie Kessler, Rabbi Modek, Rabbi Weinberg. I began.

I remember mentioning by name, at least once, every person in the room. And from the instant I opened my mouth, I found it easy to say much more than perfunctory thank-yous. I was so amazed at having served as president of the synagogue – any synagogue – that I was still bewildered and in partial disbelief that the congregation had consented to have me. Now, I know that when Susan Lobel stepped down in 1999, there weren't exactly lines of candidates milling about, anxiously awaiting their chance to take her place. Nonetheless, there were several extremely qualified possibilities – much more so than I was at the time – and that none of them had come forward still perplexed me. I had so immensely enjoyed the job that, in my naiveté I guess, I found it hard to understand why someone truly qualified hadn't jumped at the opportunity. The old adage, however, may be true: "Do what you enjoy and you'll do it well." And I had enjoyed it more than anything I'd ever done.

So, as I stood at the podium and mentioned people's names to say thank you, I wasn't only thanking them for being a great trustee, Hebrew school teacher, newsletter editor, or whatever. What I was really thanking them for was their having allowed me – in my, at first, stumbling naiveté – to have had such a great and rewarding time being president. I was still having that great time as I spoke to them now.

Chapter Twenty Eight - It's About Time

You know you've become more Jewish than you ever expected when you realize you're paying more attention to dates on the Hebrew calendar than on the secular.

The astonishing array of holidays Judaism offers, packed year-round, one after the other, is unrivaled by any religion. Judaism, in fact, is called *"the religion of holidays"* and even a casual glance at the Hebrew calendar confirms it. Despite my own very secular, non-observant background, the one thing I remember with crystal clarity from the short time I spent in Hebrew school — before I was expelled at age eleven after only a month or so for gross misconduct and instructed never to set foot in the building again — is the cycle of the Jewish holidays, beginning with Rosh Hashanah in September, i.e., in *Tishre*, every year. That the New Year should be celebrated in September, rather than in January, made enormous sense to me, because September, for a public school student, always coincided with the beginning of a new school year, and meant starting a new grade along with a whole array of brand-new teachers and new classmates. It was during the first few weeks in September that students acquired new friends, decided what clubs or teams they wanted to join, and oriented themselves toward what they hoped to achieve academically during the upcoming winter and spring semesters. When the secular New Year arrived on January 1, it was anticlimactic. All the important stuff had happened four months earlier. Also, although I definitely didn't learn much during the minuscule time I spent in Hebrew school, aside maybe from a few basics about the more than a dozen annual Jewish holidays, I vividly remember my teacher pointing out this:

"Rosh Hashanah, as you all know, is the Jewish New Year and the beginning of the High Holy Days or, as they are also called, the Days of Awe, which culminate in Yom Kippur, the Day of Judgment, ten days later. During the Days of Awe, God decides whether your sins will be forgiven and your name inscribed in the Book of Life. And during those ten days you, as a Jew, are required to demonstrate an awareness of any wrongs you may have committed, your desire to set things right, and to seek forgiveness from anyone you may have hurt during the previous year. Equally important, you may not withhold forgiveness whenever asked from those who may have hurt you. In other words, God is weighing all the good against all the evil you've done and whether your name will be inscribed in His 'Book.'"

The Reluctant Jew

But that was the very standard part of what my teacher said, and what really stuck with me was what he added almost as an afterthought:

"It may be just a coincidence, but can any of you tell me which Zodiac constellation always appears in the *Tishre* [September] night skies during the High Holy Days?"

One kid raised his hand. "My dad's an astronomy merit badge counselor for the Boy Scouts and knows all the constellations. In September, it's Libra. Right? The scales!"

Even to my eleven-year-old brain, that was amazing. During the Days of Awe, looking down over everything was Libra, the Constellation of Scales, confirming for all to see that God was weighing the good and bad each of us had done the year before and deciding which ones of us would be inscribed in His Judgment Book.

Except for Jews who have completely abandoned their historical and religious identity, like me before I joined Congregation B'nai Torah, *Rosh Hashanah*, meaning *The Head of the Year*, and *Yom Kippur*, meaning *The Day of Atonement*, are the holidays on which everyone shows up. Every synagogue the world over is so packed on those days that most have to charge steep admission fees, with tickets going on sale weeks in advance, to control the huge crowds. Even the expensive tickets, however, don't thin the numbers much, because those who can't afford them are usually allowed in anyway, *gratis*. It has always seemed a contradiction to me that *The Days of Awe*, by far the most religiously demanding of the holidays, nonetheless always attract many more secular and non-observant Jews to synagogues than any of the other holidays do. The reason, I think, is because no matter how far removed from Judaism and its philosophical outlook you may have become, attending the Rosh Hashanah and Yom Kippur services, the most solemn of the year, and allowing yourself to experience their soul-searching moods and be swept up by the blasting of the rams' horns, is a way for people to re-examine their connection to Judaism and prevent it from being completely severed. On Rosh Hashanah, the "birthday" of the world, called *Yom Hazikaron* in the Torah, meaning *Day of Remembering*, Jews look back upon the previous year, recalling the times we performed – or did not but should have – acts of kindness and good deeds. We promise ourselves, each other, and God that we will do better during the year ahead. On Rosh Hashanah eve, after a festive New Year's dinner, we greet each other with the words, *Leshanah tovah tikatevu*, meaning *May God inscribe your name in the Book of Life for a good year*. During the services the next afternoon, the famous *ram's horn*, the *Shofar*, is sounded, calling the Jewish people to action, i.e., calling upon us "to pay close attention to our lives." The chapter in Genesis that tells the story of *the binding of Isaac,* called the *Akedah,* is read, reminding us that Abraham's faith was so boundless that he obeyed God's command to offer his son as a sacrifice. At the very last moment, however, God intervened, saying, "Do not harm Isaac for now I know you have faith in me." Entangled in a bush, behind Abraham and the altar on which he had placed Isaac, was a ram with great horns. Abraham offered it to God in place of his son. Thus ended human sacrifice by Abraham, his followers, and all of his descendents – the Jews – forever. The last ritual of Rosh Hashanah is the service called *Tashlich,* meaning *to throw* or *send away.* The custom is for the entire congregation to walk to a nearby brook, stream, or river and cast away their sins, done symbolically by tossing bread crumbs into the moving water.

Those few who may not have shown up for Rosh Hashanah almost certainly will show up a week later for Yom Kippur, if not solely for religious reasons then because also of the nearly irresistible enticement of the break-fast. Anticipating that sumptuous banquet makes the required twenty-four-hour fasting period, except for the sick and very young, much easier. The reason we are commanded not eat or drink is to help focus our minds and hearts on bettering the world and ourselves, rather than on more mundane things like food. On Yom Kippur eve, the first prayer is *Kol Nidre,* meaning *all vows,* during which we ask each other and God to release us from any harmful but unintentional vows we may have made, such as "I'll kill that kid when he gets home," or "I wish she would just go and never come back," and any promises we may have made but were unable to keep during the previous year. During *Kol Nidre,* we also ask to be released in advance from any vows we may make but not keep in the future. Interestingly and understandably, it first became part of the Yom Kippur service during the 1400s in Spain, when the Inquisition forced Jews to become Christian, which most did by disingenuously reciting a *vow* of conversion, rather than face execution.

So important on the Jewish calendar is Yom Kippur, the "Sabbath of Sabbaths," that it is the only time of year considered more holy than the weekly taste of heaven called Shabbat. This is reflected, for example, not only by its intense and solemn mood, but by the fact that Yom Kippur has by far the longest synagogue service of any Jewish holiday. The morning after *Kol Nidre,* the *Al Khet* prayer, meaning *For Sins (that we have done),* is recited. It is an acrostic in which one confesses to a multitude of sins committed during the previous year using the words "*forgive us* for the sins *we* did" rather than "*forgive me* for the sins *I* did," because each Jew is required to take responsibility not just for his or her own sins, but for sins that were committed by all other Jews as well.

During the afternoon service, the Book of Jonah is read, its main theme being God's willingness to grant forgiveness to those who truly repent, as did Jonah, who at first refused to deliver this dire warning from God to the people of Nineveh, Babylonia: "Time is running short; you must mend your wicked ways or be destroyed," and instead tried to hide by boarding a ship bound for distant lands. While at sea, a huge storm gathered and Jonah, realizing that God was furious with him, said to the crew, "Throw me into the sea. It is because of me that this threatening weather has come." When they threw him overboard, the sea immediately calmed, a huge fish swallowed him, and, after several days, spit him up onto dry land. Having miraculously escaped with his life, the next time Jonah heard God's order, he obeyed at once and traveled to Nineveh, where he told the people: "Yahweh is enraged with you and will destroy your city unless you stop your wickedness and pray for forgiveness." The Ninevites heeded God's warning and He forgave them, but Jonah grew angry because he felt they did not deserve forgiveness. God, therefore, made a shady vine grow over Jonah's head to protect him from the sun, which delighted Jonah and his anger subsided. But the next day the vine died and Jonah became angry again. So God said to Jonah: "You felt sorry for the vine, which grew and died in only one day and night; shouldn't I feel sorry for the 120,000 Ninevites, who've lived and died for generations but never learned the difference between wrong and right?" This tale teaches that even when people behave wickedly, God will forgive them if they truly repent. God, in fact, was much more forgiving than Jonah. The story reminds us that during *The Days of Awe*, particularly on *Yom Kippur*, we must fully forgive – genuinely and wholeheartedly – those who have wronged us, even grievously, if their apologies are sincere whenever we're asked.

The closing Yom Kippur service is *Ne'ilah*, meaning *Shutting*, referring to the "shutting of the gates" while God makes his final decision as to the fate of each Jew and human being. It is, in fact, a final plea to God to inscribe us in the Book of Life. And then, with one long, haunting Shofar blast, Yom Kippur ends. – And the party begins. It's remarkable, but you will see far more Jews crowded together at the break-fast than on any other occasion of the year – including the Yom Kippur and Rosh Hashanah services.

The happening of both Rosh Hashanah and Yom Kippur in any one month would be enough, but on the Jewish calendar, the month of *Tishre* rocks. Almost on Yom Kippur's heels, just four days later, comes *Sukkot*, maybe the most joyous and festive Jewish holiday of them all. It lasts seven days, followed by *Shemini Atzeret* the day after – in fact, some consider it the last day of Sukkot – and another holiday, *Simchat Torah*, the day after that. *Sukkot,* also known fittingly as the Festival of *Booths,* recalls the many centuries during which Hebrew farmers constructed colorful, partly open-air shelters to camp in during the annual wheat harvests, when they had to be out toiling in their fields all day. Since the wheat harvests generally lasted a full week, it made sense to stay in these *booths,* or *Sukkas,* at night, rather than trek home at dusk every evening and then back to the fields the very next dawn. The Sukkas also symbolize the booths in which the Hebrews (we weren't called Jews yet) lived during their forty years of desert wandering, after fleeing from Egypt, and they are referred to several times in the Torah. The building of elaborate Sukkas during Sukkot has become so popular that in many places, contests are held, awarding the family with the most originally designed or beautifully decorated Sukka an all-expenses-paid one-week trip to Israel or an equivalent amount of cash. The Sukka itself, but the other symbols of the holiday in particular, are fascinating. The *Lulav,* consisting of a straight frond of palm in the center, with a branch of myrtle tied to one side, and a branch of willow tied to the other, has over the centuries come to represent three parts of the human body: the straight palm is the backbone, the oval myrtle leaves are eyes, and the oval, but much more elongated leaf of the willow is the mouth. Together with the *etrog,* a fruit native to Israel, somewhat like a lemon but larger, which represents the human heart, the idea is that these four plants make up a whole person – a complete human being – capable of performing acts of great kindness and good deeds. Another idea that has taken hold is that these different species of plants are like the Jews: all very dissimilar with diverse opinions, interests, and characteristics but bound tightly together as one unbreakable entity: the Jewish people.

Shemini Atzeret, meaning *Eighth Day of Assembly,* brings Sukkot to a formal conclusion very appropriately because it's the day on which prayers for rain were recited centuries ago, before widespread irrigation or modern farming techniques, beseeching God to make the coming year's downpours frequent and drenching so that the next Sukkot harvest would be successful. Shemini Atzeret, which happens on Tishre 21, coincides with the beginning of the rainy season in Israel, and it has been said that the reason Jews the world over recite rain prayers on that day, even though the rainy seasons in their native lands usually don't occur at that time, is so that in their minds they will be living according to the same clock as the Israelis, i.e., Israeli Standard Time, not Eastern or Central or Mountain Time, thereby maintaining an unbroken connection to the Holy Land.

Simchat Torah, which happens on Tishre 22 and means *Rejoicing in the Torah,* is my favorite holiday of all. There are fifty-two chapters in the Torah, i.e., *parshas,* corresponding to the fifty-two weeks of the year, and on the day Simchat Torah is celebrated, the last *parsha* in Deuteronomy is read and we start all over again by reciting the first *parsha* in Genesis. On Simchat Torah at JCC, and at many synagogues everywhere, the Hebrew school director, teachers, parents, and all the students position themselves around the perimeter of the sanctuary, with their backs against the four walls, facing the center of the room. Thus positioned, in a large circle, the rabbi hands one end of the Torah scroll to the Hebrew school director and then completely unfurls the Torah, 360 degrees, by walking around the room, unrolling it as he goes, and asking each person in the circle to hold up a section. Once it is unfurled, you find yourself looking upon *the entire biblical story of the Jewish people,* from Creation to the death of Moses, in a single mind-boggling glance. There, near the beginning of the scroll, are Adam and Eve, the serpent, the Tree of Knowledge, in the Garden of Eden. Then Cain and Abel and a little further along, 969-year-old Methuselah, the oldest man ever. Then Noah and the Ark, the great flood, Mount Ararat and the rainbow. Then ziggurats, multitudes, and the Tower of Babel. A little further, the stories of Abraham and Sarah, Isaac and Rebecca. Then the twins, Esau and Jacob, and then Rachel and Leah and Laban. Interwoven are descriptions of Midianites, Edomites, and Moabites. And then there, *there,* is Jacob wresting all night with the angel, and God changing his name to Israel, meaning "to struggle with the Lord." A few degrees further are the stories of Jacob's twelve sons, with Joseph becoming Egyptian prime minister, and his other sons, Judah, Manasseh, Issacar, Naphthali, Reuben, and the rest, becoming the twelve tribes of Israel. Further still are the stories – to some the actual historical accounts – of Moses, Miriam the Prophetess, Jethro and Zebulah. Stories of the Egyptians, the pharaohs, enslavement. Moses, Exodus, and freedom. Then Mount Sinai, the Commandments, the Ark of the Covenant, and tabernacle. Levites, rebels, Kuroc. The Golden Calf, Amalekites, and idolaters. The desert heat, wandering, and manna from heaven. Aaron, Joshua, Jericho. Giants and Canaanites, milk and honey. And then, no longer a dream but near and beckoning, just over a hill: The Promised Land!! – The whole story surrounding you. All of it, all at once, wherever you look. On Simchat Torah.

After Simchat Torah, there is an uncharacteristic lull in the Jewish holiday schedule. The month of October, i.e. *Heshvan,* is quiet but in *Kislev,* which usually coincides with late November to early December, comes the Jewish holiday best known the world over: Chanukah, the Festival of Lights. With the dreidels and menorahs that are its symbols, Chanukah has become well-known to virtually everyone, not least because its eight nights often overlap Christmas week, which accounts for its familiarity in even non-Jewish circles. So popular has it become that sometimes inter-religious services are held on Chanukah's first night, with the lighting of a Christmas tree done simultaneously with the lighting of the first menorah candle. Unlike some Jewish holidays — but like Christmas, which memorializes the birth of Jesus — Chanukah memorializes an undeniably real historical event. In 167 B.C.E., the infamous Antiochus VI a.k.a. Antiochus Epiphanies – a direct descendent of Seleucid, one of Alexander the Great's top generals – came to power in the Syrian portion of Alexander's Greek empire. The Syrian portion included Jerusalem, with the Second Temple and all of Judea. Almost immediately upon taking the throne, Antiochus — like Haman in the Purim story hundreds of years before him — began to detest the Jews because of their refusal to acknowledge the legitimacy of Greek religion, even though he was willing to acknowledge the legitimacy of theirs. To Antiochus, Yahweh, the Jewish God, was just another of the many gods in Greece's pantheon of deities, albeit a strange, invisible one. When Jews worshipped, Antiochus observed, they did not bow down to idols or statues, as did all other peoples, but prayed, seemingly, into thin air. One evening, a Jewish priest, Mattathias of the Hasmonean family, openly defied Antiochus by killing a Jew who had become an idol worshipper. In retaliation, Antiochus outlawed the practice of Judaism upon penalty of death, and erected statues of Greek deities in the Jerusalem temple. This caused a massive revolt and, under the leadership of Mattathias's sons, Judah the Maccabee and his brothers, the Jews ultimately overwhelmed Antiochus's forces, and in 147 B.C.E. regained total control of their ancient homeland. It had been 439 years since the Babylonians conquered Judah and it ceased to exist as a self-governing entity, but now, after a hiatus of more than four centuries, the Jews miraculously re-established an independent country. It became known as the Hasmonean Kingdom. Legend has it that when the Maccabeean forces entered the Second Temple and began clearing it of idols, they were able to locate only one small vial of holy oil. They sent for more, but when the time came to rededicate the Temple by lighting the great lamp, known as the menorah, the new supply of holy oil had still not arrived. One of the priests lit the menorah anyway and, inexplicably, the small vial of oil burned for eight days, by which time the new oil was delivered and the lamp refilled. Like the spirit of the Jewish people, the menorah never went out. Unlike the lamp, however, the Hasmonean Kingdom flickered out quickly. It lasted less than a century. In 63 B.C.E., Pompey the Great, the renowned Roman general, secured the Jews' surrender by a massive show of force, deposed Hyrcanus II, the last of the Hasmonean Kings, and Judea became a Roman province. At first, the Romans permitted their Jewish subjects a great deal of self-government and freedom. That ended, however, in 66 C.E., when the Jews revolted and, after four long years of war, with staggering losses on both sides, were crushed by Emperor Vespasian's son, General Titus. In 70 C.E., on Av 9 (*Tisha B'av*), Titus's forces completed their ransacking of Jerusalem when they burned the Second Temple to the ground. It would take the Jews nearly two thousand years to once again re-establish an independent Israel. That happened in 1948, within our own or our parents' or grandparents' lifetimes.

In Tevet (January), the month after Kislev (December), like in the month of Heshvan (November) preceding it, there is a lull, but in the next month, Shevat (February), comes *Tu B'Shevat* and in the next one, Adar (March), comes Purim. *Tu B'Shevat*, meaning *The Fifteenth Day of the Month of Shevat*, is known in Israel as the New Year of Trees and is truly the "mother" of all environmental holidays. Somewhat like "Earth Day," observed in the U.S. on April 22 by the ecologically minded, it celebrates and exalts the wonders of nature. It's a holiday that makes the hearts of all environmentalists sing. First observed in biblical times, Tu B'Shevat comes at the start of the Israeli spring season, when the trees and plants there rouse themselves from their winter slumber and begin to bloom. The Torah, in Leviticus 19:23-25, instructs: "For the first three years after a tree is planted, no man may eat its fruit. In the fourth year only, God may enjoy the fruit and it must be presented to Him as an offering. But in the fifth year, by which time a tree is strong and mature, men may harvest and eat its fruit." As a practical matter, it was impossible to keep track of the exact age of each tree, so the rabbis decided to assign one day, Shevat 15, as the birthday of them all. On that day, every tree in Israel was considered another year older and, using that system, it could always be determined when a tree had matured enough for its fruit to be harvested.

Since the re-establishment of independent Israel in 1948, Tu B'Shevat has acquired even more importance and mystique than it possessed in the biblical world. When large numbers of Jews immigrated to their ancient homeland after World War II, much of the land they settled on was eroded hill country, arid desert, infertile barrens, or festering swamp. Almost immediately, they embarked on a massive land reclamation and reinvigoration project that involved digging thousands of miles of irrigation canals, re-seeding countless acres that had lain fallow for centuries, draining hundreds of swamps, introducing modern farming techniques, and planting millions of trees to stop and reverse erosion. It has become a tradition that on Tu B'Shevat, congregants in synagogues the world over are asked to make contributions that will be earmarked specifically for the purpose of planting still more trees, millions more, every year in Israel. A rabbi of the Mishnah taught: "If you are in the midst of planting a tree when you hear that the Messiah has arrived, finish planting the tree first and only then go to meet the Messiah." This teaching was first circulated nearly 2,000 years ago when Israel was far less barren – in fact, was lush and, according to the Bible, "flowing with milk and honey" – than it had become by the early twentieth century. Yet modern ears are at least as receptive to its message as were ancient ones. Land is so limited in today's Israel that literally every square inch is precious and must, wherever and whenever possible, be nursed back to life. How's that for a bit of ancient wisdom whose meaning and impact has not dimmed with the passage of centuries, but in fact has become much more significant, given the frighteningly rapid depletion of the modern world's natural resources?

Purim, which means *Lots*, as in "to draw lots to determine who has to do something," happens on Adar 13, twenty-nine days after Tu B'Shevat is celebrated, and is party time on the Jewish calendar. And, unless I've been noticing something that's been going on only in my imagination, it seems that over the last decade or so, the partying has become wilder and wilder. On Purim, Jews are actually encouraged to drink heavily and party hard and, within the limits of decorum, get drunk. Unlike Rosh Hashanah, Yom Kippur, or Simchat Torah, which have deep religious significance, and unlike Chanukah, Sukkot, or Tu B'Shevat, which memorialize real events or practices in ancient or modern Jewish history, Purim is not religiously significant at all – God is not mentioned once in the *Megillah* – and it marks the anniversary of only *a supposedly real event* but for which there is no historical confirmation at all except for what's set forth in the Bible. In ancient Persia, according to the book of Esther, a.k.a. *the Megillah*, during the reign of King Ahaseurus (the Hebrew form of the name Xerxes, who was a real historical figure and ruled Persia from 486 to 465 B.C.E.), a man named Haman is said to have lived, who became prime minister. Somewhere along the line, Haman grew to detest the Jews, turned into a sort of ancient-world Hitler, and devised a genocide plan to exterminate them. Esther's cousin, Mordecai — presented in the Megillah as one of the most prominent Jewish leaders in Persia at the time — apparently pushed Haman over the edge when he refused to bow down to him, as was the custom of the representatives of all other peoples Persia had subjugated, and pay him appropriate reverence and respect. Haman went to the king and told him the Jews were dangerously disruptive because they refused to obey the law, did not acknowledge the king's absolute sovereignty, and might actually be moving toward rebellion. He asked Ahaseurus for and was granted permission to kill every Jew in the Persian Empire. With that, Haman cast lots *(purim)* to decide the day on which he would kill them, and Adar 13 was the date that came up. Fortunately for the Jews, however, Esther — Mordecai's much younger cousin and a woman of extraordinary beauty — had married Ahaseurus years earlier and become his queen. Unbeknownst to the king, or at least not something he thought about much, Esther was Jewish and, upon hearing about the genocide plan, she feared for her life. Esther, therefore, devised her own plan. Although queen, she had no real power and realized that if she was to have any realistic hope of saving the Jews, she would have to confront the only two men who did: Ahaseurus and Haman.

Shortly after Moredcai told Esther of Haman's plot, she prepared a lavish dinner, invited the king to attend, and requested he bring Haman with him. During the feast, Esther reminded Ahaseurus that she herself was Jewish and that if Haman's plan were allowed to go forward, she would be killed too. Ahaseurus, who deeply loved her, became enraged and ordered that on Adar 13, Haman be hanged from the very gallows on which he had intended to hang Mordecai. For that reason, Adar 13, a.k.a. Purim, has become a day of wild celebration on the Hebrew calendar. Perhaps the reason the celebrating seems to have grown wilder over the years is that the story of Esther and Mordecai's defeat of Haman, even if just legend, constantly reminds Jews of their many real victories throughout the millennia over other anti-Semites and their almost unbelievable survival as a people, intact and undaunted, retaining their traditions and customs, into modern times.

Exactly one month after Purim comes *Passover*, called *Pesach*, meaning *paschal (ceremonial) lamb* in Hebrew, which in the Jewish psyche is much more than just another holiday and joyful celebration. It is rather a re-enactment of the unquestionably single most defining event in the entire Jewish experience. It is, that is to say, for Jews, an annual renewal of the most mind-shaping happening in their almost 4,000-year history. The embedded memory of Moses leading his dispirited people from Egyptian slavery to freedom, after more than four centuries of numbing subjugation, to the very brink of the Promised Land, has never dimmed. When Jews sit down together for their first-night Seder on Nissan 15 each year, and read from their Haggadahs, they do not feel themselves to be reciting just a moving, possibly historically accurate Torah story. Instead, they look upon the Exodus as a paradigm of the ongoing struggle for human freedom fought by all people in every generation. From a Jewish perspective, in fact, the history of the world *is* the history of freedom. We've also come to look upon it as a metaphor for the personal quest embarked upon by each of us, usually in middle age, for freedom from the disappointments and failures of our often off-track and unfulfilled lives. It is this opportunity it presents – to re-calibrate the very direction of our existence and perhaps free ourselves from self-imposed psychological slavery – that accounts in part for Pesach's enormous popularity among virtually all Jews. The opportunity Pesach presents to get our lives moving forward again, i.e., to liberate ourselves from stagnation due to worrying about past failures, is priceless. It is not widely known, but there are far more copies of the Haggadah in print than even the *Tanach* itself. Moreover, it is estimated that at least 5,000 different versions of the Haggadah exist. Almost undoubtedly, even many of the most non-observant and atheistic Jews imaginable know by adulthood the Exodus story far better than they care to admit, and have probably participated in more Seders, and read from more Haggadahs, than they can remember.

Freedom, unfortunately, often comes at a high price. When the tenth plague hurled down by God caused every first-born Egyptian male to perish, but passed over and did not harm the Jews, Moses and his people took no pleasure in the suffering of Pharaoh and his slave masters. That's why during the Seder, as we recite each of the ten curses: *Blood, Frogs, Lice, Wild Animals, Cattle Disease, Boils, Hail, Locusts, Darkness, and Death of the First Born*, we dip a finger into red wine and shake a drop onto our plates. Each drop is meant to symbolize the spilling of blood – our own as well as the Egyptians' – and diminishes our joy at having been set free because of the horrifying misery it caused them.

Passover is followed by four non-biblical holidays, i.e., there is no mention of them anywhere in the *Tanach* (Hebrew Bible, consisting of the five books of Moses, i.e. *Torah*, the Prophets, a.k.a. *Nevi'im*, and Writings, a.k.a. *Ketuvim*), all of which were added to the Jewish holiday cycle only recently, in the twentieth century. *Yom Hashoah*, meaning *Day of the Whirlwind*, which happens on Nissan 27, five days after the last night of Passover, commemorates the greatest disaster ever to befall the Jews: the Holocaust, during which 8 million people, 6 million of them Jews, died from overwork or were murdered in labor and concentration camps. Interestingly, the non-Jewish word *Holocaust*, does not translate exactly with the Hebrew word *Hashoah* (whirlwind), but has a much harsher meaning, literally *burning up* or *total destruction*. Perhaps the Jews, having survived not only the whirlwind onslaught of Hitler's minions, but every previous attempt to eliminate them, felt that a word meaning "total destruction" was not quite accurate. – We are still here, we are strong. We have our own country. It is the Nazis who are gone.

In the next Jewish month, on Iyar 4, comes *Yom Hazikaron*, meaning *Day of Remembrance*. It honors and forever memorializes all the soldiers who died or suffered grievous injuries fighting for Israel during its many wars in modern times – the Independence War in 1948, the Suez Canal War in 1956, the Six-Day War in 1967, the Yom Kippur War in 1973, the

Lebanon War in 1982, the Intifada beginning in 1987, the Second Intifada which began in 2000 and the Hezbollah War in 2006. Given Israel's small population, the number of casualties has been staggering, with nearly every Israeli family having lost a father or son, uncle or nephew, brother or cousin. Since women also serve in the Israeli Armed Forces, huge numbers of female kin have been casualties too. There is no real end to the violence in sight and, in the Jewish memory, Yom Hazikaron has begun to rival even Tisha B'av, which mourns the destruction of the First and Second Temples, and has been observed as a day of sorrow on the Hebrew calendar since ancient times.

The day after Yom Hazikaron comes *Yom Ha'atzma'ut*, meaning *Day of Independence*. On May 14, 1948, when Jewish authorities declared the re-establishment of a Jewish state, the world witnessed one of the most astonishing events in history. Never before and never since have an ancient people regained territory – *captured from them by force nearly 2,000 years before* – and again taken their place among the family of sovereign countries. A year later, in May 1949, Israel became the fifty-ninth member of the United Nations. To those who believe that the refounding of Israel in modern times was wrong, because doing so displaced large numbers of Arabs, I urge them to remember this: The Jews didn't just drop out of the sky one day and start settling in droves in their ancient homeland. Rather, they fled there for their very lives after the Nazis slaughtered 6 million of them while the world stood by, feigning ignorance of the atrocities being wrought, and did absolutely nothing. Even the United States, to its discredit, a year before it entered World War II, refused to allow a shipload of Jews fleeing from the Nazis to enter port. Cuba, where the *S.S. St. Louis* first tried to dock, and most European nations at first, refused entry too. The ship was forced to head back to Germany but, before it arrived, fortunately, Belgium, Holland, France, and England changed their minds and admitted the passengers. Those who settled in England survived, but when the Nazis occupied the other three countries, the Jews from the *St. Louis* who had disembarked in them were methodically rounded up, disappeared into the extermination camps, and were slaughtered.

It is against the background of that incident, and scores of similar, equally or more horrific incidents, that the overwhelming majority of Jews worldwide realized that there would be no haven for them until they re-established their own country. That explanation, however, does not directly address or justify the situation of the displaced Arabs, many of whom lost their homes and livelihoods. But consider this: The partition plan initially put forward by the United Nations offered the Jews a state on far less territory than that which Israel eventually occupied when it counter-attacked after first being besieged from all sides by the Arab states in 1948, and again in 1967 (the Jews attacked first, but only after intelligence revealed plans for an imminent multi-nation Arab attack) and 1973. Despite the U.N. offer of just minuscule territory, the Jews immediately accepted the plan while the Arabs hysterically rejected it. They refused all discussion or compromise, even though the initial U.N. offer included mostly areas where the Jewish population already outnumbered the Arab, albeit with exceptions that the Jews very much wanted to negotiate and resolve, and did not include any part of Jerusalem. In other words, the Arabs, *who supported the Nazis during World War II*, were unwilling to accept a Jewish entity anywhere in Palestine, although the Jews were willing to forgo all territorial claims to Jerusalem and assent, as provided in the U.N. plan, to its coming under international control. It was only after the Arabs rejected any compromise, and five Arab states attacked Israel in 1948, that scores of thousands of them were displaced, fleeing from the warring armies. It must be pointed out, however, and accepted by all of Israel's supporters, that the actions of many Jews, *prior* to the Arab attack, also caused thousands to flee. There is considerable evidence of this which cannot be ignored. In 1895 Theodore Herzl himself, the father of modern Zionism, wrote: "We must expropriate gently...We shall try to spirit the penniless population [Palestinian Arabs] across the border by procuring employment for it in the transit countries, while denying it employment in our country... Both the process of expropriation and the removal of the poor must be carried out discretely and circumspectly..."[1] Then, in 1897, shortly after the First World Zionist Organization he founded met in Basel, Switzerland, Herzl made the statement for which he is most famous: "Were I to sum up the Basel Congress in a word – which I shall guard against pronouncing publicly – it would be this: 'At Basel I founded the Jewish State. If I said this out loud today, I would be answered by universal laughter. If not in 5 years, certainly in 50, everyone will know it.'" In 1937, more ominously for the indigenous Arabs, David Ben Gurion, said: "The compulsory transfer of Arabs from the valleys of the proposed Jewish state could give us something which we never had, even when we stood on our own feet during the days of the First and Second Temple."[2] Ben Gurion, who would become the first prime minister of modern Israel, constantly argued: '...the Arab problem paled in significance compared with the Jewish problem because the Arabs had vast spaces outside Palestine, whereas for the Jews, who were being persecuted in Europe, Palestine constituted the only possible haven.'[3] There are many other statements attributable to Herzl, Ben Gurion, and other Jewish leaders, some far more ominous than even these, that indicate that not only Arab aggression, but also Zionist policy, dislodged huge numbers of Arabs from their homes. There's no sense denying that such statements were actually made because doing so serves only to distort part of the history that has brought us to our current desperate circumstances in the Middle East. What we need to do is be aware of that history, all of it, so we can better understand the anger[4] of the Palestinians, which has become so intense that they've embraced terrorism and mass murder. We should not, however, ever be restrained in condemning their atrocities, and their allies', or those of Islamist fanatics elsewhere. Nor should we be restrained in pointing out the murderous cruelty and self-destructiveness – no matter how often they shout "Allah" – of their brutal, sacrilegious behavior.

A glaring example of such self destructiveness is as follows. During the '48 War, as mentioned, Israel gained not just independence, but captured the west half of Jerusalem, no part of which had it occupied before. Nevertheless, Arab and European diplomats continuously opine that if only Israel withdrew to its 1967 borders — 1967 being the year Israel gained control of the West Bank (formerly administered by Jordan) and all of Jerusalem (i.e. East Jerusalem as well as West Jerusalem) — peace would be at hand. The problem with that opinion, even aside from the recent ascent of Hamas via overwhelming majority vote of the Palestinians, and the rise of equally violent Hezbollah, is that the PLO, which supposedly has accepted Israel's right to exist, *was created before 1967*.[5] That is, the PLO, which despite any pretense to the contrary, usually behaves as though it's hell-bent on destroying the Jewish state, was created at a time when Israel controlled none of the West Bank, and only West Jerusalem. Even then, however, it refused to negotiate, and sought to kill or exile every Jew it encountered. If the PLO had come into existence after 1967, then a credible argument could be made that by Israel's withdrawing to be the pre-1967 borders, i.e., by withdrawing from the West Bank and East Jerusalem, the PLO and the Palestinians would be satisified. However, truth be told: In 1999, while the entire world hopefully looked on, Arafat walked away from the table when President Clinton and Israeli Prime Minister Barak offered him virtually everything he had publicly demanded,[6] including a return to the pre-1967 borders. He made no counter-offers, but renewed murderous terrorist attacks instead. That behavior caused a near total loss of Arafat and his cronies' credibility, and dramatically weakened the PLO. Despite its changed circumstances, however, and advent of Mahmoud Abbas as Palestinian president via free elections, does any adult really believe that the PLO at core – let alone Hamas, which has become the dominant power in the PLO, Hezbollah, Islamic Jihad, Syria, and Iran, whose president, incredibly, in this day and age, denies the Holocaust ever happened – will somehow metamorphose over the next few years? Does anyone really think that they are now, or will ever, be *genuinely* willing to recognize an Israel within the pre-1967 borders? Or even the pre-1948 borders? I don't think so. No one who is even minimally well-informed believes so anymore. This is not to denigrate the ongoing efforts by Abbas to confront the extremists and moderate their demands. His efforts, however, are as likely to result in his assassination as they are in any permanent change in PLO policy. By its actions, unfortunately , and its unremitting incitement of "Jew hatred," the supposedly moderate Fatah party of the PLO, which has now been supplanted by the even more hateful and unreservedly anti-Semitic Hamas, has repeatedly demonstrated its true intentions all too clearly. That's why the Sharon government embarked upon construction of a wall separating the Arab and Jewish populations and will not be deterred. It is, therefore, largely the behavior of the Palestinians and their own leadership, not Israel's, that has brought them to the horrendous circumstances in which they find themselves. Those circumstances include loss of freedom of movement, loss of more than 75 percent of the Palestinians' jobs in Israel, frequent incursions by the Israeli army to hunt for terrorists, massive corruption among the Palestinian leadership, abject poverty of the populace, and virtually no hope for a prosperous future. And with the advent of Hamas and Hezbollah, things will grow, and already have, considerably worse, including a cut-off of U.S. and European financial aid. All of that as opposed to Barak's offer to shut down 90-95 percent of the settlements in the West Bank, cede sizeable tracts of Israeli territory in exchange for any settlements that would remain, transfer control of East Jerusalem to the PLO, and pay billions upon billions in financial support to create tens of thousands of new jobs and jump-start the Palestinian economy. That's what the PLO walked away from. Contragulations, Yasir. Thanks for transforming lifelong Israeli doves who, until your insane behavior, were in the majority, into die-hard hawks. Thanks for destroying all trust. Mahmoud Abbas, although he seems to be trying, will likely do no better. His own people, as reward for his insisting that peaceful negotiations are preferable to terror, elected Hamas to supplant him. In addition, Hezbollah's kidnaping of two Israeli soldiers and murder of eight others in July, 2006, during their unprovoked raid, has caused the Israelis to lose all faith in a negotiated peace. The behavior of these Islamic fanatics has forced the Israelis, contrary to their best intentions and prior willingness to take great risks for peace, to become intransigent. Incredibly, the only prospects for improvement of the Palestinians' situation were the unilateral actions of the Ariel Sharon government, chief of which was returning control of all Gaza to them. This, despite the best efforts of the terrorist groups to sabotage the transfer for the sole purpose of denying Abbas the ability to claim that non-violence might work. Instead of taking advantage of the Israeli withdrawal by creating an honest, functioning government, and making use of the agricultural and industrial infrastructure the Israelis left behind, the Palestinians have descended into total chaos. As is blatantly and indisputably true and often said of the Palestinians and their supporters: "They never miss an opportunity to miss an opportunity."

Two weeks after Yom Ha'atzma'ut, on Iyar 18, comes Lag B'omer, one of the most unusual of Jewish celebrations. *Omer* means *the ripening of the barley crop*. *Lag B'omer*, an abbreviated way of saying *the thirty-third day of the counting of the Omer*, is the day on which the ancient Israelites took a break from the heavy tension that always set in during the very serious forty-nine-day "Counting of the Omer" growing season, which began on the second night of Passover and would end on Shavuot. Most ancient Israelites were farmers, and since their entire livelihoods came down to this seven-week growing period, they assiduously tended their crops, day after day, anxiously watching their progress. There were no parties, no feasts, no entertainment, no weddings, no cheerful or festive activities at all. The mood was one of deep concern and apprehension and there was no time for levity. But by the thirty-third day of Omer, people needed a diversion from their constant worry, so the custom arose that on Lag B'omer, the Jews would celebrate and be joyful. On that day, parties, galas, weddings, picnics, banquets, sports, games, and playfulness were not only allowed, but heartily encouraged. By the last day of Omer, the wheat crop (being the second crop harvested during Omer, the first being the barley crop), hopefully would be fully ripe and very plentiful, and the farmers could at last relax knowing that there would be abundant food for their families and neighbors during the coming months. Lag B'omer became part of the Jewish holiday cycle shortly after the Romans destroyed the Second Temple in 70 C.E. and the practice arose, in addition to rejoicing, of recounting the achievements of two of the most renowned of second-century rabbis, especially their resistance to Roman rule, on that day too. After the siege of Jerusalem, Rabbi Shimon bar Yochai, (c. 70 C.E. – c. 155 C.E.), the most famous student of his even-more-celebrated teacher, Rabbi Akiva, rather than obey the new Roman laws that prohibited Torah study, fled with his son into the hills of Galilee. Legend has it that they lived there in a cave for thirteen years, studying Torah and Kabala and surviving on wild game, fruits, and plants. Rabbi Yochai's students could no longer study Torah with him, but they never forgot him. Every year on the thirty-third day of the "Counting of the Omer," they came to him in the hills to once again hear his words. Tradition holds that while in the cave, Rabbi Yochai authored the single most important work of spirituality in Jewish history, the *Zohar*, meaning *splendor* or *radiance*. It is a mystical commentary on the Five Books of Moses, unrivaled by any other work to this day. Most scholars, however, attribute authorship of the Zohar to Moses de Leon, in the thirteenth century, which is when it first appeared in print. The other sage remembered on Lag B'omer, Rabbi Yochai's teacher, Rabbi Joseph ben Akiva himself (c. 50 C.E. – c. 135 C.E.), spent the first forty years of his life in ignorance but, at the urging of his wife, Rachel, devoted himself to Torah study and became the most renowned Torah master of his time. He is one of the four great sages supposedly permitted by God to enter the "Orchard," known in the Talmud as the *Pardes*, and probe the depths of Kabala. Together, Shimon Bar Kochba, as military leader, and Rabbi Akiva, as spiritual leader, organized the failed revolt against Rome that began in 135 C.E. Akiva was captured and tortured to death: his skin flayed from his body with metal combs. Eyewitnesses recount that his last words were the *Shema*. While alive, even before the revolt, Akiva was constantly threatened with arrest and possible execution by the Roman authorities for his refusal to obey their edict to stop teaching Judaism. He therefore made a plan. He instructed his students to take bows and arrows and picnic lunches and go out into the fields as if they intended to hunt. When the Roman soldiers saw the Jews on their way out "to hunt," they let them pass. But once in the fields, Akiva met them and taught Torah. For this reason, lavish all-day picnicking on Lag B'omer has become a widespread custom in Israel.

You may have noticed that despite the prohibition against rejoicing during the forty-nine-day Counting of the Omer period, from the second night of Passover to Shavuot, except on Lag B'omer, which is the thirty-third day of the Counting, *Yom Ha'atzma'ut*, nonetheless, the holiday celebrating the re-establishment of independent Israel in 1948 and a day of wild rejoicing, happens on Iyar 5, which is nineteenth day of the Counting. Also, the holiday immediately following Lag B'omer, *Yom Yerushalayim*, meaning *Jerusalem Day*, and another time of wild rejoicing, is celebrated on Iyar twenty-eight, which is the Counting's forty-second day. So what happened to the prohibition against rejoicing except on the thirty-third day? The answer, of course, is that the tradition of Counting the Omer began around the time of the Judges, some 3,200 years ago, whereas Yom Ha'atzma'ut and Yom Yerushalayim are modern holidays, and the events they celebrate just happen to have occurred during the Counting of the Omer period. In ancient times, the Counting of the Omer growing period was extremely important, but to modern Jews, the rebirth of Israel in 1948 and the reunification of Jerusalem in 1967, despite their willingness to cede East Jerusalem in exchange for peace, are much more so.

Shavuot, the Festival of *Weeks*, so named because it marks the end of the seven-week Counting of the Omer growing season, celebrates the beginning of the summer wheat harvest. In ancient Israel, if the Counting of the Omer period had been successful, farmers would reap a plentiful crop and could at last kick back. Shavuot, however, is also the anniversary of another event, one so important that some would argue that its imprint on the Jewish psyche rivals or even surpasses that of the Exodus, which we celebrated seven weeks earlier during Passover. In addition to the annual summer harvest, Shavuot celebrates the day on which God delivered the Ten Commandments to Moses, spoke to the assembled Israelite nation – 600,000 strong – and entered with them upon a holy covenant as his Chosen People. It was then, at the foot of Mount Sinai, that the Hebrews as an entire people heard God's voice and agreed to live forever by His laws as "a holy nation of priests." It is often said that although Passover and the Exodus made us free to live as we choose, Shavuot and the Torah instructed us how to live with our newfound freedom. It is interesting to note that both Christianity and Islam openly acknowledge the truth of the revelation at Sinai, i.e., accept in their own scriptures that it really happened, and that the Jews, for millennia, were God's chosen messengers on earth as "a light unto nations." After the resurrection of Jesus, however, and the refusal of the Jews to accept him as the messiah, God's grace supposedly passed to Christians from the no-longer-holy Jews, who had lost their way. When that happened, Christians believed they had become the new Chosen People, favored by God above all others. But when Muhammad heard God's words, 600 years after Jesus's crucifixion, and dictated them to his scribes as the Koran, Islam was born and God's divine grace, Muslims believed, was again transferred into new and supposedly holier hands – theirs! According to Islam, the Jews and Christians were still "Peoples of the Book" and therefore holy, but were deeply flawed. The Muslims believed that only they, the latest of God's Chosen Peoples, could lay claim to the purest and most intimate relationship that had ever existed between Him and any of His adherents. In short, Muslims and Christians believed that God spoke to them far more clearly than ever He had to the Jews.

But Jews, of course, felt differently. Their concept of and relationship with the One True God – a God of mercy, kindness, and justice for all: "God is One for everyone" (an expression derived from the *Shema*) – began during the time of Abraham, some 2,000 years before Jesus's birth, and nearly 2,600 years before Muhammad's. By the time of Moses, 750 years after Abraham died but still 1,250 years before any Christians were on the scene, and more than 1,800 years before any Muslims were, the Hebrews' relationship with God had become unbreakable, incredibly passionate, and deeply embedded into their lifestyle and philosophical outlook. They had also grown quite numerous and are referred to, albeit infrequently and only passingly, in Egyptian records. Later, artifacts dating from around 900 B.C.E. mention Israel and the House of David. Later still, Assyrian records refer to the conquest of the Kingdom of Israel in 722 B.C.E.

and the dispersal of its people throughout Assyria's territory. And tablets dating to around 586 B.C.E. talk about the Babylonian defeat of *Judah*, the Hebrew kingdom south of what had been Israel, and the forcible exile of the *Jews* to Babylon. Here, for perhaps the first time, the word *Jews* a.k.a. *Ju's*, derived from the tribal name *Judah*, appears in historical, non-biblical records. The point of this recitation is to demonstrate that the Jews – first called Hebrews, then Israelites, and ultimately Ju's – had been in existence as a distinct religious and political community for at least two millennia prior to the rise of Christianity, and nearly three millennia prior to Islam's. Although the New Testament and Koran, *retrospectively*, trace the origins of their respective religions back to Abraham, there is little question as to the true origin of both these faiths: the Jews and Judaism. To become what they did, Christians and Muslims had to pass through, absorb, reinterpret, and mold themselves to Jewish religion. For without Judaism, there would be no Christianity. The religion of Jesus while he was alive, in fact, was always Judaism, and he considered himself a Jewish rabbi, even as he hung on the cross. It is the religion about him that became Christianity. And as for Islam, Muhammad acknowledged for his entire life that the One God had revealed himself to the Jews thousands of years before he revealed himself to others. In fact, it is not inaccurate to say that Muhammad believed that Islam, at essence, was simply a more perfect form of the Judaism that had existed and been evolving for twenty-six centuries before he was born.

The attractiveness of Judaism as a system of thought and ethics, and the still-vibrant creed of an ancient people, is movingly captured during the Shavuot evening services when the story of Ruth is recited. According to the Book of Ruth, an Israelite called Elimelech, with his wife, Naomi, and their two sons, Mahalon and Chelion, immigrated to Moab during the time of the Judges, around 1200 to 1100 B.C.E., when a famine descended upon Israel. There the two sons grew to adulthood and married non-Jewish women; one married Orpah and the other married Ruth. Years later, after Elimelech and both of his sons had died, Naomi decided to return to Israel but she urged her daughters-in-law, whom she deeply loved and wanted to be happy, to stay in their native land and find new husbands to provide for them. Orpah took this advice and remained in Moab, but Ruth told Naomi the following, which is among the most deeply moving passages in the Bible: "I will not leave you. Wherever you go, I will go; wherever you live, I will live. Your people will be my people, and your God will be my God." With that, the two women set out and crossed the border into Israel. They were penniless and had no possessions besides the clothes on their backs. But Naomi had a well-to-do cousin, Boaz, who owned vast farmlands, and she remembered the Jewish custom of *gleaning*, which required that farmers permit the poor to gather stalks of grain, at the corners of their fields, to subsist upon. So Ruth gleaned and one day Boaz noticed her. Having heard of her loyalty to Naomi, he said, "You can glean in my fields throughout the harvest. You may drink from the water that is drawn from my wells and you may eat with my reapers and workers." But when Ruth reported this kindness to Naomi, the older woman realized that her cousin's words were more than just an invitation to eat and drink. She instructed Ruth: "Tonight, after Boaz has finished work and retired to his tent, go to him, uncover his feet, and lie down at them (a euphemism for "sleep with him"). Ruth obeyed. The next morning, when Ruth and Boaz awoke, he said, "I will protect you for the rest of your life. I will marry you and always love you." The Bible records that from this union, a son named Obed was born. Then Obed sired a son named Jesse and, in time, Jesse sired a son named David. – Yes David; David, the shepherd boy; David, the harp player; David, who defeated Goliath; David, who married Bathsheba; David, father of Solomon; David, who crushed Israel's enemies; David, from whom Jesus, Christians believe, descended; yes, David, hero king of Israel and most famed of them all.

Whereas Shavuot is a day of intense joy, *Tisha B'av*, meaning the *ninth day of the month of Av*, which happens just shy of two months later, is one of overwhelming sadness. It mourns the destruction of Solomon's Temple by the Babylonians in 586 B.C.E., and of the Second Temple by the Romans in 70 C.E. Solomon's Temple was erected in the ninth century B.C.E., and had been standing, undamaged, for some 400 years when Babylonian King Nebuchadnezzar's troops overran it, leveled it, and then gouged out Hebrew King Zedikiah's eyes for daring to resist. The Second Temple was completed seventy-two years later, in 514 B.C.E., and stood even longer, for nearly 600 years, until Emperor Vespasian's forces set it ablaze, with hundreds of Jews packed inside, and burned it to the ground. All that is left today is the famous Western, or as it is more often called, "Wailing Wall." Almost unbelievably, centuries later, the infamous edicts expelling the Jews from England in 1290 and from Spain in 1492 were issued on the ninth day of Av as well. The happening of those catastrophes all on the same day was no coincidence. The Romans, who had developed a deep hatred for their Jewish subjects and possessed detailed knowledge of their history, likely delayed their final assault on the Second Temple so that its destruction would exactly coincide with the date on which Solomon's Temple had been ransacked five centuries before, thus maximizing the devastating psychological impact on the Jews. Likewise, the English, and then the Spanish, undoubtedly timed the issuance of their expulsion edicts to coincide precisely with Tisha B'av, so as to ensure they would cause the deepest and most demoralizing trauma possible. On the other hand, despite its overwhelming sadness, tradition teaches that Tisha B'av is the day on which the long-awaited messiah will be born. It may be that the rabbis encouraged this idea take hold, in the hope that the Jews, even in the face of the frequent and crushing catastrophes Tisha B'av reminded them of, would never forget that for the righteous, messianic and blissful days lay ahead.

There is something deeply comforting about cyclical time, like the familiar cycle of Jewish holidays, as opposed to linear time, which is always measured as an endless progression of years. In linear time, we continuously grow old and further and further away from our childhoods, youthful dreams, and aging, eventually to be laid-to-rest loved ones. Of course, that is not to say a fountain of youth can be found simply by marking our days on the Hebrew calendar, as opposed to the Gregorian, Islamic, Chinese, or any other. But what can be said is that in Hebrew time, we always return to the same joyful celebrations, cherished moods, and meaningful lessons as in every year before. The same as we and our ancestors have done for millennia. For that reason, by focusing on the Hebrew calendar and its incredibly rich tapestry of holidays, our attention is focused on the ancient and ongoing dreams of the Jewish people – it's almost like ancestor worship – and we don't worry pointlessly about the future.

A Jewish man said to his mother on her deathbed, "Mom, are you in any discomfort? Tell me and I'll get the doctor to give you something."

"Would you stop worrying," she said. "It's Shabbat and I'm happy. You should be too."

He tried to continue, "But Mom, doesn't it hurt? You must be in terrible pain."

"Enough already! Stop trying to bring me down. On Monday, it's Purim, and I intend to party right here in the hospital. A few weeks after that, it's Pesach, and I'm going to start clearing out the *hametz* (unleavened bread) the moment Shabbat's over."

"Mom, you're much too sick, I won't allow it."

"You know, you're even a bigger *schlemiel* than I thought. Look, I'll make a deal with you. When I die, I promise, I'll tell you everything that hurts me then. But in the meantime, I'm not going to worry about it, and neither should you. In fact, I'm going to celebrate like never before. Now, light those Shabbat candles already and help me say the blessings, or please, go home and depress someone else. You can start with your brother and sister by telling them again how sick you think I am. By making them miserable, you'll probably feel much better. Right? Cut it out already!"

So there you have it: *Rosh Hashanah, Yom Kippur, Sukkot, Shemini Atzeret, Simhat Torah, Chanukah, Tu B'Shevat, Purim, Passover, Yom Hashoah, Yom Hazikaron, Yom Ha'atzma'ut, Lag Ba'omer, Yom Yerushalayim, Shavuot, and Tisha B'av,* an incredible sixteen annual commemorations in all. And this doesn't include the many other, less well-known holidays celebrated by the Orthodox. Nor does it include the most important Jewish holiday, bar none, the one celebrated every week, fifty-two times a year, *Shabbat,* the holiday the Torah commands every Jew to always keep: "And on the seventh day He rested." So now you're an expert. Right? Except for one thing: Every few years, with the passage of time, the months on the Hebrew calendar get all out of whack with the months on the Gregorian, i.e., secular calendar. It's as if the Hebrew dates move more slowly through time than the Gregorian ones.

Imagine two runners on a circular track, alongside each other at the starting line of a long-distance race. One runner is the Hebrew date Tishre 15, 5766. The other runner is the secular date October 18, 2005, which marks the same place in time, and is exactly equivalent to the Hebrew date. On the two different calendars, both are precisely the same day and correspond with the first day of Sukkot. The racetrack ahead for the Hebrew runner is the twelve Jewish months – Tishre through Elul – with the first stretch being the number of days left in Tishre. The racetrack for the Gregorian runner is the twelve secular months – October through September (which is the same period of time as January through December but in a different order) – with the first stretch being the days left in October. Now the runners dash forward, always moving at exactly the same speed relative to each other, but, interestingly, the Hebrew runner finishes the race, as measured on the secular calendar, behind the Gregorian one. They begin the race again, but this time the Gregorian runner has a head start because they don't begin the new race at the old starting line, but instead each runner begins at the point, on the Gregorian calendar, where he finished the last one. Since Tishre 15, as measured on the Gregorian calendar, lost the first race, he's no longer lined up at the same starting point as before, i.e., with Gregorian runner October 18, but now is lined up with October 7. In other words, Hebrew runner, Tishre 15, starts the second race on October 7 while Gregorian runner, October 18, starts at the same place he did in the prior race, i.e., again on October 18, eleven days ahead of the Hebrew runner. Yet, as measured on the Jewish calendar the Hebrew runner finished at exactly the place he finished the year before, i.e, on Tishre 15. During this second race, the Hebrew runner falls further behind. At the second race's end, Tishre 15 is no longer lined up even with October 7, but further back with September 27. But why? Why does this happen?[7]

It turns out that, unlike the civil calendar, which measures a year by the number of days it takes for the earth to travel around the sun, 365¼ (and then dividing those days into twelve months), the Hebrew calendar measures a year by the number of days it takes the moon to travel twelve times around the earth, 354 (each month being the number of days from new moon to new moon). In other words, the standard Jewish year is 11¼ days shorter (365¼ – 354 = 11¼) than the standard secular year or, putting it another way, the Hebrew runner, moves through a period of time 11¼ days shorter than the Gregorian one. This is the same as saying that the Gregorian runner covers a distance 11¼ days greater than the Hebrew one during a one-year period. This means that the Hebrew runner would have to race 11¼ days faster to keep up with his Gregorian counterpart. In reality, however, he doesn't run faster, and he doesn't keep up; he starts to fall behind. After only one complete race, in our analogy, the Hebrew months have fallen 11¼ days behind the secular months. This means that the first day of Sukkot, which is always Tishre 15 on the Hebrew calendar no matter what the Jewish year, and which occurred on October 18 in secular year 2005, occurs 11¼ days earlier in the next secular year, 2006, i.e., on October 7 (Oct.18 – 11¼ days = Oct. 7). After two full races, Tishre 15 on the Jewish calendar shifts even further behind, to September 27 on the 2007 civil calendar (Oct. 7 – 11¼ days = Sept. 27). This is a full three weeks further behind the secular year than it was two years earlier (Oct. 18 – Sept. 27 = 21 days, which is 3 weeks). In other words, the Gregorian runner is getting further and further out in front of the Hebrew one because, like the hare overtaking and passing the tortoise, he's faster. That is, he appears to be faster because the Gregorian runner covers more ground during the course of his year than the Hebrew one does during the course of his. The Gregorian covers a distance of 365¼ days while the Hebrew covers only 354. After yet another, third complete race, Tishre 15 would happen on September 16 in 2008 (Sept. 27 – 11¼ = Sept. 16), i.e., more than a month earlier than the date it occurred on in 2005, which was Oct. 18, when we began.

Again, this is because each complete race of our runners causes the Hebrew year to fall 11¼ days behind the Gregorian one or, saying the same thing differently, the Gregorian year to pull 11¼ days ahead. But the Hebrew calendar does not allow things to get that far out of whack because, uncorrected, this process would eventually lead to Sukkot occurring in August, in the summer, rather than when it's supposed to, in the fall. All the other Jewish holidays would start happening out of season too.

Passover, for example, would occur in winter instead of spring. To address this problem, the Jewish calendar adds a "leap month" approximately every three Jewish years. That month is known as "Adar II" and tacks an additional twenty-nine or thirty days onto the Jewish year it's used in, meaning an Adar II Jewish year is elongated by at least twenty-nine days and has thirteen months instead of twelve.[8] In fact, the Jewish years into which Adar IIs are inserted are longer than the secular years: 354, the number of days in the standard Jewish year, + 29, the number of days in Adar II, = 383, which is 17¾ days longer than the standard 365¼-day secular year. Adar II years, therefore, are faster, in the parlance we've been using, than their corresponding secular years. That's why, during an Adar II year, the Hebrew dates "catch-up" with the secular ones.

Returning to our two runners, after three full races, the additional twenty-nine days of Adar II brings Tishre 15, which, uncorrected, would coincide with Sept. 16 in 2008, approximately back to the month and day it coincided with in the base year 2005, i.e., approximately back to October 18. The "leap month" doesn't bring the Hebrew calendar and secular calendars exactly back into synch – in 2008, Tishre 15 occurs on October 14 – but close enough so that they are no longer completely out of whack. The numbers work out like this: Tishre 15 = Oct. 18 in 2005, Oct. 7 in 2006, and Sept. 27 in 2007. That is, in each successive year, Sukkot occurs 11¼ days earlier on the secular calendar than the year before. After another full race of the runners, we're in 2008 on the Gregorian calendar and, but for Adar II, the first day of Sukkot would happen on Sept. 16 (Sept. 27 – 11¼ days = Sept. 16). However, in 2008, we add an Adar II month of twenty-nine days, which causes Sukkot to occur on Oct. 14 (Sept. 16 + 29 days = Oct. 14).

And with those adjustments, that's how Jewish and secular time keep pace with each other. The Jewish calendar is purposely designed so that its months always coincide exactly with the lunar months, one lunar month being the period from new moon to new moon, while at the same time striving to make the Hebrew year coincide with the solar year as much as possible. In this way, the lunar-based Hebrew calendar never gets too far out of rhythm with the solar-based Gregorian calendar, although the Jewish holidays jump around a lot on it due to the Jewish dates falling further and further behind the Gregorian dates and then "leaping" to catch up again when an Adar II "leap month" is added.

While we're on the subject of calendars, there exists a theory about the measuring of time that says a single day 15 billion years ago, at the dawn of Creation, was much, much longer – eons longer – than a day is now. After the Big Bang, remember, the Earth and all the planets that formed from the matter it spewed out, were just super-heated balls of gas slowly condensing into molten liquid, and they would not coalesce, become solid, and begin rotating around their own axes for billions of years. A modern day, however, is dependent on the current speed of the Earth's rotation, and is measured as the period of time it takes the Earth to rotate around its axis once, just twenty-four hours. But that rotation started very slowly and did not reach the twenty-four-hour speed until untold millennia after the Big Bang. By torturing the logic of this theory a bit, an argument can be made that each day then was equivalent not to twenty-four hours, but to billions of years, with the length of each day steadily decreasing through the eons as the Earth solidified and began to rotate more and more quickly. Thus, the six days of creation could actually have taken about 15 billion years (6 'ancient' days x a mean average of about 2½ billion years for each ancient day = 15 billion years), not just 144 hours (6 'modern' days x 24 hours each = 144 hours), which estimate is in accord with modern scientific findings indicating that our universe is around 15 billion years old. In this scheme, the only 5,768 Hebrew years that the Bible tells us have passed since Creation, the current secular year being 2006, can be taken to represent the number of years modern man has walked the Earth, i.e., the period of time from the end of the sixth day until modern times. According to Genesis, recall, it was only at the end of the ancient sixth day that God created us. By then, according to the theory I'm describing, the length of each day had shortened and was equivalent to the modern, twenty-four-hour day, as opposed to before, when each day was equivalent on average to 2½ billion years. The 5,768 year estimate as to how long modern man has existed, like the 15 billion-year "age of the universe estimate," is also in the ballpark with current scientific conclusions, although it is somewhat off, since most modern anthropologists believe that modern *Homo sapiens,* i.e., Adam and Eve types, as opposed to Neanderthals and other more primitive humanoids, have existed for some 100,000 years at least. In any event, what is amazing is not the inaccuracies of the biblical writers, who believed God created the world in six "ancient" days and then rested, which turns out may actually be correct, but that they got so much right; before twenty-first-century technology and science, modern laboratories and experiments, astronauts and space exploration, carbon-14 and radiometric dating, and telescopes so incredibly powerful that now, in the twenty-first century, we can actually see stars so distant that the light they emit, although just reaching our eyes now, began traveling toward us only moments after the Big Bang, 15 billion years ago.

Speaking of time, and surprising theories about it, things happen so unexpectedly on occasion that sometimes you're knocked nearly senseless. And on Hebrew date Adar I, 1, i.e., February 23, 2004, (a "leap month," remember, is designated Adar II), that's what happened to Congregation B'nai Torah.

Chapter Twenty Nine - The Last Adventure?

On February 23, 2004, eight months to the day after I stepped down as president, Congregation B'nai Torah's irreplaceably beautiful synagogue caught fire and burned to the ground. The fire started at about 7:00 PM, when an aging electrical wire in the wall behind our memorial board sparked and ignited the old wood paneling from the inside out. Literally within seconds, smoke began pouring out from the tiny separation between the memorial board and wall, and moments afterward flames started consuming the wall's wooden panels and then, leaping overhead, the wood beams and arched ceilings. Those present tried to douse the flames with water and fire extinguishers, but it was hopeless. At a lightning pace, the fire traveled along the electrical wires inside the walls and ignited other portions of the synagogue. We couldn't save our sacred Torahs or Talmud. We couldn't save our Shofars, Menorahs, Lions of David, or *Ner Tamid*. Everything, including our entire library, all our important records, half-century-old stained-glass windows, paintings, prayer books, *tallit*, gift shop inventory, and furniture, much of it antique and unique, was destroyed.

While the synagogue burned and fifty volunteer firemen tried desperately to control it, a crowd of onlookers gathered, at least forty of them JCC members. The blaze could be seen for hundreds of yards in all directions. Soon news crews and photographers arrived. Although it was still midwinter, the crowd grew huge. One member, Gary Birnberg, captured the mood perfectly when he said, "I'm shivering inside, but it's not from the cold." Bonnie Kessler, my good friend, whom I still affectionately call Temple Wife, and who is now president of the congregation, called me from her cell phone at my office in Manhattan. Sobbing, she said, "Michael, the synagogue's on fire and they can't stop it. It's going down. Everything we've worked for all these years is gone." In the background, I could hear people crying and gasping. As the synagogue disintegrated, Bonnie gave me a depressing moment-by-moment description.

Pat Weisslander came to the phone. "We'll have to rebuild, Michael. There's not going to be much left." As she spoke, someone screamed, "Get back, the roof is collapsing!" Pat shouted, "Sorry, I've gotta go." The line went dead.

In the City, at least two and a half hours away from JCC by public transportation, I felt useless. "Was there anyone I could call or anything I could do," I thought, "to help?" Not knowing what else to do, I grabbed my phone and started calling as many congregation members as I could to let them know what was happening. Many of them, I was certain, would immediately drop what they were doing and rush to the synagogue to get one last look at the building before it was totally burned and disappeared. Within fifteen minutes, I made eight calls and successfully reached five members. All of them, exactly as I expected, along with their families, raced to JCC, picking up other members on the way. Most arrived in time to see the building an agonizing final time before it was totally consumed and reduced to a burned-out, almost unrecognizable shell. Mayer Fistal, who was the first member I had telephoned, called me back on his cell when he reached the synagogue. "Mike," he said, "there's just nothing good I can tell you. The entire building is ablaze, I can see flames shooting out of every window, the heat is brutal, and they've evacuated all the firemen. They're spraying water onto it from the trucks, but it's too dangerous for them to stay inside anymore. I tell you, Mike, it's a good thing you're not here to see this. I know what this place meant to you. They tried, really tried – there's ten fire trucks here – but couldn't save anything." I was so stunned when he said that, I momentarily lost my breath and actually stopped breathing. – And fifteen minutes later, the whole building – with the silver leaves I had bought on the Tree of Life honoring my children, the *Yizkor* plaque in memory of my mother, the bronze plaque with my name emblazoned on it, along with the names of other former JCC presidents, and the same or similar for nearly every other member of the congregation – crumbled to ashes and was gone.

As I've said before in this book, America, for the most part, is a wonderful country. So wonderful that I truly believe those of us fortunate enough to be living here are already in "The Promised Land." Almost immediately after the fire died down, even while the ashes were still smoldering, every local Christian congregation, without exception, offered JCC space in their churches or annex buildings to hold our services, meet, socialize, and run our Hebrew school and other activities for as long as we wanted. Sensitive to our needs, they even offered to remove all crucifixes and other Christian symbols from the portions of the buildings we would occupy. They offered us parking facilities, large activity rooms, huge halls where we would be able to keep our bingo games going, kitchen facilities, tables and chairs, bookcases and cabinets, financial help, and even legal help with JCC's fire damage claim against our insurance company if that would become necessary. Unsolicited, contributions began to flow in – not only from other Jews, mind you – but to a substantial extent from many of our Christian neighbors too. Most gratifying of all, perhaps, was the contribution we received from my Muslim in-laws in Louisiana, Dr. Mehmood and Audrey Patel. – God, please continue to bless this country, because in America, no matter what our religion, unlike just about any other place on the planet, we are all truly brothers.

As it turned out, within two weeks after the fire, the Greenwood Lake Volunteer Ambulance Corps made available to us, and we moved into, their empty old headquarters building on Sterling Road. It was off the beaten track a bit, and a little small, but was equipped with a new kitchen, adequate restroom facilities, several midsize rooms we could use for offices and Hebrew school classes, and two larger rooms, one of which we could use for a social hall and the other as our sanctuary. It was perfect as a temporary center of operations. Also, as fate would have it, the Volunteer Ambulance Corps Building was right across the street from Rabbi Brenda Weinberg's home and, when she found out it was being offered to us for as long as we needed it, free of charge, I'll never forget the smile that crossed her face – and mine when I saw hers – when she realized how much easier it was going to make her life and how much more time it would enable her to devote to synagogue affairs.

Although we lost our building, which had been a place of such spirituality and warmth that it helped ignite my intense interest in Judaism, and for many of us was at least like a second home, unexpectedly, we gained something from the fire catastrophe too. After we moved into the Old Ambulance Corps headquarters, for example, for some reason, our Friday night services began being more heavily attended. A good number of members who in the past had shown up only occasionally, in part because they were agnostic or even atheist and had no patience for the religious rituals, started to be regulars. Others, who had never been active at services, in helping to run the synagogue, or in any aspect of synagogue business, suddenly volunteered to join the committees we were setting up to fundraise, negotiate with our insurance company, hire an architect and builder, or pick up the ark, torahs, furniture, prayer and Hebrew school books, and dozens of other items that were being donated to us by synagogues from around the country. We were offered and accepted extremely valuable stained-glass windows, many costly works of art, and a $10,000 Tree of Life from synagogues in Queens and Manhattan. Formerly inactive members secured trucks or vans and made the arrangements to pick those things up which, logistically, required a great deal of effort. Also, we received donations of hundreds of books, *tallit*, and yarmulkes from as far away as Texas, California, and Canada. Members who were completely non-observant and non-religious, and had seldom shown any interest in synagogue affairs, made the arrangements to get those items too. The dynamics that came into play, as a result of the fire, reminded me somewhat of an extended and scattered family that, except when one of the cousins, uncles, or aunts dies, and there's a funeral to attend, seldom gets together.

Michael Grossman

But there were some religious reasons why this occurred too. Unlike Christianity, which holds that you must fully accept and believe in Jesus to be truly Christian, or Islam, which holds that you must totally submit to God to be genuinely Muslim and, in fact, means "submission," Judaism accepts those who are agnostics or even professed atheists and considers them to be authentically Jewish if: (1) they regard themselves as part of the Jewish people and, (2) their behavior is ethical. After the fire, we seemed to get much greater participation and a new surge of energy by JCC congregants who fit those two categories, i.e., who placed a very high value on ethical conduct toward others and also, for whom a major part of their identity was their connection to the Jewish people. Most of these wayward congregants, on the other hand, had little or no belief in a supreme being. What had happened was that the destruction of our synagogue presented them with an opportunity to do something very important for their congregation – help rebuild it – which did not primarily involve their having to attend services or suddenly become pious. The emphasis on services and ritual is what had caused them to keep their distance in the first place, usually showing up on Rosh Hashanah and Yom Kippur, but only rarely anytime else. This phenomenon – of being accepted as an authentic Jew even if you don't believe in God – is what makes the Jewish people more than just followers of a particular faith. You can be a bona fide Jew without, in any formal sense, practicing Judaism. It's also what makes Judaism more than just another religion. Even if you're a non-believer and completely non-observant, you're considered an adherent of Judaism just by being a member of the Jewish people and sharing their values. That's because in Judaism, how people behave is vastly more important than what they believe. In fact, if the sum total of a person's Judaism is professing an unshakable belief in Yahweh, but he does not feel a connection with other Jews who may disagree with that belief, and he behaves unethically to boot, he is considered less religious and less authentically Jewish than those who have serious doubts about God's existence but, nonetheless, feel connected to other Jews and always strive to behave justly. Judaism, particularly modern Judaism, is not just a set of take-it-or-leave-it theological propositions or be damned. Having faith in God is important, but only insofar as it causes us to be better people, i.e., results in our doing good. Judaism would much rather we always strive to do good, and thereby become better people, even without belief in God, than profess faith in God but seldom do good.

That's why, in the aftermath of the fire, Congregation B'nai Torah was able to pull together and revitalize itself. — It was as though we'd had a miniature renaissance. Just as the Jews, as a people, are more than Judaism, JCC, as a congregation, had always been more than just a building and rituals. Knowing that, or at least sensing it, enabled the many members of our congregation who had never fully embraced traditional Judaism to fully participate in the most exciting and demanding project we had ever embarked upon: rebuilding our synagogue from the ground up. The last adventure? Not a chance. After the fire we all knew, even if we never rebuilt and moved to an entirely new location, that our best days and most exciting adventures lay ahead of us.

* * *

I used to think that rabbis, priests, and all other religious leaders, and anyone else who took religion too seriously, were obstacles to democracy, modernity, progress, and rational thought. Starting from when I was very young, my observation had always been that each religion is so blindly determined to defend its own dogma that sooner or later they do or say things that make them look brainless and ridiculous, even to their own faithful. For example, to this day, I cannot get out of my mind the image of Galileo being dragged before the Inquisition in 1633 and forced to say, in effect, "Yes, I was wrong, the sun does move around the Earth," despite incontrovertible proof, even then, to the contrary. If he hadn't, he would have been imprisoned for life or worse, with the blessing and enthusiastic support of nearly the entire Catholic Church. Equally shameful, to most twenty-first-century observers looking back, is this delightful command Moses delivered when he descended from Mount Sinai and found that a good number of his people had been won over by the idol, the Golden Calf: "'Whoever is for the Lord (meaning Yahweh and only Yahweh), come here! Each of you put sword on thigh, go back and forth from gate to gate throughout the camp, and slay brother, neighbor, and kin.' The Levites did as Moses said and some three thousand of the people were slaughtered that day" (Exodus 32:25 -28). Or what about this beauty spoken not by Moses but by Yahweh himself: "If....you disobey Me and remain hostile to Me, I will act against you in wrathful hostility; I, for My part, will discipline you sevenfold for your sins. You shall eat the flesh of your sons and the flesh of your daughters. I will destroy your cult places and cut down your incense stands, and I will heap your carcasses upon your lifeless fetishes [idols]" (Leviticus 26:27-30). These instances seem like distant, unfamiliar rantings from a barbaric past because, over the centuries, fortunately, mainstream Christianity and mainstream Judaism have matured, mellowed, and become commendably tolerant. But the third monotheistic religion, Islam, in many places has not. Al Qaeda, whose enormous appeal in the Muslim world has become apparent, preaches a vicious loathing toward all non-Muslims and especially toward the West, which it perceives as the bastion of modern-thinking Christians and Jews. The unrelenting hatred it spews is directed against non-Western religions as well, including Hinduism and Buddhism. Witness the mindless destruction in Afghanistan of Buddhist statues nearly 2,000 years old by the Taliban fanatics who controlled the country before the U.S. invaded, and were in bed with and protected Al Qaeda, perpetrators of 9/11. Why did they destroy the Buddhist statues? Answer: Because they weren't Muslim; Period! Rather than treat the statues as priceless archaeological treasures, as any sane society on the planet would have, these medieval, modernity-hating, Muslim religious fanatics, and allies of Osama bin Laden, obliterated them. Forever.[1] They had been in existence, undamaged, except by the passage of time, for even longer than Islam itself. Siddhartha Guatamo a.k.a. Buddha, meaning "Enlightened One," the Indian philosopher who founded Buddhism, lived from approximately 563 B.C.E. to 483 B.C.E., more than a millennium before Muhammad, 570 C.E. to 632 C.E., was even born.

But that's the dark, frightening side of religion: ignorance and intolerance, abhorrence of outsiders, disdain for science when at odds with scripture, and sometimes, even commands to slaughter all nonbelievers. There is, however, a mind-boggling, thought-expanding, dazzlingly bright side that I stumbled across, completely inadvertently and unexpectedly, after I joined JCC and eventually served four years as its president. Aside from religion and theology, which is the philosophy about religion, and a few other branches of philosophy, there are no disciplines whose only goal is to explore man's place in the world and how we should behave in it. Judaism, Christianity, and Islam have all spun out complex webs of beliefs, ethics, rites, holy days, prayers, traditions, and laws, the sole purpose of which is to help us perceive the very purpose of our existence and guide our conduct toward and feelings about ourselves, each other, the universe, and God. Equally important, they attempt to shape and define what that amorphous word *God* means. Nor are they – I should say, need they be – hopelessly bogged down by a static, unchanging allegiance to no-longer-relevant, thousands-of-years-old interpretations of their founding scriptures. Their thinking about the world out there, *and themselves,* can and has dramatically changed; Judaism and Christianity, noticeably more so than Islam, which is the newest and arguably, therefore, most immature of the three. A tolerant, forward-looking religion – like most contemporary Judaism I know (other than the ultra-ultra-Orthodox) – is not some fossil-like, rampaging dinosaur hell-bent on devouring the modern world and dragging it backward in time to be disgorged in some ancient era that has long passed. Tolerant religion, rather, can be a source of exhilarating wonder, inspiration to justice, and an impetus to ever-increasing knowledge. The unexpected bright side of religion I stumbled across is the part that's refocused my mind on the questions I used to ask as a boy, as an innocent:

"Mom, where did we all come from? When did time begin? What was here before the Earth and living things? What was here before the Big Bang? Dad, why do people have to die? Do you really believe we have souls? Is there really a heaven? Do you think we'll go there when we die and see each other again?" And all the rest: "Mom, Dad, is there life on other planets? Does outer space go on forever? Why can't we travel faster than the speed of light? Does that mean we'll never get to see aliens from other galaxies?" Or simply, "Mom, why is grass green? Why is the sky blue? Dad, why are birds so beautiful? How come they can fly and we can't?" Thanks to that side of religion, the awe-inspiring, dazzling bright side, I can again look up at the night skies and gaze upon the stars, like when I was young, and dream. I find myself marveling once more at the world and everything in it. I'm determined to learn all I possibly can about it. I'm ravenous for knowledge. There's nothing I'm not interested in. I read, write, and study voraciously. Believe me, being religious, which for Jews, i.e., Israelites, means *struggling with God*, does not conflict with a desire to learn, change when confronted with new knowledge, and constantly find new meanings and insights. No, religion is not the obstacle I once thought it was to progress and rational thought. For me, in fact, it's my new-gained respect for and knowledge about religion that has ignited in me a desire to gain knowledge about everything else.

Epilogue

To write this book, I've had to travel a long way. For never, in my most fanciful moments, did I imagine I'd actually reach a point in life when I'd begin to seriously contemplate the existence of God. You see, in truth, in the *Introduction* to this work, I wasn't totally honest when I described my upbringing as merely anti-religious and anti-observant. More accurately, it was very nearly militantly atheistic and aggressively hostile toward those foolish or misinformed enough to still cling, in the twenty-first century, to the ridiculous notion of a supreme being. It was crystal clear to me then, based on everything I learned in school and everything I read elsewhere, that God was just something men and women had dreamed up in earlier centuries to explain things, before the long decline of superstition and its replacement, at last, by advanced Age of Enlightenment science. It was certainly clear, despite the frequent miracles the Bible claims occurred, that I had never experienced nor seen one, nor had anyone else I knew, even those who professed to be pious. Also, despite numerous biblical descriptions of God having supposedly spoken to people, sometimes repeatedly, from Abraham forward, I'd surely never heard his voice, nor ever met anyone who convinced me he had. To me, those many who still insisted on clinging to a belief in God did so mostly to help shield themselves from the approaching, horrendous anguish they would be feel by the inevitable deaths of their aging loved ones and, just as often, their slowly growing fear of their own. I felt bad for them, almost pitied them, for their inability to accept reality and need to create a "make-believe" world with a "conjured-up" heaven. No sane and rational person could possibly believe that such a fairy-tale place could exist. Even as a young boy I felt that way.

But I have not, all of a sudden, abandoned my God-skeptical, religion-reluctant, and prayer/ritual-resistant lifelong point of view. For many people, especially hardcore, doubting types like me, God is not and will probably never be a tangible, discoverable presence; but only an amorphous idea – and a whimsical, unprovable one at that. I've come to realize, however, that the whole God enterprise depends entirely – not on rituals or prayers – but on what *God* means to each one of us, the definitions of which range from the traditional "an all-encompassing, omniscient supreme being" to the very secular "the ethics shared by civilized people." At last count, there are today about 370 distinct religions or religious sub-sects being practiced in the world, many with radical and extremely odd points of view, but all with at least a slightly different take on the meaning of God. Those differences, however slight, are what distinguish them from each other.

With such diversity, and technology that makes possible the widespread and nearly instantaneous exchange of information, it is no longer possible for any one of them to convincingly argue that only its dogma speaks the truth. Such an assertion, in most democracies at any rate, would seem narrow-minded, arrogant, and silly.

With those provisos, however, it is my hope that this book may have opened a path by which even the most secular-minded, including cynical agnostics as well as rock-hard, disdainful atheists, can find their way to a new perspective on religion; i.e., toward a perhaps unexpected appreciation of what religion can offer and the surprising realization that, contrary to the conventional wisdom, religion often expands – not controls – the mind and can open it to the astonishing beauty in the world that too often lies hidden from us.

Bibliography

Aaron, David. *Endless Light, The Ancient Path of the Kabbalah to Love, Spiritual Growth and Personal Power.* New York: Berkley Books, 1998.

Ammerman, Nancy T., Jackson W. Carrol, Carl S. Dudley & William Mckinney, editors. *Studying Congregations, a New Handbook.* Nashville: Abingdon Press, 1998.

Apisdorf, Shimon. *Rosh Hashanah Yom Kippur Survival Kit.* Baltimore: Leviathan Press, 2000.

Armstrong, Karen. *A History of God: The 4000-Year Quest of Judaism, Christianity, and Islam.* New York: Alfred A. Knopf, Inc., 1993.

Asimov, Isaac. *Asimov's Guide to the Bible.* New York: Avenel Books, 1981.

Augustine, Saint. *City of God.* New York: Image Books, Doubleday, 1958.

Baha'u'llah, Shoghi. *Hidden Words of Baha'u'llah.* Oxford, England: Oneworld Publications, 1991.

Blech, Rabbi Benjamin. *The Complete Idiot's Guide to Jewish History and Culture.* New York: Alpha Books, 1999.

Blech, Rabbi Benjamin. *The Complete Idiot's Guide to Understanding Judaism,* New York: Alpha Books, 1999.

Bokenkotter, Thomas. *A Concise History of the Catholic Church.* New York: Image Books Doubleday, 1979.

Bowers, Kenneth E. *God Speaks Again: An Introduction to the Baha'i Faith.* Wilmette, Ill., Baha'i Publishing, Inc., 2004.

Browne, Lewis. *The Wisdom of Israel.* New York: Random House, 1945.

Bryson, Bill. *A Short History of Nearly Everything.* New York: Broadway Books, 2003.

Burge, Gary M. *Who Are God's People in the Middle East? What Christians Are not Being Told about Jews and the Palestinians.* Grand Rapids, Mich., Zondervan Publishing House, 1993.

Burn, A. R. *The Penguin History of Greece*. New York: Penguin Books, 1990.

Cahill, Thomas. *The Gifts of the Jews: How a Tribe of Desert Nomads Changed the Way Everyone Thinks and Feels*. New York: Nan A. Talese /Anchor Books, 1999.

Carroll, James. *Constantine's Sword, The Church and the Jews*. New York: Mariner Books/Houghton Mifflin Company, 2002.

Chopra, Deepak. *How to Know God, The Soul's Journey into the Mystery of Mysteries*. New York: Harmony Books, 2000.

Cohen, Barbara. *David, A Biography*. New York: Clarion Books, 1995.

Cooper, Rabbi David A. *God Is a Verb: Kabbalah and the Practice of Mystical Judaism*. New York: Riverhead Books, 1997.

Cunningham, Scott, *Dreaming the Divine: Techniques for Sacred Sleep*. St. Paul, Minn.: Llewellyn Publications, 1999.

Davis, Kenneth C. *Don't Know Much about History*. New York: Avon Books, 1995.

Davis, Kenneth. *Don't Know Much about the Bible*. New York: Avon Books, 1999.

Dershowitz, Alan. *The Case for Israel*. Hoboken, NJ: Wiley & Sons, Inc., 2003.

Donin, Rabbi Hayim Halevey. *To Be a Jew, A Guide to Jewish Observance in Contemporary Life*, New York: Basic Books, 1972.

Donin, Rabbi Hayim Halevey. *To Pray as a Jew, A Guide to the Prayer Book and the Synagogue Service*. New York: Basic Books, 1980.

Dosick, Rabbi Wayne. *The Business Bible, Ten Commandments for an Ethical Workplace*. New York: William Morrow and Company, 1993.

Eban, Abba. *My People, History of the Jews*, Volumes 1 & 2, New York: Behrman House Inc., 1978.

Ellis, Joseph J. *Founding Brothers, The Revolutionary Generation*. New York: Vintage Books, 2002.

Feiler, Bruce. *Abraham*. New York: William Morrow and Company, 2002.

Friedman, Richard Elliot. *Who Wrote the Bible?* San Francisco: Harper Collins, 1989.

Friedman, Thomas L. *Longitudes and Latitudes, The World in the Age of Terrorism.* Garden City, NY: Anchor Books, 2003.

Garraty, John A. & Peter Gay, editors. *The Columbia History of the World.* New York: Harper & Row, 1972.

Gevirtz, Rabbi Eliezer. *A Guide to Torah Hashkofoh, Questions and Answers on Judaism.* Jerusalem, Israel: Feldheim Publishers, Ltd., 1980.

Golinkin, Noah. *Shalom Aleichem, Learn to Read the Jewish Prayerbook.* New York: Hebrew Publishing Company, 1999.

Gomes, Peter J. *The Good Book, Reading The Bible With Mind And Heart.* New York: Avon Books, 1996.

Gordon, Noah. *The Last Jew.* New York: Thomas Duane Books St. Martin Press, 2000.

Grant, Michael. *The Twelve Caesars.* New York: Barnes & Noble Books, 1996.

Greenberg, Blu. *How to Run a Traditional Jewish Household.* New York: Fireside Books, Simon & Schuster, 1985.

Greenberg, Rabbi Sidney & Rabbi Jonathan D. Levine, compilers & editors. *Likrat Shabbat, Worship, Study and Song for Sabbath and Festival Evenings.* Bridgeport, Conn: The Prayer Book Press, Media Judaica, 1973.

Greenberg, Rabbi Sidney & Rabbi Jonathan D. Levine, compilers & editors. *Siddur Hadash, Worship, Study and Song for Sabbath and Festival Mornings.* Bridgeport, Conn: The Prayer Book Press, 1992.

Greenberg, Rabbi Sidney & Rabbi Jonathan D. Levine, compilers & editors. *Mahzor Hadash for Rosh Hashanah and Yom Kippur.* Bridgeport, Conn: The Prayer Book Press, 1977.

Greene, Brian. *The Elegant Universe,* New York: Random House, Inc., 2000.

Greene, Brian. *The Fabric of the Cosmos; Space, Time and the Texture of Reality.* New York: Random House, Inc., 2004.

Grosso, Michael. *Soulmaking, Uncommon Paths to Self-Understanding.* Charlottesville, Va.: Hampton Roads Publishing Company, Inc., 1992.

Grosso, Michael. *The Millennium Myth: Love and Death at the End of Time.* Wheaton, Ill..: Quest Books, 1995.

Gunaratna, Rohan. *Inside Al-Queda: Global Network of Terror.* New York: Penguin Group, 2003.

Halberstam, Yitta & Judith Leventhal. *Small Miracles for the Jewish Heart.* Avon, Mass.: Adams Media Corporation, 2002.

Halevi, Judah. *The Kuzari.* New York: Schoken Books, 1964.

Haugk, Kenneth C. *Antagonists in the Church: How to Identify and Deal with Destructive Conflict.* Minneapolis: Augsburg Publishing House, 1988.

Hertzberg, Arthur & Aaron Hirt Manheimer. *Jews, The Essence and Character of a People.* San Francisco: Harper, 1998.

Herschel, Abraham J. *Man's Quest for God.* New York: Charles Scribner's Sons, 1954.

Herschel, Abraham J. *The Prophets.* New York: Harper Torchbooks, 1969.

Hesse, Hermann. *Siddhartha.* Mineola, N.Y.: Dover Publications, Inc., 1999.

Hirsch, Ammiel & Yosef Reinman. *One People, Two Worlds.* New York: Schocken Books, 2002.

Howarth, Patrick. *Atilla, King of the Huns: Man and Myth.* New York: Barnes & Noble Books, 1995.

Jacobs, Louis. *The Book of Jewish Practice.* West Orange, N.J.: Behrman House, Inc, 1987.

Johnson, Paul. *A History of the Jews.* New York: Harper Perennial, 1988.

Johnson, Paul. *A History of Christianity.* New York: Simon & Schuster, 1995.

Johnson, Paul. *A History of the American People.* New York: Harper Perennial, 1997.

Johnson, Phillip E. *Darwin on Trial*. Downers Grove, IL.: InterVarsity Press, 1993.

Josephus. *The Complete Works of Josephus: Jewish Antiquities, The Jewish War, Against Apion*. Grand Rapids, Mich: Kregel Publications, 1999.

Kamentz, Roger. *The Jew in the Lotus*. San Francisco: Harper, 1995.

Kamentz, Roger. *Stalking Elijah*. San Francisco: Harper, 1998.

Katz, Molly. *Jewish as a Second Language: How to Worry, How to Interrupt, How to Say the Opposite of What You Mean*. New York: Workman Publishing, 1991.

Katz, Rabbi Mordechai. *From the Teachings of Our Sages*. Jerusalem: Feldheim Publishers, Ltd., 1987.

Keller, Walter. *The Bible as History*. New York: Barnes & Noble Books, 1995.

Kertzer, David I. *The Popes Against the Jews, The Vatican's Role in the Rise of Modern Anti-Semitism*. New York: Vintage Books, 2002.

Konner, Melvin. *Unsettled—An Anthropology of the Jews*. New York: Viking Compass, 2003.

Lamb, David. *The Arabs; Journeys beyond the Mirage*. New York: Vintage Books, 2002.

Lerner, Michael. *Jewish Renewal*. New York: Harper Perennial, 1995.

Lewis, Bernard. *The Middle East, A Brief History of the Last 2000 Years*, New York: Touchstone/Scribner, 2003.

Lewis, Bernard. *What Went Wrong? The Clash between Islam and Modernity in the Middle East*. New York: HarperCollins, 2002.

Luzzatto, Moshe Chayim. *The Path of the Just*. Jerusalem: Feldheim Publishers, 1966.

Matar, N. I. *Islam for Beginners*. New York: Writers and Readers Publishing, Inc., 1992.

Mann, Gil. *How to Get More Out of Being Jewish Even If: A. You are not sure you believe in God, B. You think going to synagogue is a waste of time, C. You think keeping kosher is stupid, D. You hated Hebrew school, or E. All of the above*. Minneapolis: Leo & Sons Publishing, 2002.

Matt, Daniel C. *The Essential Kabbalah.* San Francisco: Harper, 1996.

McAfee, John. *The Fabric of Self, Meditations on Vanity and Love.* Woodland Park, Colo.: Woodland Publications, 2001.

Mutz, John & Katherine Murray. *Fundraising for Dummies.* Foster City, CA: IDG Books Worldwide, Inc., 2000.

Osborne, Richard. *Philosophy for Beginners.* New York: Writers and Readers Publishing Inc., 1992.

Payne, Robert. *The History of Islam.* New York: Barnes & Noble Books, 1995.

Potok, Chaim. *The Chosen.* New York: Ballantine Books/Random House Publishing Group, 1967.

Renou, Louis, editor. *Hinduism, its mythology, philosophy, religious and moral practices and beliefs; its historical evolution as a religious way of life and its present role in Indian society.* New York: George Braziller, 1962.

Roche, Paul. *The Bible's Greatest Stories.* New York: Signet Classic/Penuin Putnam Inc., 2001.

Rossel, Seymour. *When A Jew Prays.* New York: Behrman House, Inc, 1973.

Rossel, Seymour. *Introduction to Jewish History, from Abraham to the Sages.* New York: Behrman House, Inc, 1981.

Rossel, Seymour. *Journey Through Jewish History, The Age of Faith and the Age of Reason.* New York: Behrman House, Inc., 1983.

Rossel, Seymour. *A Child's Bible, Lessons From the Torah.* New York: Behrman House, Inc., 1988.

Rossel, Seymour. *A Child' Bible, Lessons from the Prophets and Writings.* New York: Behrman House, Inc., 1989.

Rossel, Seymour. *Let Freedom Ring, a History of the Jews in the United States.* New York: Behrman House, Inc., 1996.

Sagan, Carl. *Cosmos.* New York: Simon & Schuster, Inc., 1960.

Sagan, Carl. *The Dragons of Eden.* New York: Ballantine Books/Random House Publishing, 1978.

Sagan, Carl. *The Demon Haunted World: Science as a Candle in the Dark.* New York: Ballantine Books/Random House Publishing, 1997.

Scharfstein, Sol. *Understanding Jewish History 1, from the Patriarchs to the Expulsion from Spain.* Hoboken, N.J.: KTAV Publishing House, Inc. 1996.

Scharfstein, Sol. *Understanding Jewish History 2, from the Renaissance to the 21st Century.* Hoboken, N.J.: KTAV Publishing House, Inc., 1997.

Shlaim, Avi. *The Iron Wall: Israel and the Arab World.* New York: W.W. Norton & Company, Inc., 1999.

Schroeder, Gerald L. *The Science of God.* New York: Broadway Books, 1997.

Shapiro, Rabbi Rami M. *Minyan, Ten Principles for Living a Life of Integrity.* New York: Bell Tower/Random House, 1997.

Siegel, Andrew Robert (adapted from material copyrighted by Fish, Sidney M., 1974). *The Hebrew Reading Crash Course, A Project of the National Jewish Outreach Program.* New York: Bloch Publishing Company, Inc., 1998.

Singer, Ellen, with Bernard M. Zlotowitz. *Our Sacred Texts: Discovering the Jewish Classics.* New York: UAHC Press, 1992.

Steinberg, Milton. *Basic Judaism.* Orlando: Harcourt Brace & Co., 1988.

Steingroot, Ira. *Keeping Passover.* San Francisco: Harper, 1995.

Strassfeld, Michael. *The Jewish Holidays: A Guide and Commentary.* New York: Harper & Row, 1985.

Strobel, Lee. *The Case for a Creator.* Grand Rapids, Mich.: Zondervan, 2004.

Tanakh, The Holy Scriptures. Philadelphia: The Jewish Publications Society, 1985.

Tate, Georges. *The Crusaders, Warriors of God.* New York: Harry N. Abrams, Inc., 1996.

Telushkin, Rabbi Joseph. *Biblical Literacy, The Most Important People, Events and Ideas of the Hebrew Bible.* New York: William Morrow and Company, Inc., 1997.

Telushkin, Rabbi Joseph. *Jewish Literacy, The Most Important Things to Know About the Jewish Religion, Its People, and Its History,* New York: William Morrow and Company, Inc., 1991.

The Book. (A modern edition of the Old and New Testaments). Wheaton, Ill.: Tyndale House Publishers, Inc., 1971.

The Koran. New York: Penguin Books, 1997.

Uris, Leon. *Exodus.* New York: Bantam Books, 1959.

Vorspan, Albert & David Sapperstein. *Tough Choices, Jewish Perspectives on Social Justice.* New York: UAHC Press, 1992.

White, Ellen, G. *Passion of the Ages.* Chicago: Homeward Publishing, 2004.

Wouk, Herman. *This Is My God, The Jewish Way of Life.* New York: Little, Brown and Company, 1979.

Notes

Chapter 10

[1] [$4,000 (4,700 − 700 = 4,000) + $700 + $700 = $5,400]

[2] [$1,100 (5,800 − 4,700 = 1,100) + $4,700 + $4,700 = $10,500] & [4,700 + 4,700 = 9,400]

[3] [$5,800 - $4,700 = $1,100) [$4,700 − $4,700 = $0]

[4] [$1,100 (5,800 − 4,700 = 1,100) + $4,700 + $4,700 = $10,500] & [$4,700 − $4,700 = $0]

[5] [$4,700 + $4,700 = $9,400] [$5,800 − $4,700 = $1,100]

[6] Beth-El could actually bet as little as $3,601 and it wouldn't change the winners/losers in the above four equations, but who can think that fast? If Beth-El bet $3,601 and JCC bet the same $4,700 in (1) above, Beth-El would win $9,401 to $9,400. In (2) it would win $2,199 to $0. In (3), $9,401 to $0. But in (4) JCC would win $9,400 to $2,199. The point is that the only reason Beth-El would want to bet $3,601 instead of $4,700 would be if we were playing with real money and Beth-El was anticipating outcome (4). In the event of outcome (4), if it was playing with real money, Beth-El would lose the match but walk away with $2,199 instead of $1,100. But we weren't playing for real money, so everything was on the line.

Chapter 11

[1] A relief on a temple wall dating from the reign of Ramses III (1195-1164 B.C.E.) in Medinet Habu, a town west of ancient Thebes on the Nile (modern Luxor, Egypt), depicts Philistine prisoners being processed by Egyptian guards. These Philistines are all at least a head taller than the Egyptians. If we presume that Hebrew slaves were about the same size on average as their Egyptian overseers, it appears there was real basis for the legend, or perhaps actual personage, of Goliath, the giant Philistine defeated by David.

[2] In 1925, at ruins on the site of Biblical Megiddo, a seal with ancient Hebrew lettering was found reading: "Shema, servant of Jeroboam." A stone at the same site bears the name: Pharaoh Sheshonk I. The Bible records that this pharaoh attacked Palestine the same year Solomon died and Jeroboam became the first king of divided Israel, the northern half of David and Solomon's formerly United Kingdom, Judah being the southern half, in about 922 B.C.E.

³ The Greek/Jewish cultural divide was known to history as early as 1150 B.C.E. when the Philistines began arriving in Canaan from the West via the Mediterranean Sea and settling the coast, the Hebrews having arrived only a century earlier from the East,* led by Joshua through Jericho, and settling the interior hill country. Recent archaeological excavations of the five major towns the Bible says were controlled by the Philistines – Askelon, Ashdod, Ekron, Gaza, and Gath – have all revealed pottery of unmistakably Greek pattern and style. This should surprise no one because the Bible states clearly: *"Have I not brought up Israel out of the land Egypt and the Philistines from Caphtor?"(Amos 9)*, which means *Crete*, the large island off the Southern Greek mainland.

*You'll recall that although Egypt lays to the west of Canaan, the Hebrews were unable to exodus using the shortest route because, among other reasons, they had to go around the territories of Moab, Edom, and Midian to avoid warfare with those peoples as much as possible. They had to head south into the Sinai Desert, skirt along the southern edge of Canaan, south of the Dead Sea, which route, by the time of Moses' death, left them poised on the east side of the Jordan River, east of the Promised Land and about five miles from Jericho.

Chapter 12

¹ Since the prophets were not sovereigns, whose battle exploits were recorded on cuneiform tablets or to whom monuments were erected, there is virtually no archaeological evidence that the prophets, as opposed to the kings of ancient Israel, ever lived. Admittedly, all we know about the prophets comes entirely from the Bible.

² Not including Moses, who was in a class by himself and lived more than two centuries before Samuel.

³ After Joshua conquered the Canaanites, the judges ruled the Israelite tribes for some 200 years, from approximately 1230 until 1020 B.C.E.

⁴ In 1845, the ruins of biblical Nineveh were discovered by British archaeologists in a tell [hill] near Mosul, Iraq. In 1847, very close by, the palace of Assyrian ruler Ashurbanipal was uncovered, with its incredible library containing 22,000 cuneiform tablets.

⁵ There is much disagreement among biblical historians as to the years when the various prophets were active, and many of the dates set forth in this book are just educated guesses.

⁶ In 722 B.C.E., 136 years before Babylonia defeated Judah, Assyria defeated the Northern Kingdom, Israel, and exiled *its* people. They vanished from history and became known as the Ten Lost Tribes.

[7] Except for the eighty-four-year reign of the Hasmonean kings, which formally began in 147 B.C.E., nineteen years after Mattathias of the Hasmonean family and his son, Judah the Maccabee, defeated Antiochus Epiphanes.

[8] All dates for the prophets' periods of activity and the reigns of Israel and Judah's kings are approximate. In fact, some of the dates listed here are different from dates given elsewhere in this book for the same persons. That's because biblical scholars differ on the dates some of these people lived by as much as two centuries.

[9] The United Kingdom split into Israel and Judah in 922 B.C.E.

[10] Israel fell to Assyria in 722 B.C.E.

[11] Judah was captured by Babylonia, Solomon's temple destroyed, and the Jews exiled to Babylon in 586 B.C.E.

[12] Persia defeated Babylonia 536 B.C.E., Jews returned to the Promised Land beginning about 532 B.C.E. and, at the urging of Haggai, the Second Temple was completed in 515 B.C.E.

Chapter 13

[1] At the Councils of Nicaea in 325 C.E. and Chalcedon in 451, the early Church set forth the doctrines of the Trinity and the two natures of Christ, one divine and one human. Nicaea, now Iznik, Turkey, was a city in ancient Bithynia, a country in northwest Asia Minor that existed as an independent nation until 74 B.C.E., when it came under the control of Rome. Chalcedon was a seaport in Bithynia at the south end of the Bosporus Strait opposite what is now Istanbul.

[2] After "Western Christendom" split into its two modern paradigms, Catholic and Protestant, a huge number of, dynamic, still evolving strands of Christian thought arose. In Medieval Catholicism, the Divine could become a living presence in mundane life via the intervention of the Saints, the blessings of the Virgin and the Pope. Post-Enlightenment Catholicism kept building on that, right down to the wonderful 19th Century conceit that the Pope is speaking for God when he speaks *ex cathedra*. But in Medieval and post-Medieval Protestantism the general drill is that you don't need somebody to "intervene" for God, just read the Bible. It's the cult of the Book. There were, however, a thousand readings of the Book and, by the time you get to the Quakers with their Inner Light, the Christian Scientists with their Christ Consciousness, the Jehovah's Witnesses with their world without Original Sin, the Anabaptists with their pacifism, the Unitarians with their Deism – by that time – you have versions of Christianity that aren't "Christian" at all in the conventional

sense. (Personal observations of Chuck Noell, co-author of *We Are All POWs*, Philadelphia: Fortress Press, 1975; and co-author/co-director of *Psycho/Dramas*, New York: McGuffin Productions, 2000 and *In The Shadow/Ground Zero*, New York: McGuffin Productions, 2001).

[3] The early Church, for all its internal squabbles, was prophetic and pacifist. It stood in a state of "opposition" to everything Rome stood for: militarism, enslavement, corruption, and cruelty. Nor was it militantly anti-Semitic since huge numbers of early Christians had formerly been Jews. Shortly after the first generation of Christians died off, however, and certainly by the time of Constantine, Christian hatred of Jews became insane. We're really talking about a pathology, maybe one better understood as a contagious disease than an outgrowth of a theological proposition or a political event i.e., for example, the existence of modern Israel. (Personal observations of Chuck Noell, co-author of *We Are All POWs*, Philadelphia: Fortress Press, 1975; and co-author/co-director of *Psycho/Dramas*, New York: McGuffin Productions, 2000 and *In The Shadow/ Ground Zero*, New York: McGuffin Productions, 2001).

Chapter 14

[1] In the ninth century in Baghdad, Jews (and Christians) had to wear black or yellow insignia, but the practice was never as widespread as it became in Europe a few centuries later.

[2] In 634 C.E., the second caliph, Umar, founded the new Islamic city of Al Basra in southeastern Iraq. It was the first Islamic city outside the Arabian Peninsula. In 1453, Constantinople fell to the Ottoman Turks. Soon, however, the Ottoman Empire began a slow but steady decline that culminated in its defeat during World War I and dismemberment by the Allies. But Turkey, the Ottomans' homeland, emerged as the most progressive, religiously tolerant, and economically advanced Islamic nation in the Middle East when Kemal Ataturk came to power, abolished the caliphate and sultanate, and established a modern, secular form of government in 1922.

[3] The other five sacraments are confirmation, penance, anointing the sick, Holy Orders, and marriage.

[4] A blow even more staggering to religious authority than Galileo's was delivered by Charles Darwin (1809-1892) with the publication of his books *On the Origin of Species* (1859) and *The Descent of Man* (1871). His theory of *evolution*, which posits that all living things are the modern descendents, through *natural selection*, of a common, primitive ancestor had such sweeping logical appeal, backed by seemingly unchallengeable scientific observations, that within a generation, huge numbers of people became agnostic or atheist. Of late, however,

Darwin's theories have come under withering attack and not, surprisingly, just from creationists or fundamentalists. Although many aspects of Darwinism are certainly true, it turns out, according to *Darwin on Trial* (1991) by Philip E. Johnson and *The Case For A Creator* (2004)* by Lee Strobel, that the fossil record to date, which Darwin predicted would confirm his hypotheses, has not conclusively demonstrated that simple, primitive creatures slowly evolved, over millions of years, into complex, more advanced creatures. For example, despite what we all read in our school textbooks, suggesting the existence of a series of a dozen or so fossils showing apelike skulls gradually transforming into human skulls, no such set of fossils actually exists. Scientists, rather, found fossil fragments they *believed* came from human ancestors. Many of those fragments are so incomplete that their discoverers simply extrapolated from them and drew pictures of what they imagined the complete skulls must have looked like. For the most part, those drawings, those extrapolations, are what appeared in our school texts. Moreover, what the fossil record does show is that during the *Cambrian Period* (approximately 500 million years ago) a multitude of complex, diverse species of animals suddenly and abruptly arose as if from nowhere. In deeper, older layers of sediment, there are virtually no fossils whatsoever of transitional species from the earlier, simpler life forms to the more complex Cambrian forms. So where are the missing links from the earlier species to the more modern species? Even soft-bodied, primitive creatures should have left some imprint and been found by now. Where is the supposedly irrefutable evidence of evolution? The most famous example of a missing link, incidentally, *Archaeopteryx,* part reptile and part bird, has been discredited. The problem with Archaeopteryx is that it lived millions of years *before* reptile physiology evolved to the point where it became similar to the physiology found in modern-day birds. If Archaeopteryx is the missing link between reptiles and birds, shouldn't it have arrived on the scene just before the onset of modern birds, and not tens of millions of years before reptiles were at all similar to them? – Believe me, I am not arguing for a theory of intelligent design, and certainly not for Biblical creation. There is, after all, no doubt that some form of evolution has taken place on a grand scale. That the bone structure of some types of modern reptiles is remarkably similar to the bone structure of modern birds, and that bird talons are covered with reptilian scales, is apropos. Also, we've witnessed evolution in our own lifetimes. Disease-causing bacteria, for example, have evolved and become resistant to once effective penicillin and other drug treatments over the course of only a few decades. Bio-engineered variation in fruit flies and mice has been repeatedly induced in laboratories. Moreover, an incredible missing link was discovered by scientists in early 2006: a 375-million year old fossil, part-fish and part-amphibian/reptile, with fishy scales and gills but also limbs in the making, the beginnings of digits, the beginnings of wrists, elbows and shoulders, and reptile-like neck bones and ribs. I still think Darwin is overwhelmingly right, but I'm perplexed, despite the recent part-fish, part amphibian/reptile fossil find, that the over-all fossil record, a century and a half after publication of *Origin*, does not give him as much unassailable support as I thought.

*If you're secular-minded, don't immediately be put off by the title *The Case for a Creator*. Although the writer has a definite point of view — that the universe was created by intelligent design and the Christian God was the designer — he raises some thought-provoking arguments. Mr. Strobel effectively attacks some aspects of the theory of evolution and leaves us with the realization that Darwin has not fully, nor at all unassailably, answered the question "Where did man come from?" On the other hand, Mr. Strobel does not propose any answer to the even more perplexing question, "Where did God come from?" and a good number of his arguments, therefore, will persuade only those who are already convinced.

Chapter 15

[1] When Muhammad went to Medina on his first *Hijra*, he was invited to mediate disputes among local tribes there which were predominantly Jewish. He became intimately familiar with their customs and, in an effort to make Islam attractive to them, selected Friday as the day for Islamic prayer, so as not to compete with the Jewish Sabbath, directed his followers to worship facing Jerusalem, and set aside Yom Kippur as a fasting day for Muslims too. When the Jews steadfastly refused to convert and occasionally allied themselves with non-Muslim Meccan chieftains against Mohammad, his attitude toward them, as reflected by increasingly harsh anti-Jewish language in the Koran, became much less friendly. By 624, he ordered Muslims to stop facing Jerusalem during prayer and face Mecca instead. Nonetheless, despite the many angry anti-Jewish Koranic passages, there was no widespread violence or unrelenting hostility toward Jews, except in rare instances, at all comparable to what existed in Middle Ages Christendom or in the Muslim world today.

[2] Annie Besant was born Anglo-Catholic, but became one of the most famous non-believers of her time. Among her best-known books is *The Gospel of Atheism*, published in 1877. Later in life, she grew religious and wrote numerous other works, including *Bhagavad Gita* (1895), The *Ancient Wisdom* (1897), *Reincarnation* (1898), *Death and After* (1901), and *Esoteric Christianity* (1905). She died believing she would soon be reborn.

Chapter 16

[1] East Bengal is now the nation of Bangladesh. Beginning in around 544 B.C.E., the now defunct "Kingdom of Bengal" was one the four major kingdoms of

ancient India. Today, the Kingdom of Bengal's territory is divided among Bangladesh, the Indian state of West Bengal, and three other Indian states, Bihar, Tripura and Orissa.

[2] The symbolism is as follows: The conch is the birth of creation, the lotus petals are the unfolding of creation, the mace and the discus are Vishnu's rewards for defeating Indra, god of storms and battle.

[3] *Tashlich* is the ceremony performed on the second day of Rosh Hashanah after the afternoon service, when Jews leave the synagogue to walk to a nearby stream or river and symbolically rid themselves of sin by throwing bread crumbs into the flowing water. The currents carry away the bread crumbs and therefore the sins.

[4] Vedanta – exploration of ultimate purposes; Yoga – contemplation, meditation, and discipline; Karma Mimasa - investigation of action; Sankhya - opposition between male and female spiritual principles; Vaisheshika – realism; Nyaya – logic with belief in god.

[5] In fact, the dynasty of Babur, who founded the Muslim Mughal Empire, which at its height included nearly all of India plus Afghanistan, ruled the subcontinent and the majority Hindus for 150 years (1556-1707).

[6] That is not to say all Hindus are pacifists in the tradition of Mahatma Gandhi. The rise to power of the fundamentalist Hindu Bharatiya Janata Party (BJP) during the past decade and a half has been accompanied by vicious outbursts of bloodshed. In 1992, for example, when militant Hindus destroyed a 500-year-old mosque in the city of Ayodhya, the ensuing rioting claimed more than 25,000 lives.

Chapter 19

[1] See also Deuteronomy 25:19, 1 Samuel 15:1-9, and 21, and Joshua 19:1-51, and there are many other passages with similar rants.

Chapter 20

[1] In 1890 Latter Day Saint (LDS) Church President Wilford Woodruff issued a Manifesto abolishing plural marriages. Since then, LDS members practicing polygamy have been excommunicated and barred from LDS Temples.

Chapter 23

[1] Babism, the precursor religion to Baha'ism, was founded by Mizra Ali Muhammad (1819-1850), who believed that he and all the other major prophets were divine manifestations of God. He wrote a new holy book, the Bayan,

meaning "Explanation," to supersede the Koran. The Bayan became part of the Baha'i sacred scriptures.

Chapter 24

¹ To finish the story: As the sun rose, Jacob looked up and saw Esau approaching with his 400 men. Expecting the worst, he rushed to meet him, bowing low.

Esau said, "What do you mean, brother, by all this company [the advance entourage and gifts] I have met?"

Jacob replied, "To gain your favor, my lord."

But Esau would have none of it. "I have enough, my brother; let what you have remain yours."

Overwhelmed, Jacob implored, "No, I pray you; if you would do me this favor, accept from me these gifts; for to see your face is like seeing the face of God, and you have received me favorably...."

And, after Jacob beseeched him, Esau accepted. The brothers were at last reconciled.

² To avoid confusion about the terms *Israelite* and *Jew*, it is helpful to review a little history. *Jew a.k.a. Ju*, you will recall, is derived from the word *Judah*, which was the name of the much larger and more powerful of the only two *Israelite* tribes to have avoided conquest by the Assyrians in 722 B.C.E. The second tribe to have avoided that fate, Benjamin, was so small that it was eventually incorporated into *Judah* and ceased to have a separate existence. The other ten tribes were forcibly dispersed throughout the Assyrian Empire, were totally absorbed by the dominant and overpowering Assyrian culture, and became known to history as "the ten lost tribes of Israel." *Judah* itself, whose territory included the city of Jerusalem, was conquered by the Babylonians in 586 B.C.E., but its members never disappeared and never lost their identity as *Jews*. In modern times, the words *Jew a.k.a. Ju* and *Israelite* (as opposed to *Israeli* which means citizen of the country of Israel) are often used interchangeably. The *Jews* are the only *Israelites*, meaning *strugglers with God*, except for the few current-day groups here and there claiming to be descendents of one of the ten lost tribes, to have survived into modern times. And while we're at it, within the tribe of *Judah* there were and, therefore, among modern Jews today are, remnants of the tribe of *Levi*, known as *Levites* (often Jews with last names like Levine or Levy), who are the descendents of Moses, and a sub-group of Levites, known as the *Kohane* (often Jews with last names like Cohen or Kahn), who are the descendents of Aaron. When Joshua led the Israelites into and conquered Canaan, i.e. the Promised Land, the tribe of Levy, unlike all the other tribes, was not given

any territory of its own. Instead, the Levites, who had been commanded by Moses to be holy men, distributed themselves among and lived with the other tribes as priests. Here's how it worked out: Jacob's twelve sons, who became the "original" but not the "final" twelve tribes, were Reuben, Simeon, Judah, Issachar, Zebulon, Benjamin, Dan, Naphthali, Gad, Asher, Levi, and Joseph. When Joseph died, which was at least four centuries before the time of Moses and Joshua, who were contemporaries, each of his two sons, Ephraim and Manasseh, attracted some of Joseph's* followers and themselves became tribal leaders. So when Joshua entered the Promised Land in around 1250 B.C.E., the configuration of sons and grandsons of Jacob, a.k.a. Israel, that had become the "final" twelve tribes of Israel, each of which existed as a distinct entity until the Assyrian conquest in 722 B.C.E., was somewhat different from the "original" list and is as follows: Reuben, Simeon, Judah, Issachar, Zebulon, Benjamin, Dan, Naphthali, Gad, Asher, Ephraim, and Manasseh. Notice that Joseph and Levi, both of whom were sons of Jacob, and became two of the "original" twelve tribes, are not on this "final" list. As above stated, Joseph had been replaced by his sons, Ephraim and Manasseh, while the tribe of Levi had disappeared as an independent tribal entity altogether. Thus, the Levites who attached themselves to the tribe of Judah are the only remnants of the tribe of *Levi* to have made it, along with the other *Jews a.k.a. Ju's*, who are the descendents of Jacob's son, *Judah*, into this century. To an extent they have even managed to preserve their distinct genetic identity by usually marrying only other Levites until modern times. As mentioned, Moses and Aaron were Levites, and today the Kohane, Aaron's descendents, are still accorded special respect. The first *aliyah* (the honor of reciting blessings over the Torah), for example, on Sabbaths, Yom Kippur, Hanukah, Purim, all fast days, and during Monday and Thursday morning services, is always given to a Kohane. If no Kohane is present then at least to a Levite. Incredibly, DNA comparisons of Levite and non-Levite Jews, now possible with modern gene-testing techniques, reveal distinguishing characteristic between the two groups in a statistically significant number of cases. There is, therefore, scientific evidence that the biblical description of the separate Israelite tribes, set down in the scriptures *more than two millennia ago*, is accurate.

* It is a bit inaccurate to describe Joseph as the leader of a tribe. Joseph, according to the Biblical account, was Jacob's eleventh son, but his first by Rachel, whom he loved so deeply, he agreed to toil for her father, Laban, fourteen years in exchange for her hand in marriage. Rachel died in childbirth while delivering Benjamin, the youngest son, about two years after Joseph was born. Of them all, Jacob favored Joseph the most and this, along with Joseph's uncanny ability to correctly foresee future events, made his eleven brothers extremely jealous. In anger one day, the brothers tossed Joseph into a pit and abandoned him there, hoping he would perish. A passing caravan of Bedouins, however, en

route to Egypt, rescued him. Once in Egypt, Joseph worked for a while in the household of a nobleman called Potiphar, but was sentenced to a long term of imprisonment after Potiphar's wife falsely accused him of raping her. In prison, Joseph's abilities to accurately interpret dreams and predict the future became widely known. These talents eventually came to the attention of Pharaoh himself, who asked Joseph to interpret a famous dream in which "seven fat cows" (the seven years of plenty) emerged from the Nile, followed by "seven lean cows" (the seven years of famine). Pharaoh was so impressed by Joseph's insights that he appointed him prime minister. Under Joseph's guidance, Egypt actually prospered during the "seven years of famine," while the surrounding areas starved, because he had instructed the Egyptians to store away huge stockpiles of surplus provisions during the previous "seven years of plenty." The famine was so bad in Canaan that Joseph's eleven brothers traveled to Egypt, hoping to purchase food there for their families and growing clans — which would soon become full-fledged tribes — back home. Since Joseph had been in Egypt for so many years and had been presumed long dead, he, unlike his brothers, never actually became the head of any Israelite clan. When the brothers arrived, they were brought before Joseph, the prime minister, whom they did not recognize. Joseph, however, immediately recognized them and, at a second meeting a few days later, tearfully revealed himself. Just as Joseph's uncle, Esau, had forgiven his brother, Jacob, for stealing his birthright, Joseph forgave all his brothers for having cruelly abandoned him in the desert years earlier. Despite their having deeply wronged him, Joseph's love for his brothers was unbreakable. In Canaan, the famine deepened. Malnutrition, even starvation, became rampant. Finally, after receiving Pharaoh's permission, Joseph rescued his brethren by inviting them to settle in Egypt, where food was plentiful and there were surpluses. The vast majority of the Israelites accepted and became established in the part of the country called Goshen. After Joseph died, as well as the pharaoh who had appointed him prime minister, succeeding pharaohs became frightened of the Israelites' growing numbers and envious of their increasing prosperity. The Israelites were enslaved, along with tens of thousands of other subject people, and remained in bondage until, 430 years after they had first settled in Egypt, Moses led them to freedom during the reign of Rameses II. After Moses died, Joshua led them back into Canaan, the Promised Land.

Chapter 25

[1] After Israel withdrew from Gaza in summer, 2005, receiving nothing in return, and with terrorist bombings and murderous rhetoric ongoing, there was a slight but perceptible lessening in anti-Jewish world opinion, especially in the West. But opinion among huge numbers of Arabs and Muslims, if anything, hardened, as evidenced by the overwhelming victory of Hamas in the first totally free election in the Palestinian territories. After listening for decades to

hysterical anti-Jewish propaganda, and cheering on the bombers, their hatred is such that they simply can't bring themselves to accept an Israel with enough territory to defend itself or, for that matter, any Israel at all.

2 A current example of the liberal left's extreme dislike of Israel was the vote on May 29, 2006 by the leadership of Britain's 69,000-member National Association of Teachers in Further and Higher Education (NATFHE), the largest such organization in the country, to boycott Israeli institutions and academics who do not publicly condemn Israel's policies in the Palestinian territories and, especially, construction of the "separation wall." The vote was 106 in favor, 71 against, and 21 abstentions. This, despite Hamas's and Iran's repeated declarations that Israel is an abomination, has no right to exist, must be destroyed, that the Holocaust never occurred, and that Europeans, especially Germans, should no longer feel remorse about past mistreatment of Jews. There was no recognition that the wall is being constructed to curtail unrelenting terrorist attacks and, in that regard, has largely succeeded. Nor has NATFHE ever voted to condemn any of Hamas's or Iran's policies, which have been increasingly venomous towards Jews, or to boycott Islamic institutions and academics who do not publicly denounce, for examples, the efforts of Afghan prosecutors to obtain a death sentence for a man who converted to Christianity in Feruary, 2006, rioting and death threats when a Danish newspaper printed cartoons of Muhammad in October, 2005, or the murder by an Islamist of a Dutch filmmaker in November, 2004 who made a documentary critical of Muslim culture.

3 On October 16, 2003 then Malaysian Prime Minister Mahathir Mohamad delivered the keynote address at the Tenth Islamic Summit Conference in Putrajaya, Malaysia. His speech was replete with passages expressing his belief that Muslims are being humiliated, oppressed, and impoverished everywhere. To him Islam's enemies are Europeans and, to a much greater extent, Jews. He said, "They [Muslim People] believe that things can only get worse. They will forever be oppressed by the Europeans and the Jews. ... It cannot be that there is no other way. 1.3 billion Muslims cannot be defeated by a few million Jews. There must be a way. ... We are actually very strong. 1.3 billion people cannot simply be wiped out. The Europeans killed 6 million Jews out of 12 million. But today the Jews rule this world by proxy. They get others to fight and die for them. ...They survived 2000 years of pogroms not by hitting back, but by thinking. They invented and successfully promoted Socialism, Communism, human rights and democracy so that persecuting them would appear to be wrong, so they may enjoy equal rights with others. With these they have now gained control of the most powerful countries, and they, this tiny community, have become a world power. ... Of late, because of their power and their apparent success, they have become arrogant. And arrogant people,

like angry people will make mistakes, will forget to think. They are already beginning to make mistakes. And they will make more mistakes. There may be windows of opportunity for us now and in the future. We must seize these opportunities."

[4] Idumaeans – In ancient Greece and Rome some of those who practiced Judaism were not ethnically Hebrews at all but Idumaeans a.k.a. Edomites. In Biblical times, Edom was a country south of the Dead Sea in what is now present-day southern Israel and Jordan. According to Genesis, the Edomites, an Arabic people, were the descendents of Isaac's son, Esau, while the Israelites were the descendents of Esau's younger twin brother, Jacob. Beginning during the reign of King David, the Edomites frequently came under the control of Israel and later, when Israel split into the Northern and Southern Kingdoms, under the control of Judah as well. According to Kings I, David exiled Edomite Prince Hadad who, some ten years later, returned and led a failed revolt against Solomon. The ancient Edomites are the only people that the Jews ever attempted to forcibly convert. To an extent, they were successful and Herod the Great, King of Judea from 39 B.C.E. to 4 B.C.E., was the son of Edomites on both sides whose ancestors were among the forced converts. Known as Idumaea in the New Testament, the country of Edom is mentioned in both Egyptian and Assyrian records.

[5] Conversos – The Spanish Inquisition was established by Queen Isabella in 1478 to ensure the sincerity of former Jews and Muslims who had recently converted to Christianity. Known as *Conversos* and *Moriscos* respectively, those judged to be heretics, i.e., backsliders toward Judaism or Islam, were executed. In 1492, all unconverted Jews were exiled from Spain. In 1496, they were exiled from Portugal. Between 1609 and 1614, more than a quarter of a million Muslims were also exiled. A few decades later, the Inquisition sought to punish and exile all persons suspected of practicing Protestantism as well.

[6] Marranos – a contemptuous term meaning *swine*, were the Jews of Spain and Portugal who had insincerely converted to Christianity to escape the Inquisition, but continued to practice Judaism in secret. Anyone the Inquisition determined to be a *Marrano* was burned at the stake. In fact, it was more prudent to remain an openly practicing Jew than to become a *Marrano* and get caught. An openly practicing Jew might lose his job, property, social standing, and ultimately be exiled, but would not be put to death. Nonetheless, tens of thousands of *Marranos* remained in Spain and Portugal, undetected, for centuries. The Spanish edict expelling the Jews in 1492, and the Portuguese edict expelling them in 1496, were not lifted until around 1834.

[7] Irving has been in the news recently again, and on February 20, 2006 he plead guilty in an Austrian court to denying the Holocaust, a crime in that country, during lectures in 1989, but claims his views have changed since then.

[8] In an article written by author and University of Florida mathematics professor, William Martin, entitled, *Who is Pushing Whom into the Sea?* that was published in the magazine, *Counterpunch,* on March 11, 2005, he quotes the following from a speech delivered on October 11, 1961 by the first prime minister of Israel, David Ben Gurion: "The Arab's exit from Palestine…began immediately after the UN resolution, from areas earmarked for the Jewish state. And we have explicit documents testifying that they left Palestine following instructions by the Arab leaders with the *Mufti* at their head, under the assumption that the invasion of the Arab armies at the expiration of the Mandate will destroy the Jewish state and *push all the Jews into the sea, dead or alive.*" Martin claims, however, that no researcher has been able to attribute that phrase 'push all the Jews into the sea…' to any Arab source pre-dating Ben Gurion. Nor, he asserts, has anyone found the 'documents' Ben Gurion implied contained the phrase. Martin believes that Ben Gurion was merely expressing his personal surmise as to the Arab armies' intentions. He goes on to discuss detailed evidence indicating that, after Israel declared itself an independent state on May 14, 1948, it was not just the invading Arab armies that caused the mass exodus of Palestinians from their villages, but the calculated and, at times, devious policies of the Jewish authorities beginning well prior to May 14, 1948 too.

Nonetheless, it appears that at least after Ben Gurion made his 1961 speech, several Arab personages have sworn that they will "drive the Jews into the sea." Also, that was clearly the invading Arab armies' intention in 1948 even if they did not actually use the phrase. More recently, in a letter published in the Egyptian newspaper, *Hadith Al-Madina,* on April 23, 2002, and in an interview the next day on a Saudi-Egyptian TV channel, *Iqrara,* the chairman of the Arab Psychiatrists Association and head of the Department of Psychiatry at Ein Shams University in Cairo, Dr. Adel Sadeq, said: "To use words that some people no longer like to use today 'We will throw Israel into the sea.' This phrase…is the truth. Either they will throw us into the sea, or we will throw them into the sea. There is no middle ground. Coexistence is total nonsense." Elsewhere in his letter and interview, although some of his statements are hateful rants, he gives an insightful explanation of the psychology of suicide bombers: "The psychological structure [of the perpetrator of a suicide attack] is that of an individual who loves life. This may seem strange to people who see the human soul as most sublime. They are incapable of understanding [the suicide attack] because their cultural structure has no concepts such as self-sacrifice and honor. These concepts do not exist in a number of cultures, and therefore they offer stupid interpretations, attesting to ignorance. But we know this well, because our culture is one of sacrifice, loyalty, and honor. Bush was mistaken when he said that the girl was killing the future when she chose to kill herself. On the contrary: She died so that others would live." In another paragraph, also insightful, he says: "When a martyr dies a martyr's death, he attains the height of bliss. As a professional psychiatrist, I say that the height of bliss comes with the end of the countdown: ten, nine, eight, seven, six, five, four, three, two, one. And then, you press the button to blow yourself up. When the martyr reaches 'one,' and then 'boom,' he explodes, he senses himself flying, because he knows for certain that he is not dead. It is a transition to another, more beautiful world, because he knows very well that within seconds he will see the light of the Creator. He will be at the closest possible point to Allah. None in the [Western] world sacrifices his life for his homeland. If his homeland is drowning, he is the first to jump ship. In our culture it is different."

Despite his condescending and often hateful tone, Dr. Adel Sadeq's comments are worth reading in their entirety and can be found on-line.

[9] Olive Schreiner was born into a strict Methodist family in South Africa, but became separated from her parents at age 12 due, in part, to her precocious defiance of their deep religious convictions. She found work as a housekeeper for her older siblings, later as a governess on an East Cape farm, and began writing drafts of her most famous books as a teenager. She traveled to Britain at age 26 with the intention of becoming a doctor but abandoned that goal shortly after starting medical school. She published her first novel, *The Story of an African Farm* (1881), when she was 28 and quickly became a star among social activists, free-thinkers, feminists, and intellectuals. Among her many works are *Dreams* (1890), *Dream Life and Real Life* (1893), *The Political Situation in Cape Colony* (1895), *An English South African Woman' View of the Situation* (1899), *A Letter on the Jew* (1906), *Woman and Labour* (1911), and, published post-mortem, *Dreams and Allegories* (1923) and *From Man to Man* (1926).

Chapter 26

[1] The quote from Marx, "Religion…is the opiate of the people" often incorrectly written as 'God is a drug for the masses' is incomplete and does accurately convey the true meaning of what he said. The full quote, from his *Critique of Hegel's Philosophy of Right*, is as follows: *"Religious distress is at the same time the expression of real distress and the protest against real distress. Religion is the sigh of the oppressed creature, the heart of a heartless world, just as it is the spirit of a spiritless situation. It is the opium of the people. The abolition of religion as the illusory happiness of the people is required for their real happiness. The demand to give up the illusion about its condition is the demand to give up a condition which needs illusions."*

Chapter 28

[1] Herzl wrote this statement in his personal diary on June 12, 1895. In its entirety it reads: "We must expropriate gently the private property on the state assigned to us. We shall try to spirit the penniless population across the border by procuring employment for it in the transit countries, while denying it employment in our country. The property owners will come over to our side. Both the process of expropriation and the removal of the poor must be carried out discretely and circumspectly. Let the owners of the immoveable property believe that they are cheating us, selling us things for more than they are worth. But we are not going to sell them anything back."

[2] This statement of Ben Gurion is from a July 12, 1937 entry in his diary.

[3] According to author Avi Shalom in his book, *The Iron Wall*, W.W. Norton & Company, New York 1999, pg. 23.

[4] What has come to be known as *The Deir Yassin Massacre*, in which Israeli irregular forces killed as many as 200 Arab men, women and children in a single small village between April 9 and April 11, 1948, occurred more than a month *before* surrounding Arab countries attacked the day after Israel declared independence on May 14, 1948. It is an event that Jews resist learning about because it challenges our conviction that *we* were the victims of fanatical Arab aggression, and not the reverse. What happened, based on eyewitness accounts, albeit often conflicting, is as follows: After Britain decided to end its Mandate in Palestine, and the United Nations recommended partitioning Palestine into separate Jewish and Arab states, violence erupted. The Arab Liberation Army, consisting of volunteers from numerous Arab countries, along with indigenous Palestinian Arabs, began attacking Jewish traffic on major roadways and Jewish communities. They succeded in cutting off the road between Tel Aviv and Jeruslaem and Jerusalem came under siege at the same time. The Haganah* launched a counterattack and its strike force, the Palmach,** captured al-Qastel, a town 2 kilometers west of Deir Yassin, which was a small but important village. Its total population was about 750 and it had previously signed a non-aggression pact with Israel. Then, on April 9, 1948, irregular Jewish militias, mostly Irgun*** and Lehi,**** entered and occupied Deir Yassin. In the process, scores of villagers died and many researchers have concluded, including Israei researchers, that the relatively large number of dead in a single village, the relatively small number of dead Israeli attackers (only 4 to 5), and the relatively low number villagers wounded in relation to deaths point to a "massacre" involving the large-scale killing of captive non-resisting individuals.

There are, however, many differing accounts. Eyewitness, Meir Pa'il, said "Villager fire inflicted heavy casualties and drove off the Irgun." Ezra Yachin recalled, "To take a house, you had either to throw a grenade or shoot your way into it. If you were foolish enough to open doors, you got shot down — sometimes by men dressed up as women, shooting out at you in a second of surprise." Yehoshua Gorodenchik remembered "In certain cases Arabs pretending to surrender revealed hidden weapons and shot at their would-be Jewish captors." Some have argued that foreign Arab fighters in the village triggered the massacre but Deir Yassin had repeatedly turned away such fighters in the past. Non-eyewitness Menachem Begin said "Iraqi soldiers were present" but no independent source has conclusively conclusively confirmed this. Begin also said "Both sides suffered heavy casualties. We had four killed and nearly forty wounded. The number of [our] casualties was nearly forty percent of the total number of the attackers."

Nevertheless, all resistance had ceased within two hours after the Irgun and Lehi entered Deir Yassin. Irgun's commander Ben-Zion Cohen said: "[We] felt a desire for revenge." Some villagers reported: that 'upon discovering an armed man disguised as a woman, one guerrilla began shooting everyone around, followed by his comrades joining in.' Dr. Alfred Engel said: "In the houses there were dead, in all about a hundred men, women and children. It was terrible. … It was clear that they (the attackers) had gone from house to house and shot the people at close range. I was a doctor in the German army for 5 years, in World War I, but I had not seen such a horrifying spectacle." Mohammad Jaber, a village boy, observed the guerillas "break in, drive everybody outside, put them against the wall and shoot them." Fahimi Zeidan stated that she encountered two captured village men and "When they [the two men] reached us, the soldiers [guarding us] shot them." When the mother of one of the killed started hitting the fighters, "one of them stabbed her with a knife a few times."

On the other hand, village resident, Ayish Zeidan, said: "The Arab radio talked of women being killed and raped, but this is not true… I believe that most of those who were killed were among the fighters and the women and children who helped the fighters. The Arab leaders committed a big mistake. By exaggerating the atrocities they thought they would encourage people to fight back harder. Instead they created panic and people ran away." And villager, Abu Mahmud, stated: "… the villagers protested against the atrocity claims: We said, "There was no rape." [Khalidi] said, "We have to say this, so the Arab armies will come to liberate Palestine from the Jews."

In any event, there is no question that the excessive number of dead villagers at Deir Yassin triggered such an intense outburst of Arab anger, that the *Deir Yassin Massacre* is always brought up whenever their own atrocities are pointed to. Many argue that the *Deir Yassin Massacre* is the incident that began the cycle of killings and revenge killings that continues to this day. That, however, is not true. As horrendous as *Deir Yassin* was, there had been several assaults on Jews (and counter-assaults by the Haganah) prior to then. On December 2, 1947, for example, shortly after announcement of the UN Partition Plan, Arabs in Jerusalem rioted and killed 62 Jews.***** Then, on December 14, 1947, fighters from the Arab Legion massacred 14 Jews near the village of Beit Nabala. Also, two days after *Deir Yassin*, on April 13, 1948, an unarmed convoy of Jewish doctors, nurses, and medical students was set upon and, despite the waving of white flags and surrendering, 77 were slaughtered.

* Haganah - meaning "Defense" in Hebrew, was the underground military organization of the Jews in Eretz Ysrael (Land of Israel) from 1920 -1948.

** Palmach - Hebrew abbreviation for "Strike Companies," was established by the British Military and Haganah on May 15, 1941 to help the British protect Palestine from the Nazis. It became the strongest Jewish fighting force in Palestine prior to Israeli independence.

*** Irgun - Hebrew shorthand for "National Military Organization," was an offshoot of the Haganah that protested against its policies of restraint and socialist leanings. It became a Zionist militia that operated in Palestine from 1931 to 1948. Former Israeli Prime Minister Menachem Begin was selected Irgun leader in February, 1944 and its ideology was a predecessor movement to modern Israel's right-wing Likud party.

**** Lehi - Hebrew acronym for "Fighters for the Freedom of Israel", the group was an armed underground faction that had as its goals the eviction of the British from Palestine, unrestricted immigration of Jews, and the formation of a Jewish State. Known also as "the Stern Gang" after its founder, Avraham Stern, it was active from around 1923 until 1948.

***** The Arab rioters were confronted by British soldiers and, during the ensuing violence, 32 Arabs were killed too.

5 The PLO (Palestine Liberation Organization) was founded by the Arab League in 1964 with its stated purpose being the destruction of Israel and its replacement by an independent Palestinian state between the Jordan River and the Mediterranean Sea. Prior to the establishment of modern Israel, which happened shortly after the end of World War II and defeat of the Axis powers (which included Turkey, formerly known as the Ottoman Empire), Palestine was a British Mandate. Prior to the end of World War I, it had been a territory of the Ottoman Empire starting in 1517 C.E., when the Ottoman Turks took control by defeating the Mamelukes. The Mamelukes were an Arab military caste, with a colorful history, composed mostly of former slave-soldiers who had converted to Islam and served the caliphs. Over time they grew powerful

and sometimes seized control of governments for themselves, including Egypt (1250 C.E.–1517 C.E.), the territory of which included Palestine. Before the Mamelukes, Palestine was controlled by other Arab and non-Arab Muslim dynasties including the Abbasids, Fatimids, and the Seljuk Turks (750 C.E. – 1250 C.E.), the Crusaders for a time (1109 C.E. – 1189 C.E) and by Muhammad and his immediate followers (614 C.E – 750 C.E.). Before that it was ruled for nearly a millennium, successively going backwards in time, by Byzantium, Rome, Greece, Persia and Babylonia (586 B.C.E – 614 C.E), except for the interim when it was ruled by the Hasmonean Jewish Kingdom (175 B.C.E – 60 C.E). Earlier still, the northern part of Palestine - ancient divided Israel - was ruled by Assyria (722 B.C.E. – 586 B.C.E.) and by Hebrew dynasties (922 B.C.E – 722 B.C.E), and the southern part - Judah - by other Hebrew dynasties (922 B.C.E. – 586 B.C.E). But from 1000 B.C.E until 922 B.C.E. the ancient Hebrews ruled nearly all of Palestine, including parts of Jordan, Lebanon and Syria, under the United Kingdom of David and Solomon. Even earlier, most of it was ruled by Israeli king Saul, and still earlier, by the Hebrew Judges, although Philistines, from which is derived *Palestine*, controlled large parts too.

[6] What Arafat couldn't swallow was Ehud Barak's insistence on abandonment of the "right of return" for Palestinian refugees who fled their homes from many parts of what is now Israel during the 1948 War. Even that, however, could have been negotiated if Arafat had demonstrated willingness to compromise. Proposals had been made by President Clinton, for example, that significant but limited numbers of refugees be permitted to re-settle in Israel on an annual basis for a fixed number of years and that reparations be paid to others.

[7] Another analogy: Imagine two discs, one on top of the other, stacked like two records of exactly the same size – the size of one year – on a phonograph. The bottom disc is divided by radial lines into twelve approximately equal spaces corresponding to the twelve secular months – October through September (which is the same period of time but in a different order as January through December). The top disc is also divided into twelve equal spaces but corresponding to the twelve Hebrew months – Tishre through Elul. The space for Tishre, in our analogy, is positioned on top of and occupies about the same amount of space as October (the month corresponding to Tishre); the space for Heshvan, the next Jewish month, is on top of and occupies about the same amount of space as November (the month corresponding to Heshvan); and so on. But now the discs begin to rotate. Interestingly, the Hebrew disc seems to rotate more slowly than the Gregorian one. Soon the space for the month of Tishre is no longer entirely on top of the space for October, but falls behind and part of Tishre starts to cover part of September, *which is the month immediately preceding October.* That is, Tishre, which covered only October when we began,

starts to overlie part of September. As more time passes, more of Tishre covers more and more of September and less and less of October. Likewise, more of the next Hebrew month, Heshvan, covers less and less of November, which it completely covered when we began, and more and more of October, which is the month immediately preceding November. And the same down the line. So as time passes the holiday of Sukkot, for example, which always happens on the fifteenth of Tishre on the Hebrew calendar, no matter what the year, no longer happens on the same date it did in October on the Gregorian calendar, as when we started, but happens earlier and earlier in October, and eventually in September. And, as even more time goes by, it happens earlier and earlier in September as the Hebrew disc falls further and further behind the Gregorian one, and the two discs get more and more out of whack.

[8] The first day of Chanukah, Hebrew date Kislev 24, 5766 – an Adar II year – corresponded exactly with secular date December 25, 2005, the first day of Christmas. That happens only a few times each century. As the next few years pass, however, Kislev 24 will occur earlier and earlier in December, or in late November, and no longer coincide with the first day of Christmas. But when future Adar II years are added Kislev 24 will again occur around December 25, and the cycle of Kislev 24 occurring earlier and earlier in December, and then leaping to catch-up with December 25, will be repeated. Occasionally, it will occur exactly on December 25 but the next time that will happen, causing the first day of Chanukah to precisely coincide with the first day of Christmas, won't be until Kislev 24, 5785 (December 25, 2024), again on Kislev 24, 5796 (December 24, 2035), and for the last time in this century.

Chapter 29

[1] In February, 2006 a 41 year old Afghan man was arrested for converting to Christianity and faced a possible death sentence nder Afghanistan's Sharia law for "rejecting Islam." Under intense U.S. pressure, an Afghan court rejected the case and instructed Afghan prosecutors to review the defendant's "mental condition." Although the man has been released from prison and is now seeking asylum in another country, the case is not over. Many local clerics and large numbers of demonstrators insist he be executed."

Index

A

Aaron 193, 291, 321, 324, 336, 337
Abraham xv, xvi, 9, 10, 52, 57, 75, 76,
    101, 104, 136, 144, 152, 156,
    157, 169, 204, 206, 207, 208,
    252, 256, 257, 272, 288, 291,
    303, 304, 319, 322, 324, 326
Abravenel, Don Isaac 135
Adam 291, 310
Adar I 310
Adar II 309, 310, 347
Aesop 137
Affan, Uthman Ibn 157, 158
Afghanistan 125, 158, 169, 316, 335, 347
Ahab, King 89, 92, 97
Ahaseurus, King 294
Ahaz, King 91, 92, 96
Akedah 288
Akiva, Rabbi 79, 301, 302
Alaric 112, 114, 116
Alexander the Great 78, 256, 292
Ali, Caliph 122, 157, 158, 332
Allah 154, 157, 169, 198, 203, 275, 299, 342
Al Khet 282, 288
Al Qaeda 315, 316
Amalekites 195, 291
Ambrose 112
Amoraim 70
Amos 86, 90, 96, 97, 99, 204, 330
Ananias 104, 105, 108
Antiochus Epiphanies 55, 72, 78, 256, 262, 292
Antipas, Herod 79, 95, 106, 340
Aquinas, Thomas 130, 146
Arabs xv, 91, 92, 115, 121, 122, 156,
    157, 158, 202, 270, 271, 297,
    298, 325, 338, 343, 344, 345
Arafat, Yasser 65, 201, 255, 270, 346

Aristotle 138, 140
Artaxertes 78
Asher 2, 337
Asimov, Isaac 90
Assad, Hafez 65
Assyria 77, 88, 89, 90, 91, 92, 93, 97,
    98, 173, 264, 304, 330, 331, 346
Assyrian Empire 93, 97, 173, 336
Athaliah, Queen 92
Augustine 103, 110, 111, 112, 113,
    114, 259, 263, 264, 266, 267, 321
Augustulus 115, 118
Augustus, Emperor 79, 105

B

Baal 94, 97
Bab, The 245, 246
Babylonia 72, 78, 87, 93, 98, 110, 289, 330, 331, 346
Baha'i xiv, 213, 242, 243, 244, 245,
    246, 247, 321, 336
Baha'ism 243, 244, 245, 246, 335
Baha'u'llah 242, 243, 244, 245, 246, 321
Bakr, Abu 122, 157, 158
Baptists 146, 147
Barak, Ehud 201, 270, 346
Bar Kochba xiv, 79, 110, 119, 131, 258, 302
Bar Kochba Rebellion xiv
Bathsheba 67, 68, 86, 97, 305
Benedict XVI, Pope 107, 145
Benjamin 2, 77, 151, 264, 321, 336, 337
Ben Gurion, David 298, 341
Besant, Annie 159, 334
Bhagavad-Gita 165
Big Bang 309, 310, 317
Bill of Rights 136, 151, 152, 260

349

Bin Laden, Osama 316
Blacks 209, 268, 269
Blood Libel 254, 267
Boaz 304, 305
Book of Life 286, 287, 289
Buddha 112, 165, 167, 243, 316
Buddhism 166, 167, 169, 316
Bukharin yarmulke 41, 45, 196, 246
Byzantine Empire 114, 115, 116, 126, 157
Byzantium 114, 115, 116, 119, 122, 123, 126, 346

C

Cajuns 160
Camp David Accords 65
Canaanites 10, 76, 159, 194, 195, 291, 330
Castes 165, 167
Catholic Church 35, 100, 107, 115, 116, 118, 119, 122, 140, 142, 143, 144, 145, 146, 282, 315, 321
Cave of Machpelah 60
Chanukah xiv, 31, 55, 177, 291, 292, 294, 307, 347
Chosen People 94, 103, 104, 120, 256, 257, 261, 262, 264, 271, 303
Christendom 26, 35, 111, 114, 116, 119, 120, 121, 122, 125, 126, 128, 129, 131, 157, 221, 222, 254, 258, 262, 266, 270, 271, 272, 331, 334
Christianity xi, xv, 26, 99, 100, 101, 102, 103, 104, 107, 108, 110, 111, 112, 114, 117, 121, 122, 131, 137, 141, 148, 149, 151, 152, 156, 159, 163, 165, 166, 169, 170, 173, 208, 210, 213, 222, 245, 259, 260, 261, 263, 264, 271, 303, 304, 314, 315, 316, 321, 324, 331, 334, 339, 340, 347
Christians xv, 26, 27, 32, 35, 100, 102, 103, 104, 105, 107, 108, 110, 111, 112, 117, 119, 121, 122, 126, 127, 128, 129, 131, 132, 133, 140, 141, 143, 144, 145, 152, 153, 154, 156, 157, 159, 161, 167, 169, 173, 174, 191, 192, 193, 199, 211, 213, 246, 259, 260, 261, 262, 263, 264, 266, 271, 303, 304, 305, 315, 321, 332
Claudius, Emperor 105, 257, 264
Clement VI, Pope 131
Clinton, Bill 201, 346
Columbus 135, 138, 210
Constantine 110, 111, 113, 114, 115, 117, 119, 122, 259, 260, 261, 264, 266, 322, 332
Constantinople 115, 116, 122, 123, 124, 127, 145, 332
Conversos 210, 340
Copernicus 139, 149
Crusades 121, 125, 126, 127, 129, 130
Cyrus the Great 95, 173

D

Dan 2, 87, 337
Daniel 85, 86, 154, 326
Dante 136, 137
Darius, King 78
Dark Ages 122, 131, 152, 265
Darwin, Charles 332
David 7, 9, 10, 67, 68, 77, 81, 84, 86, 87, 96, 97, 138, 139, 215, 261, 303, 305, 311, 329, 340, 346
Days of Awe 55, 56, 286, 287, 289
Da Vinci, Leonardo 139
Deborah 77, 85, 268
Declaration of the Rights of Man 152
Deir Yassin 343, 344, 345
Descartes, Rene 151
Deuteronomy 56, 77, 78, 93, 194, 195, 291, 335
De Leon, Moses 134, 301
Diaspora xv, 79, 110, 119, 131, 132,

210, 258
Disputations 130
Divine Rights of Kings 152
Dominicans 146
Dutch 1, 50, 132, 135, 137, 175, 209, 211, 238, 279, 339

E

Earth Day 293
Edom 92, 98, 330, 340
Edomites 91, 92, 291, 340
Edward I, King 133
Egypt 18, 58, 65, 69, 76, 77, 92, 93, 94, 95, 108, 115, 125, 127, 128, 129, 207, 211, 262, 267, 290, 329, 330, 338, 346
Einstein, Albert 150
El 52, 53, 54, 55, 56, 57, 59, 60, 61, 62, 63, 94, 207, 329
Eleazar Ben Yair 79
Elijah 73, 86, 89, 96, 97, 172, 325
Elisha 86, 89, 90, 96, 97
Elohim 94, 277
England 126, 130, 133, 143, 147, 148, 150, 163, 209, 211, 254, 297, 305, 321
Enlightenment, The 149, 151
Ephraim 2, 187, 337
Episcopal Church 148
Esau 98, 250, 251, 291, 336, 338, 340
Esther xiv, 72, 294, 295
Etrog 290
Evangelicalism 148
Exodus 9, 10, 193, 207, 256, 291, 295, 296, 303, 315, 328
Expulsion Edicts 134, 305
Ezekiel 86, 96, 98
Ezra 78, 343

F

Fatima 158
Ferdinand, King 135
First Temple 77, 78, 87
Fourth Lateran Council 130

France 57, 117, 118, 123, 126, 128, 130, 134, 138, 142, 209, 255, 297
Franciscans 146
Franklin, Benjamin 151
Franks 117, 118, 123, 124, 125, 127, 152

G

Gad 2, 337
Galileo 113, 114, 119, 149, 150, 315, 332
Gandhi, Indira 168
Gandhi, Mahatma 170, 335
Ganesha 164, 169
Ganga 164, 169
Garden of Eden 291
Gaza 330, 338
Genesis xi, xvi, 76, 139, 206, 207, 221, 250, 252, 288, 291, 310, 340
Geonim 69, 70
George III, King 152
German 132, 134, 137, 140, 142, 145, 150, 344
Germany 117, 118, 123, 126, 144, 209, 255, 267, 297
Ghetto 152, 265, 266
Gideon 77, 85
Gnosticism 109
God xiv, xvi, 1, 4, 10, 15, 18, 25, 26, 32, 46, 54, 56, 57, 72, 73, 75, 76, 77, 78, 84, 85, 86, 87, 89, 92, 93, 94, 95, 97, 98, 101, 102, 103, 104, 105, 106, 108, 109, 110, 111, 112, 113, 120, 140, 141, 146, 147, 148, 150, 152, 156, 157, 158, 159, 163, 165, 168, 169, 173, 187, 188, 191, 192, 193, 194, 195, 198, 204, 206, 207, 208, 211, 216, 221, 222, 223, 242, 244, 245, 247, 248, 249, 250, 252, 253, 254, 255, 256, 257, 259, 260, 261, 262, 263, 264, 266, 268, 271, 272,

275, 276, 277, 280, 286, 287,
288, 289, 290, 291, 292, 293,
294, 296, 302, 303, 304, 310,
312, 314, 316, 317, 319, 321,
322, 324, 325, 327, 328, 331,
334, 335, 336, 342
Goliath 62, 215, 305, 329
Gospels 107, 108, 109, 156, 259
Greece 78, 79, 115, 116, 137, 256,
257, 262, 292, 322, 340, 346
Greeks xiv, 72, 78, 108, 109, 137, 138,
173, 255, 256, 257, 258, 263,
270, 272
Greek Orthodox Church 115, 116,
122, 145
Gregorian calendar 307, 309, 347
Gutenberg, Johannes 149

H

Habakkuk 86, 96, 98
Hadrian, Emperor 79, 131, 132, 258
Haganah 343, 345
Haggai 78, 86, 94, 96, 98, 331
Haifa 242, 244, 246
Hajj 157
Haman xiv, 72, 140, 292, 294, 295
Hamas 270, 338, 339
Haran 76, 251
Harvey, William 149
Hasmonean Kingdom 79, 110, 256,
292
Hebrews xiv, xv, 76, 91, 94, 95, 97,
108, 156, 249, 263, 264, 290,
303, 304, 330, 340, 346
Hebrew calendar 18, 21, 286, 295,
297, 306, 307, 308, 309, 347
Hecataeus of Abdera 256
Herodias 106
Herod the Great 79, 95, 106, 340
Herzl, Theodore 298
Heshvan xiv, 291, 293, 346, 347
Hezekiah 92, 93, 96, 97
Hijra 157, 334
Hillel 84, 261

Himalaya 164
Hindus xv, 156, 160, 161, 162, 163,
164, 167, 168, 169, 172, 174,
335
Hippocrates 138
Hitler, Adolph 267
Hobbes, Thomas 151
Holland 118, 135, 139, 297
Holocaust 100, 142, 145, 267, 268,
270, 275, 296, 339, 341
Holy Roman Empire 114, 117, 118,
119, 121, 122, 126, 134, 138,
152, 260
Hosea 86, 90, 96, 97
Hoshea 91
Hyrcanus II 79, 257, 292

I

Independence War 296
India xv, 119, 132, 133, 135, 155, 160,
161, 163, 164, 165, 166, 167,
168, 169, 172, 173, 174, 209,
213, 335
Inquisition 100, 102, 113, 129, 130,
135, 139, 146, 208, 209, 264,
265, 270, 288, 315, 340
Intifada 297
Iran 123, 125, 127, 169, 173, 244, 246,
255, 339
Iraq 123, 124, 125, 129, 155, 158, 330,
332
Irving, David 268, 270
Isaac 10, 52, 57, 75, 90, 135, 150, 157,
206, 207, 250, 251, 256, 288,
291, 321, 340
Isabella 135, 340
Isaiah 75, 86, 92, 96, 97, 98, 212
Ishmael 156, 157
Islam xi, xv, 99, 100, 114, 115, 119,
120, 121, 154, 155, 156, 157,
158, 159, 161, 163, 166, 168,
169, 170, 191, 192, 195, 200,
202, 205, 243, 245, 249, 271,
303, 304, 314, 315, 316, 321,

325, 326, 334, 339, 340, 345, 347
Israel xvi, 1, 2, 8, 13, 41, 51, 57, 59, 65, 66, 71, 75, 76, 77, 80, 84, 85, 86, 87, 88, 89, 90, 91, 92, 93, 96, 97, 98, 110, 115, 120, 126, 144, 145, 146, 152, 155, 169, 173, 174, 192, 193, 194, 198, 201, 202, 207, 242, 244, 246, 252, 254, 255, 258, 263, 264, 270, 274, 277, 290, 291, 293, 294, 296, 297, 298, 302, 303, 304, 305, 321, 322, 323, 327, 329, 330, 331, 332, 336, 337, 338, 339, 340, 341, 343, 345, 346
Israelites xvi, 2, 76, 77, 85, 90, 91, 95, 194, 211, 301, 304, 317, 336, 338, 340
Iyar 156, 296, 301, 302

J

Jacob xvi, 2, 10, 58, 67, 75, 76, 84, 98, 104, 157, 206, 207, 250, 251, 252, 256, 277, 291, 336, 337, 338, 340
Jainism 167, 169
Jains 167, 168, 169, 174
James, Jesus's brother 259, 263
James II, King 150
James the Apostle 105
Jefferson, Thomas 151
Jehovah's Witnesses xiv, 213, 215, 217, 220, 221, 222, 223, 224, 331
Jehu, King 90, 92
Jeremiah 73, 86, 93, 96, 98
Jeroboam, King 71, 77, 87, 88, 90, 91, 96, 329
Jerrahi 185, 191, 195, 199, 200, 202, 203, 204, 205
Jerusalem 72, 77, 78, 79, 86, 87, 92, 93, 94, 96, 98, 105, 106, 107, 108, 121, 122, 123, 124, 125, 126, 127, 128, 129, 145, 157, 173, 201, 202, 254, 256, 258, 292, 293, 298, 301, 302, 323, 325, 334, 336, 343, 345
Jesuits 146
Jesus xiv, 26, 32, 35, 100, 101, 102, 103, 104, 105, 106, 107, 108, 109, 110, 111, 112, 119, 121, 122, 133, 139, 140, 141, 142, 145, 146, 147, 148, 152, 156, 165, 169, 173, 221, 222, 245, 254, 258, 259, 260, 261, 262, 263, 264, 266, 270, 271, 275, 292, 303, 304, 305, 314
Jews xiii, xiv, xv, xvi, 9, 10, 18, 25, 26, 27, 28, 32, 35, 42, 44, 46, 72, 78, 79, 80, 84, 85, 87, 93, 98, 99, 100, 101, 102, 103, 104, 105, 106, 108, 109, 110, 111, 112, 119, 120, 121, 123, 125, 128, 129, 130, 131, 132, 133, 134, 135, 136, 138, 139, 140, 141, 142, 143, 144, 145, 148, 152, 153, 156, 157, 159, 161, 164, 167, 168, 169, 172, 173, 174, 182, 184, 188, 191, 192, 193, 195, 199, 201, 202, 205, 208, 209, 210, 211, 212, 213, 223, 246, 247, 249, 254, 255, 256, 257, 258, 259, 260, 261, 262, 263, 264, 265, 266, 267, 268, 269, 270, 271, 272, 273, 274, 277, 287, 288, 289, 290, 292, 293, 294, 295, 296, 297, 298, 301, 302, 303, 304, 305, 306, 312, 314, 315, 317, 321, 322, 324, 325, 326, 331, 332, 334, 335, 336, 337, 339, 340, 341, 343, 344, 345
Jezebel 88, 89, 97
Joab 68
Joel 52, 86, 96, 97, 148
Johnson, Paul xi, 105, 106
John Paul II 35, 145
John the Baptist 104, 106
John XXIII, Pope 35, 68, 69, 100
Jonah 85, 289

Joseph xi, 58, 60, 68, 69, 105, 108, 145, 148, 213, 291, 302, 322, 327, 328, 337, 338
Josephus 104, 105, 325
Joseph of Bethlehem 105
Joses 105
Joshua 2, 10, 76, 77, 91, 131, 159, 254, 291, 330, 335, 336, 337, 338
Josiah, King 82
Judah 2, 67, 71, 72, 77, 78, 84, 86, 87, 88, 89, 90, 91, 92, 93, 96, 97, 98, 173, 263, 264, 291, 304, 324, 329, 330, 331, 336, 337, 340, 346
Judah the Maccabee 72, 331
Judaism xi, xiii, xv, xvi, 6, 8, 9, 10, 11, 18, 35, 37, 38, 41, 44, 45, 52, 63, 78, 84, 85, 99, 100, 101, 102, 104, 105, 106, 110, 121, 133, 141, 155, 158, 159, 163, 167, 169, 172, 173, 174, 188, 191, 192, 200, 202, 205, 208, 210, 213, 217, 221, 222, 223, 242, 245, 246, 249, 255, 260, 261, 262, 263, 264, 266, 271, 275, 277, 280, 286, 287, 292, 302, 304, 313, 314, 315, 316, 321, 322, 323, 327, 340
Judas Iscariot 107
Judea xiv, 79, 95, 106, 119, 256, 257, 258, 292, 340
Judges 58, 59, 231, 232, 330
Julian the Apostate 111, 117, 260

K

K'aba 156, 157
Kali 164
Kant, Immanuel 151
Karma 163, 165, 335
Kepler, Johannes 150
Ketuvim 296
Kingdom Hall(s) 217, 219, 221, 224, 225, 227
Kislev xiv, 291, 293, 347

Kochba, Shimon bar 79, 258, 302
Kol Nidre 46, 47, 288
Koran 121, 157, 161, 191, 192, 195, 203, 205, 271, 303, 304, 328, 334, 336
Krishna 165, 244
Kristallnacht 267
Kuroc 291

L

Laban 251, 291, 337
Lag B'omer 301, 302
Leah 60, 187, 251, 291
Leap Month 309, 310
Lebanon War 297
Levi 336, 337
Leviticus 194, 221, 293, 315
Levy, Asser 209
Lipstadt, Deborah 268
Locke, John 151
Louis XVI, King 152
Luke 106, 108, 109
Lulav 290
Luther, Martin 35, 140, 143, 146, 147
Lutheranism 146

M

Maariv 19
Madison, James 136, 151
Maimonides 111, 112, 113, 129
Malachi 85, 86, 96, 98, 99
Manasseh 2, 93, 291, 337
Manetho 256
Mani 112
Mark 107, 108, 109
Marranos 135
Martel, Charles 118, 134
Mary 30, 31, 32, 33, 34, 105, 106, 108, 160
Mattathias 55, 72, 256, 292, 331
Matthew 4, 108, 109
Matthias 107
Maxentius 110, 259
Mayflower 211

Mecca 156, 157, 334
Medina 157, 334
Menahem 91
Menasseh 172, 173, 174
Menassehites 173, 174
Menorah 177, 292
Mesha 89
Methodism 147
Methuselah 291
Micah 86, 96, 97, 212
Michelangelo 139
Middle Ages xiii, 120, 123, 136, 159, 265, 334
Midian 330
Midianites 291
Mincha 19
Moab 89, 90, 92, 304, 330
Moabites 91, 291
Montesquieu, Charles 151
Moors 118, 125, 134
Mordecai xiv, 294, 295
Mormonism 148
Mormons 148, 213
Moses 2, 7, 9, 10, 56, 76, 94, 101, 104, 108, 134, 159, 164, 173, 193, 194, 206, 207, 243, 245, 252, 261, 267, 271, 291, 295, 296, 301, 303, 315, 330, 336, 337, 338
Mount Sinai 120, 211, 271, 291, 303, 315
Muhammad 121, 122, 156, 157, 158, 159, 173, 192, 193, 244, 245, 246, 271, 303, 304, 316, 334, 335, 339, 346
Musaf 19
Muslims xv, 35, 116, 119, 120, 121, 122, 123, 124, 125, 126, 127, 128, 129, 130, 131, 132, 153, 154, 155, 156, 157, 158, 159, 160, 167, 168, 173, 174, 191, 195, 199, 205, 246, 254, 271, 303, 304, 315, 334, 338, 339, 340

N

Nachmanides 130
Nahum 86, 96, 97
Nanak 168
Naomi 304, 305
Naphtali 2, 91, 291, 337
Napoleon 119, 123, 152
Nataputta, Mahavira 167
Nathan 86, 87, 96, 97, 260
Native Americans 209, 269
Nazis 144, 145, 202, 269, 296, 297, 298, 345
Ne'ilah 289
Nebuchadnezzar 72, 87, 93, 110, 305
Nehemiah 78
Nero, Emperor 107, 108, 259
Nevi'im 296
Newport Jewish community 208
Newton, Isaac 150
New Testament 102, 103, 105, 106, 107, 109, 222, 259, 304, 340
Nineveh 85, 97, 289, 330
Nirvana 163
Nissan 18, 295, 296
Noah 291, 323
Northern Kingdom 77, 87, 88, 97, 330
Nostra Aetate 35, 100, 145
Nureddin 125

O

Obadiah 86, 96, 98
Odoacer 115
Old Testament xiii, 8, 85, 94, 109, 121, 133, 264
Omri, King 91
Oneida Perfectionists 213
Orpah 304

P

Paleologus VIII, Michael 116, 127
Palestine 8, 57, 89, 105, 129, 202, 267, 270, 298, 329, 341, 343, 344, 345, 346

Palestinians 200, 201, 202, 254, 299, 321, 341
Pale of Settlement 152
Palmach 343, 345
Parsha(s) 237, 291
Passover xiv, 18, 55, 97, 295, 296, 301, 302, 303, 307, 309, 327
Paul xi, 35, 101, 105, 106, 107, 109, 111, 141, 145, 259, 260, 263, 266, 322, 324, 326
Persia 78, 93, 95, 110, 173, 192, 245, 294, 331, 346
Pesach 295, 306
Peter 107, 115, 123, 130, 135, 140, 142, 145, 209, 260, 323
Peter the Hermit 123, 130
Pharaoh(s) xiv, 58, 69, 87, 88, 93, 256, 296, 329, 338
Philistines 10, 85, 86, 91, 92, 94, 329, 330, 346
Pirkei Avot 165
PLO 65, 345
Pompey, General 257, 292
Pope(s) 35, 68, 69, 100, 116, 118, 119, 123, 126, 127, 128, 130, 131, 134, 141, 144, 145, 146, 331
Portugal 135, 138, 209, 340
Potiphar 58, 338
Presbyterian(s) 27, 147
Promised Land 72, 76, 78, 85, 93, 94, 110, 157, 173, 206, 208, 211, 213, 291, 295, 312, 330, 331, 336, 337, 338
Protestant Reformation 136, 140, 147
Protocols of the Elders of Zion 254, 266, 267
Punjab 168
Purim xiv, 37, 292, 293, 294, 295, 306, 307, 337

R

Rachel 10, 60, 187, 251, 291, 302, 337
Rameses II 338
Rebecca 10, 187, 250, 251, 291

Rehoboam 71, 77, 91, 96
Reincarnation 163, 165, 167
Renaissance 113, 116, 117, 119, 122, 123, 129, 131, 136, 137, 138, 139, 141, 142, 149, 151, 159, 265, 327
Reuben 2, 67, 291, 337
Richard the Lionheart 126
Rishonim 69, 70
Robin Hood 126
Romans xiv, 26, 104, 105, 107, 108, 110, 111, 115, 119, 122, 131, 142, 173, 254, 255, 256, 257, 258, 259, 261, 263, 270, 272, 292, 301, 305
Roman Empire 111, 112, 114, 115, 116, 117, 118, 119, 121, 122, 126, 134, 138, 152, 259, 260, 261
Rome 79, 95, 105, 107, 110, 112, 113, 114, 116, 117, 118, 119, 122, 123, 137, 140, 142, 143, 144, 145, 146, 152, 254, 257, 258, 262, 263, 266, 302, 331, 332, 340, 346
Rosh Hashanah 12, 15, 17, 18, 19, 22, 40, 45, 46, 47, 56, 185, 229, 286, 287, 288, 289, 294, 307, 314, 321, 323, 335
Rousseau, Jean Jacques 151
Russell, Charles Taze 220
Russia 132, 168, 255, 265
Russian Revolution 265
Ruth 304, 305

S

S.S. St. Louis 297
Sabaeans 191, 192
Saladin 125, 126, 127, 129
Salomon, Haym 212
Samaritans 77, 91
Samson xiii, 10, 77, 85
Samuel 7, 9, 10, 57, 77, 84, 85, 86, 87, 95, 96, 97, 330, 335

Sarah 10, 11, 64, 65, 72, 187, 291
Saul, King 346
Saul of Tarsus 106
Schreiner, Olive 272, 342
Second Isaiah 86, 96, 98
Second Temple xiv, 78, 79, 94, 98, 105, 108, 110, 258, 292, 293, 298, 301, 305, 331
Seleucid 292
Septuagint 259
Seventh Day Adventists 148
Shabbat 59, 155, 185, 187, 191, 239, 288, 306, 307, 323
Shakers 213
Shakespeare 140
Shavuot 131, 301, 302, 303, 304, 305, 307
Shema 87, 120, 302, 303, 329
Shemini Atzeret 131, 289, 290, 307
Sheshonk, Pharaoh 87, 88, 329
Shia 158, 213, 243
Shiite 244, 246
Shiva 282
Shoah 45
Siddhartha 165, 166, 167, 316, 324
Sikhs 167, 168, 169, 174
Silva, Flavius 79
Simchat Torah 289, 290, 291, 294
Simeon 2, 337
Simon 79, 107, 142, 323, 324, 326
Socrates 138
Solomon 10, 71, 72, 77, 80, 87, 90, 91, 96, 98, 110, 261, 305, 329, 331, 340, 346
Solomon's Temple 72, 77, 98, 110, 305
Southern Kingdom 77, 90, 91, 264
Souza, Thomas De 210
Soviet Union 57, 79
Spinoza, Baruch 151
Stern Gang 345
Stuyvesant, Peter 135, 209
Suez Canal War 296
Sukkot 131, 289, 290, 294, 307, 308, 309, 347
Sunni 158, 213
Sura(s) 192, 193

T

Tacitus 104, 257
Taliban 158, 169, 316
Tanach 70, 203, 296
Tannaim 70
Tashlikh, Tashlich 19, 20, 21
Ten Commandments 9, 261, 262, 272, 303, 322
Ten Curses 296
Terach 57
Tevet 293
Theodosius I, Emperor 114
Tiglath-Pileser 91
Tishre xiv, 18, 21, 286, 287, 289, 290, 307, 308, 309, 346, 347
Tish B'av 45
Titus, General & Emperor 79, 258, 293
Torah xi, xii, xiii, xvi, 18, 54, 56, 59, 70, 75, 107, 108, 112, 132, 156, 163, 164, 165, 175, 176, 191, 193, 195, 231, 233, 234, 235, 236, 237, 238, 241, 246, 247, 250, 277, 279, 281, 287, 289, 290, 291, 293, 294, 295, 296, 301, 302, 303, 307, 310, 311, 323, 326, 337
Tourquemada, Tomas De 134, 135, 146
Transmigration of Souls 168
Tree of Knowledge 291
Turkey 106, 115, 123, 124, 135, 331, 332, 345
Turks 116, 122, 124, 332, 345, 346
Tu B'Shevat 293, 294, 307

U

Umar I, Caliph 121
Umma 119, 120, 122, 123, 126, 127, 128, 129, 130
United Nations 57, 110, 202, 254, 297, 343

Urban II, Pope 116, 123
Uriah the Hittite 68, 86

V

Vespasian, Emperor 258, 293, 305
Vishnu 164, 165, 169, 275, 335
Voltaire 119, 151, 152, 260

W

Washington, George 135, 142, 208
Watchtower Bible and Tract Society of
    Pennsylvania 220
West Bank 201, 254
World War I 266, 332, 344, 345
World War II 79, 145, 202, 273, 293,
    297, 298, 345

Y

Yahweh 78, 93, 94, 98, 169, 193, 263,
    275, 289, 292, 314, 315
Yochai, Rabbi Shimon bar 301
Yoga 335
Yom Ha'atzma'ut 297, 301, 302, 307
Yom Hazikaron 287, 296, 297, 307
Yom Kippur 15, 17, 18, 20, 21, 22, 40,
    45, 46, 47, 56, 65, 211, 212, 282,
    286, 287, 288, 289, 294, 296,
    307, 314, 321, 323, 334, 337
Yom Kippur War 296
Yom Yerushalayim 302, 307

Z

Zechariah 86, 91, 98
Zedikiah, King 87, 93, 96, 305
Zephaniah 86, 96, 98
Zionism 298
Zohar 134, 301
Zoroaster 112, 173, 192, 243, 245

Printed in the United States
72920LV00004BA/88-123